THE HONOR OF THINKING

Cultural Memory
in
the
Present

Mieke Bal and Hent de Vries, Editors

THE HONOR OF THINKING
Critique, Theory, Philosophy

Rodolphe Gasché

STANFORD UNIVERSITY PRESS

STANFORD, CALIFORNIA

2007

Stanford University Press
Stanford, California

Printed in the United States of America on acid-free, archival-quality paper

Library of Congress Cataloging-in-Publication Data

Gasché, Rodolphe.
    The honor of thinking : critique, theory, philosophy / Rodolphe Gasché.
        p. cm.—(Cultural memory in the present)
    Includes bibliographical references and index.
    ISBN-13: 978-0-8047-5422-4 (cloth : alk. paper)
    ISBN-10: 0-8047-5422-5 (cloth : alk. paper)
    ISBN-13: 978-0-8047-5423-1 (pbk. : alk. paper)
    ISBN-10: 0-8047-5423-3 (pbk. : alk. paper)
    1. Thought and thinking—Philosophy. 2. Lyotard, Jean François. I. Title.
B105.T54G37 2007
128'.3—dc22

                                                                2006026637

Typeset by Westchester Book Group in 11/13.5 Adobe Garamond

Contents

Acknowledgments

Several parts of this book have been published before. The first chapter, "Critique, Hypercriticism, Deconstruction," appeared in *Cardozo Law Review* 13, no. 4 (1991): 1115–1132, under the title, "Critique, Hypercriticism, Deconstruction: The Case of Benjamin." Chapter 2, "The Sober Absolute," was written for *Studies in Romanticism* 31, no. 4 (1992): 433–453, where it appeared under the title "The Sober Absolute: On Walter Benjamin and the Early Romantics." Reproduced courtesy of the Trustees of Boston University. A portion of Chapter 3 was published under the title "Sublimely Clueless: On the Foundation of Marriage in Statutory Law," in *Cardozo Law Review* 26, no. 3 (2005): 921–942. © Cardozo Law Review. Chapter 4 first appeared in *Enlightenments: Encounters between Critical Theory and Contemporary French Thought,* ed. H. Kunneman and H. de Vries (Kampen, The Netherlands: Kok Pharos, 1993), 121–140. Reprinted by permission of Peeters Publishers. Chapter 6, "Under Heading of Theory," was published in *Institutions in Cultures, Theory and Practice,* ed. R. Lumsden and R. Patke (Amsterdam: Rodopi, 1996), 103–129. Chapter 7 appeared in *Germanistik und Komparatistik: DFG-Symposium 1993,* ed. H. Birus (Stuttgart: Metzler, 1995), 417–432. Chapter 8 was previously published in *After Poststructuralism: Writing the Intellectual History of Theory,* ed. T. Rajan and M. J. O'Driscoll (Toronto: University of Toronto Press, 2002), 129–151. Reprinted with permission. A portion of Chapter 9 entitled "Archéologie et Frivolité" was included in a special issue of *L'Herne* on Jacques Derrida, ed. M.-L. Mallet and G. Michaud (Paris: Editions de l'Herne, 2004), 172–178. Chapter 11, "Saving the Honor of Thinking," was first published under the title "Saving the Honor of Thinking: On Jean-François Lyotard," in *parallax* 6, no. 4 (2000): 127–145. Used by permission of *parallax* (www.tandf.co.uk). A short portion of Chapter 12, entitled "The Sublime, Ontologically Speaking," was included in *Yale French Studies* 99 (2001): 117–128. A reduced version of Chapter 13 was published in a French translation by G. Leroux under the title "L'expérience aporétique aux origines de la pensée: Platon, Heidegger, Derrida," in *Études françaises* 38, nos. 1–2 (2002): 103–121. Finally, a first draft of Chapter 14 appeared in *Epoché* 10, no. 2 (2006).

Introduction

Honor is a title of respect that is bestowed on something or someone because of proven worth or merit—or perhaps simply because of rank. It can also distinguish a person who demonstrates integrity—that is, consistency and steadfastness in his or her beliefs and actions. But what could it mean to speak of the honor of thinking? In what sense can thinking be distinguished by this term, which has a decidedly pompous ring in many languages? Indeed, the word "honor" resonates differently in various languages; for instance, the English "honor" and the French *honneur* are certainly less charged than the German *Ehre*, which continues to resonate with the culturally normative role it has played in the past as a social and cultural regulator. Is it because of thinking's special accomplishments, of its position or status, that thinking can claim a mark of honor? If this is the case, then the question at once becomes: higher than what? Or is it because of the high-minded principles in strict conformity to which thinking operates that it could be seen as honorable? Then again, perhaps the honor of thinking is determined by that with which thinking concerns itself? Perhaps, certain issues, topics, or objects—rather than others—are more conducive to "honoring" thinking. Let us also bear in mind that honor is always good public esteem, and it presupposes the communal—if not the general—recognition of what is thus distinguished. Is this to say that to refer to the honor of thinking is to allude to an essential public nature, task, and role that would be its own? Is this emphasis on the honor of thinking a reminder that thinking pertains to humankind as such and that its thrust is by nature universal? How could we make such a weighty claim without seeming preposterous? Furthermore, does the title *The Honor of Thinking* not also invoke a concept of honor that would be specific to thinking—say, a philosophical conception of honor distinct from what is commonly understood by this term—a concept that is only somewhat in tune with the connotations of the term in specific languages? Finally, does such talk of the honor of thinking not also suggest that its honor is in question—perhaps even in jeopardy—and that, therefore, expanding on it is an urgent necessity? What precisely is it that is imperiled in thinking? Is it its own self-understanding, the principles that it is supposed to uphold and to which it should conform, or its claim to universality? Or is thinking putting its own honor in danger by misinterpreting itself, by conceiving of itself merely as intellect or as merely a means for something else? Is the honor of thinking then something in need of being saved? If, indeed, the honor of thinking is at stake, we must ask precisely what it is that might threaten the alleged honor of thinking. In other words, is the honor of thinking threatened merely by external causes or does thinking itself endanger its own inmost honor?

As an homage to the philosophical accomplishments of Jean-François Lyotard, this book borrows its title, *The Honor of Thinking*, from his opus magnum, *The Differend: Phrases in Dispute*, which, in its preface, raises the question of "how to save the honor of thinking."[1] We will explore this question in the two chapters of this book that are devoted to Lyotard, in which some of the aforementioned matters are addressed within the framework of Lyotard's thought. But the demarcation of thinking from critique, theory, and philosophical thought that this book's subtitle suggests warrants a broader introductory sketch of the issue of the honor of thinking, and, in particular, of the reasons why critique, theory, and philosophy may not fully live up to the exigencies of thinking.

According to Immanuel Kant, dignity (*Würde*) and nobility (*Adel*) set human beings apart from all other beings. Yet, if these characteristics pertain to human beings, and to them alone, it is insofar as they are capable of reason (*Vernunft*)—not because they are in possession of understanding (*Verstand*), hence, capable of rational thinking as differential and cognitive thinking (*Verstandesdenken*), for as *animalia rationalia*, they still belong to nature. Only insofar as human beings are persons (rather than merely natural, or sensible, beings)—that is, insofar as they are subjects of moral and practical reason—are they endowed with a dignity that raises them above all things and other living beings. Put differently, what makes us recognize our dignity as well as that of every other human being and, consequently, what leads us to show respect for ourselves and others is that each and every human being as a being capable of self-thinking incarnates nothing less than mankind as a whole. As a person, the human being is, therefore, an end or a purpose in itself. According to Kant, dignity as "an absolute inner worth," implies that the "human being cannot be used merely as a means by any other human being (either by others or even by himself), but must always be used at the same time as an end." He remarks that the acknowledgment of the human being's dignity is the acknowledgment of "a worth that has no price, no equivalent for which the object evaluated could be exchanged."[2] In sum, the dignity or nobility that the human being as a moral being capable of reason can lay claim to is that of universal mankind. Dignity and nobility are, thus, terms that indicate universal rank.

Kant, in the *Critique of Pure Reason,* is faced with antinomies that derive from reason's striving to extend its domain beyond the limits of experience, thus soaring to lofty ideas; he at first acknowledges the "dignity and worth" of philosophy manifest in such a progressive extension of the employment of reason. If nonetheless, for Kant, the honor (*Ehre*) of reason is at stake in such an extension, it is because by thus seeking to give satisfaction to the highest ends with which humanity is most closely concerned, reason finds itself "compromised by the conflict of opposing arguments," and hence divided against itself. Indeed, what these opposing arguments put into question is not only the unity of reason, but also its universality. Consequently, the imperative "to defend . . . the honor of human reason," as the early Kant formulates it, derives above all from the fact that "reason" stands for the human being's highest aspirations and expectations.[3] In *Rogues,* Jacques Derrida refers to these Kantian statements, as well as to Edmund Husserl's call for a rehabilitation, or *Ehrenrettung,* of reason in order to suggest that today the honor of reason is at stake, and that it is, perhaps, "a matter of saving the honor of reason"; but it is also in order to uphold the intractable demand of the unconditional—which is intrinsically linked to what is called reason—against all calculating thought.[4] Furthermore, as Derrida's discussion of Husserl's diagnosis of a crisis of European rationality caused by the naturalistic and objectivist turn of the sciences reveals, it is reason itself that is responsible for its crisis, because the calculating rationality of the modern sciences is reason's own product. This calculating rationality, which has made European rationality sick, cannot be surrendered because it is a legitimate form of reason itself, but the unconditional and the incalculable must nonetheless be upheld against it.[5] It follows from this that the need to save the honor of reason, in the face of the crisis undergone by reason, does not originate in some historically accidental and limited situation but responds to an internal division of reason that is intrinsic to reason itself. But, if the need to save the honor of thinking derives from conflicting demands of reason itself, can one then not also say that to save the honor of reason is the most elementary movement of reason itself? Perhaps reason has to be constitutionally saved from itself, and it is only reasonable, first and foremost, in bringing its unconditional demands to bear on calculating rationality.

However, what can it mean to speak of the honor of thinking, and, eventually, of the necessity "to save the honor of thinking"? Apart from making reference to Lyotard, my emphasis on thinking in the demand to save the honor of thinking also elicits Martin Heidegger's privileging of thinking over philosophy, although Heidegger, to my knowledge, never speaks of the honor of thinking or of the need to save it. Indeed, among the contemporary thinkers, Heidegger is the one, who, after the turn most forcefully asserted the primacy of thinking over all forms of philosophizing. Thinking is the counter-concept to both philosophical and scientific thought as representational and calculating thought. Furthermore, all of the thinkers whose work will be discussed in part 3, "Philosophy"—Michel Foucault, Gilles Deleuze, Lyotard, and Derrida—are driven by Heidegger's question, "What is called thinking?" Therefore, in the following pages, Heidegger's claim for a primacy of thinking will be given special attention.[6] From the perspective of common sense, no less than from that of philosophical thinking, such a concern with thinking alone is usually presumed indifferent to the realm of the practical. Heidegger, by contrast, in the "Letter on Humanism," for instance, remarks that "thinking acts insofar as it thinks. Such action is presumably the simplest and at the same time the highest, because it concerns the relation of Being to man."[7] But as Hannah Arendt, for one, observes, to hold that thinking is acting is a dishonest claim. In the name of honesty (*Ehrlichkeit*), one must, she writes, insist on distinguishing thinking as contemplation—in other words, as a concern with what is essential—from praxis.[8] However, thinking, as understood by Heidegger, is not contemplation—that is, a theoretical gazing at the essence of what is—and does not stand in contrast to praxis, as is the case with theory. Yet, the title, *The Honor of Thinking*, rather than merely speaking of honesty—that is, the uprightness, integrity, or truthfulness of thinking—evokes the honor of thinking. But, how and when does the question of honor become an issue? Even when thinking is understood as contemplation, that is, when—rather than being of the order of an apprehending response to what calls upon thought to be addressed in a thinking mode—it is regarded as (merely) thoughtful gazing at what is essential for the sake of thinking alone, the rank of that which thinking contemplates decides its honor. If, furthermore, the object of contemplation concerns things or situations that calculating thought ignores, and to which it blinds itself, then thinking is already no longer merely contemplative. Whether thinking addresses that which metaphysical thought has, for essential reasons, been unable to think—in other words, Being itself—or whether it understands itself as being truly thinking only on the condition that it respond to extreme encounters (such as speaking up when a victim has been wronged absolutely, that is, deprived of even the means of testifying) or when and where situations are aporetic and undecidable, the very act of thinking is no longer merely contemplative and inconsequential. But, apart from the kinds of objects that thinking addresses, the form of thinking bears on its honor as well. The honor of thinking is at stake at any moment when thinking is subject to external constraints and subservient to, among other things, ideological, pragmatic, or religious concerns. A form of thinking that does not also produce and secure, in Kantian terms, self-thinking and the autonomy of the person, surrenders its honor. Could one not argue therefore that it is in this sense (at least, but certainly not limited to it) that one has to understand Heidegger's claim that thinking is praxis in an eminent sense? Undoubtedly, if thinking can be understood as the highest form of doing, it is not because thinking would create a subject who by his very autonomy stands in an opposition to the world and to others, but because it relates the human being to the meaning of Being without which the human does not come into its essence and, from which alone, all his other activities can become meaningful.

When we oppose thinking to philosophy, it is not a question of confronting the latter with what one could call "mere thinking," that is, a mental activity directed without any discrimination toward objects in general.[9] On the contrary, for Heidegger, thinking is a highly determined mode of being (rather than an activity) not only insofar as it is understood as an apprehending (*Vernehmen*), or hearing (*Hören*), but also through what thinking apprehends, and to which as a hearing it belongs. If the essential nature of thinking is, as Heidegger contends, "determined by what there is to be thought about: the present (*Anwesen*) of what is present, the Being of beings," then it is clear that to philosophize is not yet necessarily to think.[10] Indeed, to think Being and to question it as the opening or clearing that grants the appearance of all beings is not the matter of philosophy. What determines the essence of thinking remains concealed to philosophy as philosophy and constitutes what Heidegger terms philosophy's "unthought." If, consequently, philosophizing is no guarantee in itself that thinking occurs, it is not simply because in our times philosophizing has become more than ever a ludicrous thing or a pompous pretension. Largely a thing of the academy and part of the so-called humanities, doing philosophy today consists mostly of historical or textual commentaries on the texts of the tradition; of critically probing, in conformity with certain disciplinary and institutional constraints, criteria and rules, arguments taken out of context; or of epigonic variations on previous philosophical accomplishments, however brilliant. As is well known, this situation is, according to Heidegger, the consequence of philosophy's development as metaphysics into the independent sciences in which it finds its legitimate completion. As Heidegger writes, "Philosophy is ending in the present age. It has found its place in the scientific attitude of socially active humanity."[11] This diagnosis of philosophy's ending in the present does not mean that there are no philosophies anymore, nor that philosophizing no longer takes place, but we must remember that even when preoccupation with philosophy and its problems is serious, this is not yet evidence of any readiness to think. Heidegger writes: "The learned world is expending commendable efforts in the investigation of the history of philosophy. There are useful and worthy tasks, and only the best talents are good enough for them, especially when they present to us models of great thinking. But even if we have devoted many years to the intensive study of the treatises and writings of great thinkers, the fact is still no guarantee that we ourselves are thinking, or even are ready to learn thinking. On the contrary—preoccupation with philosophy more than anything else may give us the stubborn illusion that we are thinking just because we are incessantly 'philosophizing.'"[12] Indeed, it is not only because philosophy has come to an end in our age that we are not yet thinking according to Heidegger, but also because philosophy itself—that is, qua metaphysics—has deterred the need to think. Such a claim, however, in no way implies any disrespect for philosophy, nor a disparagement of its greatness, but only an awareness that philosophizing and thinking are not the same. For Heidegger, thinking is a possibility of philosophy, one that the completion of philosophy as it evolves into the sciences has not yet been able to address precisely because of what philosophy is about. Rather than a "*last* possibility," that is, "the dissolution of philosophy in the technologized sciences," the possibility of thinking that has not yet been actualized is a "*first* possibility," or "a possibility from which the thinking of philosophy had to start, but which as philosophy it could nevertheless not experience and adopt." Thinking thus remains a task, one that is still "reserved for thinking in a concealed way in the history of philosophy from its beginning to its end, a task accessible neither to philosophy as metaphysics nor, and even less so, to the sciences stemming from philosophy."[13] Compared to "the greatness of the philosophers" and their philosophizing, thinking and its task are "less (*geringer*) than philosophy." Great philosophy is already less assuming, more modest, and even more sober-minded than technology and the sciences, in which the extreme possibilities of philosophy have found their completion; this is even truer of thinking whose direct or indirect effects are felt even less than those of philosophy. But if in distinction to great philosophy, thinking remains unassuming, it is "because its task is only of a preparatory, not a founding character."[14] Rather than creating epochs, or even worldviews, thinking only seeks to awaken the not yet actualized possibility of philosophy at the very moment at which the latter has come to an end. The thinking in question is itself, therefore, something still to be learned, and that from which thinking receives its essential determination—the matter of thinking—is itself something that always remains in need of being secured. Even though this thinking has a rigor of its own, it does not have the assurance and security that institutionalized rules of philosophizing, which have been handed down to us, traditionally provide. To quote Arendt, this thinking is "thinking without bannister," thinking without guardrails.[15] The contours of the possibility for which thinking prepares, therefore, remain uncertain, and thinking qua thinking necessarily runs the risk of missing the mark.

Putting the emphasis on thinking serves thus, first and foremost, to demarcate it from philosophy and philosophizing. The reference in the title of this book to the honor of thinking acknowledges this necessity of distinguishing between the two. However, setting thinking and philosophy apart is not merely a matter of breaking free from philosophy's legitimate exigencies, nor a declaration that anything goes. But, even in order to be able to think only a little bit, a strategically calculated and highly vigilant suspension of the institutionally established norms of philosophy as an academic discipline and also of the seemingly legitimate demands of philosophical thought in the metaphysical tradition is required—particularly, if thinking is to do justice to the conflicting demands from within the tradition itself. Now, as we have seen, thinking, for Heidegger, is entirely suspended from and determined by the unthought of philosophy as metaphysics, that is, by thinking's relation to Being as the clearing for the unconcealment of beings. Although the Heideggerian question of Being is a question that cannot be bypassed, we cannot allow the Heideggerian determination of Being to monopolize thinking. There may be "more" than the Opening, or clearing, of Being to which thinking needs to open itself up. In order to remain thinking, thinking cannot let itself be saturated, not even by the call of Being. If it is to be true to itself, thinking must remain constitutionally open to respond even to the call(s) of what remains as yet unforeseeable and unthinkable. It may therefore be necessary to "think thinking otherwise," as Derrida has put it.[16] Given Heidegger's appropriation of the term "thinking" for a responsiveness in thought to Being, "thinking" may even be too charged a concept for what still remains to be thought.

Let us recall Heidegger's assertion that thinking is perhaps the highest form of praxis. Such a claim is, of course, meant to counter the objection that action, rather than thought, is what is lacking. But if Heidegger suggests that it could well be that "man for centuries now acted too much and thought too little," this is not because "the time of theory" has come, as Theodor W. Adorno once proclaimed in the sixties, arguing that the call for "action now" chains thought and brings it to a halt precisely where thinking would have to continue in order to arrive at the place where finally something could be changed.[17] Indeed, Heidegger's affirmation that thinking is perhaps the highest form of praxis also means that thinking is not of the order of the theoretical, for only theory stands in direct opposition to praxis. Undoubtedly, Heidegger acknowledges that the way in which the Greeks conceived of *theoria* emphasized its grand nature and lofty design. They understood *theoria* and the *bios theoretikos* as the highest form of doing, and the most perfect form of human existence, not in the least because the Greeks, who, according to Heidegger, thought in a unique way out of their language, also heard in the word *theoria* the word *ora,* that is, "the respect we have, the honor and esteem we bestow." Thus apprehended, *theoria* is "the reverent paying heed to the unconcealment of what presences."[18] But if thinking as the highest form of doing is not theoretical, this also means that it is not theoretical in the sense of what Greek *theoria* has become in the modern sciences. Certainly, the Greek conception of *theoria* is itself not without ambiguities, but the refusal to conflate thinking and theory is rooted in the need to demarcate thinking from what theory has come to mean in the modern sciences, which largely dominate our understanding of theory today. As Heidegger remarks, "The interest of the sciences is directed toward the theory of the necessary structural concepts of the coordinated areas of investigation. 'Theory' means now supposition of the categories, which are allowed only a cybernetical function, but denied any ontological meaning."[19] Theory in the modern sense is a deductive system in view of the explication of given facts, and, hence, is dependent on a naturalistic view of the world, which theory advances while being grounded in it. For the present purpose, it will suffice to recall that modern science—hence, theory—is grounded in the fundamental experience of Being that characterizes the metaphysical ground-situation of Western science and cognition, that is, in the experience of that which presences as object in objects and which consists in securing and entrapping what presences in such objectness. But even if the doing of thinking is not theoretical in the sense of the theory of the sciences, it is nevertheless not practical in our common sense. Although theory implies a clear distinction from praxis, the latter shares with it the same representational relation to Being as presence-at-hand. By contrast, the deed of thinking is "neither theoretical nor practical, nor is it the conjunction of these two forms of behavior."[20]

Undoubtedly, the title of this work, *The Honor of Thinking*, seems to suggest a supremacy of thinking over theory. However, registering reservations with respect to the concept of theory in no way entails a suspicion of theory for, say, annihilating the specificity of that which it deals with, abandoning concreteness for lofty abstractions, or for simply being obscure and convoluted. Resistance to theory does not amount to hostility against theory. Declarations against theory are hopelessly naive, and even self-contradictory. This is the case whether their authors profess to follow an approach that is more American (i.e., a pragmatist approach in the humanities) than continental (i.e., a theoretical approach) or whether they are terrified of becoming politically irrelevant by deferring to theory, and, therefore, intend to go it alone without theory. In contrast, Heidegger's reticence to embrace theory is founded in thinking's broader task. Yet, he never disregards theory; on the contrary, he fully recognizes the technical interpretation of thinking that it entails, whatever some of its disastrous consequences may be, as what also constitutes the grandeur of the metaphysical heritage of the West. Heidegger's reservations regarding theory are fueled by what modern theory has faded out from early Greek *theoria* in whose shadow, and in reaction to which, it still proceeds. But we should not limit ourselves to Heidegger's reservations in expressing a guardedness with respect to theory while revaluing thinking. Contemporary developments in literary theory are a further motivation for registering a reticence regarding "theory." Indeed, what has come to be known as "theory" in many of North America's literature departments, is, in fact, a specifically North American phenomenon and artifact: "theory" (or Theory), otherwise unspecified, is not theory in the sense of the modern sciences, but basically means continental philosophy.[21] Whatever the specific cultural and, especially, academic reasons for such a translation have been, the reason for resisting calling "continental philosophy" theory is that the label "theory" divests so-called continental philosophy of nothing less than its character of thought and philosophical nature. Furthermore, because theory in this sense neither encompasses continental thought in the entirety of its tradition nor pays attention to what motivated its developments, it is unaware of the exigencies of that tradition for interpreting the texts that are part of it; it is thus more often than not highly eclectic and selective, referring above all to contemporary developments in French philosophy and literary studies—that is, to what came to be known as French postmodern thought. Therefore, to uphold thinking in the face of "theory" is also to resist the impoverishment of continental thought that the label "theory" produces and to advocate a responsibility toward the tradition of continental philosophy as a whole, without which a critical break in a thinking mode with this tradition makes no sense. Finally, to reassert thinking over theory is also to take into account the fact that, paradoxically, the one thinker whose writings have become eminently associated with theory in this latter sense—Jacques Derrida—has time and again asserted that deconstruction is not a theory, and has, for essential reasons, no theoretical status. The advocates of "theory" pay no attention to the fact that deconstruction cannot be theoretical either if it is not to be another philosophy even when it takes the form of a philosophical or theoretical inquiry. Indeed, compared to what theory has always meant, Derridean thought does not aim at epistemologically totalizing and mastering regions of given objects.[22] It is, therefore, theoretical neither in a philosophical nor in a scientific sense. But, in addition to questioning the criteria that would make a theory of it, deconstruction is also a manner of thinking intimately interlaced with ethical and political concerns, and in this sense, not theoretical either.[23]

Nonetheless, to highlight thinking and to demarcate it from theory is not at all to argue for its irrelevance, nor to insinuate some supremacy of thinking over theory. Thinking does not occur in the denigration of theory or in the cutting of all ties to it, leaving it behind for a new approach that would be exempt from all theoretical implications, as it were. Thinking is neither a new fad nor a novel activity nor a domain that has only lately come into being. In the case of Heidegger, we have already pointed out that, compared to theory, thinking pursues a more modest task, namely, to link theory back to *theoria*. The characteristic modesty of thinking is also what intrinsically inhibits it from making any claims to priority. But Derrida does not, as Richard Rorty holds, "simply drop theory."[24] Rather, what is at stake in Derrida's resistance to theory is the demand "to exceed the theoretical rather than to hinder it and take positions 'against theory.' "[25] A thinking that exceeds the theoretical does not leave it behind but comprises the confrontation of theory with the structural limits that its very enabling conditions impose on its totalizing and stabilizing enterprise. It also follows from this that thinking does not make theorizing obsolete—totalization and mastery remain as necessary as ever, except that theory needs to face both the structural limits of its conditions of possibility and the metaphysical (but also ideological and political) character of many of its claims. Theory continues to have its place, but "reformed," as it were, within and with respect to thinking.

But what about the relation of thinking to critique or criticism? On the surface, the question is, of course, also motivated by the fact that like "theory," the words "critique" and "criticism" are used today in ways otherwise unspecified. Indeed, literary criticism in the English-speaking world is still referred to simply as "criticism," and in the wake of the importation of French thought of the sixties and seventies into North American literature departments, "critique" and "criticism" have become synonymous with "theory." "Critical theory," distinct in all respects from the critical theory of the Frankfurt School, has been the title of a more theoretical approach to literary studies. But setting thinking apart from critique and criticism does not only, or even primarily, take issue with this relatively recent phenomenon, for the concept of critique has a long and complex history within philosophical thought. In particular, since the Enlightenment, critique belongs to the fundamental capacities of our cultural identity and self-understanding. But what is critique or criticism in the first place? Needless to say, no elaborate or general definition of critique is to be expected here, but only the bare contours of the concept are provided so as to make the necessity of a demarcation of thinking from critique plausible.[26]

As they are commonly understood, critique and criticism have a negative ring and mean faultfinding and unfavorable judgment. But given that the concept of critique in modernity has its origins in Descartes' effort to establish an indubitable foundation for the explanation of what is by way of methodical and universal doubt, critique also entails a new and radical negativity of thought.[27] But is this the sense of "critique" when critique is contrasted with thinking? Is thinking distinct from critique because it is essentially positive and affirmative? Or, by contrast, could it be that from the perspective of thinking, critique is not sufficiently negative? Finally, what if the distinction in question derives from thinking's irreducible nature to the binary opposition of negativity and positivity? When critique as faultfinding does not occur just for its own sake, it involves judgment about the truth or merit of what is judged—in other words, it presupposes a definite standard of what is essential. The negativity of critique is thus a function of a self-evident positivity held to be fundamental and unshakable. Furthermore, since the notion of critique derives from the Greek verb *krinein* (to separate, to distinguish, to choose, to decide), critique entails the assumption of the possibility of clear-cut, pure distinction and discrimination. The reticence of thinking with respect to critique derives from these unquestioned, if not uncritical, presuppositions of self-evident truth and purity that underlie, and essentially determine the concept of critique. Let us also remind ourselves of the fact that throughout the eighteenth century, which Kant, in *Critique of Pure Reason,* labeled "in especial degree, the age of criticism" and to which our use of "critique" today remains largely indebted, critique was above all critique of prejudice and established authority, and hence was intimately tied to a conception of the human being as capable of self-thinking, hence autonomous, and free from religious and political authorities.[28] However fitting and necessary such criticism was and is today, thinking cannot take the Enlightenment ideas of freedom and of the autonomy of the human individual simply at face value. Not to interrogate the presuppositions of these ideas would, paradoxically, imply a lack of critical vigilance on the part of thinking.

But no discussion of the concept of critique and criticism can skirt the Kantian concept of critique. Indeed, notwithstanding Kant's statement that his age is the age of criticism, the concept of critique only really became a concept in its own right with Kant's radical conception of critique as a self-critique of reason by way of which reason subjects itself to its own standard and achieves self-knowledge, as well as a knowledge of its inherent boundaries. It is true that in the eighteenth century, a theory of critique had already come into existence in which critique was deemed the art of judgment in general (*ars judicandi*); however, only Kant's understanding in his critical philosophy of critique as the self-policing of reason elevated the concept of critique to the level of a key concept and endowed it with a discreteness that retrospectively became the signature of the century.[29] Notwithstanding the progressive dissolution of the radicality of the Kantian concept of critique, which, as some have argued, had already begun with Kant's immediate followers, it is this conception that supplied critique's prominence, which for us today is a given, and put it on par, as it were, with theory.[30]

The radicality of critique in the Kantian sense—which has been heralded by many as inaugurating an epochal change—is owed, at first, to its thorough destruction of the pretensions and dialectical illusions of reason. But critical destruction is not an aim in itself. By inquiring, for example, in the *Critique of Pure Reason,* into the sources of theoretical cognition, the task of critique is limited to the, indeed, rather modest ambition to overcome dogmatism and skepticism alike by securing the minimal, but firm, foundation for the much more ambitious project of establishing a future metaphysics. In *What Is a Thing?* Heidegger takes a brief look at the origin of the term "critique" in the Greek verb *krinein* and suggests that Kant's understanding of critique and criticism, like the original meaning of the Greek word, has no negative connotations. He writes: " 'Critique' comes from the Greek *krinein,* which means 'to sort' (*sondern*), 'to sort out' and thus 'to lift out that of special sort' (*das Besondere herausheben*). This contrast against others arises from an elevation of a new order. The sense of the term 'critique' is so little negative that it means the most positive of the positive, the positing of what must be established in advance in all positing as what is determinative and decisive." Since, of course, such positing of what is determinative and decisive entails "separation and lifting out of the special, the uncommon, and, at the same time, decisive," critique, by implication, also acquires a negative meaning.[31] Indeed, as we have seen, *krinein* is also rendered as "to separate," "to sever," "to distinguish," and "to decide." But let us also remind ourselves of the fact that in the eighteenth century, critique became a concern of its own in conjunction with the emerging philosophical discipline of aesthetics. As Heidegger remarks: "Critique meant establishing the standard, the rules, legislation; and this at the same time means the elevation of the general over against the special [*dem Besonderen*]. In this contemporary direction of meaning lies Kant's use of the term 'critique.' "[32] Needless to say, the positive that is exhibited in Kant's radical review of the faculty of pure reason is reason's proper nature—its elements and the rules that govern its different possibilities.

Whence, therefore, comes the urge to demarcate thinking from critique? Is it because criticism, even in its Kantian radicality, is not sufficiently critical and leaves out certain presuppositions on which it rests from its critical undertaking? Is critique hampered from within by the positivity that it seeks to throw into relief? Does not even Heidegger's fundamental understanding of critique, which, by relating it to its early Greek meaning as a contrasting of the decisive, then also fail to think critique to its end? As Gilles Deleuze has remarked, "Kant is the first philosopher who understood critique as having to be total and positive *as* critique. Total because 'nothing must escape it'; positive, affirmative, because it can not restrict the power of knowing without releasing other previously neglected powers." But he also emphasizes that rather than making good on his general project of a radical critique, "Kant merely pushed a very old conception of critique to the limit, a conception which saw critique as a force which should be brought to bear on all claims to knowledge and truth, but not on knowledge and truth themselves; a force which should be brought to bear on all claims to morality, but not on morality itself."[33] According to Deleuze, Friedrich Nietzsche, who "in the *Genealogy of Morals,* wanted to rewrite the *Critique of Pure Reason,*" was the first to realize the project of a critique, which, as an internal or immanent critique, puts also reason itself into question insofar as it is not only the faculty that is judged, but also the judging faculty.[34] All-pervading critique, for Deleuze, is the strength of active forces that turn negation into the power of affirming sense and values, creating the new and the future. "Critique is destruction and joy, the aggression of the creator. The creator of values cannot be distinguished from a destroyer, from a criminal or from a critic: a critic of established values, reactive values and baseness."[35] Yet, is thinking's reservation regarding critique adequately described by characterizing Kant's critique, or any other forms of critique, as "a false critique" to be opposed to Nietzsche's "true critique," thus reintroducing the value of truth that internal critique, precisely, was supposed to overcome?[36]

As Philippe Lacoue-Labarthe has argued, the credit owed to Kant for having initiated an epoch-making event rests less on the critical nature of his thought, through which, for the first time, metaphysics puts itself into question, and more on what such a critique presupposes—namely, that, in order to be a critique, "critique must reminisce [*remémorer*] the whole of metaphysics *ab initio.* From this perspective, critique is the first philosophical anamnesis of philosophy and, hence, the first belated [*après-coup*] resounding, in the figure of lucidity, of the Platonic decision."[37] In other words, the self-critique of reason that Kant stages throughout the three *Critiques* rests not only on the confrontation of the whole of philosophy hitherto, but also on the lucid recognition of the Platonic decision to sever philosophical thought from its others, in particular, from the arts. If Kant's critical enterprise opened up a new age, it is precisely because it entails revisiting the Platonic decision and opens thinking up again to its others. But does this opening up of thinking not also throw a critical light on criticism as well? By putting the Platonic distinction into question, does Kant not also put the metaphysical understanding of critique as pure separation into question? Is he not forced to acknowledge intrinsic limits to the need, however necessary, to sever the necessary from the accidental, the essential from the contingent, the pure from the impure, and so forth? Furthermore, does this problematization of the Platonic decision not also imply that freedom from impurity, hence clear-cut binarism, is, rather than a fact of essence, essentially of the order of a demand and thus something that can only be accomplished and striven after but never be achieved in a full and unequivocal manner? Rather than objecting to Kant's criticism on the basis that it is not sufficiently critical because it is too timid to realize in full its severing nature, we should examine the inherent limits of critique's ability both to put what is decisive into relief by contrasting it against others and to radically accomplish the operation of critical severing, which thus come into view. Kant's criticism would thus not only be a radical criticism that puts the dogmatic assumptions of critique into question, but would also be the beginning of thinking. If thinking can neither entirely embrace critique nor become its full incarnation, this is precisely because of an inherent dogmatism of all critique: the critical idea is founded not only on the assurance or *doxa* that binary severing is ultimately possible without also being rendered impossible from within, but also on the uncritical faith in the salutary nature of what critique tries to sever off in strokes of uncontaminated purity and the desirability of thus achieved purity and ideality. By questioning the critical ground of assumptions on which critique rests, as well as that which necessarily limits critique from within, thinking is unconditionally critical of all the conditions on which the critical idea is grounded. Such a criticism of critique turns thinking into a hypercriticism, as it were.

Let us call to mind one more time that like the notion of "theory," "critique" is used as a name for the practice of close reading, rhetorical reading, or "deconstructive" reading in the North American academy as a result of the reception of so-called French postmodern thought—particularly, of deconstruction. Ironically, no one has more clearly resisted identifying deconstruction with critique than Derrida. Yet, according to Derrida, deconstruction, although critical of critique, "does not seek to discredit critique. Deconstruction unrelentingly relegitimizes the necessity and the heritage of critique without, however, neither renouncing the genealogy of the critical idea nor the history of the question and supposed privilege of interrogative thought."[38] Deconstruction can give rise to critical effects because of its unconditional criticism of the dogmatism of critique, but "it is even *critique* in an essential manner," a "radical critique," more precisely, a "hypercritique."[39] Whatever the subject matter that thinking consists in, critique belongs to thinking in an essential way. However, to the extent that critique has its roots in an uncritical ground set of presuppositions, it itself needs to be thought. Hypercritique directed at critique seeks to exceed critique without, however, compromising it in the least. In thinking critique otherwise, radical and interminable hypercritique expropriates critique from all reassuring certitudes, above all from the certitude of disposing of unequivocal, definite, and determined oppositions, and opens it up to what, therefore, is by definition indeterminate, incalculable, and unforeseeable—to what exceeds binary determination, and which, therefore, escapes the categorization sought by the latter. Hypercritique makes critique into a duty, but by submitting it to criticism, it also outlines within critique a space for that which is other than the determinable and the determined other that critique severs from its opposite, and which as a noncategorizable other remains an other yet to come.[40]

The preceding discussion of critique, theory, and philosophy concerns some specifically internal threats that puts thinking into question. The honor of thinking is, indeed, at stake when thinking is conflated with "critique," "theory," and "philosophy." Yet, if critique, theory, and philosophy imperil thinking from within, this is because they necessarily arise from within thinking itself and accomplish tasks that are intimately tied to it. However, there is not *one* thinking that critique, theory, and philosophy threaten with annihilation. Thinking is not a unified and separate undertaking. Rather, thinking is multiple from the start and takes shape only by way of such differentiation and multiplication of its forms. But although it takes place in the shape of these various undertakings that are critique, theory, and philosophy, it is also what ceaselessly questions these formations and expands on their inherent limits. Thinking occurs in no other way than by way of the uncompromising vigilance regarding the unquestioned presuppositions of the different forms in which it segregates.

During the years of my apprenticeship of philosophy, different teachers, approaches, experiences, encounters, and events formed my sense of the philosophical. Derrida's seminar titled "Theory of the Philosophical Discourse," which I attended at the Ecole Normale Supérieure in Paris in 1968–1969, during the first year among several that I spent at this institution, was definitely the decisive event that shaped my understanding of philosophy. There I began to understand that the unquestionable and irreducible uniqueness of philosophy as a disciplinary discourse rests on structures, which, while enabling the autonomy of the philosophical, at the same time tie it to its many others—particularly, to literature situating it within a complex economy that also prevents the philosophical from ever severing itself completely from these others. Henceforth, the task of thinking for me became one of investigating these enabling and disabling structures constitutive of the philosophical, including those of critique and theory. To continue thinking within the legacy of Derridean thought is to pursue the legitimate demands of theorizing and criticism without, however, ceasing to be critical of both the dogmatic presuppositions and the certitudes of theory and critique. Indeed, fidelity in thinking in response to that legacy consists above all in preventing the conceptual and categorial grid that informs philosophical thought from closing thought upon itself and of eliminating the possibility, first and foremost, of something that would not let itself be identified by what Kant referred to as the "form of thinking." This form of thinking, however necessary, must be rethought so as to secure a space within it for the possibility of events so singular and so new that they do not let themselves be determined in distinction from and in opposition to what already obtains.

The essays collected in this book were written over more than ten years. Initially, *The Honor of Thinking* was planned as a systematic book, but circumstances did not permit my carrying the project through in such a form. Although each one of the essays in this book can be read independently, without heeding the order in which they appear here, what holds them together will not elude the shrewd reader, although it is perhaps visible at times only by way of dotted lines. By focusing these introductory remarks on the rationale for dividing the book into three sections—"Critique," "Theory," "Philosophy"—and explaining its title, I hope to have provided the reader with the hints necessary to construct the broader picture that should emerge from these essays, one that relates to the task of thinking. This task arises not only at the end of philosophy as the project of another beginning of thought, that is, as a beginning in which thinking turns upon the unthought of the metaphysical tradition and thus realizes an originary possibility of philosophy: one that was forgotten in the development of metaphysical thought. Rather, the task in question consists in thinking thinking otherwise—in other words, in meeting the challenge of the unthinkable to thought. Only in this extreme confrontation with the demand to account for the unaccountable, the unpredictable, the impossible, and the still-to-come can thinking ultimately be true to its name.

PART I

CRITIQUE

1

Critique, Hypercriticism, Deconstruction

The challenge of deconstruction is how to distinguish between intentional objects in thought without judging and deciding; in other words, how to do justice to what requires recognition on the basis of its singularity. Deconstruction demands demarcation that proceeds without a criteriology, or that is not critical. And yet, it is precisely as a critique—in the sense of literary criticism—or as a critique of philosophy understood either as an antiphilosophy or as a Kantian investigation of the transcendental condition of possibility of knowledge, if not of philosophizing, that deconstruction has often been presented. This misjudgment of its thrust could have easily been avoided by a more careful scrutiny of Derrida's texts.

That deconstruction is not a critique is stated in a rather unambiguous and decidedly propositional manner throughout Derrida's writings. Among the many possible references, here are two examples: The first is from the "Ja, or the faux-bond," where Derrida writes: "deconstruction is not a critical operation; it takes critique as its object; deconstruction, at one moment or another, always aims at the thrust confided in the critical, critico-theoretical agency, that is, the deciding agency, the ultimate possibility of the decidable; deconstruction is a deconstruction of critical dogmatics."[1] The second comes from "Lettre à un ami japonais," where Derrida writes that "deconstruction is neither an *analysis* nor a *critique* . . . in a general, or Kantian sense. The authority of the *krinein* or of *krisis* (decision, choice, judgement, distinction) is itself, in the same way as the whole apparatus of transcendental criticism, one of the essential 'themes' or 'objects' of deconstruction."[2]

Although altogether distinct from a critical operation, deconstruction is not without relation to critique. It is an operation first and foremost upon the critical faith in the possibility of pure distinction and in the critical value of an immaculate, uncontaminated, invulnerable, and impenetrable limit. This is evident from Derrida's concern with the fatal necessity of the contamination of fundamental originarity, from his early text *Le problème de la genèse dans la philosophie de Husserl*, to his most recent writings.[3]

Yet, although deconstruction deals with critique, it is not a critique of critique. The constructive operation is not carried out in the name of critical values. It does not seek to establish more rigorous criteria for the theoretical enterprise. Nor is deconstruction anticritical. In spite of its interrogation of the possibilities of pure distinction, deconstruction recognizes the necessity of distinguishing, and even the occasional *critical* (and scientific) power of critique. Indeed, while deconstruction operates on the faith and the values of pure distinction, it does not affect the limits within which the critico-theoretical enterprise (philosophical or literary) generates distinctions that have antidogmatic consequences. But where such differentiation and discrimination takes place in the perspective of values of purity, fundamental originarity, and decidability, deconstruction questions the claims made.

In order to demarcate deconstruction from critique, I turn to a brief analysis of Benjamin's essay "Critique of Violence" and Derrida's discussion of that essay in "Force of Law: The 'Mystical Foundation of Authority.' "[4] Although Benjamin's work, and the essay on violence in particular, occasionally arouses alarm because of the ambiguity of some of its statements and operations, because of its particular interpretation of Jewish thought, and because of its disquieting proximity to such thinkers as Georges Sorel, Ludwig Klages, and Carl Schmitt, to name a few, his writings have come to be seen, at least by some literary critics, as situated in the neighborhood of deconstruction. It is, therefore, all the more important to show that what Derrida brings to bear on his reading of Benjamin's essay on violence is quite different from Benjamin's concerns. In spite of its inhibiting hermetism—which would require a careful analysis of its own—the stated intentions as well as the argumentative strategies of "Critique of

Violence" are not akin to those of deconstruction.[5] As the title of the essay clearly and unequivocally suggests, Benjamin intends to treat violence critically, to subject it to a critique. But what does Benjamin mean by "critique"? What characterizes, in his eyes, "a critical approach" (*eine kritische Fragestellung*), and what, in particular, are the criteria (*Massstäbe*) needed to distinguish between the "more precise critical approach," he advocates, and ordinary critiques (*CV*, 236)? A critique, Benjamin tells us, is rooted in a philosophy that enables, on the one hand, a "scheidende und entscheidende Einstellung," a discriminating, separating, demarcating approach, and on the other, a decisive, deciding, ruling approach (*CV*, 251).[6] Such separation and decision require criteria, extrinsic or intrinsic distinguishing marks or characteristics by which a thing can be judged, estimated, distinguished, and decided upon. A critique of violence must therefore seek first to establish what Benjamin calls the "criterion for violence itself (*der Gewalt selbst*) as a principle" (*CV*, 236). In seeking to determine "the only secure foundation of . . . critique," Benjamin grounds himself on a "philosophy" of the history of violence, singling out one species or function of violence whose analysis yields the criterion for determining violence as such (*der Gewalt überhaupt, der Gewalt selbst*) (*CV*, 240). A very determined, and hence clearly distinguishable, kind of violence provides the criterion for deciding on violence itself as a principle. By this criterion, violence as a principle is *set apart,* cut off from all other kinds of violence with which less critical critiques of violence may have been concerned. This more precise critical approach, with its criterion of violence itself, aims at breaking the circle (*Umlauf*) of the "dialectical rising and falling in the . . . formations of violence," that is, "the law of oscillation" (*Schwankungsgesetz*), which rules not only the history of all other functions and genres of violence, but the less precise critical approaches as well (*CV*, 251).

Now, if Benjamin can make use of one particular kind of violence to determine violence itself as a principle, it is because this form of violence is not just any ordinary form. As previously illustrated, the criterion for violence as violence must be capable of setting it apart from all other species of violence. Benjamin achieves this demarcation by making demarcation the very criterion of violence itself. Benjamin's more precise critique of violence sets violence apart on the basis of violence's own separating and deciding power. His critique shows violence to be critique—separation and decision—a *scheidende und entscheidende Einstellung.*

With this gesture of thought, Benjamin's "Critique of Violence" also distinguishes itself from critique in the common sense and, in spite of some allusions to the contrary, from critique in the philosophical, particularly Kantian, sense. Benjamin's more precise concept of critique differs from critique as skillful judging and as an investigation from a transcendental point of view by turning critique into a principle, into the metaphysical, ontological idea of the starting point (*die Idee ihres Ausgangs*) of the "philosophy" of the history of violence (*CV*, 251). Schematically speaking, Benjamin's essay succeeds in radically divorcing critique from both the common use of the term and the history of the concept in Kantian thought by ontologizing a methodological concept.

Benjamin's strategy in "Critique of Violence" does not so much concern itself with preserving at any cost distinctions that already exist between different kinds and functions of violence, or between different kinds of philosophical or legal positions on violence, but with performing and securing such distinctions in the first place. His scheme is to cut through the relations, connections, and correlations that still exist between the traditional theoretical definitions of the various forms of violence. These traditional definitions do not permit distinction to have the cutting edge sought by Benjamin's critical approach. From the beginning of the essay, Benjamin determines "the task of a critique of violence . . . [to be] that of expounding its relation to law and justice" (*CV*, 236). His ensuing analysis of the relation between violence imposed by fate and the law seeks to demonstrate that precisely no such relation can ultimately be justified. In contrast, divine violence is said to relate to just ends not "as means at all but in some different way" (*CV*, 247). But let us first reconstruct the major argumentative steps of Benjamin's demonstration of the absence of all relation between violence in the legal sense, violence as means, and just ends.

The question that Benjamin raises right at the start of his essay is "whether violence, as a principle, could be a moral means even to just ends" (*CV*, 236). He sets out to distinguish the "diametrically opposed" theses on violence posited by natural law and positive law (*CV*, 237). This diametrical opposition stems from natural law's conception of violence as "a product of nature" (*CV*, 237). Benjamin makes positive law his starting point—though only a starting point—first and foremost because positive law sets itself apart from a natural determination of violence, nature always being associated by Benjamin with the lowest and most ensnaring forms of fate. He also opts for positive law against jusnaturalism, because in contradistinction to the latter, positive law undertakes "a fundamental distinction between kinds of violence" (*CV*, 237). Jusnaturalism not only engages in a natural justification of violence; the distinction that it makes between violence as a means for either just or unjust ends is not fundamental. Thus, Benjamin's strategic privileging of positive law rests on its more fundamental separating and cutting power.

Yet, however radical the diametrical opposition of the two assessments of violence may be, they partake in one fundamental dogma that links them intimately together, the dogmatic assumption that "just ends can be attained by justified means, justified means used for just ends" (*CV*, 237). Therefore, the conceptual antagonism between jusnaturalism and positive law over violence cannot be as absolute as it might seem. Jusnaturalism and positive law embrace each other through the "circular argument," on which they are grounded (*CV*, 237). Benjamin's aim throughout the essay consists of trying to break that circular argument, by seeking "mutually independent criteria both of just ends and of justified means," to show that between just ends and justified means—and more generally between violence as a means and just ends—there is an "irreconcilable conflict" (*CV*, 237). Yet, if the domains of ends and means can be shown to be irreconcilable, or more precisely, incompatible (*unvereinbar*), jusnaturalism and positive law, losing all common ground, drift apart and become opposed to each other in an unheard-of fashion. With their underlying dogmatic assumption destroyed, both legal accounts of violence would finally be clearly and radically distinct. Such a move would enable Benjamin to further radicalize his claim that positive law contains an insight into the nature of violence that is far more fundamental than that of jusnaturalism and that can be extracted from it before relinquishing once and for all the two antagonistic legal positions.

In his pursuit of such a demarcation, Benjamin takes up the distinction made by positive law, one that promises to be more fundamental than that undertaken by natural law: the distinction between sanctioned and unsanctioned violence. Indeed, the critical question of "the meaning of this distinction"—of "what light is thrown on the nature of violence by the fact that such a criterion or distinction can be applied to it at all"—insinuates an even more radical demarcation since it can only be carried out from "a standpoint outside positive legal philosophy but also outside natural law" (*CV*, 238). In other words, the historico-philosophical view of law and violence that this very critical move presupposes leads to a rejection of, and departure from, both legal conceptions of violence. The position on violence that emerges from this departure is absolutely distinct from—that is, without relation to—what has thus been shed as ballast by the critical operation.

The fundamental distinction set forth by positive law is that between sanctioned and unsanctioned violence—more precisely, a violence whose ends are based on the presence of a general historical acknowledgment and one whose ends are not. Yet the distinction in question presupposes another difference, the difference between natural ends, which lack historical acknowledgment, and legal ends, which are defined by such sanctioning. As Benjamin's discussion of the legal conditions in contemporary Europe shows, the distinctions between sanctioned and unsanctioned violence is aimed at replacing all natural ends by legal ends, and thus at monopolizing violence in the name of the law. The meaning of the distinction at the heart of positive law implies that violence *should not* exist outside the law. Positive law wishes to separate violence from all natural ends. Positive law wants to denaturalize violence, to set it radically apart from the realm of nature.

The interest of the law in monopolizing violence, in making it unavailable as a means to serve the natural ends of individuals, is that the law qua law is grounded on violence; it is the result of a violent institution. Hence, all existence of violence outside the law is a threat to the law. The monopolization of violence by the law serves to "preserve the law itself" (*CV*, 239). The meaning of the fundamental distinction on which positive law is based thus begins to come into view. Benjamin's analysis of one of the forms in which violence is still permissible outside the legal system— the right to strike—reveals that the distinction in question testifies to the recognition that violence is lawmaking. Violence can overthrow a legal system, modify it, and institute a new one. If Benjamin has privileged positive law for its distinction between sanctioned and unsanctioned violence, it is precisely because that very distinction is an implicit acknowledgment that violence is essentially lawmaking. This characteristic of violence is, he adds, "the only secure foundation of its critique" (*CV*, 240). It provides a first hint of what the criterion for violence as a principle is, by determining violence as the "basis for, or a modification to, relatively stable conditions

(*Verhältnisse*)," in contrast to its definition by jusnaturalism as "the means to secure directly whatever happens to be sought" (*CV*, 240). Violence is most fundamentally lawmaking and not "predatory violence" (*CV*, 240). This means that violence does not give birth to laws sometimes, or accidentally; it does so necessarily. With fatal necessity, violence institutes the law, that is, relatively stable relations. The correlative implication is that the law is always based on an act of violent institution and violence pervades its system throughout. Benjamin's analysis of the meaning of the distinction constitutive of positive law takes him a step closer toward securing violence as a principle.

Violence as lawmaking violence is, indeed, a distinguishing trait that hints at what Benjamin ultimately shows to qualify violence as violence, because in lawmaking violence, violence appears to be nonmediate (*nicht mittelbar*)—not to have its essence in being a means to an end. If violence institutes the law, it happens in an immediate fashion. This also explains why Benjamin so forcefully insists on keeping the complementary characterization of violence as law-preserving apart from violence as lawmaking, although in the end the latter is unmasked as a manifestation of mythic violence.

Within sanctioned conditions or relations (*Verhältnisse*), violence takes on the shape of law-preserving violence. Here, violence is at the service of legal ends. It has become *mittelbare Gewalt,* a means for "the representation and preservation of an order imposed by fate" (*CV*, 241). Although the law is said to originate in lawmaking violence—that is, as we shall see, in "violence crowned by fate"—Benjamin notes that law-preserving violence, which is characterized as a "threatening violence" that is "threatening, like fate," must remain distinct from lawmaking violence (*CV*, 242). Indeed, where, as in the case of the police, the distinction between those two functions of violence becomes blurred (*die Trennung . . . aufgehoben ist*), an "unnatural combination (*Verbindung*)," a "spectral mixture," occurs (*CV*, 242). If the police are so detestable for Benjamin, it is because they weave tight relations and mix what is to be kept separate so thoroughly that "nothing essential at all" can any more be encountered in the phenomenon in question, which consequently escapes "critical evaluation" (*CV*, 243). To intertwine lawmaking violence and law-preserving violence is the high point of mythic violence. Although lawmaking violence is nonmediate violence, it institutes more or less stable relations, or *Verhältnisse*. Therefore, it is mythic violence. Law-preserving violence makes violence subservient by tying violence up with (legal) ends. Therefore, this violence is crowned by fate. But, in the police, even those two distinct manifestations of fateful violence become linked to one another. This obfuscates what, as a criterion for violence *itself*, could slash the mythic network, or text, apart and sets violence free from its mythic manifestations: violence's immediacy. In the sphere of fate, violence is tied to what it is not. It is not itself anymore and has its "criterion" in something other than violence.

Benjamin concludes his development up to this point by noting that "all violence as a means is either lawmaking or law-preserving. If it lays claim to neither of these predicates, it forfeits all validity" (*CV*, 243). In other words, even lawmaking violence is not *simply* nonmediate. The relations that it institutes as law in whatever nonmediate fashion contaminate it. Lawmaking violence, because it is a means, is impure violence. And because of its linkage as a means to an end, it is terribly ambiguous (*zweideutig*). Ambiguity, however, is *the* characteristic of the order of fate. It is the result of mixing what has to be kept apart, of contaminating the pure by linking it up with what it is not. Yet the ambiguity that hovers over all lawmaking (and law-preserving violence, in all its forms), must be dispelled and broken. Benjamin intends to demonstrate that "all the violence imposed by fate, using justified means [is] of itself in irreconcilable conflict with just ends" (*CV*, 247). In other words, Benjamin sets out to break the circle of the fundamental dogma that "just ends can be attained by justified means, justified means used for just ends" (*CV*, 247). As a means, violence, whether lawmaking or law-preserving, cannot possibly stand in a relation to just ends.

As Benjamin's discussion of the nonviolent forms for resolving conflicts evidences, the issue in question is not that of the purity of means. Pure means, that is, nonviolent means, such as the general strike (within certain limits), can, through a "severing of relations," achieve a limited undoing of the order of fate and the law (*CV*, 239). But pure means, because they are still means, cannot ever hope to achieve a deliverance from the spell, or, literally, to untie the binding circle (*Erlösung aus dem Bannkreis*), "of all the world-historical conditions of existence obtaining hitherto" (*CV*, 247). Only violence can succeed in this. Hence, Benjamin concludes, it becomes necessary to investigate "other kinds of violence than all those envisaged by legal theory" (*CV*, 247). He argues that such "a different kind of violence" can only be one "that certainly could be neither the justified or unjustified means to those ends, but is not related to them as means at all but in some different way" (*CV*, 247; trans. mod.). In short, only a violence that has no (mediate) relation to what it is to achieve can succeed in dispelling and unraveling the texture of the law instituted in lawmaking violence. Such other violence, therefore, must be an end in itself—a violence that has its criterion in itself and not in an outside that could contaminate it. It must be a violence so pure that all possible relations as a means to ends are cut off. It can only be immediate, nonmediate violence. And it must be shown that this kind of violence is the essence of violence and that, hence, violence as a means stands in a relation of incompatibility with justified as well as just ends.

The subsequent task that Benjamin faces is to dispel all possible similarity between nonmediate and mythic violence. Mythic violence, indeed, stands in a relation of resemblance to the kind of violence advocated by Benjamin, in that in its most archetypal form, it is not a means to an end, but "a mere manifestation of the gods" (*CV*, 248). The critical gesture by which the link of resemblance is cut rests on the proof that, rather than being capable of deciding about what he had termed "the impossibility of conclusive pronouncements" (*Unmöglichkeit bündiger Entscheidung*), or "the ultimate insolubility of all legal problems," mythic violence is not only closely related (*nächstverwandt*), but it is identical to lawmaking violence (*CV*, 247; trans. mod.). Although mythic violence is nonmediate violence at first, qua power-making violence, it is a setting of the "boundary stone on the frontier between men and gods" (*CV*, 248). "Power [is] the principle of all mythic lawmaking," in the same way as "the establishing of frontiers . . . is the primal phenomenon of all lawmaking violence" (*CV*, 248–249). The same uncertainty and ambiguity characteristic of the sphere of fate, from which burst mythic violence, distinguish the "demonically ambiguous way" in which legal violence strikes (*CV*, 249). This "deliberate (*planvolle*) ambiguity" of both mythic and lawmaking violence is a function of their boundary setting. Benjamin writes that "where frontiers are decided the adversary is not simply annihilated" (*CV*, 249). Mythic violence, in the same way as lawmaking violence, is "not actually destructive" (*CV*, 248). The differences that it institutes, the limits that it traces, the laws it establishes are not radical, not clear-cut, not absolutely severing. What has been separated by frontiers is characterized by ambiguity, and deliberately so, since mythic and lawmaking violence, however nonmediate, are also mediate violence in that they institute the law as an end with violence as the means. However important the characterization of lawmaking and mythic violence as nonmediate has been along Benjamin's critical itinerary, it now becomes clear that both forms of nonmediate violence are not pure. They are contaminated by mediate violence, and thus terribly ambiguous. But the critical distinction between both kinds of violence is nonetheless decisive. It is a call for destroying this ambiguity—the links between both kinds of violence—by posing "again, in the last resort, the question of a pure immediate violence that might be able to call a halt to mythic violence" (*CV*, 249).

Such pure nonmediate violence is called "divine violence." The principle of its end making (*Zwecksetzung*) is justice (*CV*, 248). This pure violence, free of all mediate contamination, is "the antithesis in all respects" to mythic violence (*CV*, 249). If the latter "sets boundaries, the [former] . . . boundlessly destroys them" (*CV*, 249). Pure violence does so by cutting through the relations that make up the fateful realm of the mythic. By destroying the ties woven by myth, pure violence destroys the ambiguous limits, frontiers, and boundaries that have been erected by mythic violence in its manifestations as lawmaking violence. Pure immediate violence unbinds boundlessly by severing the connections that were established between itself and all possible historical ends. It is for this reason that Benjamin can characterize this divine violence as *schlagende Gewalt*, as "striking" or "slashing violence." This violence is critical in that it radically tears asunder what has become related, or what has been distinguished in the mode of *Grenzsetzung*, of "frontier setting," that obtains in the sphere of law. Divine violence, pure violence distinguishes itself as a setting apart, as a cutting off of all references to any other. And if Benjamin can say that whereas mythic violence "is bloody power over mere life for its own sake" and hence is based on an impure and interested relation to mere life—that is, its destruction of life is merely surgical—then divine violence is "pure power over all life for the sake of the living," or the soul of the living (*des Lebendigen*) (*CV*, 250). Divine power is absolutely lethal to merely natural life, "for with mere life the rule of the law over the living ceases" (*CV*, 250). Mere life, as Benjamin stresses in particular in the essay on Goethe's *Elective Affinities* (written at the same time as the essay on violence), is the sphere of the mythic interconnectedness of guilt. The uncompromising destruction of life is a just (*gerecht*) expiation because it takes place in the name of the living, of *der Lebendige*, insofar as the latter is not merely seen as a natural being who is biologically alive, but partakes of *das Lebendige*.

Das Lebendige, or *Lebendigkeit*, is what transcends mere life. Benjamin notes that it refers to "that life in [man] . . . that is identically present in earthly life, death and afterlife" (*CV*, 251). It is what, in human beings, separates them from themselves as bodily beings, and the mere life in them. It is of the order of the divine *krinein* itself—the act of creation—to which it points, thus exceeding life, which Benjamin puts into the same class as goods, rights, and the like (*CV*, 251). *Das Lebendige*, by contrast, manifests its divine belonging by transcending, through active destruction, life itself, "the marked bearer of guilt" (*CV*, 251).

Yet, the distinctions that Benjamin reclaims from the law and myth; from fate's attempt to weave connections, nets, and texts; from any attempt to blur difference are not yet complete. Pure violence has been demarcated with all necessary rigor from its manifestations in mythic violence, and from all the eternal forms bastardized by myth with law (*CV*, 252). Yet pure violence must still be distinguished from what human beings might construe as its manifestation. Indeed, Benjamin states that, although revolutionary violence is that "highest manifestation of unalloyed violence by man," it is impossible for humankind "to decide when unalloyed violence has been realized in particular cases. For only mythic violence, not divine, will be recognizable as such with certainty, unless it be in incomparable effects, because the expiatory power of violence is not visible to man" (*CV*, 252). Pure violence is different from what, in the eyes of men's critical and deciding powers, is a manifestation of that very violence. It thus separates itself from its own decidable manifestations. Yet this does not imply that it would itself be tinged by the ambiguity characteristic of mythic violence. If pure violence separates itself from itself in its appearances, it is because it is deciding, separating, dividing violence. It is nothing but critique. And therefore, its certain manifestation can only occur in "incomparable effects," that is, in effects that have no relation to anything, that are separated in their uniqueness from everything else, that are decisive and deciding events in and for themselves. With this last gesture, Benjamin has undertaken to set pure violence radically free from all decidable manifestations, and he has done so by construing it as the power of separation itself, even separating itself from itself. It is nothing but the power of distinction, and hence, Benjamin writes that "divine violence, which is the sign [*insignium*] and seal but never the means of sacred execution, may be called sovereign [*waltende*] violence" (*CV*, 252). Divine violence reigns as the *insignium* and the seal, as a marking and distinguishing activity.

This activity sets it apart. It is the slashing (*schlagende*) occurring of itself. A decisive criterion has, thus, been found, which can establish violence in its purity, free from all contamination by and entanglement with otherness. What establishes divine violence in its own right, *as itself*, is separation itself. The purity of divine violence can only consist in this violence's infinite separation of itself from everything else. In the same way as *das Lebendige,* which in mere life is the transcending power destructive of life itself, divine violence is (nothing but) unrelenting, infinite separation. This separation is what Benjamin calls divine justice.

With this final gesture, Benjamin has concluded his critical wrenching of distinctions from the demonically ambiguous realm of the law's interconnecting and mixing of heterogeneous kinds of violence. By arguing that pure violence, violence so pure that it cannot be recognized with certainty in its manifestations, is pure *krinein,* he has unequivocally shown the divine and undecidable *krinein* to have its essence in decision itself. This sets violence apart as a principle that has the criterion for itself exclusively within itself.

In "Force of Law: The 'Mystical Foundation of Authority,'" Derrida refers to Benjamin's concern with the function of distinguishing in "Critique of Violence," as a "hypercriticism" (*FL*, 979).[7] As demonstrated, Benjamin's obsession with critique compels him to establish the object of his critique—violence—as the very essence of the critical operation itself. By seeking to find a criterion for violence as a principle, critical separation and decision is, moreover, raised to an ontological and metaphysical status. It *is* the divine *itself*. In the name of this divine violence, which Benjamin has isolated in a critical strategy oriented toward pure rupture, he rejects (*verwerflich,* which is one of the last words of the text) all other forms of violence by severing all ties to them. Benjamin's hypercritical operations toward a notion of pure destruction (of the law and the realm of fate) rests on slashing relations and on casting off what, consequently, has become incommensurable with the purity of divine decision.

In "Force of Law," Derrida takes up Benjamin's trust in the possibility of critique and decision by pointing out the "radically problematic" nature of his conceptual divisions (*FL*, 981). This confidence in the critical enterprise goes hand in hand with what is called the "terrible ethico-political ambiguity of the text" (*FL*, 1024). Indeed, he notes, the "Critique of Violence" belongs, in 1921, to the great anti-parliamentary and anti-"*Aufklärung*" wave on which Nazism so to speak surfaced and even surfed in the '20's and the beginning of the '30's. (*FL*, 975)

Beyond the affinities that it maintains with the worst (the critique of *Aufklärung*, the theory of language and fallen language, the critique of representation and of parliamentary democracy, etc.), is a temptation [left] open . . . to the survivors of the victims of the final solution, to its past, present or potential victims . . . to think of the holocaust as an uninterpretable manifestation of the divine violence insofar as this divine violence would be at the same time annihilating, expiatory and bloodless. (*FL*, 1044)

Of this text, Derrida remarks that "it lends itself to an exercise in deconstructive reading" (*FL*, 979). Indeed, Benjamin's distinctions and oppositions, the "ambiguous and laborious movement on [his] part to preserve at any cost a distinction or correlation without which his whole project could collapse" (*FL*, 1001), "seem to me to call more than ever for deconstruction; they deconstruct themselves, even as paradigms for deconstruction" (*FL*, 977). Obviously, the deconstruction of Benjamin's critical operation takes place "beyond Benjamin's explicit purpose" (*FL*, 977). It is not of Benjamin's signature, *if* signing is limited to assuming responsibility for the explicit intentions of the text. Explicitly, the whole strategy Benjamin uses to organize his text serves his effort to establish the most rigorous distinction between divine violence and all other sorts of violence by letting them go. The responsibility for all the operations that constitute Benjamin's hypercriticism: the concept of a nonmediate violence (*FL*, 1025), the interpretation of divine violence as respecting the living (*FL*, 1027), the distinction between the Greek and the Jew (*FL*, 1037), his interpretation of Judaism in particular, and finally, his own signature (divine violence itself) is given to Benjamin. That is, Derrida "leaves the responsibility for all of the decisive pieces of the mechanism for decision in Benjamin's text" to Benjamin (*FL*, 1025). Consequently, if deconstruction is not to be an external operation brought to bear on Benjamin's essay, "this deconstruction [must be] in some way the operation or rather the very experience that this text . . . first does itself, by itself, on itself" (*FL*, 981). A deconstructive reading has to demonstrate that "deconstruction [is] at work, in full negotiation: in the 'things themselves' and in Benjamin's text" (*FL*, 1003). It is to be shown that such an "auto-hetero-deconstruction" of the text ruins the latter's critical purpose, as well as the signature that in the name of divine violence would wish to decide upon its achievement and destiny (*FL*, 981).

I do not retrace here Derrida's various steps through which the text of Benjamin is put "to the test of a certain deconstructive necessity" (*FL*, 1035). I only take up the principle that marshals his reading of Benjamin's attempt to distinguish and decide. Derrida writes that "what threatens the rigor of the distinction between the two types of violence [lawmaking and law-preserving violence], is at bottom the paradox of iterability. Iterability requires the origin to repeat itself originarily, to alter itself so as to have the value of origin, that is to conserve itself " (*FL*, 1007–1009). Because iterability, "inscribes the possibility of repetition [that is, of law-preserving violence] . . . at the heart of the originary [that is, lawmaking violence]" (*FL*, 997), Benjamin's text ruins the distinctions at the very moment it tries to make them. Now, this paradox of iterability is a "law or . . . general necessity. . . . It has an *a priori* worth" (*FL*, 1009). For a priori reasons, then, conservation is inscribed from the start in the essential structure of the lawmaking foundation. Derrida notes that Benjamin knows, and even knows very well, that his text is ruined in advance by this law (*FL*, 1007). Proof of this is, according to Derrida, that Benjamin rejects at one point both forms of violence. It must, however, be noted that Benjamin does not reject both forms of violence on the basis of a recognition of the a priori law in question. The distinction between lawmaking and law-preserving violence, as much as its subsequent rejection, is fueled by the concept of a nonmediate violence. Indeed, as I hope I have been able to show in my exposition of Benjamin's argumentative strategies, lawmaking violence can be rejected once its concept has yielded a concept of a nonmediate violence. If it must be rejected, it is because lawmaking violence as lawmaking can at best only be a phantom of such pure violence. The rejection of the distinction of the two functions of violence takes place in the horizon of the desire for an immediate violence that would not institute an order of law. Nor does Benjamin's text, in my view, recognize that what motivates his critique—the thought of a pure nonmediate violence—is itself subject to the a priori law of iterability. Even if he would, as Derrida suggests with respect to what Benjamin establishes about the "dialectic of up and down" of the founding or conserving violence of the law, "to some extent recognize this law of iterability that insures that the founding violence is always represented in a conservative violence that always repeats the tradition of its origin and that ultimately keeps nothing but a foundation destined from the start to be repeated, conserved, reinstituted," no such recognition leads to a complication and subsequent rejection of the ultimate distinction he makes (*CV*, 1031–1033). If, in the end, divine violence appears to be undecidable, it is because its own concept of pure distinction requires that it must be different from its own manifestations. Whatever Benjaminian gestures could be shown to undermine the thought of such a pure violence, they are not deliberate; they certainly are not thematized. Hence, if the a priori law of iterability does, for principled reasons, contaminate the purity of divine violence, it is because the very "thing" itself of a pure nonmediate violence cannot *not* yield to what it so violently excludes—the mediate, the law, mere life. It is not necessarily the text in its common understanding that would reflect, or reveal traces of the a priori law's contaminating effects. In other words, if the text deconstructs the distinctions that Benjamin wishes to establish in absolute purity, it is because the a priori law of iterability causes his text to open itself up—by the very "things" that it seeks to secure—to what ruins it as a text as well. It is in this sense, I believe, that one must read what Derrida, in "Force of Law," writes about the status of the deconstructive text:

The text *Zur Kritik der Gewalt* consists of this strange exposition: before our eyes a demonstration ruins the distinctions it proposes. It exhibits and archivizes the very movement of its implosion, leaving instead what we call a text, the ghost of a text that, itself in ruins, at once foundation and conservation, accomplishes neither and remains there, up to a certain point, for a certain amount of time, readable and unreadable, like the exemplary ruin that singularly warns us of the fate of all texts and all signatures in their relation to law. . . . Such would be (let it be said in passing) the status without statute, the statute without status of a text considered deconstructive and what remains of it. The text does not escape the law that it states. It is ruined and contaminated, it becomes the specter of itself. (*CV*, 1007)

In short, if the a priori law of iterability deconstructs Benjamin's attempt to isolate, in all purity, a thing such as pure nonmediate violence, and if this very attempt is itself (as the signature by which Benjamin signs adieu to his text suggests) a possible manifestation of that very same violence, then it is because such a thing as pure violence, or a text such as the pure manifestation of divine decision, must, with necessity, ruin itself. But since this necessity is that of "the thing itself" and of the text as the performance of the divine *krinein*, it is one that operates on a level different from what is usually called a text. As a result, the deconstructive operation takes place against all textual appearances, contrary even to the "evidence" that, toward the end of "Critique of Violence," Benjamin has, indeed, succeeded in achieving the purpose of his critique. Deconstruction, let it be said in passing, is, therefore, not a critical operation, nor is it an operation akin to literary or textual criticism. What Derrida calls texts is the (always singular) "law" between what we call a text and the spectral, or nonphenomenal, text, into which the first implodes.

The critique of violence must be thoroughly distinguished from deconstruction. As a critique, it is based on the security and confidence of mastering the threat of contamination. By naming it, Benjamin hopes to contain it. By referring to it as demonic ambiguity, contamination is put into its place and ejected from the sphere of the divine. It becomes the exact counterpart of the divine—without relation to it. Deconstruction by contrast, insofar as its essential "theme" is critique, is what Derrida calls "*différantielle* contamination," a thought that excludes the possibility of all rigorous distinction, of establishing itself in purity and without a contaminating relation to an other (*FL*, 997). Deconstruction, rather than lending itself to a severing of relations by letting the other go in the same way as one lets a ballast go to soar up into purer realms, attempts to do justice to the other that is the object of all decisions. More precisely, deconstruction is responsibility—a responding to, first and foremost, the other in its alterity— before all critical separation, division, and decision. This other is the referent against, from, and with which distinction occurs. Yet, this other, before any division (or contract, for that matter), is infinite because it is irreducible, and it is irreducible because it is "the other's coming as the singularity that is always other" (*FL*, 964). Deconstruction responds not so much to the other constituted through a critical division as to the always singular "appearing"—the irreducible contingency that it happened to be occuring or coming—that all critical decision presupposes. No relation (logical or dialectic) is capable of mastering the singularity of this otherness, or of doing justice to it. No severance of relations in a hypercritical spirit can succeed in ridding itself of this irreducible event of the "appearing" of the other; it will always have been the denegation of a response to the other's coming. Yet as a response to that coming in its irreducible singularity, deconstruction is owed to the other, and hence infinite, as well. Deconstruction is infinitely responsible toward the singularity that sustains and undercuts the "decision that *cuts,* that divides," to mere life, for instance, which in the name of the living is pushed, if not sold off, by the critical operation (*FL*, 963).

It is in the spirit of such justice that, "in saying *adieu* or *au-revoir* to Benjamin," the deconstructive text, signed by Derrida, "nevertheless leave[s] him the last word. I let him sign, at least if he can," Derrida writes. "It is always necessary that the other sign and it is always the other that signs last. In other words, first" (*FL*, 1037).

The Sober Absolute

According to Philippe Lacoue-Labarthe and Jean-Luc Nancy in *The Literary Absolute*, Walter Benjamin's dissertation "The Concept of Criticism in German Romanticism" has revolutionized traditional studies in German Romanticism. Indeed, Winfried Menninghaus remarks that Benjamin's dissertation is the most frequently cited work in studies on that period of German thought. The reason for the breakthrough effect of Benjamin's dissertation is quite clear: his analysis of the major concepts characteristic of Jena Romanticism—the concepts of art, literature, critique, irony, and so on—is fundamental in that he shows these concepts to be the cornerstones of a very specific philosophical position distinct from those of the contemporary major power brokers: Kant and the German Idealists.[1] Even though Benjamin's assessment of the specificity of Romantic thought was made on the basis of the few writings accessible at the time, and, moreover, on a narrow selection of the available material, there is no doubt that his dissertation continues to provide a correct and fruitful view of the early Romantic philosophical conceptions. Yet it also remains true that the dissertation is thoroughly flawed, not only for philological reasons, but for discursive-argumentative reasons as well. As Menninghaus has forcefully shown in *Unendliche Verdopplung*, Benjamin's work abounds with loose argumentation and makes such free use of citations that they are made on occasion to say the exact opposite of what they say in their original context. Furthermore, the exegeses of some concepts (such as the major one of reflection) are essentially limited and distorted. The semantics of a number of fragments is either consciously perverted or forced in certain directions. Finally, the dissertation makes an extremely selective use of the material, selective to the point of being silent about, and perhaps to the point of annihilating, what does not fit his conception. This is especially true for the first part of the dissertation in which Benjamin lays the general philosophical foundation for his analysis of the chief concepts of Romantic thought. And yet, in spite "of these numerous and partly more than marginal violences," Benjamin's "derivation of the cardinal concepts of Romantic poetology from the theory of reflection" remains valid. But even the first part, "On Reflection," where Benjamin finds "the trace of a dominating systematic signification of the Romantic concept of reflection with its two 'moments' of immediacy and infinity," as Menninghaus notes, demands admiration in spite of all its philological and argumentative difficulties.[2] The question thus arises as to what explains this strange paradox of an interpretation that yields correct results despite its poor textural basis and systematic distortion. From where does the surprising confidence that Benjamin demonstrates in his violent penetration of the recalcitrant text material originate? Menninghaus suggests that Benjamin's sagacious analysis of early German Romanticism follows not from any brilliant intuition, but from his own theoretical proximity to the fundamental problems raised by Friedrich Schlegel and Novalis. Menninghaus writes: "The avenues of Benjamin's access to the Romantic theory of reflection are already preprogrammed by his own largely Romantic theory of language."[3] The divining rod with which he approaches the sparse corpus of the Romantics' writings available to him would thus be made up of conceptions and concepts intimately related to the Romantic project itself. At first sight such a conclusion seems warranted. This thesis of a fundamental affinity of Benjamin's thinking to that of the Romantics seems plausible not only because a great number of topics that Benjamin deals with throughout his career—from the question of translation to that of the mechanical work of art, not to speak of the notion of critique—are already broached in the dissertation, but also because his own theories on these subjects appear closely related to what in the dissertation he had claimed to be the Romantics' position on these matters. However compelling and fruitful such an affinity may be in accounting for what Benjamin does in his dissertation, its limits come to light as soon as the specificity and originality of Benjamin's own thinking is established. Above all, it is incapable of accounting for Benjamin's repeated, if not systematic, criticism of Romantic philosophy. Indeed, "The Concept of Criticism in German Romanticism" is anything but a wholesale appropriation or celebration of Romanticism. Its presentation of the main axioms of Romantic thought is not without ambivalence. At times Benjamin shows little sympathy for, indeed, even direct hostility toward, the Romantics' insights. As we shall see, he accuses the Romantics of obscurity, of failing to clearly differentiate between their concepts, of having become embroiled in unresolvable contradictions, of having developed a metaphysics of limited interest, and finally, and not least, of having committed the philosophically unforgivable crime of confusing and mixing levels of thought—a *metabasis allo eis genos.* In the following, I bring Benjamin's criticism of the Romantics into relief in order to precisely determine his point of departure from Romanticism. The vehicle for this demonstration is the concept of critique itself.

Benjamin understands his objections to Romanticism as philosophical objections. More generally, he conceives his overall approach to the Romantics as a philosophical one. From the very beginning of the dissertation, the task to write a "history of the concept of criticism" (as opposed to a "history of criticism itself") is said to be a "philosophical or, more precisely, a problem-historical task (116).[4] The qualification in question is necessary because Benjamin distinguishes two philosophical tasks: one is concerned with a historical problematic; the other is systematic. The dissertation is limited to a philosophical inquiry of the first type, but pushes its investigation, as Benjamin notes, to a point where it indicates, "with complete clarity, a systematic connection" (183). In the introduction to the dissertation, Benjamin gives some indication as to how he wants the terms "philosophical" and "problem-historical" to be understood. After having demarcated such a task from questions concerning the history of philosophy and the philosophy of history, he evokes "a metaphysical hypothesis": "the whole of the history of philosophy in the authentic sense is at the same time and ipso facto the unfolding of a single problem" (117). His analysis of early German Romanticism focusing on a historical problematic, is, I hold, geared toward exhibiting this one single problem of philosophy in the historical configuration of Romantic thought. Once this philosophical task has been achieved, it would be possible to proceed to a systematic evaluation of the way this problem has taken shape in Romanticism and to eventually solve the difficulties that it poses. In order to bring the single problem constitutive of all philosophy as such in to view, one must "determine the entire philosophical bearing (*Tragweite*)" of the Romantics' positions, Benjamin remarks (158). It is a matter of analyzing the Romantics' concepts—and in particular the concept of critique—in a manner that brings out what they contain in themselves and what is clear from the subject matter they address, a manner that treats the concepts "in accordance with [their] most particular philosophical intentions (*nach seinen eigensten philosophischen Intentionen*)" (160). In other words, a philosophical analysis, that is, an analysis regarded from a problem-historical perspective, has to focus on what, from a philosophical viewpoint, are the most proper intentions of the Romantics' concepts, as well as on Romanticism's "positive and negative aspects" (158). Obviously, an analysis of this kind will have to stretch the meaning of the concepts well beyond what the Romantics themselves intended.

Benjamin undoubtedly accords to the early Romantics a very special privilege: for him, Romantic criticism's superiority is at least twofold. Romantic criticism is "the decisive overcoming of aesthetic dogmatism" (154). Indeed, "the Romantics, unlike Enlightenment, did not conceive of form as a rule for judging the beauty of art, or the observance of this rule as a necessary precondition for the pleasing or edifying effect of the work. Form did not count for the Romantics either as a rule in itself or even as dependent on rules" (158). But Romanticism did not only repudiate the eighteenth century's celebration of conventional aesthetic rules, it also "surmounted the destructive moments intrinsic to the theory of *Sturm-und-Drang*," with its "boundless cult of creative power understood as the mere expressive force of the creator" (154). By finding "the laws of the spirit in the work of art itself " (154), early Romanticism thus enjoys the historical privilege of having overturned both the major aesthetic ideologies of the time.

Early German Romanticism's privileged position is further accentuated by a comparison with contemporary criticism. Although contemporary criticism shares with Romantic criticism the overcoming of dogmatism, this overcoming "has come to be taken for granted as legacy of modern criticism," and Benjamin notes that the criticism of the nineteenth and twentieth centuries has once again sunk below the Romantic

standpoint in that it makes the artwork into a mere by-product of subjectivity (154–155). Although it is in truth the offspring of Sturm and Drang
aesthetics, modern criticism overlooks the fact that the liberating negation
of dogmatism by the Romantics rested on the presupposition of the artwork's immanent and objective laws. This negation "secured [indeed] a
basic concept that could not have been previously introduced into the theory with any definiteness: the concept of the work" (155). With this, the
Romantics deduced, "from the side of the object or structure [*Object-oder
Gebilde-Seite*], that very autonomy in the domain of art that Kant, in the
third *Critique*, had lent to the power of judgment" (155). Contemporary
critical thought, by contrast, according to Benjamin, is "not determined
by any theory but only by a deteriorated praxis" (155)—for it, critique is
what is most subjective. Romantic theories of art criticism hold a definite
advantage. Today, the "problematic of German philosophy of art around
1800, as exhibited in the theories of Goethe and the early Romantics, is
[still] legitimate," one reads toward the end of the dissertation (183).

Although from a theoretical viewpoint, Benjamin believed, the Romantics' position on art criticism has not been surpassed, this does not
mean that he uncritically promoted a return to their theories. In spite of
his unmistakable valorization of Romantic thought, quite the opposite is
true: "The basic cardinal principle of critical activity since the Romantic
movement—that is, the judgment of works by immanent criteria—was attained on the basis of Romantic theories which in their pure form certainly do not completely satisfy any contemporary thinker" (155). The
philosophical or historical-problematic presentation of early Romantic
thought thus has a critical edge. Indeed, if for such an analysis it is a matter of drawing out the Romantic concepts' proper philosophical intentions, a certain ambiguity of Benjamin's approach comes into view: to
analyze the Romantic concepts of art criticism according to their own
most proper philosophical intentions means to measure them against the
single problem constitutive of philosophy and to critically radicalize concepts whose own radicality, in the words of Benjamin, is grounded in "a
certain lack of clarity (*eine gewisse Unklarheit ist der Grund dieses Radikalis-
mus*)" (176).

A philosophical investigation of critique is warranted, Benjamin
claims, "because criticism contains a cognitive factor" (116). This generaliz-
ing statement acknowledges the fact that the Romantics inherited the concept of critique from Kant. As Benjamin remarks, they raised this concept

"to a higher power, since by the word 'criticism' they refer to Kant's total historical achievement and not only to his concept of *Kritik*" (142). As a result, the epistemological underpinnings of their concept of criticism still had to be made manifest. Although with Romanticism, it is a matter of "criticism as the criticism of art, not as epistemological method and philosophical standpoint" (117), their "higher criticism" (142), as they familiarly called it, "stands completely upon epistemological presuppositions" (116). It therefore becomes indispensable to explicate, isolate, and exhibit that theory of knowledge, and this is Benjamin's task in the first part of his dissertation titled "On Reflection."

Right from the start, it becomes clear that, for the Romantics, epistemology and metaphysics were intimately linked. Their philosophy, as presented by Benjamin, comprises a theory of the Absolute as a medium of reflection, and a theory of absolute or immediate intuiting of this Absolute. With the idea of the Absolute as a "medium of reflection" (Benjamin is responsible for coining the expression), the Romantics laid the groundwork for an entirely original philosophical position in the aftermath not only of Kant, but of Fichte as well. By releasing reflection from the restriction to a self-positing "I" that it had in Fichte, by extending reflection—and that also means immediate cognition, according to Benjamin—to mere thinking, or thinking in general, reflection becomes "the infinite and purely methodical character of true thinking," Benjamin writes (128). Apart from thus reintroducing infinity into the sphere of theoretical knowledge, a sphere from which it had been excluded by Fichte, the early Romantics redefined infinity, seeing it no longer, in contradiction to Fichte, as a continuous advance, but rather as an infinitude of connectedness. And rather than implying emptiness, for the Romantics, infinity was a "full infinitude (*erfüllte Unendlichkeit*)" (126). But, as Benjamin argues, this immediacy of knowing in reflection is also different from the immediacy of intellectual intuition that Fichte ascribed to the self-knowing and self-positing "I." The immediacy characteristic of Romantic thought is *intellectual*; not grounded on thinking's intuitive nature, it is purely conceptual.

It must be noted that, for the Romantics, thinking is "proper to everything, for everything is a self" (128). Consequently, the medium of reflection is both the infinity of interconnected centers, infinitely increasing or potentiating reflection, and also the immediate knowing that these centers have of themselves and others. The Absolute as a medium of reflection is the totality of these thinking centers. This succinct presentation of the Romantic Absolute must suffice for the moment. A more detailed picture of it will arise when, in a moment, I proceed to a discussion of the difficulties that Benjamin has with this conception. First, however, I must briefly address the Romantics' contention that this whole—the Absolute, or the System—can also be absolutely grasped. If there is, indeed, such a thing as an absolute grasping of the whole in a mode of comprehension that is not intuitive, as in the sense of *unanschaulich*, but intellectual, it is because the whole, as the center of all centers, grasps itself without mediation "in closed and completed reflection" (129). Indeed, if Schlegel can search for "a non-intuitive intuition (*unanschauliche Intuition*) of the system" (139–140; trans. mod.), it is because the Absolute, as the very medium of reflection, cannot escape the logic of reflection. Everything is thinking, and hence thinking must grasp itself reflectively, that is, immediately, as well.

This theory of the reflexive medium and its absolute comprehension does not merit Benjamin's undivided approval. Although his objections appear as marginal and passing remarks, as footnotes, and are never developed or even substantiated, they occur with such frequency and insistence that the task of reading "The Concept of Criticism" becomes the task of construing their underlying rationale.[5] Of this theory, Benjamin says that it "was delineated according to circumscribed metaphysical concerns (*in begrenztem metaphysischen Interesse*)" (192); in other words, it is of limited use or importance to metaphysics. Moreover, any attempt to clarify, from a "purely critical, logical interest," what of this theory the Romantics have left in the dark risks ending in darkness as well. It is a theory, Benjamin concludes (in a footnote), that "leads in its totality to purely logical, unresolvable contradictions" (192).

Let me try then to elicit from Benjamin's critical remarks throughout the first part of the dissertation the reasons for the preceding devastating appraisal of the Romantics' theoretical presuppositions of their concept of art criticism. First, I circle back to the question of releasing reflection from the bounds of the "I." With Fichte, the Romantics shared the insight that "the epistemologically valid [*massgebende*] form of thinking" is the thinking of thinking. It is a form of immediate knowing and "constitutes for the early Romantics the basic form of all intuitive knowledge and thus attains its dignity as method; as knowledge of thinking it comprises all other, lower-level cognition under itself" (127). For Fichte, thinking as the thinking of thinking—or in Benjamin's terminology, second-level reflection directed upon first-level reflection whose subject matter is mere thinking, with its correlative, thought—achieves completion in the self-positing "I." Yet such thinking occurs incessantly, according to the Romantics, and in everything. "Accordingly," Benjamin writes, "the thinking of thinking turns into the thinking of thinking of thinking (and so forth), and with this the third level of reflection is attained. . . . The third level of reflection, compared with the second, signifies something fundamentally new" (129). For Fichte, the thinking of thinking is constituted by "the original form [*Ur-Form*], the canonical form of reflection" (129). However, for the Romantics, this epistemologically authoritative form of thinking is made up by the infinitizing thinking of thinking of thinking that constitutes the medium of reflection. According to the Jena Romantics, this boundless thinking is not only the form of intuitive cognizing par excellence, but in its universality, it comprises all other forms of thinking as well.

Although Benjamin discards the objection that the Romantics' theorem is abstruse by referring to its axiomatic presuppositions, first and foremost to the assumption that infinitude for them is filled and substantial, his discussion of the relation between the *Ur-Form* of thinking and the Romantic conception of absolute thinking begins to show clear signs of strain. Benjamin holds that "in face of the Absolute," "the rigorous original form" (129) of reflection dissolves. This dissolution (*Zersetzung*) manifests itself through a "peculiar ambiguity" (129) in the third-level reflection. Indeed, the rigorous *Ur-Form* of second-level reflection in the third-level reflection occupies the position of both the object and the subject of thinking. The strict form of reflection is thus assailed and shaken by this ambiguity, Benjamin remarks, stressing that "this ambiguity would have to unfold into an ever more complex plurality of meanings at each successive level" (129). He sums the matter up in the following passage: "On this state of affairs rests the peculiar character of the infinitude of reflection to which the Romantics laid claim: the dissolution of the proper form of reflection in face of the Absolute. Reflection expands without limit or check, and the thinking given form in reflection turns into formless thinking which directs itself upon the Absolute" (129).

Two things need to be underlined at this point. First, reflection, strictly speaking, becomes formless. From being characterized by self-limitation and the continual coiling back upon itself that marked Fichte's

"I," reflection becomes unbounded and thus able to direct itself upon the Absolute. Second, the Absolute itself becomes characterized by increasing, and ultimately inextricable and irredeemable, ambiguity. As Benjamin argues, in "a line of thought that was not thought through by the Romantics with full clarity," they, and Schlegel in particular, "saw, immediately and without holding this in need of a proof, the whole of the real unfolding in its full content, with increasing distinctness up to the highest clarity in the Absolute" (130). The thesis of a continuity between the two kinds of reflection, the *Ur-Form* of reflection and absolute reflection, is for Benjamin the bone of contention. With Benjamin's emphasis on the unbounding of the strict form of reflection, that is, of the lower form of reflection, and the ambiguity of absolute reflection, a problem, indeed, surfaces. The Absolute, rather than yielding the desired clarity, becomes characterized by increasing ambiguity—and, as evidenced in essays written before the dissertation, or at the same time, for Benjamin, this is the terrible signature of nature, fate, myth—and more generally, of the profane. It is the disastrous consequence of directing the illimitable and, hence, formless form of the strict kind of reflection upon the Absolute itself. As Benjamin remarks in the footnote to which I have already referred, the logically unresolvable problems with which the theory of the medium of reflection is ridden climax in "the problem of primordial reflection [*Urreflektion*]" (192). As a result of the contention that there is a steady continuity between lower forms of reflection and absolute reflection, the Absolute loses its distinctness, its univocity, in short, everything that separates it from the lower orders.

Yet, what about the Absolute itself? It grasps itself, as well, in immediate reflection, or cognition, Benjamin notes. He writes: "Reflection constitutes the Absolute, and it constitutes it as a medium. Schlegel did not use the term 'medium' himself; nonetheless, he attached the greatest importance to the constantly uniform connection in the Absolute or in the system, both of which we have to interpret as the connectedness of the real, not in its substance (which is everywhere the same) but in the degrees of its clear unfolding" (132–133). For the Romantics, the movement in the medium of reflection is made up by either the potentiation of reflection or its decrease—to quote Novalis with Benjamin, by "reciprocal elevation and reduction" (133). But in the footnote to which I have already made recourse several times, Benjamin takes issue with this contention. After having remarked that in spite of statements to the contrary, cognition for the Romantics could only mean intensification or potentiation of reflection, he writes: "Reflection may very well be intensified, but can never be diminished. Only a breaking off [*Abbrechen*], never a lessening, of heightened reflection is thinkable. Therefore, all interrelations among centers of reflection—not to mention their relations to the Absolute—can rest only on intensifications of reflection" (191–192; trans. mod.). For reasons of principle, what Benjamin says here about the intensifying reflections between the centers, or from the center to the Absolute, is valid for what happens in the Absolute as well. Indeed, Benjamin's critical statement, which gives the Romantics the lie, is an objection (*Einwand*), an "isolated critical remark," he claims (192). What he objects to is not only the illimitable potentiation of reflective cognition in the relation of the centers to one another, and in particular to the Absolute, but also, especially, its use as a model for understanding the way the Absolute comprehends itself. To conceive of the Absolute as grasping itself in a process of a continually increasing reflection is, for Benjamin, an illegitimate projection of forms (or unforms) or movements specific to lower orders onto the Absolute itself.

I have pointed out already that the Romantics believed that "as a virtuality, even an absolute immediacy in the grasping of the context [or the Absolute], of reflection is thinkable" (126). On Schlegel, Benjamin writes that he did not attempt "to grasp the Absolute systematically, however, he sought conversely to grasp the system absolutely. This was the essence of his mysticism" (138). What Benjamin thinks of such a possibility becomes clear when he says that "the perilous character [*das Verhängnisvolle*, another word linked to the order of fate] of this venture did not remain hidden" from Schlegel himself (138). Indeed, when Benjamin claims that Schlegel characterizes in an unsurpassable way this idea of the absolute comprehension of the system with the question, "Are not all systems individuals?" (139), Schlegel's mystic is denounced as mysticism. Just as much as Schlegel neglected "to distinguish profane mysticism (*Mystizismus*), something inauthentic, from the higher mysticism (*Mystik*)" (196) (*versäumen*, to neglect, is another significant Benjaminean term), he paid insufficient attention to the difference between the Absolute and individuality. If Schlegel's attempt to characterize the Absolute as an individuality fell on unsympathetic ears with Benjamin, it is, as we shall see in a moment, because, according to the latter, it rests on an illegitimate mixing of levels of thought.

For Benjamin, such immediate grasping of the Absolute in the case of the Romantics must be clearly demarcated from what takes place with the mystics. Whereas mystics call upon intellectual intuition and ecstatic states, the Romantics are indifferent to intuitability.

Rather (to put it in a summary formula) [Schlegel] searches for a nonintuitive intuition [*unanschauliche Intuition*] of the system, and he finds this in language. Terminology is the sphere in which his thought moves beyond discursivity and intuitability. For the term, the concept, contained for him the seed of the system; it was, at bottom, nothing other than a preformed system itself. Schlegel's thinking is *absolutely conceptual*—that is, it is linguistic thinking. Reflection is the intentional act of the absolute comprehension of the system, and the adequate form of expression for this act is the concept. (139–140; trans. mod.)

The absolute grasping of the Absolute is thus based on a nonintuitable individuality of the Absolute, an individuality provided by concepts rather than names: "It is in the concept alone that individual nature— which Schlegel . . . vindicates for the system—finds its expression" (140). Such individuality, however intellectual, is still an individuality. And as such, Benjamin seems to suggest it is incommensurate to the Absolute.

Benjamin admits that some, but only some, propositions of this, in his eyes, dubious theory of the medium of reflection have achieved a peculiar fruitfulness in the theory of art.[6] Art is a determination of the medium of reflection, however, it is not a privileged one, as Benjamin sees it, because for the Romantics all things are centers of reflection. Yet, it is argued in the dissertation that the Romantic theory of art in which the medium of reflection is one of forms "reaches the metaphysical depth of Romantic thinking immediately and with far greater certainty [than in other Romantic determinations of the medium]" (149). Hence, this theory should, while permitting a grasp of the greatness of Romantic thought, also be the privileged place where this thought can be critically examined.

After having recalled that all the laws that generally hold for objective knowledge (and that Benjamin had discussed in his exposition of the early Romantic theory of the knowledge of nature) hold good in the medium of art as well, Benjamin claims that the task of art criticism becomes determined as "knowledge in the medium of reflection that is art" (151). Benjamin writes: "Criticism when confronting the work of art is like observation when confronting the natural object; the same laws apply, simply modified according to their different objects" (151). If observation in the realm of natural objects means moving or inciting a thing into self-consciousness, then criticism achieves the same goal in the medium of art.

"Thus, criticism is, as it were, an experiment on the art work, one through which the latter's reflection is awakened, through which it is brought to consciousness and to knowledge of itself " (151). Hence, the cognition to which Romantic art criticism gives rise is the work's self-cognition. Criticism in the medium of reflection is not only entirely objective, but for the Romantics, it is also entirely positive: "the ultimate intention of . . . critique," Benjamin says, is "the intensification of the consciousness of the work" (152).

Every critical understanding of an artistic entity is, as reflection in the entity, nothing other than a higher, self-actively originated degree of this entity's consciousness. Such intensification of consciousness in criticism is in principle infinite; criticism is therefore the medium in which the restriction of the individual work refers methodologically to the infinitude of art and finally (*endlich*) is transformed [*übergeführt*] into that infinitude (*Unendlichkeit*). For it is self-evident that art, as medium of reflection, is infinite. (67)

Romantic criticism is predominantly positive in that through its intensification of the self-consciousness of the work, the artwork becomes transported, or converted into Art itself. Compared to this positive transformation, the moment of self-negation, that is, the destruction of the work in its limitation, is negligible. By dissolving the single work into the medium of art, Romantic critique renders the finite absolute. It perfects it, as Benjamin's remarks on Schlegel's paradigmatic critique of Goethe's *Wilhelm Meister* indicate: "the critique is not meant to do anything other than discover the secret tendencies of the work itself, fulfill its hidden intentions. It belongs to the meaning of the work itself—that is, in its reflection that the criticism should go beyond the work and make it absolute. This much is clear: for the Romantics, criticism is far less the judgment of a work than the method of its consummation" (153). Thus, in a letter to Schleiermacher, Benjamin reports, Schlegel refers to his critique of *Wilhelm Meister* as the *Übermeister* (152). Criticism, indeed, is "perfecting, positive" (154), in that it is an *Übersetzung*, a translation of the necessarily incomplete work into its own absolute idea.

For Benjamin, this idea of critique as translation hinges on the Romantics' conception of the artwork in terms of form understood as self-limited reflection. As form, the work of art is necessarily a contingent reflection of the medium of reflection. Critique, consequently, must drive these self-limited reflections outside themselves and dissolve the original reflection into a higher reflection. He writes: "In this project [*Arbeit*], criticism depends on the germ cells of reflection, the positively formal moments of the work that it resolves into universally formal moments. It thus represents the relation of the individual work to the idea of art and thereby the idea of the individual work itself" (156).

In short, then, critique in the medium of art is an objective movement in which self-limited reflection, or form, is released through a potentiation of the reflection frozen in the singular work and through which that work becomes dissolved into the medium of reflection, the continuum of forms, the idea of Art itself. While discussing this concept of critique in view of the Romantic theory of assessment, Benjamin introduces a term that shows to what extent critique is anchored in the work. "Criticizability (*Kritisierbarkeit*)" (160) is an objective characteristic of the artwork and is the reason why critique, as well, is "an objective tribunal [*Instanz*] in art" (164). This criterion of art—criticizability—summarizes, as Benjamin puts it, "the entire art-philosophical project of the early Romantics" (179). It formulates in no uncertain terms the dependence of Romantic art criticism on the Romantics' understanding of the work as formed, that is, limited, reflection, and hence the objective need to free reflection from its contingent limitation as work into the medium of reflection itself.

Critique—a concept that, as Benjamin had noted, is an exemplary instance of the Romantics' mystical terminology—is thus a positive concept: "To be critical meant to elevate thinking so far beyond all restrictive conditions that the knowledge of truth sprang forth magically, as it were, from insight into the falsehood of these restrictions" (142). But according to Benjamin, this generally positive valuation of critique notwithstanding, the Romantics also "understood how to preserve and apply the unavoidable negative moment of this concept" (142). One would have expected him to refer here to the inevitable destruction of the work that comes with its elevation into the Absolute, or to Schlegel's valorization of polemics as the extermination of the mass of bad art, an extermination required before productive critique can begin.[7] Instead, Benjamin picks out the "vast discrepancy between the claim and the accomplishment of their theoretical philosophy" (143) in order to suggest that by characterizing their own theoretical pretensions as critique, the Romantics admitted the very failure of their enterprise—of critique as a positive procedure and of the attempt to relate the finite to the infinite, first and foremost. Critique also names the "necessary 'incompleteness of infallibility,'" "the inescapable insufficiency of their efforts" (143) to grasp the Absolute absolutely, Benjamin claims. With this we can proceed to Benjamin's fundamental objections against what the Romantics called "critique." Yet Benjamin's fascination with Romantic thought is also a fact. Hence, my task will be double. Apart from establishing what it is that he finds fault with, I try to determine not only the reasons for his critique, but to outline succinctly his own conception of critique.

In the chapter "The Idea of Art," Benjamin notes that Romantic art theory culminates in the definition of the medium of absolute reflection as art, or, more precisely, as the idea of Art. Since "the organ of artistic reflection is form, the idea of art is defined as the medium of reflection of forms. In this medium all the presentational forms hang constantly together, interpenetrate one another, and merge into the unity of the absolute art form, which is identical with the idea of art. Thus, the Romantic idea of the unity of art lies in the idea of a continuum of forms" (165). Benjamin's critique of Romantic criticism commences by putting into question the Romantics' philosophical competence to determine the nature of this unity of forms, or Absolute, on which their whole theory of art and art criticism is based. Benjamin concedes that Schlegel's philosophical efforts "indicated how much [he] strove for . . . determinacy (*Bestimmtheit*)" (168). Yet, making "the most intensive efforts to give expression to the determinateness and fullness in which he conceived [the] idea" (166), he merely came up with the concept of individuality, Benjamin claims. Undoubtedly, when speaking of the reflection medium of forms, Schlegel characterized it as an individual. To conceive of the unity or continuum of absolute forms, the Absolute, in short, as an individual, is, for Benjamin, to strain concepts and to "grasp at a paradox. Otherwise the project of expressing the highest universality as individuality was not to be consummated" (166–167). He admits that in making recourse to this paradox, Schlegel aspired "to secure the concept of the idea of art from the misunderstanding of those who would see it an abstraction from already given empirical artworks" (167; trans. mod.). This "valuable and valid motive" is the reason why Schlegel's thought about the individuality of the Absolute is not simply "an absurdity or even an error," Benjamin concedes (167). Yet, Schlegel, by characterizing the Absolute as an individuality, "simply gave a false interpretation to a valuable and valid motive" (167).

It was certainly correct, Benjamin continues, to try "to define this concept [of art] as an idea in the Platonic sense, as a *proteron te phusei,* as the real ground of all empirical works" (167).[8] But it was a mistake—indeed a huge mistake, the mistake par excellence—to hope to achieve this with the help of the concept of individuality. Schlegel, in Benjamin's eyes, "committed the old error of confounding 'abstract' and 'universal' when he believed he had to make that ground into an individual" (167). Only because he confused the universal and the abstract could Schlegel have sought to determine the Absolute as individuality, or a "work." For Schlegel, individuality is intellectually and conceptually purified—as is obvious from his reference to the "invisible work which takes up into itself the visible work" (167). His characterization of the unity of art, the continuum of forms, or art itself as a work is an infringement upon the rule that forbids mixing genres of thought. Benjamin also calls it a "mystical thesis" (167). Benjamin thus criticizes Schlegel for not having clearly grasped the philosophical nature of the highest universal and for having contaminated it with concepts that belong to another ontological sphere. Even the sphere of pure concepts is incommensurate with the realm of the idea, or the Absolute. Schlegel was a mystic for Benjamin in that he believed that pure concepts such as "individuality" or "the invisible work" could bring the Absolute within reach. Benjamin has no quarrel with the Romantics about the necessity of thinking the Absolute; he parts company with them when they bring the Absolute into the intellects' range. Made present as an individuality, or a work, the Absolute is stripped of what makes it absolute, that is, cut off not only from all sensible but all intellectual presentation as well. As individuality or work, the Absolute has been surrendered to the profane.

To present (*darstellen*) the idea of art "in conceptual concentration" (169) is, indeed, a function of the Romantics' theory of reflective intensification. In his discussion of the "poetry of poetry," another Romantic attempt to present the idea of Art itself, Benjamin describes it as "the comprehensive expression for the reflexive nature of the Absolute" (170–171). He adds: "It is poetry conscious of itself, and since, according to early Romantic doctrine, consciousness is only a heightened spiritual form of that *of* which it is conscious, it follows that consciousness of poetry is itself poetry. It is poetry of poetry. Higher poetry . . ." (171). In short, the Romantic theory according to which the centers of reflection can be elevated to the medium of reflection itself through reflexive intensification condemns the medium of reflection, or the Absolute, to being only the heightened reflection of whatever is reflectively raised to that higher level. By holding that the totality of all works is a work—however invisible or purely intelligible it may be—is to determine the Absolute as a mere potentiation of the singular works that it embraces. Such an understanding of the Absolute (or of consciousness) entails a loss of the force of transcendence and the relativization of difference. Against the backdrop of this Benjaminian critique, another aspect of his suspicions about the concept of reflection comes into view. A reflection that knows only intensification, and not the possibility of diminishing, presupposes and asserts a continuity between the profane and the Absolute that can make the Absolute tangible only as something profane.

Benjamin makes the distinction between the profane and the Absolute in an effort to further specify what the Romantics understood by art criticism and what they saw as its task. The distinction is borrowed from Schlegel himself. "The organ of transcendental poetry, as that very form which in the Absolute survives the downfall of profane forms, Schlegel designates as the symbolic form," Benjamin remarks (171). After having denounced the ambiguity of "symbolic form" and discarded the mythological content of the expression, which in that sense "does not belong to the context" in which the distinction between profane and symbolic form is made, he defines the latter as "the imprint [*Ausprägung*] of the pure poetic Absolute in the form itself" (171). Symbolic form is exhibition, or presentational form (*Darstellungsform*), purified of and distinguished from the profane forms of exhibition through its reference to the idea of art or the Absolute. Yet the "purification" or "survival" of symbolic or absolute form after the downfall of everything profane is a function of a reflection that elevates itself to the Absolute. "The 'symbolic form' is the formula under which the range of reflection for the work of art is concentrated," Benjamin notes (171). Yet precisely for that reason, the important distinction between profane and symbolic or absolute form becomes blurred. It loses its cutting edge. When Benjamin remarks in a footnote that for the Romantics "the presentational form does not need to be wholly profane [but] through sustained purity, it can have a share in the absolute or symbolic form and in the end turn into it" (197), it is clear that for him, the latter form is only the reflectively enhanced profane form.

Art criticism, Benjamin suggests, is the reflective movement between the poles of this dulled distinction. He writes: "Criticism of art exhibits this symbolic form in its purity; it disentangles it from all the inessential moments to which it may be bound in the work, and finishes with the dissolution of the work" (172). Benjamin could subscribe to this definition of criticism as pursuing the double task of *Ablösung* and *Auflösung* in the perspective of the Absolute. Yet he is quick to add that "in the framework of Romantic theories, despite all conceptual coinages, full clarity can never be reached in the distinction between profane and symbolic form, between symbolic form and critique." Such lack of sharpness "forces itself on our attention" (172), he declares without elaborating. But have not we seen that for reasons of principle—conceiving the relation between profane form and symbolic form as one of reflection—the Romantics could not make this distinction as sharp as their own philosophical intentions would have it? At this juncture, Benjamin makes an explicit statement that dramatizes the gist of what up to this point had mainly been implicit in his objections: "Only at the price of such hazy demarcations can all the concepts of the art theory which the Romantics ultimately undertook be drawn into the region of the Absolute" (172). In other words, Romantic art criticism is anything but critical: it fails to distinguish and to set apart as trenchantly and vigorously as the concept of criticism calls for. As a consequence, the Absolute—the critical concept par excellence—is not only not demarcated from the profane with the necessary rigor, but everything profane is drawn into the region of the Absolute, polluting what, in principle, is to be kept pure of all alien ingredients. The positivity of Romantic critique thus becomes suspicious. But this positivity, with its attendant lack of a discriminating and analytical rigor, is not accidental. It stems from the Romantics' metaphysical credo of a continuity between the profane and the Absolute. Criticizability, Benjamin notes, presupposes transition (*Übergang*) from the realm of ideas, or "the archetypal realm to the single works, such as exist in the medium of art from the absolute form to the single forms" (181). It rests on the assumption as well that all singular works can "vitally coalesce into the unity of the ideal itself" (181). Indeed, as Benjamin holds, "art was the region in which Romanticism strove to carry through most purely the immediate reconciliation of the conditioned with the unconditioned" (181). Criticizability—the principle that the entire art-philosophical work of the early Romantics sought to demonstrate—is thus tied up with what impedes criticism and against which criticism ought to prevail: transition, continuity, reconciliation between what can be brought together only at the price of paradox, false interpretation, or, in other words, a complete surrender of the critical notion of the Absolute to the profane.

However, such radical abandonment of the highest universal to the region of the profane is also an accomplishment of major—and fatal—proportions. Benjamin makes this point in the course of his analysis of the Romantic concept of the novel. For the Jena Romantics, the novel is the "comprehensible manifestation (*fassbare Erscheinung*)" (173) of the continuum of forms, or the poetic Absolute. "It is this thanks to prose. The idea of poetry has found its individuality (that for which Schlegel was seeking) in the form of prose; the early Romantics knew no deeper or better determination for it than 'prose'" (173). But what is "prose" if it is to be the most proper individuality of the poetic Absolute? In order to conceive of prose's "unifying function," its role as the "creative ground," of poetical forms (174), it is necessary that it be understood in all its senses, that is, in an indistinct and equivocal manner. Prose certainly has the meaning of "*ungebundene Rede*" (178), of a writing style distinguished from poetry by its greater irregularity, its variety of rhythm, and its greater proximity to ordinary speech. Benjamin makes it quite clear that "prose" does not mean "ornate prose," which—and in this he follows Novalis—"has nothing at all to do with art but which concerns rhetoric" (197). For Benjamin, prose is something transparent and colorless (*farbloser . . . Ausdruck*) (174). But in addition to its proper meaning, prose has a figural, improper meaning, namely prosaic, plain, ordinary, sober. Furthermore, this improper meaning cannot properly be distinguished from the proper. This lack of differentiation, this ambiguity of meaning predestines prose to become the comprehensible manifestation of the Absolute. Yet if only "the purely prosaic [form of prose] fulfills this task" of conferring individuality upon the Absolute, the individuality in question can only be a "prosaic unity" (174). However paradoxical it may seem to conceive of the prosaic, the plain, or the sober as the highest possible manifestation of the idea of art or of the poetic Absolute, it is "in truth [a] very profound intuition . . . an entirely new basis for the philosophy of art. On this ground rests the entire philosophy of art of early Romanticism, especially its concept of criticism," Benjamin claims (173). It is also a conception "historically rich in consequences" (175). Indeed, Benjamin hints that with it began a new era of thought, an era that extends into the present. With the Romantics began the epoch of absolute sobriety.

Benjamin points out that the Romantics shared this "fundamental philosophical conception" (175) of the prosaic with Hölderlin, although the realm of Hölderlin's thought remained only a "promised land" for them (198). Still, as far as the "principle of the sobriety (*Nüchternheit*) of art" (175) is concerned, he stands in a philosophical relation to them.

This principle is the essentially quite new and still incalculably influential leading idea of the Romantic philosophy of art; what is perhaps the greatest epoch in the West's philosophy of art is distinguished by this basic notion. Its connection with the methodological procedure of that philosophy—namely, reflection—is obvious. In ordinary usage, the prosaic—that in which reflection as the principle of art appears uppermost—is, to be sure, a familiar metaphorical designation of the sober. (175)

Benjamin's demarcation of this conception of art from that of Plato's further shows that the greatest epoch in the Western philosophy of art, an epoch that began with the Romantics, is characterized by a sobering of the Absolute. The Absolute becomes desacralized, dedivinized by reflection—in an intellectual and conceptual process of an intuiting no longer intuitive (*anschaulich*), but soberly rational, down-to-earth (and hence distinct from the mystics' intellectual intuition of the whole). But not only is reflection sober, the Absolute to which it becomes potentiated—the medium of reflection and the continuum of forms—turns prosaic as well. It is an Absolute only relatively different from the profane forms, one that has been divested of its separating and discriminating force. The sober Absolute is an Absolute that has forfeited its transcendence.

On this principle of absolute sobriety rests the concept of Romantic criticism. It proceeds on the assumption that the core of the work is "filled with prosaic spirit" (176). Art, for the Romantics, is mechanical, akin to manufacturing, and has its seat entirely in the understanding (175–176). Benjamin writes: "By means of mechanical reason, moreover, the work is soberly constituted within the infinite—at the limit-value of limited forms" (176). If the Absolute—what transcends everything profane as the highest universal—achieves presentation as "work," it has become something inherently profane: profanity itself. And the incarnation of such prosaic spirit in a comprehensible shape is no less profane.

To exhibit this prosaic kernel of all art is the "final contentual determination" of criticism, Benjamin argues (177). "Criticism is the presentation of the prosaic kernel in every work. In this, the concept 'presentation'

(*Darstellung*) is understood in the chemical sense, as the generation of a substance through a determinate process to which other substances are submitted" (178; trans. mod.). The *Darstellung* of the prosaic present in every work—the profane Absolute—is a production on the basis of potentiating reflection.

This legitimation of criticism by its prosaic nature and the prosaic nature of its task has some distinctive consequences. On several occasions, the dissertation shows that, for the Romantics, critique has no pedagogical aim. Its function is not to assess or judge the work. Romantic critique "needs no motivation," Benjamin claims (178). In other words, critique is not a function of a purpose heterogeneous to the work; rather, it is exercised for its own sake. "Criticism is . . . a formation whose origin is occasioned by the work but whose continued existence is independent of it. As such, it cannot be distinguished in principle from the work of art" (177). It has the same ontological nature as the work of art. Like the work from which it originates, critique is, according to the Romantics, a fact (*Faktum*). Benjamin quotes Schlegel: "A so-called *recherche* is a historical experiment. The object and the result of this experiment are a fact. Whatever is to be a fact must have strict individuality" (178). As a fact, then, critique is indistinguishable from the work. Although a potentiation of reflection, critique has no deciding or transcending thrust. This sheer positivity marks critique's departure from what must have been its ownmost philosophical intention—to separate what cannot be of the same nature. But what of the prosaic Absolute presented by critique? Presented in the individualizing mode of prose, the sober Absolute appears as something absolutely prosaic—itself a fact, only the potentiation of the transitory contingency of the singular work. Benjamin notes: "By limiting itself in its own form, [the work of art] makes itself transitory in a contingent figure, but in that fleeting figure it makes itself eternal through criticism" (182). Absolutizing the created work, rendering it eternal, criticism presents the Absolute as fact. Yet in spite of the fact that criticism is indistinguishable from the work, Schlegel, paradoxically yet inevitably, valued criticism "more highly than works of art" (185) because the critical activity of absolutizing the work is higher than the creation of art, Benjamin concludes. "This can be illustrated in an image as the generation of dazzling brilliance [*Blendung*] in the work. This dazzling—the sober light—extinguishes the plurality of works. It is the idea" (185). These final lines of Benjamin's dissertation speak a final critical word about Romantic criticism. The sober light of the prosaic Absolute that criticism exhibits in all works is a blinding light. It is so dazzling that it becomes deceptive. In its brilliancy, all differences fade absolutely. Its spell, the fascination it exerts, is that of the fact—of the Absolute become secular.

Benjamin's massive and intransigent criticism of the Romantic conception of art and its concept of criticism thus seems finally to be an outright rejection. And yet, this conception is said to have inaugurated "perhaps the greatest epoch in the West's philosophy of art" (175). His recognition of and admiration for the Romantics' achievements is evident, and hence I must return to the question of Benjamin's relation to early Romanticism, to his debt to the Romantic concept of criticism that he so vehemently criticized. Considering the unyielding and unrelentingly negative critical gesture that dominates the whole of the dissertation, Benjamin's own concept of criticism arises from motifs that appear only in an understanding of the most extreme implications of Romantic theory. Indeed, the greatness of Romantic thought is linked to its conception of a secular Absolute, of critique as the primarily positive dissolution, and the connection of the finite to such an Absolute—in other words, to Romantic thought's total relinquishing of transcendence. From everything we have seen, such a conception of the Absolute, and of the critical relation as a movement in the continuum between the finite and an equally finite infinite, cannot satisfy Benjamin. His critique of the Romantic Absolute and the Romantics' notion of criticism is made in the name of the proper philosophical intentions of the very concepts, according to which the Absolute has to be distinguished absolutely and critique must be a movement or rigorous separation, demarcation, scission. Compared with the Romantic concept, his is an *Übercritique* in the sense in which Schlegel could speak of his critique of *Wilhelm Meister* as the *Übermeister*—an ultracriticism or hypercriticism. Benjamin agrees with the Romantics that all critique must take place in view of the Absolute, but in view of an Absolute that is absolutely transcendent, radically distinguished from everything profane or finite. Between it and the latter, no continuity is thinkable. Yet critique is a relating to such an Absolute. It is the movement of transcendence in the realm of the profane or finite. However, because the Absolute— or rather truth, as Benjamin would call it—is entirely of another order than the profane, all critical relation to it must necessarily lack the certitude of truly transcending the given. Such certitude is not in the power of the critical act. For Benjamin, critique's eventual success in pointing to the Absolute, in enacting a pure separation or difference, can be guaranteed only by the Absolute itself. Yet even such authentication of the critical relation by the Absolute, were it to occur, would be beyond the cognitive reach of all critique. In contradistinction from the Romantic epistemological optimism that constituted the bedrock of their concept of critique, but whose price was a total sobering of the Absolute, Benjamin's concept of critique is characterized by an essential agnosticism. It is a critique, however, and as such it must take its aim at the Absolute and seek to sever it from itself in absolute purity. Hence, of that Absolute, nothing can be known, and least of all that the Absolute has authenticated the critical relation to begin with.

With this, both the rationale for Benjamin's critique of the Romantics and his debt to them come to view. He shares with them the insight into the inexorably sober nature of the critical relation. Yet this sobriety, with the extremist implication of a radical loss of transcendence within early Romanticism, becomes for Benjamin the sign that the transcending gesture of critique depends on a redemptive justification. Although beyond critique's own reach, such justification is required by what it, as critique, must mean according to its own most philosophical intention. If all critique is finite, and if, by itself, it can reveal only a sober Absolute, the pure distinction that it calls for as *krinein* (and the absolutely Other toward which it nevertheless incessantly gestures) requires that critique be contingent on a relation to an Absolute whose power would finally fulfill its critical intention. Paradoxically, the universal sobriety in which Romantic thought loses itself turns into the thought of an absolutely "non-sober" Absolute capable of a post-factum endowment of the transcending movement of critique, of conferring actual transcendence upon critique. No finite certitude, no empirical security guarantees that such a conferral has taken place or shall occur. However, in order to avoid squandering (*versäumen*) the possibility of such a conferral by which the very intentions of critique would become fulfilled, critique must be critical to the outmost—unrelentingly and uncompromisingly negative. Of such criticism, Benjamin's dissertation on the Romantic concept of positive critique is a most fulfilling example.

3

Critique, Authentic Biographism, and Ethical Judgment

According to Walter Benjamin, "biographical considerations . . . do not enter at all into commentary and critique" (309). Conversely, "in the realm of biography, there is neither commentary nor critique" (325).[1] Given that commentary and critique concern works of art, and biography a human life, these statements, made in the essay, "Goethe's Elective Affinities," not only radically hold apart commentary and critique from the biographical, and vice versa, they also assert a radical difference between work and life. Benjamin's cutting criticism of Friedrich Gundolf's *Goethe,* who in this influential book conceives of Goethe's life as a work and interprets the latter's writings as an emanation of a heroicized life, could thus suggest that as a literary critic Benjamin would be concerned with Goethe's work alone, intent on engaging the text of the *Elective Affinities* in, say, an immanent, or even textual, reading. However, this is a deceptive conclusion. Indeed, in "Goethe's Elective Affinities" Benjamin interlaces his interpretation of the text with philosophical, theological, and moral issues that originate in his own work, issues that ultimately disqualify all purely immanent, or textual, analysis on the basis that such an analysis is merely an extension of the mythical dimension of Goethe's work, which, as we will see, rather than the truth content, is only the material content of Goethe's novel.[2] But above all, Benjamin's essay is just as much concerned with certain biographical aspects of Goethe's life as it is a commentary and a critique of *Elective*

Affinities. Although Wilhelmine Herzlieb, the object of Goethe's passionate though unreturned love, served as the primary model for Ottilie, with this late work, Goethe, as Benjamin emphasizes, sought to come to terms with the negligences (*Versäumnisse*) in his erotic life. Benjamin writes: "it is the figure—indeed the name—of Ottilie which spellbound Goethe to this world, so that he could truly rescue someone perishing, could redeem in her a loved one" (354). Furthermore, considering Benjamin's dedication to Jula Cohn, who, as has repeatedly been reported, stood as a model for Benjamin's characterization of Ottilie and for whom he had, in particular during his marriage to Dora, a passionate affection that remained unrequited, Benjamin's essay on Goethe is also intertwined with facts regarding his own life.[3] Needless to say, Benjamin scholars have been aware of this biographical and, as Bernd Witte terms it, "existential" aspect of Benjamin's essay.[4] But by generally taking this private reference as being only of anecdotal significance, most critics have not only overlooked, if not repressed, Benjamin's consistent allusions to Goethe's life, but they also elide the issue of biography. Indeed, in spite of Benjamin's constant exhortation to keep biographical considerations from intruding on commentary and critique, and vice versa, this concern with the life of the author is so preponderant in the text that the question of what their precise link is amounts to a theoretical question that no reading of the essay can avoid.[5] In the following study, which limits itself to a discussion of Benjamin's interpretation of *Elective Affinities* and the relation of this novel to Goethe's biography (that is, without taking up the autobiographical aspect of the essay), I explore what the precise relations are between critique and biography, between work and life, between domains, that is, that ostensibly must be kept from mingling. Indeed, if Benjamin's concern in the essay is one with the "matter of essence and the truth in the work and in the life" (327), work and life, critique and biography must be interrelated in some essential fashion. If, furthermore, for Benjamin, truth, rather than an epistemological concept, is an ethical concept, then what ties work and life, critique and biography together must necessarily have moral implications. But what does Benjamin understand by "work" and "life" in the first place? How does he define the task of critique and biography?

I.

Right at the outset of "Goethe's Elective Affinities," Benjamin remarks that even though the essay devotes considerable attention to philological detail, it is not meant as a commentary but as a critique. "Critique seeks the truth content (*Wahrheitsgehalt*) of a work of art; commentary, its material content (*Sachgehalt*)" (297). As a critique, Benjamin's essay is thus dominated by the question of the truth content of the literature under consideration, whereas the concern with philological detail and material content is subordinated to this quest. However, primarily interested in the way critique and commentary are interlinked, Benjamin does not yet elaborate here on what the truth content of a work consists in. By contrast, the material content, that is, the object of commentary, is said to be made up of the "concrete realities (*Realien*)" displayed by a work, which appear "striking and curious" to later critics as historical accessories (297). More precisely, since Benjamin distinguishes between the "matter (*Sache*)," or "facts of the matter (*Sachverhalt*)" and the "material content (*Sachgehalt*)," it is clear that though the material content concerns the "concrete realities," it is not identical with them. Indeed, as Benjamin puts it later, "the concrete realities [are] in the material content" (313). The material content, or "the meaning of the concrete realities" in a work, is not something that is given immediately (298). In fact, "not the existence but for the most part the meaning of the concrete realities in the work will no doubt be hidden from the poet and the public of his time" (298). The material content of the concrete realities in a work may sometimes be intuited (*ahnen*) by the poet and his contemporaries, but without having a clear conception of it. This is basically the undertaking of commentary. What it takes for commentary to grasp the content of the concrete realities depicted in a work will occupy us later. For the time being, let us only emphasize that, as the comparison between the critic and the paleographer reveals, the importance of the task of commentary, which establishes a clear conception of the material content of a work, derives from the fact that the material content "refers" to the truth content, which thus is, in principle, distinct from the former. Benjamin emphasizes that "the most essential contents of existence are capable of stamping their imprint (*auszuprägen*) on the world of things" (298). Although "there is truth only in objective things [*Sachen*], just as objectivity [*Sachlichkeit*] lies in truth," the material content is not yet the truth content of a work (326). The material content, in itself, is blind, and thus "the blind earth-stratum of mere material content is [not] to be taken for the truth content" in a work (327).

At this juncture of Benjamin's essay, only the truth content's obscurity is underlined: it is deeply sunk into an artwork's material content, and, therefore, remains hidden from view. Furthermore, when, as a result of the history of a work, "the material content and the truth content, united at the beginning of a work's history, set themselves apart from each other in the course of its duration," the truth content "remains to the same extent hidden as the material content comes to the fore" (297). But setting itself apart from the material content, the truth content determines a work's life—its immortality. Aided by the duration of the work, which already severs the truth content from its material and time-bound content and which thus prepares for its critique, critique aims at further insulating both and increasing in this manner the power of the truth content. Yet, to further the life of a work, critique must resort to a commentary on the material and historical content of a work. Commentary serves to interpret in a work what with time has become striking and curious and which thus distracts from the truth content bound up with it. Its aim is to interpret away, as it were, everything in a work that covers up its hidden truth, and thus to set it free. Benjamin writes:

If, to use a simile, one views the growing work as a burning funeral pyre, then the commentator stands before it like a chemist, the critic like an alchemist. Whereas, for the former, wood and ash remain the sole objects of his analysis, for the latter only the flame itself preserves an enigma: that of what is alive (*des Lebendigen*). Thus the critic inquires into the truth, whose living flame continues to burn over the heavy logs of what is past and the light ashes of what has been experienced. (298)

Whereas commentary focuses only on the concrete realities, which with time die out in a work (*absterben*), in order to establish their meaning, critique focuses on what in the work consumes its historical and material content and makes it alive, or, rather, endows it with a life that transcends history. The process by which a work in its duration separates its truth from the material content into which it is sunk—a process that thus prepares for the work's critique—defines the aim of critique as a concern with the enigma of the life of a work that manifests itself through the consummation of "the life of the material content" (298), that is, of everything in the work that has historical character, and thus belongs to time. The truth of the work, or "eternal being" (298), with which critique is concerned, is thus intimately associated with the process by which a work reduces its material content—the past and what has been experienced, or rather lived (*erlebt*)—to ashes. This truth, which constitutes the work's being alive (*Lebendigkeit*), is a hidden truth—an enigma.

The critic stands before the work, and critique searches for its truth content, which, as we have seen, is linked to the work's being alive in a process of turning to ashes everything in it that is of historical nature. Although work and human life are thoroughly different, artworks have thus clearly a life of their own. Historical distance to the work prepares critique, which only continues to advance the separation of the truth content from the material content that began with the growth of the work. Furthermore, the critic's "object" is the enigma of the work's being alive—that is, of the living flame of truth that burns everything in the work that is historically transient. His aim, however, is not to unravel this enigma. Critique does not penetrate the work of art; if it seeks the truth content of works, it is not by directly prying it out. Benjamin addresses the way in which critique relates to artworks more explicitly in the opening pages of the last part of the essay. The simile by which this question is introduced recalls that the works to which critique relates are artwork, works of the beautiful arts. He writes:

Let us suppose that one makes the acquaintance of a person who is handsome and attractive but impenetrable, because he carries a secret with him. It would be reprehensible to want to pry. Still, it would surely be permissible to inquire whether he has any siblings and whether their nature could not perhaps explain somewhat the enigmatic character of the stranger. In just this way critique seeks to discover siblings of the work of art. And all genuine works have their siblings in the realm of philosophy. It is, after all, precisely these figures in which the ideal of philosophy's problem appears. (333)

In the face of beautiful art, critique keeps a respectful distance. Its objective is not to dispel art's impenetrable strangeness by revealing the secret that it carries within itself. As Benjamin later explains, any revelation of what lies behind the beautiful appearance reduces it to the ordinary.[6] All critique seeks to achieve is to "somewhat" explain the enigmatic character of the beautiful works. Presuming a relation between artworks and works of philosophy, critique, in its search for the truth content of works, thus shifts its investigation toward the siblings of the works of art, in the hope that they "perhaps" can shed some light on the enigma of artworks. Just as the growing work itself prepares critique in that it severs material and truth content, so does the affinity that exists between genuine works of art and works of philosophy permit critique to pursue its task by turning away from the artwork to philosophy. More specifically, the family relations that exist between art and philosophy enable the critical quest that arises as a demand from the artworks' internal separation of truth content and material content, without intruding upon the enigma of the works.

But what precisely makes the works of philosophy siblings of those of art? Both are related insofar as "the ideal of philosophy's problem"—which in philosophy cannot be obtained by questioning, that is, in a form that presumes an answer or solution to the question or problem—comes into an appearance in the works of art. The affinity with "the ideal of the problem" is thus what constitutes the "precise relation [of works of art] to philosophy" (334). What does this rather obscure notion of "the ideal of the problem" refer to? As Benjamin explains, philosophy is involved in a manifold of problems, or questions, to which it seeks to give solutions, or answers. But the whole of these problems is not something that itself can be problematized, or made the object of a question, without falling into an infinite regress. No question is able to encompass the unity of philosophy, which transcends the totality of all its problems and solutions. The unity in the solution of all its problems taken together is something other than what can be (intraphilosophically) construed as a response to a question, or a solution to a problem. Benjamin writes: "The concept of this nonexistent question seeking the unity of philosophy by inquiry functions in philosophy as the ideal of the problem" (334).[7] In a language vaguely reminiscent of Kant's critical treaties, "the idea of the problem" designates the ultimate unity of philosophy, which as such cannot be established in the questioning, or problematizing, mode or, more precisely, cognized in a theoretical mode, but which nonetheless can and must be thought. Consequently, "the ideal of the problem" refers to the "higher magnitude of power" characteristic of the idea of the whole of philosophy's problems, here called the "ideal," which Kant associates with the ideas of reason.[8] Now Benjamin avers: "Even if, however, the system is in no sense attainable through inquiry, there are nevertheless constructions (*Gebilde*) which, without being questions, have the deepest affinity with the ideal of the problem. These are

works of art" (334). Because it escapes questions and problems, "the ideal of
the problem" in philosophy is constitutionally unknowable, hence, philosophy's enigma, as it were. This impenetrable secret is precisely what relates
the works of philosophy to those of art. Now, in conformity with its
essence, "the ideal can present (*darstellen*) itself solely in a multiplicity"
(trans. mod.). As a presentation, it shines forth into an appearance in a
manifold of artworks; to be precise, it presents itself in these works by
deeply burying itself in them. "Buried in a manifold of works," the "ideal
of the problem" is thus also the artwork's enigma. It must be excavated,
and this is, according to Benjamin, the business of critique. Critique "allows the ideal of the problem to appear in the work of art in one of its manifestations. For critique ultimately shows (*aufweisen*) in the work of art the
virtual possibility of formulating (*virtuelle Formulierbarkeit*) the work's
truth content as the highest philosophical problem" (334). This, then, is
how the philosophical sibling of the artwork can somewhat illuminate the
enigma of the latter. The truth content of the work of art is, as we have
seen, the prime "object" of critique. This content now reveals itself to be a
unique presentation of the "ideal of the problem," and thus critique's concern with the artwork's truth content mirrors "the highest philosophical
problem," that is, the problem of unity, or totality. But since the "ideal of
the problem" finds presentation only in a manifold of works of art (that is
never as such), the work of art's sibling clarifies its enigmatic character only
somewhat. In no way, therefore, does the affinity of art and philosophy blur
their difference. As Benjamin emphasizes, "the work of art does not com-
pete with philosophy itself " (334). Indeed, only because of their difference,
can they stand in a "most precise relation."[9]

   The role of critique is to excavate and further "the ideal of the
problem"—the nonproblem of the unity of philosophy, as it were, because
philosophy cannot pose this issue in the questioning mode that is peculiar
to it—which in works of art finds a presentation. Such excavation and
furthering consist in demonstrating "in the work of art the virtual possibility of formulating the work's truth content as the highest philosophical
problem." By tying the truth content of the work of art to the highest philosophical problem—one that cannot be solved—the truth content becomes
capable of being virtually formulated. By establishing this virtual possibility
regarding the artwork's truth content, critique "somewhat" sheds light on
the enigma of beauty.

That before which [critique] stops short, however—as if in awe of the work, but equally from respect for the truth—is precisely this formulation itself. That possibility of formulation could indeed be realized only if the system could be the object of inquiry and thereby transform itself from an appearance of the ideal into the existence of the ideal—an existence that is never given. As such, however, it says simply that the truth in a work would be known not as something obtained in answer to a question, to be sure, but to be recognized as something that is demanded (*nicht als erfragt, doch als erfordert sich erkennen würde*). (334; trans. mod.)

Although the linkage of the work's truth content to "the ideal of the problem" makes it virtually formulatable, critique refrains from actually formulating this content. Respect for both the work and truth prohibit such formulation. Actualizing a formulation of the truth content would presuppose a solution to the highest philosophical problem concerning the unity of all philosophical problems. It would require that the ideal be determined intraphilosophically. At that moment, the ideal would make an act of presence in the work rather than shine forth in the work. However, like the Kantian idea, "the ideal of the problem" cannot ever manifest itself in propria persona without ceasing to be what it is, that is, without becoming infinitely inconspicuous, or ordinary, or plain. Therefore, by insisting only on the merely virtual possibility of formulating the ideal of the problem, critique acknowledges that the truth content of beautiful works cannot be obtained in the questioning mode. Thus, if Benjamin concludes that the truth content of artworks, which is the prime concern of critique, cannot be reached in the questioning mode (in Kantian terms, theoretically cognized) but can be known only "as something that is demanded"—more precisely, as something required, called for, or exacted—the truth content of a work is, in holding to Kantian terminology, clearly of the order of a practical, or moral, idea. Distinct from commentary, critique would, therefore, be practical in essence. As criticism's intent, the truth to which everything beautiful is connected, and whose virtuality can be determined in philosophy, is of an order akin to ethical truth. It is discernible in "every true work" (334) as something that beauty demands or calls upon, and, which, as we will see hereafter, interrupts its semblance, its shining. Guided by philosophy, the critical reflection on beautiful works seeks to interpret the work in light of a truth that demands that its material content be severed off and that "manifests" itself, precisely, in or as this separation, which animates the work and constitutes its being alive.

However, in "Goethe's Elective Affinities," Benjamin not only explores the novel by commenting on its material content in order to critically isolate its truth content, but he also lays out the rudiments of a biography of Goethe's life that is structured in terms of the same categorial divide. Let me, therefore, bring to mind again the statement that "biographical considerations . . . do not enter at all into commentary and critique" (309). If the prime intention of "Goethe's Elective Affinities" is critical, as Benjamin claims at the beginning of the essay, why then does the essay start off with an inquiry into "the production of a Goethe (*das Goethesche Schaffen*)" (298), what Goethe wished to express (301), and what Goethe himself thought of his work (309–310)? Furthermore, what is the reason for the extensive investigations of "that which is most hidden in Goethe" (314), "the mythic forms of life in the existence of the artist" (316), "the power of primeval forces in the life of this man" (317)? If, conversely, "in the realm of biography, there is neither commentary nor critique" (325), how is one to understand the fact that the categories of truth content and material content also pertain to the life of the artist insofar as he or she is a human being? Benjamin writes, indeed, that "the material content of the life lies open . . . and its truth content is hidden" (324–325). But besides conceiving thus of human life in relation to truth in a way similar to what obtains in the case of artworks, the imagery that Benjamin uses to describe the artwork's process of growing serves him as well to portray the life of the aging Goethe. Comparing Goethe to the early Romantics, Benjamin writes that "the laws that they vainly sought to satisfy by converting, and thus by extinguishing their lives, kindled in Goethe—who also had to submit to these laws—the highest flame of his life. It burned away the dross of every passion" (329). Consequently, if the task of criticism were defined as the search for the truth content of a work, why would the presence of a hidden truth content in the life of the artist ban all critique from the realm of biography? Does Benjamin, in "Goethe's Elective Affinities," keep critique and biographical considerations as neatly separated as the above statements would have it? The distinction made between Gundolf's mythologizing biography of Goethe and "the great modesty of authentic biographism" (324) may be a first indication of a more complex relation than one of mutual exclusion of critique and biography. Undoubtedly, Benjamin's objection to Gundolf's *Goethe* is that "Goethe's life is not rigorously distinguished from that of the works" (324). But even though life and work, biography and critique are not to be allowed to mingle and must be dealt with separately, this very separation does not prevent one from shedding light on the other. With the statement that "every work is able, like *Elective Affinities,* to shed a light on the life and essence of the author," a significant relation between work and life comes into view. But before refining that relation, it is necessary to recall that according to the rudimentary lineaments of an authentic biography of Goethe sketched out in the essay, a life, in the same way as a work, contains a material and a truth content. If art criticism investigates the material content of works in a concern with the formulatability of its truth content, thus preserving the enigma of the work's life, authentic biographism grasps the material content of a life "precisely for the sake of what has not been understood in it." Genuine biographism, Benjamin holds, is an "archive containing the documents (by themselves undecodable) of this existence" (324). However, if the two tasks are distinct because commentary and criticism have no place in biography, and the biographical has no place in the critical treatment of works, it remains that the critical working out of the truth content of Goethe's late work serves to shed light on the author's life and, through the thus interpreted life, on the works. But apart from this interaction of critique and biography, critique in its very limitation to works, may, in the last resort, be subservient to another concern, one that is only "anticipated" by the truth content of the beautiful works—the truth content of a life.

I return to the distinction between material and truth content, which, as we have seen, pertains as much to works, insofar as they are alive, as to human life, although human life is never of the order of a work, as we will see. I begin by recalling that Benjamin chooses what is not just an example among others, namely marital relation, to further elaborate on, first, the notion of the material content and, second, on the latter's relation to the truth content. After the contention that no "thought was more foreign [to the European Enlightenment thinkers than] that the most essential contents of existence are capable of stamping their imprint on the world of things" and that, therefore, the works of the Enlightenment's main representatives are distinguished by extreme abstraction and "poverty of their material contents" (above all, but not exclusively, Kant's critical work that maps "the bare woods of reality" and Goethe's "quest for the seeds of eternal growth"), Benjamin remarks that only "in the literary works of Goethe's old age" a "renewed material content" again becomes available. It is at this point that he introduces the topic of marriage to illustrate the extent to which the search for the material content was foreign to the times.

"How clearly the most sublime spirits of the Enlightenment had a premonition of the content [*Gehalt*] or an insight into the matter [*Sache*], yet how incapable even they were of raising themselves to the perception of its material content [*Sachgehalt*], becomes compellingly clear with regard to marriage" (298–299). Benjamin's discussion of marriage offers a possibility of clarifying the distinction between concrete realities and their meaning (or material content), and provides an opportunity of glimpsing the way commentary establishes such meaning, or content, and how it "refers" to the truth content.

It is, of course, not by accident that marriage is singled out in an essay on Goethe's late work, *Elective Affinities.* For, as Benjamin holds, "it is marriage, as one of the most rigorous and objective articulations of the content of a human life, that in Goethe's *Elective Affinities* attests, also for the first time, to the author's new meditation, turned toward the synthetic perception of the material content" (299). No wonder, then, that although Benjamin repeatedly states that marriage is not the central theme of Goethe's novel—rather the dissolution of marriage, and the forces that such dissolution sets free, constitutes its theme—he consistently returns to this issue in his analysis of the work as well as of Goethe's life.[10] But before taking up Goethe's understanding of marriage, Benjamin turns to Kant's late work, *The Metaphysics of Morals,* and its definition of marriage as "the union of two persons of different sexes for the purpose of lifelong possession of their sexual organs," and whose end is not, according to Kant, the natural end of begetting and rearing children (299). Benjamin characterizes this definition as "the most sublime product of a *ratio* that, incorruptibly true to itself, penetrates infinitely deeper into the facts of the matter (*Sachverhalt*) than sentimental ratiocination. Of course the material content itself, which yields only to philosophical perception (*Anschauung*)—or, more precisely, to philosophical experience—remains inaccessible to both [Kant and Goethe], but whereas the latter leads into the abyss, the former attains the very ground where true knowledge is formed" (299). Yet, however penetrating, the definition in question concerns exclusively the matter of marriage, and although it grasps this matter at a depth beneficial to the understanding of its content (and thus also its relation to truth), its content escapes Kant's thought. Not only that, as a "most sublime product" of reason, this definition of marriage by one of the most sublime thinkers of the Enlightenment is not only limited to being a merely material definition, "in the consciousness of its cluelessness [regarding the content of marriage, it is, as Benjamin disparagingly remarks] sublime" (300).[11] Benjamin, seemingly oblivious of the fact that Kant's definition of marriage, in *The Metaphysics of Morals,* occurs in the context of "The Doctrine of Right," that is, his inquiry into the rational laws that regulate the *exterior* relations (such as acquisition and possession of property) between persons, but also the rights to persons akin to rights to things (i.e., the conditions under which one person can possess another without infringing on his or her autonomy), accuses Kant of making "his gravest mistake when he supposes that from his definition of the nature of marriage which takes solely its 'natural moment,' namely sexuality into account, he could deduce its moral (*sittliche*) possibility, indeed, its moral necessity, and in this way confirm its juridical reality" (299).[12] Undoubtedly, Kant's definition of marriage is one in terms of rational laws. In the "The Doctrine of Right," marriage is a contract between free persons according to a priori rational laws that permit them to mutually possess each other like things, yet without jeopardizing their independence. The rational laws, however, that inform marriage as defined by Kant are legal laws, that is, laws directed merely to external actions and thus distinct from the ethical laws that he broaches in "The Doctrine of Virtue," and which concern the morality of actions. The juridical institution of marriage as expounded in the "Doctrine of Right" is not justified in ethical terms properly speaking because the latter refer only to internal freedom and use of choice. It is justified only in terms of the rationality of the laws that regulate the exterior relations between persons. No deduction of its morality in the sense of ethicality is intended here; however, as Kant remarks, if in addition to fulfilling their exterior legal obligations to one another, the persons who have contracted marriage fulfill them in accordance with internal grounds for the determination of their acts, then their actions are also ethical. Yet, Benjamin claims that "from the objective (*sachlichen*) nature of marriage [as described by Kant], one could obviously deduce only its depravity—and in Kant's case this is what it willy-nilly amounts to" (299). To substantiate Kant's sublime cluelessness of the material and truth content of marriage, Benjamin refers to Kant's (legal) definition of sexual commerce as "the reciprocal use that one human being makes of the sexual organs and sexual capacities of another" and the idea that such use can be either natural or unnatural, in which latter case, it concerns either another human being or an animal (300). Speaking of the natural, or unnatural, ends of marriage, Kant misses out on what Benjamin sees as the divine end of the marriage relation, which alone saves it from the natural depravity that Kant highlights so effectively. But, as we have seen, for Benjamin even the material content of marriage remains concealed to Kant. Yet, Benjamin credits Kant for his rigorous insight into the matter of marriage and for thus reaching "the very ground where true knowledge is formed" (299). Indeed, the "strict allusion to the natural component of marriage—sexuality—does not obstruct the path to the logos of its divine component—fidelity," in the Kantian explanation (326). On the contrary, by ruthlessly pursuing the natural dimension of marriage by which the latter's complete depravity becomes exposed, another aspect of marriage comes into view. Indeed, for Benjamin, the complete depravity of marriage as a legal institution reveals, in a negative fashion, the imprint of a transcendent end of the marriage relation. Obviously, what Kant construes as the ethical obligations that can, and even should, be present in marriage on top of the legal ones are not what Benjamin has in mind when he speaks of the material, and truth, content of marriage. Assuming that, in *The Metaphysics of Morals,* Kant seeks to deduce the material content of marriage from the facts of the matter regarding marriage, Benjamin objects that the material content can never be deduced from the matter. The material content, even more so the truth content, transcends matter.[13] To conceptualize the way both relate, he has recourse to the image of the seal.

Just as the form of a seal cannot be deduced from the material of the wax or from the purpose of the fastening or even from the signet (in which one finds concave what in the seal is convex), and just as it can be grasped only by someone who has had the experience of sealing and becomes evident only to the person who knows the name that the initials merely indicate, so the content of the matter cannot be deduced by means of insight into its constitution or through an exploration of its intended use or even from a premonition of its content; rather, it is graspable only in the philosophical experience of its divine imprint, evident only to the blissful vision of the divine name. (299–300)

Solely philosophical perception and experience—something clearly missing in Kant, who has gained only an insight into the constitution of the matter of marriage—is capable of bringing the content of the matter in question, as well as its truth, into view. Several things need to be underlined here: first, no relation of deduction exists between a matter and content; the matter is only the occasion for the presentation of its content, which is thus transcendent with respect to the matter; second, philosophical perception and experience alone can serve as a guide to making out any content of a matter, whether it is the material or truth content. Consequently, if commentary seeks the material content, it needs philosophy to achieve this goal. But if Kant proved unable to grasp the material content of the matter that he penetrated so effectively, to which philosophical perception and experience does Benjamin refer? As will become clearer in what follows, commentary, whose task it is to find the material content by way of a detailed philological analysis of the concrete realities featured, whether in a work of art or by way of a penetrating analysis of the facts of the matter in the case of an institution such as marriage, cannot achieve this goal without comprehending these realities, or facts, morally. Indeed, when Benjamin writes that the material content of matrimonial bond, rather than being defined by the juridical norm, is morally constituted and has a "moral character," the suggestion is that the reason for its existence is to express a "continuance in love" (301–302). The content of the bond in question is thus determined by fidelity. Yet, this moral comprehension by commentary of the realities of marriage by which its material content becomes determined is itself dependent on philosophical perception and experience. As Benjamin understands such perception and experience, it is intrinsically one of the divine, more precisely, the divine name, in its imprint in the matter—in short, of the presence of the divine in the matter (of marriage) in the form of the word, or language. Indeed, after having argued that Kant's elaboration of the natural component of marriage does not obstruct the logos of its divine component, Benjamin explains: "For what is proper to the truly divine is the logos: the divine does not ground life without truth, nor does it ground the rite without theology." Logos, here, is understood as the "ground" where words "ought to stand and give an account of themselves" (326–327). The divine component of marriage, by which love "becomes master of this world" and which thus secures "its supernatural duration" (345), in short, fidelity, is the imprint of the divine name in the shape of verbal responsibility and transparency, on its material configuration.[14] The material content of a matter such as marriage is thus intimately linked to the truth content of a matter. It follows from this that critique, which seeks the truth content, is another term for the philosophical perception and experience in question, whose ultimate aim is the blissful vision of the divine name. Yet, as Benjamin states, material content and truth content are not only interlinked, they are the same: "the achieved insight into the material content of subsisting things finally coincides with insight into their truth content. The truth content emerges as that of the material content. Nonetheless, the distinction between them—and with it the distinction between the commentary and the critique of works—is not futile, insofar as the striving for immediacy is nowhere more misguided than here, where the study of the matter and its intended use, like the intuition of its content, must precede each and every experience" (300). If this distinction is not to be abandoned it is because, at least in the commentary and critique of works, any critical grasp of the truth content of a work inevitably presupposes the grasping of the material content through a patient commentary on the concrete realities displayed by the works, and their moral comprehension. Although, ultimately, material content and truth content are the same, this identity does not abolish difference. In fact, identified as the same, their difference, or transcendence, with respect to the matter becomes even more exacerbated. The truth content to which the material content points is even more "detached" from the material realities than the material content. Furthermore, as we will see, it is necessary to distinguish degrees when speaking of material content; perhaps only the highest material content coincides with the truth content.

Recall that in spite of the privilege that marriage enjoys as an example in the context of the attempt to differentiate between material content and truth content, marriage is not the subject matter of Goethe's novel. Benjamin writes: "The subject of *Elective Affinities* is not marriage. Nowhere in this work are its ethical powers to be found. From the outset, they are in the process of disappearing. . . . In its dissolution, everything human turns into appearance, and the mythic alone remains as essence" (302).[15] Not marriage, but its dissolution occupies the center of the novel. It is its real subject matter, as well as the forces that such dissolution sets free. Probing Goethe's insight into the material content of marriage, Benjamin argues that although the poet "never really did obtain pure insight into the moral constitution of this bond," in his descriptions of the "declining relation (*untergehendes Verhältnis*)," "Goethe in fact touched on the material content of marriage" (301). By showing "that [the] norm of law makes itself master of a vacillating love" (345) and that the forces that arise from the decay of marriage, whose only legitimation is that of "an expression of continuance in love," are "the mythic powers of the law," Goethe indicates that, rather than being "justified in law (that is, as an institution)," marriage becomes the juridical relation only in its decline (301). By breaking up, marriage, if grounded on the law, releases those mythic forces on which the law itself rests.[16] The dissolution of marriage is "pernicious only because it is not the highest powers that produce it. And solely in this disaster-vexed-into-life (*aufgestörten Unheil*) lies the ineluctable horror of the proceedings" in the novel (301). In the first part of "Goethe's Elective Affinities," which, in a manuscript page titled "Zu den Wahlverwandtschaften. Disposition," is called "The Mythic as Thesis"—part two is titled, "Redemption as Antithesis" and part three, "Hope as Synthesis,"[17]—Benjamin establishes the material content of Goethe's book as the mythic.[18] He writes: "Nowhere, certainly, is the mythic the highest material content, but it is everywhere a strict indication of it. As such, Goethe made it the basis of his novel. The mythic is the real material content of the book" (309). Apart from introducing a difference of degrees between at least two kinds of material content—the real and the highest material content—this passage makes the important point that the characters of the novel are distinct from human beings in that they are "entirely rooted in nature" (304). As the parsimony of their names demonstrates—there are only seven names in a novel of such size, Benjamin notes—these highly cultivated beings go their ways in muteness. Yet, for Benjamin, the name is what links the human creature as a singular creature to the creator, or divine Word. The name, therefore, amounts to a summons to the creature in its very singularity to face God, and to justify itself in speech before him. Almost anonymous, language is not the element of the characters of the novel. Theirs is a "fateful kind of existence, which encompasses living natures in a single nexus of guilt and expiation" (307). They "are subject to forces that cultivation claims to have mastered, even if it may forever prove impotent to curb them" (304). Fate, as Benjamin explains, "unfolds inexorably in the culpable life" (307). Culpable life is "mere life," that is, natural life from which the "supernatural life in man" has disappeared. He writes: "When they turn their attention away from the human and succumb to the powers of nature, then natural life, which in man preserves its innocence only so long as natural life binds itself to something higher, drags the human down" (308). This guilt that the characters of the novel have incurred is not ethical, because they are not bound to language and do not account for themselves. Their guilt is natural guilt, one that "befalls human beings not by decision and action but by negligence and celebration"

(308). Like Ottilie, they all "vegetate without decision . . . lingering, at once guilty and guiltless, in the precincts of fate" (337). The characters' lack of expression, their silence, and hence the missing clarity of their actions reveal the absence in their life of something higher and show them to be "members [who] live out their lives under a nameless law, that fills their world with the pallid light of a solar eclipse," rather than daylight, in the clarity of which decision occurs (305). Theirs is thus "a lost life" (304).

"From the start, the characters are under the spell of elective affinities." They yield, as Benjamin argues, to "the particular harmony of the deeper natural strata" (304), such as "the magnetic power of the interior of the earth" (303). For the characters of the novel, "marriage seems a destiny more powerful than the choice to which the lovers give themselves up" (308). Indeed, "the violated law stands opposed to such choice, powerful enough to exact sacrifice for the expiation of the shattered marriage" (309). Marriage is something endured by the characters, whereas its dissolution sets free the powers of fate, that is, those powers on which marriage, as a juridical institution, is founded. The inevitable outcome of "the somber ritualistic tendencies" (310) of all the events in the novel—the setting free of the mythic powers by the violated statutory laws, as a result of which even "seemingly dead things acquire power" (308)—is Ottilie's "sacrifice for the expiation of the guilty ones" (309).

The characters of the novel are not only subject to the mythic forces of mere natural life, of a life forsaken by higher powers, but also "they must themselves manifest the violence of nature, for at no point have they outgrown it" (303–304). Because these fictional characters are both ruled by the forces of myth, and are its very agents, Benjamin construes the material content of the *Elective Affinities* as the mythic. Keeping in mind that this material content is not the novel's "highest material content" (309), what are the implications of this diagnostic? What does this recognition entail as far as the understanding of the novel as an object of critique is concerned? And what does it say about the task of critique itself? As Benjamin contends, because they are entirely entangled in a fateful nexus of guilt, neither the novel's characters, nor what occurs between them, can be judged ethically. In fact, according to what he terms to be a universal insight (*allgemeinern Erkenntnis*), he claims that

the characters in a fiction (*Dichtung*) can never be subject to ethical judgment. And, to be sure, not because such judgment, like that passed on human beings, would surpass all human discernment. Rather, the grounds of such judgment already forbid, incontrovertibly, its application to fictional characters. It remains for moral philosophy to prove in rigorous fashion that the fictional character (*erdichtete Person*) is always too poor and too rich to come under ethical judgment. Such a judgment can be executed only upon real human beings. Characters in the novel [of the *Elective Affinities*] are distinguished from them by being entirely rooted in nature. And what is crucial in the case of fictional characters is not to make ethical findings but rather to understand morally what happens (*das Geschehen moralisch zu erfassen*). (304; trans. mod.)

What is true of the fictional characters in Goethe's novel, who cannot be judged ethically because they are entirely under the spell of nature and, hence, inextricably interconnected in a nexus of guilt, is true of all characters in a fiction. The basic reason for this is precisely their fictional character, that is, their origin, not in an act of creation but in an act of formation, as well as their embeddedness in a textual web. The interconnectedness in guilt of Goethe's figures is one manifestation of such textual entanglement. In the case of *Elective Affinities,* the essentially anonymous characters who, "deaf to God and mute before the world," live a life before language are incapable of any ethical decision. Under the sway of the forces of the mythic, "rendering account eludes them, not because of their actions but because of their being. They fall silent" (304–305). Ethical action, for Benjamin, is intrinsically linked to language, that is, to accounting to others for one's deeds. Speaking of Ottilie's "decision" to die, a decision that she keeps from her friends, Benjamin emphasizes that "this hiddenness touches the root of the morality of her decision. For if the moral world shows itself anywhere illuminated by the spirit of language, it is in the decision. No moral decision can enter into life without verbal form and, strictly speaking, without thus becoming an object of communication" (336). But language is constitutive of ethical decision in still another way: without the word's interruption of the threads of the weblike interconnectedness of mere, that is, mythic, nature, no true decision is conceivable. But being mute before the world and bereaved of language, the characters of Goethe's novel are also deprived of a relation to the divine. Goethe's beings are deaf to God, that is, deaf to the Word. These characters cannot be judged ethically because in their world "the ethical never lives triumphantly but lives only in defeat" (312).[19] Consequently, if the characters' linguistic poverty excludes them as objects of an ethical judgment, that is, of a judgment whose grounds lies in the human being's ability to decide and account for his actions, it remains that in the case of fiction it is necessary "to understand morally what happens." In the case of fiction, determining "the content of the course" (309) requires establishing "the moral content" of what occurs (312). In other words, what is required with fictions is to grasp the whole of what is described—what happens in a work in its totality—from a moral perspective. What such a judgment of the entirety of what happens in the novel amounts to becomes clear when Benjamin writes that the observation that the fictional characters of Goethe's novel "have lost the sense for what is ethical" is to be understood "as a judgment not on their actions but rather on their language. Feeling, but deaf, seeing, but mute, they go their way: deaf to God and mute before the world. Rendering account eludes them, not because of their actions but because of their being. They fall silent" (304–305).[20] Critique and commentary, which pertain only to artworks, are not to treat fictional characters as if they were life persons. This is, certainly, one sense of what Benjamin means when he observes that critique and commentary are not to mingle with the biographical. But although commentary and critique, which aim at bringing the material and the truth content of a work of art into view, exclude an ethical judgment regarding the characters, commentary and critique are in need of morally understanding what happens, that is, the meaning of the subject matter. If the content of that matter is established through commentary and critique, this establishment takes place through a moral judgment upon the whole of what happens in a fiction. Benjamin's very conclusion that the material content of the *Elective Affinities* is the mythic is based on nothing less than a moral judgment, one that concerns the absence of language and, hence, of all relation to the divine from the world and life of its protagonists. Commentary, critique, and moral judgment are intrinsically tied together.

This moral judgment, however, cannot come to the work from the outside. If it is a true work of art, the work itself must prepare the judgment in question. As we have seen, the subject matter of the novel, including its content, is the mythic. However, if the *Elective Affinities* were nothing but a stage for demonic forces, it would not be a work of literature, a work of *Dichtung*. From the domain ruled by the mythic forces, critique has to separate off "a special domain (*gesonderter Bereich*)" in the novel, which interrupts the forces of myth and makes it possible "to isolate [a] layer in which the meaning of [the] novel autonomously reigns. Where the existence of no such special domain can be proved, we are dealing not with a literary work of art but solely with its precursor: magical writing" (323). Speaking of *Elective Affinities,* Benjamin writes, that, therefore, "a purer promise (*Verheissung*), no matter how darkly the myth holds sway in it, must already be visible there" (329). The task of critique, then, is to locate in the work this domain, which is separated off from the textual and mythic fabric of the novel, cuts its interlacings, and dispels the twilight that reigns in the novel in order to provide "insight . . . into the luminous kernel of redemptive content" (323). Needless to say, this content, which is distinct from the mythic material content, constitutes "the highest material content" and, consequently, is connected, if not identical, to the work's truth content. As Benjamin forcefully argues in his essay, the novella "The Wayward Young Neighbors" inserted in the novel performs the break (*Bruch*) with the mythic content, if not even with the form of the novel itself. In this novella, which "ennobles (so to speak) the form of the novel," to such a degree, indeed, that *Elective Affinities* "stands further removed from other novels than those novels stand from one another" (330), the lawful character of its form, "namely, the untouchability of the center— that is to say, the mystery (*Geheimnis*) as an essential characteristic," stands out in exemplary fashion. Benjamin writes: "For in it, the mystery is the catastrophe, which, as the animating principle of the story, is conducted into its center, while in the novel the significance of the catastrophe, the concluding event, remains phenomenal" (331). In contrast to Ottilie's self-inflicted death, which, as Benjamin explains, is anything but the result of a conscious decision, the young girl's leap into the river, which constitutes the center of the novella, is the novella's mysterious enlivening power. However enigmatic, and "so difficult to fathom," this catastrophe causes "in the novella a brilliant light to hold sway. From the outset everything, sharply contoured, is at a peak. It is the day of decision shining into the dusk-filled Hades of the novel" (331). The light that reigns in this novella, which in the novel "confronts the novel," dissolves the ambiguous twilight that dominates the events in which the characters of the novel are embroiled. It does so because the impenetrable mystery, or enigma, of the catastrophe at the center of the novella is that of decision, that is, of ethical and responsible action. This mystery of decision, which dissolves all ambiguity and brings everything into sharp relief, is the enlivening force of the novella and, ultimately, of the *Elective Affinities* as a whole. The enigma of the decision is what makes this work alive; it is the living flame of its truth—its highest material, if not truth content—that is, the prime "object," as we have seen, of literary critique.

Let us remind ourselves of Benjamin's claim that without the presence in the novel of a separate domain interrupting the mythic forces at play, *Elective Affinities* could not be a work of literature, or a work of art. Before expanding on the events narrated in the novella, and the promise of redemption from the forces of myth to be found there, we must first deepen our understanding of what, according to Benjamin, constitutes art. In the analysis devoted to Ottilie in part 3 of the essay, it is pointed out that Goethe, in his depiction of Ottilie, goes "against the laws of novelistic form" (338). By bestowing on Ottilie the appearance of the beautiful as her essential content as a living being, he removes her "from the epic plane in which the writer reigns" and transmits "a strange vitality to her for which he [as writer] is not responsible" (338). Rather than artistic skill, conjuration, indeed, is at play in the presentation of Ottilie's beauty. He writes:

> In *Elective Affinities* . . . the daemonic principles of conjuration irrupt into the very center of the poetic composition. For what is conjured is always only a semblance— in Ottilie, a semblance of living beauty—which strongly, mysteriously, and impurely imposed itself in the most powerful sense as "material." Thus, the aura of Hades (*das Hadeshafte*) in what the author lends to the action is confirmed: he stands before the deep ground of his poetic gift like Odysseus with his naked sword before the ditch full of blood and like him fends off the thirsty shades, in order to suffer only those whose scanty words (*karge Rede*) he seeks. (339; trans. mod.)

Leaving, for the time being, a discussion of Benjamin's characterization of the author himself in abeyance, I reflect only on what is asserted with respect to the style and composition of the novel. As a result of the demonic conjuration of Ottilie's beauty, which represents the center of the novel, the composition of the novel, and in particular the novel's second part, has as Benjamin remarks, "formulaic quality" (339). Even more problematic are those features of the novel, he holds, that "can in no way be disclosed to the purely receptive intention—those correspondences which reveal themselves only to philological research that completely eschews aesthetics. In such correspondences the presentation encroaches, quite undeniably, upon the domain of incantatory formulas. That is why it so often lacks the ultimate immediacy and finality of artistic vivification—why it lacks form" (339). In short, in *Elective Affinities*, the formal laws of the novel are transgressed, and more often than not, its style and composition are mythic in nature. To be precise, it is formless, but formlessness, and the ensuing lack of distinction, is a mythic feature par excellence. Because numerous aspects of the novel eschew aesthetics, it follows as well that the novel's status as a work of art is uncertain. If form is what artistically vivifies a work of art, *Elective Affinities* all by itself does not seem to truly be one. And yet, as Benjamin observes, in this novel the form of the genre "does not so much construct figures, which often enough on their own authority insert themselves formlessly as mythic figures. Rather, it plays about them hesitantly—in the manner of an arabesque, so to speak; it completes and with full justification dissolves them" (339). In other words, although the formal qualities of the genre do not shape the novel's figures, which impose themselves with demonic force into the poetic composition, the poet's formal gift is still at work in this novel in that it fends off these mythic figures by completing and dissolving them "with full justification," suffering only one figure whose scanty words he seeks, the figure of Ottilie. This is the reason why the novel is not merely a piece of magical writing. The destruction of the novel's figures, all of which are of ghostly origin, takes place, in *Elective Affinities,* by way of form that, like Odysseus' naked sword, trenchantly dissolves these figures' turbid power.[21]

Art has nothing in common with conjuration. Like divine creation, its negative counterpart—demonic conjuration—claims "to bring forth a world from nothingness." However, art, or more precisely, the world of art, does not spring from nothingness. As Benjamin forcefully argues throughout the essay, the artist does not create. "The artist is less the primal ground, or creator, than the origin, or form giver [*Bildner*], and certainly his work is not at any price his creature but rather his formation [*Gebilde*]" (323–324; trans. mod.). As a work, the artwork "emerges not from nothingness but from chaos" (340). Chaos, as Benjamin explains, is a state without distinctions, and, hence, it is without limits. Chaos, as a state of existence from which all difference is absent, is the correlate of the mythic interconnectedness of guilt. Where everything is thoroughly interconnected, distinction, hierarchy, and order are lacking. Chaos is the ultimate outcome of the life of myth, "which without master or boundaries, imposes itself as the sole power in the domain of existence" (316). It is dominated by the same; in it, everything eternally recurs. In contrast to creation, which wrenches a world from nothingness, and conjuration, which, by mixing elements of chaos, engenders by means of formulas the semblance of a world that also pretends to be distinct from chaos and to have a life of its own, art, for its part, does not produce something from mythic chaos that would be clearly severed off from its substrate. Form, Benjamin argues, "enchants (*verzaubert*) chaos momentarily into world" (340). The "material" of art is thus mythic chaos, that is, mythic life in which everything is interconnected, and all difference is blurred. Artistic form bestows again on this chaos an order of differences and hierarchies. The thus re-differentiated chaos becomes transfigured into the shape of a world. In other words, since Benjamin understands the mythic state of the world as the created world in the state of the Fall, the work of art, by bestowing order on mythic chaos, restores the world, as it were, to its initial state. More precisely, the work of art transforms the fallen world back again into a fragment of divine creation. However, because this enchanted world is not produced from nothing, it cannot last longer than the flash of a moment. Its life must appear transient lest it be mistaken for an object of creation or demonic conjuration. Benjamin writes: "no work of art may seem wholly alive without restraint (*gänzlich ungebannt lebendig erscheinen*) without becoming mere semblance and ceasing to be a work of art. The life undulating in it must appear petrified and as if arrested in a single moment. That which in it has being is mere beauty, mere harmony, which floods through the chaos (and, in truth, through this only and not the world) but, this flooding-through, seems only to enliven it" (340; trans. mod.). In order to avoid becoming mere semblance, and, hence, demonically conjured life, the life that seems to flood through chaos and to enliven it must be arrested. The appearance of life that seems to enliven the chaos that artistic form metamorphoses into a world by reimposing differences needs to be interrupted and petrified in order to prevent it from becoming a mere appearance of life. Paradoxically, this interruption of appearance is what constitutes the artwork's specific life, the life of a transient moment. At this juncture of his argument, Benjamin introduces the notion of the "expressionless (*das Ausdruckslose*)."[22] He writes:

What arrests this semblance, stays the movement, and interrupts (*ins Wort fällt*) the harmony is the expressionless. The life in question grounds the mystery while this petrification grounds the content (*Gehalt*) in the work. Just as interruption by the commanding word is able to bring out the truth from the evasions of a woman precisely at the point where it interrupts, the expressionless compels the trembling harmony to stop and through its objection [*Einspruch*] immortalizes its quivering. In this immortalization the beautiful must vindicate (*verantworten*) itself, but now it appears to be interrupted precisely in its vindication, and thus it has the eternity of its content precisely by the grace of that objection. The expressionless is the critical violence which, while unable to separate semblance from essence in art, prevents them from mingling. It possesses this violence as a moral dictum (*moralisches Wort*). In the expressionless, the sublime violence of the true appears as that which determines the language of the real world according to the laws of the moral world. For it shatters whatever still survives as the legacy of chaos in all beautiful semblance: the false, errant totality—the absolute totality. Only the expressionless completes the work, by shattering it into a thing of shards, into a fragment of the true world, into the torso of a symbol. (340)

This passage, which, in a most condensed form, contains the basic tenets of Benjamin's conception of art and the artwork, would require a lengthy commentary. In the present context, only several remarks must suffice. The form that gives the work its internal harmonious movement and unity constitutes the artwork's semblance of life. As we have seen before, this life is the enigma of the work of art, its hidden truth. Precisely because what floods through the work is only a semblance of life (as opposed to the life of an *ens creatum*), its quivering needs to be brought to a standstill. Otherwise this life would amount to mere semblance, that is, to mythic life. The expressionless, likened by Benjamin to the Hölderlinean concept of the caesura, performs this interruption. As a result of this arresting cut, the inner life of the work becomes "frozen" into a moment, immortalized, as it were. Because the petrifaction of an artwork's undulating life grounds its content, the work's material content is tied to momentary, unique, and singular animation of mythic chaos through artistic form. According to Benjamin, the expressionless, which causes this interruption and petrifaction of the life that seems to animate chaos and which, thus, immortalizes this quivering life, is "a category of language and art and not of the work or of the genres" (340). The expressionless, therefore, juts into the work from beyond, so to speak. Whereas the form that transforms chaos into a world, and thus enlivens the work, is a category of the artwork as a work, the expressionless, to the extent that it interrupts "along with harmony, every expression" (341), concerns the media of linguistic and artistic expression.[23] As an extra-aesthetic category of sorts, the expressionless refers to language's origin in the divine word, that is, in the infinite language of the creative Word.[24] The expressionless confronts the work of literature, which qua work is of the order neither of creation nor conjuration but only formed from chaos, with language's divine essence.

Indeed, if by interrupting the quivering life of the work, the expressionless immortalizes its beautiful harmony, it does so precisely by forcing it to face eternal truth and to account for itself before the creative Word. The way in which the expressionless intervenes in the quivering life of the work is of the order of a violent intervention. It is violent insofar as the expressionless, or "the sublime violence of the true," in the shape of "the laws of the moral world" (in short, in the form of a moral dictum), determines the language of the real world. Benjamin's simile compares the expressionless to the "commanding word," which "bring[s] out the truth from the evasions of a woman precisely at the point where it interrupts."[25] This "commanding word" not only interrupts all the woman's evasions and excuses, but also it forces her to abandon language as a way for evasion and lies and to face language as the medium in which one renders accounts. The commanding word orders her to make a truthful use of language, a use conformed with language's divine origin. With this word, which demands unequivocal clarity and full transparency regarding all one's deeds and words, we are thus in the sphere of ethics. In the order of the language of the real world, the expressionless, for its part, is the moral equivalent—language under the laws of the moral world—of the sublime violence of truth, that is, of language no longer as a medium of expression, but of rendering accounts.

Immortalized, that is, stopped in its quivering, and face to face with the expressionless as the eternal nature of the Word, the beautiful, as semblance that is, must thus vindicate itself as well. However, because the expressionless freezes the mere semblance of life in the work of art, the latter's efforts to respond to the demand to responsibly account for itself are interrupted as well. Benjamin writes that it has thus "the eternity of its content precisely by the grace of that objection." In other words, the beautiful work of art does not acquire its immortality on its own account, but only from beyond itself, that is, by the grace of the transcendent Word. Just as the truth is extracted from the evasions of the woman at the precise point where the commanding word interrupts, just so does the (truth) content of a work spring from the interruption by the expressionless of the expressive nature of its language. This truth content is thus less the result of an active vindication of the beautiful by itself than something that the work receives by the grace of the violent protest, or objection, of the expressionless. In the same way that the demand for vindication is not only forced upon the evasive woman, and that truth is brought forth by the interruption of her evasions—that is, not by herself, but by the commanding word itself—the eternal content of the work is not the effect of beauty's self-vindication, but a gift of the interruption. Suppose the woman would spontaneously admit to what she has been up to, or the quivering harmony in the work would account for itself; both accounts would remain imbued with semblance. Yet, no mingling of semblance and essence is to occur in true works of art.

According to Benjamin, the expressionless is "the critical violence which, while unable to separate semblance from essence in art, prevents them from mingling." The creative Word alone possesses the violence required for absolute separation. The expressionless, however, is only in the literary work of art, the repository of the divine Word (in the same way the commanding word is the repository of the divine Word in the real world). As we have seen, mere beauty and mere harmony are indications that the life that artistic form bestows on mythic chaos is only a semblance of life. Every beautiful semblance remains indebted to chaos. This legacy of chaos in beautiful semblance corresponds to the unity that the quivering harmony bestows upon beautiful works, which Benjamin qualifies as "the false, errant totality—the absolute totality."[26] Just as the ideal of the problem, which cannot be thematized in philosophy's problematizing mode, becomes just one more problem when articulated in philosophy, so does the harmonious unity of a work of art remain tributary to mythic interconnectedness and must be demarcated from the unity of the "true world." The latter cannot be grasped as such in the world opened up by a work of art. But the critical violence of the expressionless prevents the latter's unity from mingling with what remains in the artwork as the heritage of mythic chaos. This violence shatters the work, but by preventing semblance and essence to mingle, the critical intervention of the expressionless also completes the work, as it were. It completes it precisely as a fragment of the true world. Insofar as the expressionless, as that which within language yields to the moral law (and actualizes the sublime violence of truth), performs within the artwork the critical operation that prevents semblance and essence from mixing, the expressionless is that which, in the work, ultimately, makes the operation of the critic possible. In the same way as the expressionless, as moral dictum, violently interrupts beautiful semblance in the work, literary criticism, or art criticism, inevitably does violence to the work. Just as the expressionless does not radically separate semblance and essence, but only prevents them from mingling, so too is critique limited to merely preventing their mixture. Critique interrupts the work, and breaks it up into shards, with the effect of showing it as a fragment of truth. Furthermore, critique can have this power only as a moral dictum of sorts.

It follows from this that the judgment that critique must render about the moral significance of what happens in the novel—as a result of which its material content is found in the mythic—is made structurally possible not only by the novella that is inserted in the novel, but also, on a deeper level, by the interruption of a work of art's expressive sphere by the expressionless required by true art in general. The expressionless confronts the expressive medium of art, above all its language, with language's destination to serve as a medium in which the artistic work must vindicate itself before language as such. The expressionless, as that which in the artistic work testifies to the creative Word, interrupts all beautiful semblance—the appearance of life in the artwork and what of this life remains indebted to chaos. By virtue of this power to interrupt the semblance, and the power to summon the artwork to vindicate itself before the eternal—in an objective vindication, of sorts—the expressionless, in relation to the artwork, is the creative word in the quality of the moral dictum. Made possible by the expressionless, which prevents the mingling of essence and semblance in the work, critique is therefore ethical through and through.

As we have seen from the start, works of art are alive. This, indeed, is their enigma. Before we turn to a clarification of the difference between works and the life of their authors, in order to further probe the distinction that Benjamin makes between critique and biography, we must reflect on what kind of life it is, that is, whose flame burns in true works of art. Even though the artist is not a creator, but a form-giver, and, consequently, his work is "not at any price his creature but rather his formation [*Gebilde*] . . . the form too, and not only the creature, has life" (323–324; trans. mod.). However, notwithstanding the many parallel structures that Benjamin describes between works and lives, the life of a work and that of a creature are not of the same order. Benjamin claims that "the basis of the decisive difference between the two is this: only the life of the creature, never that of the formed structure [*des Gebildeten*], partakes, unreservedly (*hemmungslos*), of the intention of redemption" (324). Whereas the life of the creature not only partakes in the intention of redemption, but also does so without restraint, the work of art is strictly inhibited from such participation. If this is so, it is because the work is only formed chaos, a momentous flickering up of the true world. As we have seen, the life that quivers in an artwork, although not the product of demonic conjuration, is only a semblance of life and as such is indebted to mythic chaos. Only the interruption of this life by the expressionless lights the flame that makes a work immortal. But this true life of the work consists of nothing but the burning to ashes of everything that is linked to the expressive medium in the work, in short, its entire material content. What brings works of art truly alive is the expressionless that interrupts all semblance of life, their harmony and expression. As previously illustrated, the expressionless does not radically separate the essence from semblance, but only prevents both from mingling. The immortal life peculiar to true artworks is merely that of the flame that feeds, and continues to consume, their material content, reminding us, as it were, of the divine nature of language and of its true destination as the medium in which created life must render account to the divine Word. Because works have only a semblance of life, there is no life to be redeemed in them. As works, however, in which the expressionless interrupts semblance, and thus brings them alive, this very interruption that causes them to be true works of art is indicative of the promise of redemption in the domain of created life. In seeking the truth content of works, which is not the same as unraveling their truth content, critique is thus limited to reflecting on the enigma of their life. Although this life is radically different from that of human beings, its consuming flame, in which all material content, that is, in the case of *Elective Affinities,* the mythic, is ablaze, is indicative of truth events in the life of their author and serves to shed a light on it.

II.

In his discussions of Kant's definition of marriage in *The Metaphysics of Morals,* Benjamin calls to mind that this definition is now and again remembered as "a curiosity of his senile period" (299). Indeed, according to Benjamin, it is in one of his late works that Kant, though clueless as regards its material content (*Sachgehalt*), by highlighting the depravity of marriage as an institution, penetrated the facts of the matter (*Sachverhalt*) of marriage infinitely deeper than most of his contemporaries. Mozart's

treatment of marriage in *The Magic Flute,* which Benjamin sets alongside
Kant's definition and which he credits for having had a premonition of the
content of marriage (*Ahnung des Gehalts*)—its material content—as con-
sisting in "the feeling of fidelity" and steadfastness, also takes place in a
work composed just before Mozart's death.[27] Both "represent the most extreme and at the same time most profound views of marriage which the
age possessed" (300). As far as Goethe is concerned, *Elective Affinities* is the
first of his works of old age in which a renewal of material content (as opposed to its general neglect in the period of the Enlightenment)—one that
concerns marriage as well—becomes available. Not only are Kant, Mozart,
and Goethe praised for having rediscovered in their old age the facts of
matter (of marriage, for example) and for having penetrated them and,
possibly, suspected their content, but also the theory of art and of the artwork developed in "Goethe's Elective Affinities" is predicated entirely on
the works Goethe produced in his later years. Indeed, according to Benjamin, *Elective Affinities* marks a turning point in Goethe's life. Together
with *Truth and Poetry, East-West Divan,* and the second part of *Faust, Elective Affinities* is a document of penance (328). "In his old age, Goethe had
penetrated profoundly enough into the essence of poetry to feel with horror the absence of any occasion for poetry (*Gesanges*) in the world that surrounded him, yet wanted to stride solely and forever [upon the] carpet of
truth" (329). Even though he abhorred religion, he submitted, without
converting, to its laws. These laws, Benjamin argues, kindled in Goethe
"the highest flame of his life. It burned away the dross of every passion"
(329). And he concludes that, "if in the series of these works from his old
age *Elective Affinities* is the first, then a purer promise, no matter how
darkly the myth holds sway in it, must already be visible there" (329).
Only in these late works, is the semblance of the artwork's life interrupted,
and in them alone is the truth alive that makes them truly immortal. It
thus becomes increasingly clear that between the works and the life of an
author an intrinsic relation obtains. True works of art, works in which a
promise must be visible, mirror the event in the life of the author of a purification from the forces of myth. Only those works are true works that
mirror human life in view of its "redemption in eternal life" (320).

If "Goethe's Elective Affinities" take on Gundolf's *Goethe* in a highly
polemical fashion, it is certainly not because of Gundolf's possibly unsatisfactory analysis of Goethe's late production. Nor is it merely because of

the prominent literary critic's "almost impenetrable terminology" (325), "the almost unfathomable perversion of the mode of thinking of this work" (327), "the confusion instituted by the conflation of truth and myth" (326), "the blood-thirsty mysticism" (of the remarks on marriage, for example) (326), and so forth, but because in this biography of Goethe, according to which "among all the works of Goethe the greatest is his life" (324), "Goethe's life is not rigorously distinguished from that of the works" (324). By forgoing such a distinction, Gundolf "eliminates every moral concept from the horizon," Benjamin asserts. Apart from the accusation of "the blasphemous profundity" of which Gundolf is the target (given that the negligence to separate works and life leads to a characterization of the artist as a heroic creator), the prime reason for Benjamin's fierce critique of this powerful and influential biography is the complete lack of a moral perspective regarding both life and work.

Indeed, Gundolf's book seeks "to portray Goethe's life as a mythic one" (323), that is, as a life distinct from human life—the life of hero, who as a "representative of mankind before its gods," lacks the "moral uniqueness of responsibility" specific of human life (322). As a demigod, the poet is assigned a task that he has to accomplish for the sake of mankind. Tasks, however, have no place within "the moral domain" (322); they never come from God from whom man only receives exactions. Yet, however critical of Gundolf's *Goethe,* Benjamin admits that the latter's "conception demand[s] consideration because mythic elements operate in the existence of this man, [and] it demands it all the more in the contemplation of a work [*Elective Affinities*] to which, because of it mythic moments, it could appeal" (323). We have already seen to what extent the material content of *Elective Affinities* is constituted by the mythic. But in his essay, Benjamin also consistently underscores the mythic elements in Goethe's life. Part 1 of the essay, especially, forcefully makes this point. Not only is the Olympian's personal existence clouded (*Trübung*) like murky water, a "dark, deeply self-absorbed, mythic nature . . . in speechless rigidity, indwells Goethean artistry" (314). If Benjamin lingers on the author's statements about *Elective Affinities*, it is certainly not in order to let the path of critique be staked out by them. "To wish to gain an understanding of *Elective Affinities* from the author's own words on the subject is wasted effort" (313). Biographical considerations, as we have seen, do not enter into commentary and critique. If Benjamin nevertheless pays attention to Goethe's own thoughts about his work, it is because they say something about his life. Even if he recognizes that Goethe, undoubtedly, had to meet contemporary judgments and defend his work, Benjamin's main argument is that Goethe's statements seek to "forbid access to critique" (313) and to keep, by the apologetic and mystifying nature of his remarks, the secret of the work. Although "Goethe's contemporaries were aware—not through insight but by feeling—of the mythic content of the work" (311), the thoughts he expressed regarding his work were precisely aimed at concealing this mythic content. Yet in doing so, Goethe's artistry submits to the powers of myth given that "all mythic meaning strives for secrecy" (314). This is also the reason for the poet's "indifference toward criticism" (315). Faced with criticism, the Olympian grows silent, becomes mute. But, both "the rejection of all criticism" and "the idolatry of nature," which, significantly enough, is manifest in the author's self-advertisement of the novel, "are the mythic forms of life in the existence of the artist" (316). In spite of all his research into nature, Goethe's concept of nature was never defined by him conceptually and thus remained ambiguous. Lacking any internal differentiation, nature grows into a monstrosity that subjugates all existence. Nature, in Goethe, is just another name for the almightiness of the mythical. It is to this "incomprehensible ambivalence of nature" (316) that Benjamin refers when he writes: "As olympian, he laid the foundation of the work and with scant words rounded out the dome" (314).

But, as Benjamin emphasizes, the power of primeval forces is also "terribly clear . . . in the life of this man" (317). "Something dark . . . in the gravest way, has cast a shadow on the existence of [this] man," as the idea of the demonic—which accompanies Goethe's vision throughout his life—demonstrates. His concern with astrology, with signs, and with oracles further reinforces this shadow, since fear is the price that Goethe paid for his intercourse with demonic forces: first and foremost, the fear of death, "a heathen concern" par excellence; the fear of life as well; and, above all, the "fear of responsibility . . . the most spiritual of all those kinds of fear to which Goethe's nature subjected him" (317–319). Benjamin avers: "It is the foundation of the conservative position that he brought to the political, the social, and in his old age probably the literary, too. It is the root of negligence (*Versäumnis*) in his erotic life. That it also determined his interpretation of *Elective Affinities* is certain. For it is this work of art that sheds light on the foundations of his own life—

foundations which, because his confession does not betray them, also remain concealed from a tradition that has not yet freed itself from the spell of that life" (319–320; trans. mod.). Goethe's words, as we have seen, are intended, knowingly or not, to conceal the moral content of this work. Indeed, if, in the novel in question, "the ethical never lives triumphantly but lives only in defeat . . . the moral content of the work lies at much deeper level than Goethe's words lead one to suspect" (312). Its moral content is tied to the question of negligence, which, as Benjamin notes, "was of the first importance in so many relations of Goethe's life," as well as to the recognition of "the irretrievability of what he had neglected" and the attempt "still to embrace in feeling what was lost" (313; trans. mod.).

Before further inquiring into the moral content of this late Goethean novel, a clarification of Benjamin's contention that this work sheds light on Goethe's life, more precisely, on what "is most hidden in Goethe" (314), is certainly warranted. This will also be an opportunity to evaluate this contention in light of what is said about the relation of commentary and critique, on the one hand, and biography, on the other hand. On the opening pages of part 2 of Benjamin's essay, the point is made that "every work is able, like *Elective Affinities,* to shed light on the life and essence (*Wesen*) of the author" (320). Yet, this possibility does not, as is the case both in the usual, or commonsensical, reflection on this issue and in almost all modern philology (particularly that of Wilhelm Dilthey, for whom life is the sole ground of all poetry, and, therefore, the starting point for all research), amount to deriving (*ableiten*) the poetic work as a product from the essence and the life of the author. If this goal of deriving the work from the life is characterized as the *proton pseudos* of the method of modern philology, it is because this approach, based on a misunderstanding of the essence of human life—one that anticipates Gundolf's presentation of the poet as a demigod—mixes commentary and critique and biographical consideration. Such an approach not only lacks an understanding of the true nature of works, it also misconstrues the essence of the life of a human being. If, as Benjamin holds, works can shed light on the life and essence of the poet, the starting point has to be the work, because only the latter can reveal something of substance regarding its own content and essence, which, in turn, can shed a light on its author. If, indeed, the aim is to achieve knowledge about the relationship between the creative artist and the work of art, then one must begin with the examination of the work, which, even though it too contains a secret—the secret of its life—the work alone permits verifiable results, as opposed to a life of whose essence, "a complete and final intuition," cannot be revealed (321). Benjamin writes that "the sole rational connection between the creative artist and the work of art consists in the testimony that the latter gives about the former" (321). Consequently, "wherever insight addresses itself to content and essence, the work must by all means stand in the fore-ground. For nowhere are these more lastingly, more distinctively, and more comprehensibly evident than in the work" (320). Whereas the life of a hu-man being cannot directly be cognized, his manifestations and expressions permit us to gain some knowledge about it. "Not only does one gain knowledge of the essence of a human being solely through his outward manifestations (and in this sense the works, too, are a part of his essence); no, such knowledge is determined first and foremost by the works. Works, like deeds, are non-derivable" (321). Qua outward manifestations of the essence of a human being, works are compared to deeds, the implication being that as such works belong to the moral sphere. Like deeds, they have to be understood from that which, according to Benjamin, constitutes the human being: the relation of the human being before its creator, or divine Word—that is, the relation to the logos, to which he must render ac-counts. From what concerns us here—namely, the relation of the artist and his works—two things, at least, follow: first, the life of the artist is de-fined exclusively within the theological horizon in question; and second, works, though not already necessarily ethical deeds, are judged within the horizon of the human being's relation of responsibility to God. If, the works, then, correctly understood, can shed some light on their author, it is on his or her life as a human being, that is, as a finite creature before the infinite.

But what does Benjamin mean when he claims that works like deeds are non-derivable? As we have already seen, modern philology, by seeking to derive the works from the life of an (heroically stylized) author, mis-construes the essence not only of the works, but also that of the author's life. Traditional biography conceives of the totality of a life as a finite totality. But, as Benjamin notes, the totality of life is infinite, an infinite relation. It is because of this infinite relation, therefore, that, "in the realm of biography, there is neither commentary nor critique." For, indeed, "only the material content of the life lies open, however, and its truth content is hidden. Certainly the particular trait and the particular relation can be illuminated, but not the totality" (324–325). Yet, as we have seen, the works of an author, correctly interpreted, can shed a light on this life. However, to traditional biographism, "all knowledge of the author, according to his totality, his 'nature,' is rendered vain through neglect of the interpretation of the work. For if this, too, is unable to render a complete and final intuition of the essence, which for various reasons is indeed always unthinkable, then, when the work is disregarded, the essence remains utterly unfathomable. But even insight into the life of the creative artist is inaccessible to the traditional biographical method" (321).[28] What Benjamin terms "authentic biographism" is based on the recognition that the totality of a life cannot be made fully transparent; not only does authentic biographism, therefore, proceed "with great modesty," but also it is, for the same reason, characterized by a "faithful attitude (*treue Gesinnung*)," one that is respectful of what in a life remains undecodable (324). Such biographism, which seeks to shed light on the poet's life, is conscious of the fact that however great the work, it is only one among many other elements in a life. Hence, it proceeds on the assumption that "the work can clarify the life of the artist only in a wholly fragmentary way, more in development than its content" (321). But authentic biographism also concerns only one aspect of the life of a human being in still another sense. Authentic biographism addresses only that part in the life of a human being that concerns him or her as a human being, that is, his or her being in the face of the divine. Benjamin writes: "The primacy of the biographical in the picture one forms of the life of a creative artist—that is, the depiction of his life as that of a human being, with that double emphasis on what is decisive and what is undecidable in the ethical sphere—would have a place only where knowledge of the fathomlessness of the origin excludes each of his works, delimited according to their value and their content, from the ultimate meaning of his life" (321). That part of the life of a human being that genuine biographism takes into consideration, and that grounds the primacy of the biographical in the overall picture of a human being's life, is his or her life as a human being, that is, his or her ethical life. It is the life of decision in the face of "what is undecidable in the ethical sphere," a life where a decision is exacted from the human being at the precise time and place where it is impossible for him or her to decide. In his discussion of the lovers in the novella, Benjamin underlines that decision is not "the

nothingness of choice," which originates in a "chimerical striving for freedom," or in "a falsely conceived freedom" (332). Choice is never equal to
"the greatness of the decision" (346). Whereas choice draws down mythical fate on its agents, decision "tears to bits" the interconnection of guilt
that constitutes fate and relieves its actors from fate altogether. Comparing
the relations of the characters in the novel with those in the novella, the
former being drawn to each other in passion and by choice, the latter by
true love, Benjamin writes that decision, "annihilates choice in order to establish fidelity (*Treue*): only the decision, not the choice, is inscribed in the
book of life. For choice is natural and can even belong to the elements; decision is transcendent" (346). As a result of the decisions that they make,
the lovers of the novella "no longer have a fate and . . . they stand at the
place where the others [the characters of the novel] are meant to arrive
some day" (332). Thanks to their decision, they show themselves to be human beings who dwell in the ethical sphere. Indeed, whereas "from the
standpoint of destiny, every choice is 'blind'" (309), decision, which occurs in the ethical sphere, implies clarity and unequivocalness. Furthermore, ethical life is grounded in the relation of the naked creature to the
creator (the creative Word), at the price of destroying all relations to others. In other words, it is grounded on the human being as an individual
who stands "alone before . . . God" (322). In this relation, no transindividual or superhuman norm obtains according to which the human being is
to act. An ethical relation is accomplished solely in "moral uniqueness"
(322), in other words, in a relation where, no longer a representative of
mankind, the individual must decide without any pregiven rule in the face
of what is thus undecidable. In an ethical relation, the individual is not to
have advance knowledge of the rule according to which he or she will have
to act. In this manner alone will the individual achieve the "moral uniqueness of responsibility" (322) without which there exists, strictly speaking,
no morality. By contrast, heroic, or mythic, life (that of the characters of
the novel), "attains neither to the sphere of individual particularity (*indi-
vidueller Sonderart*) nor to that of moral uniqueness (*Einzigkeit*). The type,
the norm, even if superhuman, distinguishes the hero from the individual;
his role as representative separates him from the moral uniqueness of responsibility. For he is not alone before his God; rather, he is the representative of mankind before its gods. In the moral domain, all representation
is of a mythic nature" (322).

As we have already pointed out, if moral uniqueness of responsibility is possible only in the relation of the individual in all its creatural nakedness before his God, this relation entails the violent severing from all others, including especially those who are closest to oneself. Benjamin stresses "the annihilating character of true reconciliation" (343). It is only on this condition that the individual act of rendering accounts becomes the individual's own act, one for whose uniqueness he alone is responsible before his God. Benjamin can thus write that rather than between an individual and his fellow men, "true reconciliation exists only with God. Whereas in true reconciliation the individual reconciles himself with God and only in this way conciliates other human beings, it is peculiar to semblance-like reconciliation that the individual wants others to make their peace with one another and only in this way become reconciled with God" (342). If ethics, rather than being grounded on the relation between the individual and his God, rests on intersubjective relations, it becomes semblance-like, precisely because it shies from the violence and destruction that is required not only in order to come face to face with one's God, but also in order to achieve the uniqueness of moral responsibility, without which all talk about morality remains mere semblance. Such uniqueness is, as we have seen, accomplished in a situation from which all pregiven, transindividual, or superhuman norm is not only absent, but also is violently discarded. Furthermore, decision, in which ethical relation culminates, must tear apart the weblike structures of intersubjective relations that all reconciliation among human beings, rather than with God, tends to preserve, if not to tighten. Compared to the characters of the novel for whom no true reconciliation is possible because the noble consideration of the educated and well-mannered characters "only increases the distance in which the figures of the novel know themselves to stand," the characters of the novella, who, because they engage in a "bizarre quarrel," thereby achieve a "reconciliation and with it the peace in which their bond of love endures." Benjamin adds: "Because true reconciliation with God is achieved by no one who does not thereby destroy everything—or as much as he possesses (*soviel an ihm ist*)—in order only then, before God's reconciled countenance, to find it resurrected. It follows that a death-defying leap marks that moment when—each one wholly alone for himself before God—they make every effort for the sake of reconciliation. And only in such readiness for reconciliation, having made their peace, do they gain each other"

(342–343). If the ethical relation demands the annihilation of all ties to others for it to have been grounded in the face-to-face with the creator, it becomes a relation between individuals in their creatural singularity at the moment when it is extended to other human beings. However, such a relation by which an individual can enter into reconciled relations to other such individuals can solely be accomplished by first shedding everything he or she shares with others so as to be singled out in all his or her nakedness before his or her God as *this* individual and then transgressing the rules of "tolerance and gentleness" in his or her relations to fellow men. Without violence, and painful ruptures, without actions such as that of the commanding word that interrupts a wife's evasions, in short, without a certain brutality, no true reconciliation with God, and, subsequently, with others, is possible. As Benjamin furthermore suggests, the moral law requires breaking with "bourgeois custom," and "noble considerations," in short, with all the conventional rules that govern human behavior in civil society and that are characterized as "impious caution, or circumspection (*unfromme Vorsicht*)" (343; trans. mod.). Even though the individual, once reconciled with his or her God, will find everything that he or she has destroyed resurrected again, the violence required to free him- or herself from the bonds of natural and conventional, or mere, life remains nonetheless a violence, a violence in an emphatic sense.

This, then, is also the point where we can return to the question left in abeyance, namely, to the question of in what sense works like deeds are underivable. Undoubtedly, given that, as Benjamin holds, "human life cannot be considered on the analogy of a work of art" and that, furthermore, "through the concept of the work, a strictly circumscribed sphere of its own is established—one which the life of the poet is unable to penetrate" (325), the underivability of the works refers, at first, to the impossibility of explaining the works on the basis of biography, understood in its traditional sense as the narrative of the author's natural, or mere, life. Poetry, Benjamin writes, "does not descend from God but ascends from what in the soul is unfathomable; it has a share in man's deepest self" (323). If life and works have to be held rigorously apart, it is because works originate in the human being's transcendence of mere life even where this does not take the express form of a stepping forward in creatural nakedness before the divine Word. Just as in the case of deeds, so too do works originate in man's deepest self, that is, in what is unfathomably singular about him and subject to a responsibility that is also always only his very own and, hence, absolutely unique. From what we have seen so far concerning the moral uniqueness of responsibility, that is, of the need required by true morality to take full responsibility for the rules according to which one makes a decision precisely where no decision seems possible, a moral act, in a true sense, cannot be derived from any preestablished norm. If works, like deeds, are underivable then this means also that works, in a way, have an ethical dimension. From the perspective of genuine biography, works, although distinct from life, have to be evaluated in a way similar to the judgment about deeds. Yet, similar to deeds, works, insofar as they as they arise from the artist's singular relation of responsibility, are indeed capable of illuminating the life of their author to some extent.

Now, if works and deeds are underivable in the sense that we have seen, it follows that their material content cannot be mythic throughout. In the case of *Elective Affinities*, this means that it must be possible "to isolate [a] layer in which the meaning of that novel autonomously reigns." It is, precisely, the presence of "such special domain" that distinguishes the literary work—the literary work that is a work in a genuine sense—from "its precursor: magical writing" (323). "No matter how darkly the myth holds sway in [the novel, 'a purer promise'] must already be visible there" (329). Benjamin locates "the luminous kernel of redemptive content" (323) in a sentence of the novel, which he characterizes as the caesura of the work, "in which, while the embracing lovers seal their fate, everything pauses, [and which] reads: 'Hope shot across the sky above their heads like a falling star.' They are unaware of it, of course, and it could not be said any more clearly that the last hope is never such to him who cherishes it but is the last only to those for whom it is cherished" (354–355).[29] Because, as Benjamin notes, "reconciliation is entirely supermundane and hardly an object for concrete depiction in the novel" (343), and because hope of reconciliation is always only one to those for whom it is cherished, this hope symbolized by the falling star is only that of the narrator for his characters. Benjamin writes: "With this comes to light the innermost basis for the 'narrator's stance.' It is he alone who, in the feeling of hope, can fulfill the meaning of the event" (355).

Let us call to mind again that the characters of a novel cannot be judged ethically, such judgment being possible only in the case of human beings and not in the case of fictional characters who, in *Elective Affinities*, are, moreover, entirely caught up in the forces of mythic nature. Ethical judgment is warranted only in the case of human beings for whom alone there is "redemption in eternal life" (320). Only human life is capable of a reconciliation with God and, hence, of redemption in eternal life, one that presupposes the radical destruction of natural, or mere, life. In that case, however, the hope that the falling star symbolizes for the lovers of the novel is exclusively that of the author or narrator for his characters. From beyond the novel, independently of the laws of its form, the narrator's stance interrupts the fateful unfolding of the events in order to inscribe a glimmer of hope for his characters. This demonstration of an autonomous domain in the novel, one that can be clearly distinguished, though not simply severed, from its material content, completes as it were the task of critique insofar as it concerns the truth content of the work. As a symbol, the falling star represents what "of the mystery in the exact sense of the term indwells the work" (355). Its truth content, distinct from its material content, is the "mystery of hope" (355).[30] This, then, is also the point where one can clearly begin to see how Benjamin's contention that the works can shed a light on the life of their author is to be understood. It is also the point at which the relation between work and life, as well as between critique and biography, becomes tangible.

As the preceding discussion has shown, in spite of the asserted essential difference between works and a human life, numerous parallel structures obtain not only between the works and a life, but also between the critical approach to works and the authentically biographical approach to a human life. Works not only are alive; in the same way as Benjamin distinguishes mere life from human life with respect to human beings, they too know a "life of the material content" (298) that is distinct from their being alive (*Lebendigkeit*). Let us bring to mind again that the artwork's siblings in philosophy can shed some light on the artworks. The "the ideal of philosophy's problem" (334), which shines forth in works of art, and thus comes in them into an appearance, provides the works with a unity, or totality. However, for this unity, which, in the artwork, is the accomplishment of form, not to be a mere semblance of life—that is, "the false, errant totality—the absolute totality" (340)—the work's totality must be interrupted by the expressionless. Only in this way does the work, rather than becoming a demonic conjuration of life, achieve its being alive and its immortality. In distinction from the totality of the work of art, which is finite, a human being's life is an infinite totality thanks to the creature's relation to the infinite that disrupts the totality of its mere, or natural, life. If critique shows works of art to illuminate the life of their author (in a way similar to the philosophical siblings that shed light on artworks), it is, first, because it locates the artworks' life in the fire that animates it and that burns away its historical junk, thus endowing it with immortality. As such, works are testimony to the author's expiation of all his earthly concerns by way of which the redemption of his life in eternal life becomes a virtual, yet in no way certain, possibility. If the life of the work consists in the flame that burns its historical content to ashes, the life that transcends mere life is that of the flame that burns away, in Benjamin own words, "the dross of every passion" (329). The role of critique is to show that those works that interrupt what their unifying form still owes to chaos and the mythic are a "reflection" of their author's break with mere life for the benefit of creatural life, thus, of that kind of life that alone is susceptible of being redeemed. Critique that pertains exclusively to works nonetheless takes place in view of what they reveal about, or, more precisely, of what they signify with respect to, their author's life. In essence, the critical treatment of works is subordinated to the ethical concern with saving life—the life of a human being who, as is the case with Goethe, had been entangled in the forces of the mythic.

Indeed, just as the material content of *Elective Affinities* cannot be its highest content, so too is the material content of Goethe's life not limited by the mythic. "Whenever an insight into Goethe's life and work is in question, the mythic world—however visibly it may come to light in them, too—cannot provide the basis of knowledge. A particular mythic moment may very well be an object of reflection; on the other hand, where it is a matter of the essence and the truth in the work and in the life, the insight into myth, even in its concrete relations, is not final. For neither Goethe's life nor any one of his works is fully represented in the domain of myth" (327). If this is so, it is essentially because a work, if indeed it is an artistic one, originates in what is most unfathomable in the self—its uniqueness as that of a creature and the uniqueness of its responsibility. Furthermore, if neither Goethe's life nor any one of his works belong entirely to the realm of the mythical, it is, after all, because human life is a life for which redemption in eternal life is a promise. Benjamin avers: "If, insofar as it is a question of the life, this is warranted simply by its human nature, the works teach it in detail, to the extent that a struggle which was kept secret in life emerges in the last of them" (327). As regards its essence of truth, Goethe's life is not entirely dominated by the mythic, and if this is the case, it is simply because it is a human life. No doubt, the mythic was present in the existence of Goethe, but in its totality, his life is not fully subject to the dark forces of the mythic. It is here that the works, and in the case of Goethe, his last works, come in to provide a unique testimony. If they shed a light on the life of the author, it is precisely because they are witness of a struggle kept secret in Goethe's life, the struggle to escape the forces of the mythic. A significant difference between these late works and Goethe's earlier ones becomes manifest when Benjamin remarks that "only in these [late] works does one encounter mythic elements in the content (*Gehalt*) and not just in the subject (*Stoffen*)" (327; trans. mod.). What this demonstrates is that in *Elective Affinities*, Goethe, though still without clear knowledge of the truth content of his work, has raised himself, at least, to a premonition, if not to (philosophical) insight, into the material content of the mythic and, hence, to an awareness of the essence of this subject matter. Consequently, the "testifying force" of Goethe's works of old age does not concern "the mythic world alone, or at its deepest level . . . [the mythic in] Goethe's existence. For there is in him a struggle to free himself from its clutches, and this struggle, no less than the essence of that world, is attested to in Goethe's novel" (327; trans. mod.). If, in *Elective Affinities*, Goethe gained insight into the material content of, above all, the institution of marriage, and its subjection to the norm of law (though, as Benjamin notes, no clear insight into its divine destination), this throws a light on a struggle in Goethe's life with the institution in question:

In the tremendous ultimate experience of the mythic powers—in the knowledge that reconciliation with them cannot be obtained except through the constancy of sacrifice—Goethe revolted against them. If he made a constantly renewed attempt during the years of his manhood—an attempt undertaken with inner despondency, yet with an iron will—to submit to those mythic orders wherever they still rule (indeed, for his part to consolidate their rule, in just the way this is done by one who serves the powerful), this attempt broke down after the final and most difficult submission of which he was capable, after his capitulation in the more than thirty-year struggle against marriage, which struck him as the threatening symbol of arrest by the mythic powers. And a year after his marriage, which had forced itself on him at a time of fateful pressure, he began *Elective Affinities*, with which he then registered his protest—a protest that unfolded ever more power-fully in his later work, against the world with which he had concluded the pact in the years of his manhood. *Elective Affinities* constitutes a turning point in this body of work. With it begins the last series of his productions, from no one of which he was able to detach himself completely, because until the end their heart-beat was alive in him. (327–328)

Whereas the productions of his manhood drew from Goethe's life, largely under the spell of the dark powers of the mythic, his later life came under the influence of a poetry that struggles for freedom from precisely those powers. "The final phenomenon of this literature that governed his life, and indeed ultimately even the duration of his life, was the conclusion to *Faust*" (329). If the last series of works "attests to and accompanies his purification (*Läuterung*), which was no longer allowed to be a liberation," it is, Benjamin muses, perhaps because "by a terribly punishing irony . . . poetry [became] the tyrant of his life," as retribution for having fled from the exigencies of life into the domain of literature during his youth (328). Critique, which establishes "the moral significance of his meditation in old age on the material contents," shows them as documents of "masked penance" (328; trans. mod.). What they reveal about his life is that al-though Goethe was not allowed to convert to religion, as the Early Ro-mantics did, he wanted "to stride solely and forever upon the carpet of truth." According to Benjamin, its laws aroused in him responsibility and kindled "the highest flame of his life. It burned away the dross of every passion" (329).

Among Goethe's late novels, *Elective Affinities* is the first in which "a purer promise, no matter how darkly the myth holds sway in it, [is] al-ready visible" (329). Even though Benjamin takes his clue for situating the truth content of the novel as a glimpse of hope shooting above the lovers' heads like a falling star from a biographical fact reported by Sulpiz Bois-serée, according to whom, the rising of the stars, on a journey to Heidel-berg, steered Goethe toward speaking of *Elective Affinities* and about how much he had loved Ottilie, it is the work itself that is to illuminate Goethe's life. The task of critique, based on a previous commentary of the matter and the formulation of its content, is to establish the existence of the promise in question that breaks with the forces of myth. Yet, con-cerned at first with the truth content of the works, the aim of the critique of works is, ultimately, to demonstrate that a life qua human life, even if it does not raise itself consciously above the entanglements with the mythic forces, is as such capable of redemption. It is the struggle with these forces, however secret, that gives a life its infinite totality. Although critique and commentary must keep the work free from the life intruding in it, and whereas biography must avoid construing a life as a work, critique is eminently ethical, in that its aim is to save—to save a life as a human life, by demonstrating that, however inconspicuously, it manifests a relation to truth. By doing so, critique cherishes hope—the hope of redemption—for this life.

Toward an Ethics of *Auseinandersetzung*

In a process now all too predictable, critical and theoretical concepts such as "critical theory," or "deconstruction," are abandoned, long before their full potential has even begun to be tapped, in favor of seemingly new and more promising terms. *Auseinandersetzung* is one such notion now beginning to make its appearance in texts of literary and cultural criticism. As opposed to the alleged abstraction of critical theory and the obscurantism of deconstruction, *Auseinandersetzung* promises a more intimate and more engaged, if not more visceral, relation to texts, works, or thoughts. In *Auseinandersetzung*, the critic comes face to face in a direct confrontation with the thought of an Other. Out of the ensuing clash of ideas, real and concrete issues are broached, while the debate itself mobilizes energies that testify to the urgency and seriousness of the problems in question. Moreover, *Auseinandersetzung*, by virtue of its greater intimacy and engagement with texts or ideas, takes shape as a relation in which critical vigilance, paired with truly concrete concerns, guards against dogmatic positions and conclusions. In confrontation as *Auseinandersetzung*, opponents meet stripped of ideological masquerade. It is a debate that suggests honesty, responsibility, and a shared commitment to things that truly matter.

It is no secret that the term *Auseinandersetzung* is lifted from Heidegger. Returning to what this term implies and seeks to achieve in its original context, the following discussion of *Auseinandersetzung* intends not only to confront its current use with its strict definition, but also to set conditions for fruitfully putting this term to work. Indeed, recourse to *Auseinandersetzung* either as a refuge from concepts that have come under attack, or from unresolved difficulties adhering to these concepts, may serve to recontextualize and clarify the very nature of criticism and deconstruction. There is at least a chance that a sustained and informed confrontation with the Heideggerean concept in question could lead to a productive reevaluation of the critical and deconstructive "relation." This debate, however, may show *Auseinandersetzung* to be more than a simple alternative to the relations in question. Located in an array of positions from which to choose, *Auseinandersetzung* may represent a privileged vantage point from which insight into the limits, promises, and achievements of critique and deconstruction may be gained. It is in view of such critical reevaluation that the subsequent developments have been undertaken.

Auseinandersetzung is a term that, in the midthirties, abruptly appears in Heidegger's work, in particular, in his lectures on Nietzsche and in *Introduction to Metaphysics*. From the outset, this word, devoid of any anterior philosophical meaning, indicating, in addition to its juridical meaning of partition, only the explication of something, a debate or dispute, functions as a *terminus technicus*. The Nietzsche lectures advance the term in question as *the* philosophical and hermeneutic mode of relating to the subject matter of a philosopher's thought. It serves to conceptualize the relation to that which, in a thinker's thought, resists access by its very nature, to any extraneous approach, namely, that which cannot "be determined anywhere else than from within itself." *Auseinandersetzung* is the exclusive relation to that which, in a thinker's thought, is "true philosophy,"[1] that is, to what in his thought obeys the law of thinking, thinking's own law. As such, it dictates a bracketing of anything that in thinking is of heteronomous origin, anything that would reveal concerns extrinsic to those of thinking itself.

In the "Author's Foreword to All Volumes," Heidegger notes that the object of *Auseinandersetzung*, for which these lectures are to pave the way, is to be *the matter* (*die Sache*) of Nietzsche's thought. *Die Sache* is *der Streitfall*, Heidegger continues, showing that he has in mind the original Germanic meaning of *die Sache* as legal matter, legal case, a case taken to court. *Auseinandersetzung* thus understands that which, in the thinking of a philosopher, is determined only from within itself, as a point in question, a case or conflict under dispute. More precisely, "the matter, the point in question, is in itself a confrontation (*Auseinandersetzung*)."[2] The philosophically autonomous core of a thinker's thought is *Auseinandersetzung* not only also because it must be construed or established through the proceedings of the debate, but also because having in itself the structure of debate, *the matter* itself invites the confrontational relation in which *the matter* is to be determined as what it is. Being responsive to such a *matter* of thinking is neither talking *about* it nor judging it *from outside*, but rather entering into a relation of *Auseinandersetzung* with it. Thinking, insofar as it is determined only from within itself, invites only one mode of responsible response, namely, one of *Auseinandersetzung* with the case in dispute.

The reason that Heidegger proposes in the first pages of "The Will to Power as Art" for the fact that such an *Auseinandersetzung* with Nietzsche's thought has not yet begun, that even its prerequisites are still to be established, reveals a decisive structural feature without which any debate with that which has the law in itself cannot take place. He writes: "Nietzsche's thought and speech are still too contemporary for us. He and we have not yet been sufficiently separated (*auseindergesetzt*) in history; we lack the distance (*Abstand*) necessary for a sound appreciation of the thinker's strength."[3] From this we see that any debate of the kind in question requires a setting apart, a distance across which the thinker's strength may come into view and justice may be done to his specific achievements. As long as Nietzsche remains caught up in present-day concerns, no glimpse of him as a true philosopher can be had. But the distance implicit to all *Auseinandersetzung* must also be seen as a function of the definition of *the matter* of thinking itself, that is, as that which is determined solely from within itself. If what matters in thinking is thinking free from all heteronomy, then thinking itself is constitutive of the distance that allows any appreciating *Auseinandersetzung* to get off the ground. Although confrontation assures that a thinker's thought be recognized in its true strength, such strong thought itself engenders the distance required to appreciate it. *Auseinandersetzung* debates that which in thinking is determined by itself alone, but it does so from a respectful distance, allowing such thought to unfold from itself and in itself.

Before further discussion of the complex structural features of the notion of *Auseinandersetzung* now beginning to emerge, let me first open the dictionaries. *Auseinander*, the Grimms' *Deutsches Wörterbuch* tells us, is the result of drawing together in one word what remains separate in living speech while at the same time inverting the natural order of the words, that is, putting the preposition *aus* in *ein aus dem andern* ahead of the other words. This operation engenders what the Grimms call a hardened and motionless linguistic mass. If moreover, *auseinander* is connected to verbs implying an idea of separation or dissection, "a variety of the most ponderous compounds arise."[4] *Auseinandersetzung* is one of them. This linguistic monster solidifies in one ponderous compound, what, by nature is discrete, distinct, and separate and what can only be drawn together by neutralizing the sense of separation inherent to both *ein aus dem anderen* and *setzen*. In *Trübner's Deutsches Wörterbuch*, Goetze prefaces his presentation of the historical evolution of the meaning of the term by noting that it is a very weak verb in New High German and has no ground (*nirgends Boden hat*) in any of the dialects. According to Goetze's dictionary, the legal meaning of *auseinandersetzen*, referring to the partition of the common property of parties who have shared ownership, is historically primary. The verb later acquired the more general meaning of a "clarification of a legal matter, of awarding to each litigant what is properly his or her own," but it was subsequently transposed by representatives of the Enlightenment, Johann Christian Gottsched, for instance, to the realm of literary representation where it acquired the meaning of "presenting in such a manner that all viewpoints are given due attention (*zu ihrem Rechte kommen*)." The contemporary use of the word in the sense of explaining, examining, presenting, or laying out, Goetze adds, derives from this meaning of *auseindersetzen*.[5] Finally, in *Handwörterbuch der deutschen Sprache*, from a purely semantic account of the term, J.C.A. Heyse determines that *auseinander* signifies "a development (*Entstehen*), a succession or consequence (*Folge*), of one thing from another, or a distancing (*Entfernung*) of one thing from another. Consequently, *auseinandersetzen properly* means, to set apart from one another; *improperly,* to elucidate or explain a representation to some one by dissolving it into its components; *sich über etwas auseinandersetzen,* is to annul or dissolve the community with others regarding a matter, to reach a settlement about such a matter (a heritage, for instance)." He concludes saying that *die Auseinandersetzung* can be taken in *all* the meanings of the verb.[6]

Yet, how are we to understand Heidegger's use of the term? Speaking of the necessity of an *Auseinandersetzung* with Nietzsche in the appendices to his 1941–1942 lectures on "Nietzsche's Metaphysics," Heidegger writes: "We take the word *Auseinandersetzung* literally. We seek to posit his and our thought apart from and into a relation of opposition to one another (*ausser einander und in das Gegeneinander über zu setzen*); but in a thinking, and not in a comparative mode."[7] Heidegger's literal understanding of the term stresses the *separation* of the two kinds of thoughts, the *distance* thus created between them, as well as the relation of *adverseness* into which they come to stand, or rather, into which they are *set*, or posited. Consequently, the common meaning of *Auseinandersetzung* as debate and confrontation, explanation and exposition, ought not to incur on its philosophical meaning. Still, the literal (*wörtlich*) meaning of the term is not exhausted by the traits of separation, distance, and adverseness, and furthermore, Heidegger makes it such a compound of traits that it literally ceases to be a word.

As shall become increasingly clear, Heidegger's valorization of the word derives from both the history *and* semantics of *Auseinandersetzung*. As a philosophical term, *Auseinandersetzung* is a term not to be found in the dictionaries, for it combines the semantically primary meaning of setting apart, or distancing, with the historically primary meaning of awarding each party what is properly its own. In other words, *Auseinandersetzung* is a formation that draws together, in one intimate linguistic whole, meanings thoroughly alien to one another. The word, if it still is one, allows semantically and historically irreducible senses of *auseinandersetzen* to dwell together. Moreover, the different ways Heidegger writes the word—*Auseinandersetzung, Aus-einandersetzung, Aus-einander-setzung*—suggest a complex synthesis in which multiple and different modes of separation and belonging together cohabit. Finally, it also means struggle, conflict, and is thus, as we shall see, a translation of *polemos*.

Yet, linguistic condensation is not the sole means by which Heidegger forges this new philosophical concept. He furthermore differentiates *Auseinandersetzung* from critique by determining it as genuine or authentic critique. He writes: "Confrontation (*Auseinandersetzung*) is genuine criticism. It is the supreme way, the only way, to a true estimation of a thinker. In confrontation we undertake to reflect on his thinking (*seinem Denken nachzudenken*) and to trace it in its effective force, not in its weaknesses. To what purpose? In order that through the confrontation we ourselves may become free for the supreme exertion of thinking."[8]

As genuine critique, confrontation is not negative. In *What Is a Thing?* Heidegger remarks that the common meaning of critique is "faultfinding, a pointing to errors, emphasis on incompleteness and the corresponding rejection."[9] In the appendices to the original lectures on "The Will to Power as Art" (written between 1936 and 1937 and published in volume 43 of the *Gesamtausgabe*), Heidegger is clear about this. We read: "*Auseinandersetzung ≠ Bemängelung.*" Nor does it manifest itself as a polemic. But confrontation as genuine critique must also be distinguished from the meaning of critique that emerges in the second half of the eighteenth century, particularly in the context of reflections on art and aesthetics, where it signifies "fixing standards, rules, where it means legislation, that is, an emphasis of the universal over the particular."[10] Finally, Heidegger's genuine critique has nothing in common with critique in the Kantian sense. From Heidegger's developments with respect to Kant's use of the term in *What Is a Thing?* we can conclude that *Auseinandersetzung* is not identical with a systematic mapping, based on the model of intelligibility particular to modern mathematics, of the powers of pure reason. It is not the method by which reason comes to know itself and through which it achieves its most intimate rationality.

What then is genuine critique? It is critique in the originary sense, Heidegger holds in *What Is a Thing?* The established root of critique is *krinein,* commonly translated as "to separate," "put asunder," "distinguish," "decide," and so forth. In conformity with this originary meaning of the word *krinein,* concepts of criticism, ranging from the common notion of criticism as estimation to its dialectical form based on determined negation, have consistently articulated a faith in the possibility of pure, if not absolute, distinction. The critical operation thrives on the dream of a pure difference guaranteeing that the separated suffers no contamination by that from which it is cut off and allowing the determination of essence to proceed in a realm free of all intrusions and within which decision is clear and without ambiguity. This is the philosophical meaning and thrust of critique established by the tradition out of the original meaning of *krinein.* But is it in this sense that we are to understand *Auseinandersetzung?* In *What Is a Thing?* Heidegger too makes recourse to the original Greek word *krinein.* Yet, he translates it as follows: " 'sondern,' 'absondern,' und so 'das Besondere herausheben,' " in English: to separate, to isolate, and *to thus bring out the particular.* From the beginning, Heidegger's translation subordinates separation to the end of bringing out the particular. However, before drawing out the consequences entailed by this translation for an understanding of "confrontation," we need to read in full this passage wherein Heidegger establishes the originary meaning of critique:

"Critique" comes from the Greek *krinein* which means: "to sort" (*sondern*), "to sort out" and thus to "lift out that of special sort" (*das Besondere herausheben*). This contrast [*Abheben*] against others [*gegen anderes*] arises from an elevation [*Hinaufheben*] to a new order. The sense of the word "critique" is so little negative that it means the most positive of the positive, the positing of what must be established in advance [*im voraus angesetzt*] in all positing [*Setzung*] as what is determinative and decisive. Therefore, critique is a separation and lifting out of the special, the uncommon and, at the same time, decisive [*des Massgebenden*], therefore, and only in consequence, is it also a rejection of the commonplace and unsuitable. [11]

Critique in a genuine sense is thus neither negative nor determined by the goal of establishing an invulnerable limit. Rather than a severing of one thing from another in pure difference and free of all contamination, critique, in the authentic sense, serves to raise what is separated into its proper rank precisely by contrasting it to what it is separated from. Critique secures propriety and property as it locates its possibility in the other. Critique allows particularity to arise on both sides of the divide; indeed, it is the very condition through which something can come into its most proper own. In this sense, critique is the same as *Auseinandersetzung*. In the operation of setting apart by setting against, the particular is posited as such for the first time. Genuine critique is thus what is most positive, since the very possibility of innermost propriety, which, however, is only what it is against, what is on the other side of the divide and vice versa, rests on the decision that it brings about. *Auseinandersetzung* understood this way, is thus as much characterized by the setting apart as by the intimate interrelation of what occupies the respective sides of the division.

Before I analyze this complex economy of *Auseinandersetzung* occurring in one thinker's dialogue (*Zwiegespräch*) with the subject matter of another thinker's true philosophy—Nietzsche, in this case—it may be appropriate to recall that for Heidegger, in *Introduction to Metaphysics*, *Auseinandersetzung* translates as *polemos*. In the following, it will indeed be necessary to demarcate *Auseinandersetzung* as *polemos* from the confrontation that characterizes the genuine dialogue of philosophies. *Polemos* is, of course, not just any war, struggle, or conflict, nor is it war, struggle, or conflict in general. It is also distinct from "the merely polemical . . . the intrigues and machinations of human beings within the present-at-hand."[12]

Rather, *polemos*—the reference, obviously, is to fragment 53 of Heraclitus—names the "originary struggle, for it allows those that struggle to originate as such in the first place; it is not a mere assault on the present-at-hand.[13] The *polemos* of fragment 53, Heidegger writes, "is a strife that holds sway before everything divine and human, not war in the human sense. As Heraclitus thinks it, struggle first and foremost allows what essentially unfolds to step apart in opposition [*lässt im Gegeneinander das Wesende allererst auseindertreten*], first allows position and status and rank to establish themselves in coming to presence. In such stepping apart [*Auseinandertreten*], clefts, intervals, distances, and joints open themselves. In con-frontation [*Auseinandersetzung*], world comes to be."[14] In other words, *polemos*, seen not as "mere quarreling and feuding but the strife of the striving [*der Streit des Streitbaren*] [that] sets the essential and the unessential, the high and the low, into their limits and that makes them manifest,"[15] shows *Auseinandersetzung* not only to be a separation that enables the particular to be what it is in contrast to what it is set against, but a unification as well. Heidegger remarks: "Confrontation [*Auseinandersetzung*] does not divide unity, much less destroy it. It builds unity; it is the gathering (*logos*). *Polemos* and *logos* are the same."[16] *Polemos* binds together in that it gathers in an intimate bond what stands in a relation of the highest antagonism. In this sense, *polemos* is the same as *Geist*, spirit, of which Heidegger writes in *Erläuterungen zu Hölderlins Dichtung*: "Spirit reigns as the sober but audacious *Aus-einandersetzung* which institutes everything present into the clearly distinct boundaries and arrangements of the present's presencing. Such *Aus-einandersetzen* is essential thinking. The 'Spirit's' ownmost proper are the thoughts. Through them everything, because it is separated (*auseinandergesetzt*), belongs together. Spirit is unifying unity. This unity lets the being-together of everything real appear in its gathering."[17] Heidegger's comments in the appendices to volume 4 of the *Gesamtausgabe*, as to what he identifies as Hölderlinean guiding words— *Alles ist innig*—reveal intimacy (*Innigkeit*) as indeed the very criterion for what is in a mode of *Auseinandersetzung*. Heidegger remarks: "*Alles ist innig*. This means: One is appropriated into the Other (*Eines ist in das Andere vereignet*), yet in such a way that in this appropriation it remains in its own (*in seinem Eigenen bleibt*). More precisely, through this appropriation into the Other it acquires its ownness to begin with: gods and men, earth and sky. Intimacy does not signify a fusion and dissolution of differences.

Intimacy names the belonging-together of what is alien to one another, the happening of *Befremdung* [of being taken (aback) by the Other, or alien]."[18] Setting apart is thus the condition under which *Befremdung* can occur, that is, a being-affected by the Other through which selfhood is granted to self. The being-appropriated into Other, by which One, or self, is always already disappropriated, is at the same time the very relation in which One, or self, acquires, through the Other, selfhood and Oneness. The proper and the Other here stand in a relation of mutual implication and disimplication. In *Auseinandersetzung* as *polemos*—and as *logos,* which is the same thing—a harmonious ringing takes place in which there is no priority, neither of the One nor of the Other. Indeed, One and the Other both presuppose *das Walten der Befremdung.*

　　Everything we still shall see shows *Auseinandersetzung* as genuine critique, as the "method" of the dialogue between philosophies, to exhibit the same basic attitude as in the originary struggle, *polemos.* Still, differences obtain between *polemos* and genuine critique that prove significant for any evaluation of the ethics of *Auseinandersetzung.* If in the following I thus try to underline not only the parallels between the play of the proper and the Other in *polemos* and genuine critique, but also the differences, it is in order to circumscribe, with as much precision as possible, certain limits that haunt the dialogue between thinkers. Undoubtedly, *Auseinandersetzung* has a clear advantage over critique, for rather than putting separation to work as a means to exclude the Other, or non-proper, in *Auseinandersetzung*, separation, as the space from which *Befremdung* occurs, is the very condition by which not only justice is done to Other, but in which the constitution of propriety shows itself to be a function of the Other's (dis)appropriating address. Yet it seems that *Auseinandersetzung* is not identical to the harmonious interplay between the One and the Other, the harmony of differences in play characteristic to *polemos. Auseinandersetzung* is oriented. It follows a path and has a purpose. As the introductory pages to Heidegger's *Nietzsche* demonstrate, *Auseinandersetzung* with Nietzsche's thought seeks to determine to what extent the few thoughts that determine the whole of Nietzsche's thinking remain thought-worthy. Such evaluation, moreover, is not disinterested. If it is true that one must get on the way (*unterwegs*) to *die Sache* of Nietzsche's thinking, it is true too, that the debate with him—the *Auseinandersetzung* with the matter of Nietzsche the philosopher—*comes from* somewhere and *goes somewhere.*

Indeed, through confrontation with the Other, Heidegger's thought seeks to achieve an essential historicality for itself.[19]

Before addressing this question of *Auseinandersetzung*'s orientation let us first see how as a struggle, a debate, or a confrontation, it adheres to the basic features of the original struggle of *polemos*. In the addendi to volume 43, Heidegger describes the *Zwiegespräch* between thinkers in the following way: "Only in *Auseinandersetzung* does creative interpretation become possible, an interpretation in which Nietzsche comes to stand with respect to himself into his strongest position (*auf sich selbst in seiner stärksten Stellung zum stehen kommt*)."[20] Only through *Auseinandersetzung* does Nietzsche, or the thought of any other great thinker, acquire a relation to itself, which is, moreover, of the strongest kind. In *Contributions to Philosophy*, Heidegger notes that "*Aus-einandersetzung* with the great philosophies—as basic metaphysical positions in the history of the guiding-question—must proceed in such a way that every essential philosophy comes to stand as one mountain among mountains—and thus to bring about what is its most essential."[21] The confrontation in question allows the opponent to stand in what is greatest about him, to acquire his strongest properties. In addition, by reflecting on the opponent's thinking, on its effective force rather than on its weaknesses, he who confronts a thinker becomes free as well "for the supreme exertion of thinking."[22] *Auseinandersetzung* is consequently a relation "in which the opponent is chosen, and in which we and he are brought into a position of confrontation, more precisely, into a struggle for the essential."[23] By being intended in a manner such that the opponent comes to stand in a relation of strength with respect to himself, and that he who confronts the opponent becomes thus capable of the supreme task of thinking, *Auseinandersetzung* virtually guarantees that rather than leading to antagonism, the struggle, free from extraneous concerns, will be solely for what is essential and determined from within itself. Heidegger continues: "Such 'bringing the-opponent-into-position' requires the development of the most essential questions; the opponent must be unfolded from the innermost depth of his work to what is most extreme about him."[24] In short, an *Auseinandersetzung* begins only when the most essential questions are being raised, that is, when a confrontation with Nietzsche, for instance, "is at the same time conjoined to a confrontation in the realm of the grounding question of philosophy."[25] In other words, a confrontation requires not only that a thinker and his opponent come to stand in their strongest position with respect to themselves, but also that the struggle be over the most essential, that is, the most binding concern and thereby entail an essential intimacy between the opponents. In the addendi to volume 43, Heidegger remarks that "the rigor of *Auseinandersetzung* is possible only when it is based on the most intimate affinity or relationship. It is possible only where there is a Yes to the essential."[26] Genuine critique binds together as much as it sets apart. In *Auseinandersetzung, logos* or *Geist* dominates as much as *polemos*, or *Streit*. In confrontation, the essential is fought for, and gained (*erstritten*) in opposition, and hence mutually. This essential, causing the opponents to coil into what they are in strength and most properly as they struggle over something that they share, is constitutive of confrontation in the strict sense and suggests that ultimately it is not the opponents that truly matter in this conflict, but rather that for which the struggle is waged, since it is the struggle that assigns the places of the opponents. And yet, without the opponents' strife, nothing essential could occur. Is thus the *Auseinandersetzung* between dialoguing thinkers, or rather between One and the matter of the true philosophical thought of the Other, identical with the appropriating and disappropriating play of the proper and the Other that we have encountered with the originary struggle? Is it comparable to the harmonious constitution of One and Other in mutual *Befremdung* that we had seen to characterize *polemos*?

At this point, and before attempting an answer to the preceding question, we do not escape the issue of the range, or sweep, of *Auseinandersetzung*. As a relation in which thinkers, or rather the matter of their thought, comes to stand in what most powerfully characterizes them, and in which justice is done to the Other as Other, a question arises as to the specificity of *Auseinandersetzung*. Is it a relation valid for all dialogue, or a model with only one application, restricted to the dialogue with Nietzsche's thought alone? Is the very nature of Nietzsche's philosophical achievement such that any appropriate relation to it must have the form of *Auseinandersetzung*, and is this relation to Nietzsche unique? Although evidence points to a certain generalizability of *Auseinandersetzung* as the structure for all thinking dialogue, there seems to be a certain tension in Heidegger's writings, especially in those from the midthirties concerning this question. Undoubtedly, in *Contributions to Philosophy*, he speaks at one point of Nietzsche's *Auseinandersetzung* with Schopenhauer;[27] in the lectures on "Thinking and Poetry" from 1944 to 1945, he even seems to suggest an *Auseinandersetzung* with Hölderlin's poetry;[28] and more importantly, in the seminar of 1968 at Le Thor, he is said to have spoken of the necessity "to embark on an *Auseinandersetzung* with Hegel, in order for Hegel *to speak* to us."[29] But, is it not significant that in *Contributions to Philosophy*, after having reviewed the different stages in the history of metaphysics in need of historical treatment—Leibniz, Kant, Schelling, Nietzsche—that only in the case of Nietzsche is such treatment called an *Auseinandersetzung*? Heidegger speaks here about daring "to come to grips [*die Auseinandersetzung wagen*] with *Nietzsche* as the one who is nearest but to recognize that he is farthest removed from the question of being."[30] Finally, what is the significance of the fact that Heidegger elaborates the concept of *Auseinandersetzung* itself exclusively in the Nietzsche lectures, and only with respect to his debate with the latter? In response to these questions, I would argue that *Auseinandersetzung* is primarily cut to size to fit the debate with Nietzsche, this thinker still too close to be engaged in a just dialogue, with respect to whom the distance across which his true philosophical contribution, his strongest self, can come into view, has yet to be attained. But, as we now shall see, there is certainly another reason that might hold the key to why confrontation is cut to shape to Nietzsche more than to any one else.

In the addendi to "The Will to Power as Art," Heidegger notes that the battle positions in a genuine *Auseinandersetzung* "must be historical—Nietzsche's and ours, and this again in the perspective of the mountain range (*in der Richtung der Höhenzüge*) of the essential history of philosophy."[31] Indeed, *Auseinandersetzung* is a kind of debate that *comes from*, and is *waged from* and *for* what Heidegger calls in *Nietzsche*, but in particular in *Contributions to Philosophy*, "*der andere Anfang*," the other beginning. Once that has been established, a definite limitation of *Auseinandersetzung* to the case of Nietzsche's thought will not fail to come into view. Nietzsche, we are told at the beginning of "The Will to Power as Art," proceeds "within the vast orbit of the ancient guiding question (*Leitfrage*) of philosophy."[32] This guiding question, which has been *the* question of the history of metaphysics, is the question constitutive of "the first beginning" (*der erste Anfang*), and consists of the question: "What is Being?" It is a question that inquires into the essence of beings in terms of existence, in terms of an *existing* essence. In what is to follow, it is essential to distinguish this guiding question from what Heidegger calls the grounding question (*Grundfrage*), the question: "What is the truth of Being?" This question does not itself unfold in the history of philosophy as such, yet it inaugurates "the other beginning." Now, as Heidegger remarks, his lectures on Nietzsche intend "to elucidate the fundamental position within which Nietzsche unfolds the guiding question of Western thought and responds to it. Such elucidation is needed in order to prepare a confrontation (*Auseinandersetzung*) with Nietzsche. If in Nietzsche's thinking the prior tradition of Western thought is gathered and completed in a decisive respect, then the confrontation with Nietzsche becomes one with all Western thought hitherto."[33] As is well known, Heidegger's point in *Nietzsche* is that Nietzsche completed the guiding question, which he persisted to think, and thus has brought the whole of Western thought into a view that, presupposing a distance to this whole, implicitly harbors an other beginning. Showing that Nietzsche has brought the first and, as Heidegger stresses, greatest beginning, to an end—and has thus become "a transition"— Heidegger has also brought his opponent into the position in which he stands to himself in his strongest relation. In the above-mentioned addendi, he notes that to be a transition is "the highest that can be said of a thinker. A transition, that prepares transitions to the second beginning."[34] Moreover, in *Contributions to Philosophy*, Heidegger writes, "the transitional [das Ubergängliche] constitutes the actual struggle."[35] From this it follows that the true opponent, Nietzsche at his strongest, as transition and authentic struggle, is in himself *Auseinandersetzung*. In him, and for the first time, the first and the second beginning are at war. Thus, it would seem that the mode of dialogue called *Auseinandersetzung* must be restricted to Nietzsche, that is, to the only thinker who, by having completed the first beginning, is in virtual transition to the other beginning. *Auseinandersetzung* seems to be limited to a debate in the name of the other beginning. As Heidegger emphasizes, such a debate with Nietzsche has not yet begun because we are still too close to him. Any *Auseinandersetzung* requires that we be sufficiently set apart from Nietzsche. Indeed, what must come into view is that Nietzsche, bringing the first beginning to an end, has achieved a position of exteriority of some sort to it. As Heidegger remarks in *Contributions to Philosophy*, in order to experience what began in and as that beginning, it is necessary to take up a distant-positioning (*Fernstellung*). "For *without* this distant-positioning—and only the positioning in the *other* beginning is a sufficient one—we always stay insidiously too close (*verfänglich*) to that beginning. . . . Only the distant-positioning to the first beginning allows the experience that the question of truth (aletheia) necessarily remained unasked in that beginning and that this *not* happening determined Western thinking in advance as 'metaphysics.' "[36] In short, then, *Auseinandersetzung* is strictly speaking a debate with a position characterized by distance (*Fernstellung*), namely, distance to the first beginning, which as such is at least virtually in transition to the other beginning. *Auseinandersetzung* presupposes that the subject matter to be confronted has set itself *apart* from the first beginning and that this distance is what unites the thinkers in opposition. *Auseinandersetzung* requires a distance to one's opponent that permits a sight of the extent to which the thinker has already taken a position of distance from the first beginning. However, since, according to Heidegger, Nietzsche occupies this privileged position in the history of Western thought of having brought himself in opposition to the whole of Western thought, while at the same time being furthest away from the grounding question, from the *Seinsfrage*, Nietzsche must be the opponent par excellence, the exemplary thinker whose matter, unlike that of any other thinker in the history of metaphysics, demands a confrontation in the mode of *Auseinandersetzung*.

The role of the other beginning constitutive to any appreciation of what Heidegger calls *Auseinandersetzung* clearly shows it as an oriented debate. Heidegger's contention that bringing the opponent into a position of strength is the condition by which he becomes free "for the supreme exertion of thinking," rings with ambiguity. *Auseinandersetzung* has the look of an unequal struggle in which justice is done to the Other for the mere benefit of the *explicit* development of the question that, while remote to Nietzsche, is Heidegger's opening question. But let us not come to a hasty conclusion. Indeed, as Heidegger would have it, what counts in this debate is not the person "Nietzsche," or "Heidegger" for that matter, but the essential Yes that both share, the Yes to the essential question. Moreover, the unfolding of that question in an *Auseinandersetzung* with a properly posited Nietzsche could well be the unfolding of a kind of thought that, according to its very nature, while potentially harboring in itself the promise of an other beginning for all the voices that have made up the whole of the Western metaphysical tradition, the whole of the first beginning, is only to be gained in a biased struggle. To sustain such a point, I return to the question of the first and the other beginning.

The necessity of the other beginning, Heidegger reminds us in *Contributions to Philosophy*, arises from the originary positing of the first beginning itself. More precisely, the first beginning does not only explain the necessity of the other beginning, but it also necessarily sets the other beginning apart from and opposite to itself. "The *Auseinandersetzung* with the necessity of the *other* beginning from out of the originary positioning of the first beginning (*Die Auseinanderandersetzung der Notwendigkeit des anderen Anfangs aus der ursprünglichen Setzung des ersten Anfangs*)."[37] The first beginning is characterized by the experience and positing of the truth of beings (*die Wahrheit des Seienden*), yet since what thus became disclosed in the first beginning, "being as being, necessarily overpowers everything," the question concerning truth as such is not asked here.[38] Indeed, the more extreme the forgetting of the question of truth becomes, the more imperiously metaphysics sets the space for another beginning apart from and opposite to itself. However, with the other beginning, only that which could not be questioned in the first beginning—as a result of the sheer overpowering disclosure of being as being—is questioned: truth itself. By explicitly asking the question of the truth of being, the other beginning conceptualizes what in the first necessarily receded into oblivion in order for there to be a first beginning in the first place, but from which alone the first beginning draws its true meaning. In the confrontation with the first beginning, this first beginning—metaphysics, in other words—is not denounced as error. No demarcation of the other beginning from the first can possibly be a turning down or belittling.[39] On the contrary, to cite Heidegger, "Leaping into the other beginning is returning into the first beginning, and vice versa. But returning into the first beginning (the 'retrieval') is not displacement into what has passed, as if this could be made 'actual' again in the usual sense. Returning into the first beginning is rather and precisely distancing [*Entfernung*] from it."[40] In the *Auseinandersetzung*, the other beginning is only the repetition of the first beginning, yet in such manner that the explicit questioning of the forgotten question constitutive of the first beginning leads to a deepening of it, and hence to its complete recasting. Heidegger writes: "From a new originariness the other beginning assists the first beginning unto the truth of its history—and thus unto its inalienable and ownmost otherness (*zu seiner unveräusserlichen eigensten Andersheit*), which becomes fruitful solely in the historical dialogue of thinkers."[41] In short, in the *Auseinandersetzung* between the first beginning and the other beginning and necessarily set forth by the first, the first beginning, by coming into its own, by achieving what it is most properly, and hence what is most inalienably other about it, becomes the greatest of the beginnings. In addition, only by having come to an end, by having in its most extreme position reached its own limits, is it possible, in the confrontational dialogue, for the first beginning to fulfill that greatness.

What, then, does this imply for the dialogue, the confrontation between Nietzsche and Heidegger? If the other beginning, from which the *Auseinandersetzung* takes place, is the condition under which Nietzsche's thought can be established in its greatest strength, in what is most proper to it, then an *Auseinandersetzung* not only is what does justice to Nietzsche's thought, but also it takes place in a place necessarily called upon by that thought itself. Hence, the unequal struggle at which we pointed, as well as the orientation of the confrontation toward enabling Heidegger to exert the supreme task of thinking, is demanded by *the matter* of Nietzsche's thought itself. For without it, the thought of the thinker cannot achieve what is most inalienably other about it and, hence, also what is most inalienably proper to it. *The matter* of Nietzsche's thinking—in itself *Auseinandersetzung*—itself entails a certain injustice, or delay in justice, such that justice can be done to *the matter* in the first place.

Although Nietzsche's thought necessitates from within a certain injustice on Heidegger's part in order that it be recognized in its greatest strength, this necessary injustice, this limitation of justice to do justice, is at the same time the condition by which Heidegger will be able to exert the supreme task of thinking. The very specificity of Heidegger's philosophical achievement is a function of that interpretation called upon by Nietzsche's thought "itself." Consequently, what looked at first like an unequal relation by virtue of the historical nature of the battle positions now appears to have all the characteristics of the rather harmonious play of contestants in the originary struggle of the *polemos*. Undoubtedly, interpreting Nietzsche's thought from the perspective of the other beginning restricts it to representing "only"—an " 'only' [that] is not a delimitation but the demand for something more originary"[42]—a completion of the first beginning. In that, however, Nietzsche's thought achieves a greatness it could not have had by itself in itself. For there is no such thing as a thought; even a thought exclusively determined from within itself, which is solely of itself, is only thought. The thought of the other beginning, by contrast, is a thought whose necessity has always been required by the first beginning. It is what it is "only" insofar as without it, the first beginning could never have been the greatest beginning. In the *Auseinandersetzung* between Nietzsche's thought and Heidegger's thinking, the necessity of the latter's thought is staged in view of the needs of the first. But, the thought of the other beginning requires also that it be demarcated from what it must construe as the first beginning, and this demarcation reflects the thought of the other beginning into its own. In *Auseinandersetzung*, the bias is shared. One and the Other, the first beginning and the other beginning, Nietzsche and Heidegger, without priority, reflect each other into their own by calling upon the respective Other's biased approach.[43] In such *Auseinandersetzung*, one thinker's thought and that of another play into by playing against one another. This movement shares the allure of dialectics, but differs from it in the important respect that in it, the One and the Other, far from being poles destined for eventual supersession, constitute themselves as themselves to begin with. Their irreducible, inalienable difference from one another hinges upon the mutual call for disappropriation. More importantly, however, *Auseinandersetzung* differs from dialectics in what might be called the *generalized biasing*, or *systematic slant*, that characterizes its movements. As we have seen, only in view of the thought of the other beginning does Nietzsche achieve what is most inalienably proper to him, and conversely, Heidegger's own thought comes into its own only through its demarcation from a Nietzsche "reductively" interpreted as having completed the first beginning. Unlike critique, *Auseinandersetzung* accords a necessary, constitutive function to the Other. Yet, it is also clear from what we have developed so far that the possibility of recognition of the Other and *Befremdung* of the One by the Other hinge on a presentation of the One and the Other from a special angle. *Auseinandersetzung*, and thus the existence of a One and an Other in the first place, is only possible on the condition of a slanted, slightly unjust understanding that does not see the One and the Other as being what they are solely in and out of themselves. This injustice not only causes Nietzsche to appear in his greatest strength and hence as Other to begin with, but also makes Heidegger's "supreme exertion of thinking" *merely* the humble recasting of the first beginning. Consequently, one slant counterbalances the other. No dissymmetry prevails here, and hence, in *Auseinandersetzung*, the One and the Other merely secure their respective places by unseating one another in a movement of reciprocal reference, or *Befremdung*. Yet, although this symmetric play between the One and the Other seems to reveal a definite limitation on the ability of *Auseinandersetzung* to take in the Other as Other, it also brings into view a clear limit on the extent to which propriety—the ownmost in its inalienable Otherness—may be attributed to an opponent in dialogue. It is in light of this essential limit, without which there would not be any *Auseinandersetzung*, that the following remarks by Heidegger on the limits of greatness must be read. In the addendi to "The Will to Power as Art," Heidegger remarks that to valuate a thinker does not mean to overlook what he has not overcome. The fateful belongs to greatness, he notes.[44] While *Auseinandersetzung* is not a finding fault or scoring of mistakes, it is nonetheless "a fixing of limits." "Limits belong to greatness. They do not exist in order to be regarded as something faulty, for they are the border—of the other and the created," Heidegger writes.[45] Confrontation as genuine critique thus points out the *necessary* limits to greatness, limits that belong intimately, inalienably to thinking. If these limits become thematic, in *Auseinandersetzung*, "it is in order to take up the task once again and to know the necessity of the limits. The limits of all greatness—the moment of its birth."[46] The very Otherness of greatness calls for the repetition of a thinker's thought, demanding that *the matter* be taken up again, and in thinking its limits, be developed, or rather, be thought further.

5

More than a Difference in Style

Intellectual debate in the academy prides itself only on its arguments, the search for truth being its prime objective. It takes place, it would seem, in dispassionate and disengaged fashion, largely without feud or altercation. Where disputatiousness is nonetheless unleashed, it is attributed to the extravagance, or idiosyncrasy, of the participants and thus is characterized as a regrettable aberration within the precincts of disinterested debate. With the furtherance of truth its sole objective, the rules governing the culture of intellectual debate in the university concern only the way of constructing well-formed propositions and how to interpret and set those propositions into a correspondence with other propositions, or even something other than propositions. Undoubtedly, the downplaying of polemics in academic culture betrays a desire to secure a culture that is properly academic and, hence, demarcated from the world beyond the university. But apart from its syntactic and semantic dimension, intellectual discussion inevitably has a pragmatic aspect as well. Within the academic culture, argumentative debate seeks not only to clarify issues, to make points, or to foster scholarly contribution, but in arguing intellectual debate, it also *does* something. It has a performative character. Once pragmatic consideration is given to the intellectual debate in the university, the boundaries between university culture and general culture become much less clear-cut (though they are not thereby annulled). And yet, the axiomatics hidden underneath intellectual debate cannot any longer be ignored. With it then comes the obligation to do something practical about the "style" of such debate.[1] Furthermore, if the performative nature of debates is taken into account, the very possibility of a neat distinction between the syntax and semantics of discussion may become blurred as well. What this may imply is that contrary to established belief in academic culture, the search for what is true and false is inherently bound up with the performative dimension of debate, and on occasion—it is, after all, necessarily a possibility that can always happen—truth might not even be the primary objective of academic discussion. In any event, consideration of the pragmatic dimension of intellectual debate obliges one to acknowledge not only the philosophical, but also the ethical and political axiomatics that support theoretical discussion. It demands as well that one do something about this axiomatics *in* theoretical discussion.

I.

Active confrontation with the norms that regulate the ways theoretical discussion is conducted may be all the more urgent where the debate concerns what is commonly described as a branch of semiotics, namely the discipline of pragmatics itself. Indeed, as Jacques Derrida has pointed out with respect to J. L. Austin's speech act theory, it is not a theory like others. "By contrast with *all* the other sciences, the theory of speech acts has as its object—lest we forget—speech acts, in other words, language, language said to be ordinary in languages said to be natural." Yet, since "theoretical utterances are speech acts," a theoretical discourse such as speech act theory cannot for principial reasons be a theory in a classical sense. Because its objects are acts of speech in ordinary language, "the process of abstraction and idealization" required by theory, which is always a "non formalizable residue, a residue not idealizable by the theory of language," is significantly limited (69; trans. mod.).[2] "This discourse . . . finds itself an integral part—part and parcel, but also *partial*—of the object it claims to be analyzing" (71). Furthermore, if speech act theory brings to light the performative nature of acts of speech, including those of theoretical utterances, its own pragmatic nature prevents it from ever achieving the purity of a theory. Since Austin's admitted difficulty in finding single and simple criteria of grammar and vocabulary for distinguishing constative from performative statements is a direct consequence of an analysis of language that puts "linguisticism and the authority of the code," in short, the *theory* of language, into question (19), one can safely venture for the same reason that the distinction between the syntactic, semantic, and pragmatic dimensions of an utterance becomes fluid and that it is no longer possible to confine speech act theory to a theoretical discipline such as pragmatics. Nor can a discussion of its theoretical claims call for a purely theoretical approach because of the performative aspect of the discipline.

For intrinsic reasons, then, the debate on speech act theory is, more than any other debate, inseparably tied to questions about the ethics of discourse. As Derrida suggests in "Limited Inc a b c . . . ," "Speech act theory is fundamentally and in its most fecund, most rigorous, and most interesting aspects . . . a theory of right or law, of convention, of political ethics or of politics as ethics. It describes (in the best Kantian tradition, as Austin acknowledges at one point) the pure conditions of an ethical-political discourse insofar as this discourse involves the relation of intentionality to conventionality or to rules" (97). Speech act theory is an investigation not only of what one does with words that confronts the normativeness of linguistic acts, but it gives particular consideration as well to acts of speech that have overt ethical-legal-political implications, such as promising, making excuses, pretending, and so forth. But, according to Derrida, speech act theory is also "compelled to reproduce, to reduplicate in itself the law of its object or its object as law; it must submit to the norm it purports to analyze" (97). But to the extent that this law is identical with the "ethical conditions of a *given* ethics" (122), the definition, in speech act theory, of what constitutes the objects and concepts of its analysis in their ideal purity, of what, for example, seriously represents a promise, rests on unquestioned ethical assumptions. With the prescriptive normativeness that imbues all its concepts and ideal objects, speech act theory is therefore not only not a theory in a strict sense anymore, it is a theory that, by taking the law of a given ethics at face value, "exclude[s], ignore[s], relegates[s] to the margins other conditions no less essential to ethics in general, whether of *this given* ethics or of *another*, or of a law that would not answer to Western concepts of ethics, right, or politics" (122). This inevitable reduplication in speech act theory of the norm it purports to analyze would require speech act theory to constantly reflect on what it is itself doing when discussing acts of speech, or when debating speech act theory. Speech act theory implicitly demands of its theoreticians that they be attentive at all moments to what they are doing when arguing. It follows that any discussion about speech act theory must address the performative dimension of debate, lay open the axiomatics—the rules and conventions—that guide the debate, and question the prescriptive normativeness, its limits and pre-suppositions, that inform any claim made and every move made.

Revisiting his debate in 1977 with John R. Searle about Austin's speech act theory, Derrida remarks in the exchange of letters with Gerald Graff titled " Afterword. Toward an Ethic of Discussion" that in retro-spect the theoretical or philosophical "content" of the debate matters little (given that these contents have been elaborated elsewhere in much greater detail). In contrast, he argues, the pragmatic aspect of the debate and the "questions of right, morality, and of politics" in academic culture in gen-eral invite further deciphering. But these questions, as well as Derrida's in-tention to make the ethical and political axiomatics of academic discussion legible, framed his contribution to the debate from the beginning. Refer-ring to his response to Searle, he notes that in "Limited Inc a b c . . ." "he tried to *say* something [about the violence that permeates discussion in the academic world and] also tried, at the same time, to *do* something" (111) about it. Given the axiomatics at the heart of Searle's version of speech act theory—"the values of propriety and property, of the proper name, of copyright (the rights of the author)," for instance—it became a "*duty* to treat it both theoretically and practically" (113).

However, before I engage the "Derrida-Searle debate" itself, let me briefly describe how this debate came about in the first place. Founded in the late seventies by Samuel Weber, the journal *Glyph* was intended as a forum for the publication of the work of a group of individuals, many of whom, at the instigation of Richard Macksey, then the director of the Hu-manities Center, had joined the Johns Hopkins University. They shared a common interest in new developments in continental thought, especially in France, and more precisely in those innovative aspects of it that could be made fruitful for the study of literature, and textual studies in general, in North America. As Weber noted in his programmatic foreword to *Glyph 1*, the aim of the journal was to graft the "problematization of the repre-sentational framework of Western Metaphysics" by certain European thinkers onto the universe of discourse prevailing in the English-speaking world, in order to seek "a transformation of investigative concepts and procedures [in that universe of discourse] consonant with the specific dif-ferences of the Anglo-American scene."[3] But *Glyph* aspired as well to be-come a forum for the discussion of certain trends in Anglo-American philosophy at the cutting edge of philosophy and literary studies and their impact on developments of the avant-garde of continental, particularly French, philosophical and critical thought. This was then the context in which John R. Searle was invited in 1977 to engage Derrida's discussion of Austin's speech act theory in the essay "Signature Event Context." It is not inappropriate to recall that no English version of Derrida's essay existed at the time. Searle having requested a translation, Jeffrey Mehlman and Samuel Weber translated "Signature Event Context," in order to meet Searle's conditions for agreeing to respond. Both the translation of Derrida's essay on Austin and Searle's "Reiterating the Differences: A Reply to Derrida" appeared in the first issue of *Glyph*. Derrida's lengthy response to Searle "Limited Inc a b c . . ."—was published in *Glyph 2*.

Given Derrida's point-by-point rebuttal of Searle's criticism of his interpretation of Austin, it would be tedious to rehearse the debate in all its particulars. I will thus limit myself to some general remarks. I recall first that Searle's discussion of "Signature Event Context" takes place out of context. Not one single reference to another work by Derrida in the "Reply" suggests even a minimal familiarity with the latter's writings. Thus, when taking up, at one point, the problematic of writing, the "Reply" merely replays the then current misunderstanding in North American academia of this central notion.[4] Second, less surprising (because less well known), but not for that matter less significant, is another context of which the "Reply" takes no account. In fact, "Signature Event Context," was written at a time of intense scholarly exchanges between Oxford philosophers and philosophers at the Ecole Normale Supérieure in Paris. During the late sixties and early seventies, several working seminars initiated by Derrida, Alan Montefiore, Anthony Kenny, Jonathan L. Cohen, and others took place at regular intervals both at Oxford and Paris. At no point does Searle suspect Derrida's familiarity with the Anglo-American tradition of philosophizing. It should also be noted here that since Émile Benveniste presented the idea of the performative (though without calling it by that name) in a 1958 essay and became the first linguist to discuss Austin's speech act theory, the pragmatic theory of language has been a decisive reference in the sixties and seventies in France.[5] Needless to say, this interest was fueled by the need to overcome some limitations of structuralism. Searle should also have taken into account another contextual aspect of Derrida's discussion of Austin's speech act theory. Derrida refers to it when he writes in "Limited Inc a b c . . ." that " 'Signature Event Context' analyzes the metaphysical premises of the Anglo-Saxon—and fundamentally moralistic—theory of the performative, of speech acts or discursive events. In France, it seems to me that these premises underlie the hermeneutics of Ricoeur and the archeology of Foucault" (39). Third, Searle is entirely oblivious of the transcendental, or rather quasi-transcendental thrust of Derrida's inquiry in "Signature Event Context." Missing out on the nature of the investigation, and fixed on what Derrida himself calls the "all too evident," or "self-evident," if understood in merely empirical, or "real," terms, namely that "a written sign carries with it a force that breaks with its context," or that the "unity of the signifying form only constitutes itself . . . by the possibility of being repeated in the absence . . . of its 'referent' " (9–10), Searle never confronts the thrust of Derrida's argument. By focusing, for instance, on the traits recognizable "in the classical, narrowly defined concept of writing," "Signature Event Context" seeks to demonstrate that these traits are "generalizable." As "the nuclear traits of all writing," "they are valid for all orders of 'signs' and for all languages in general but moreover, beyond semio-linguistic communication, for the entire field of what philosophy would call experience, even the experience of being," or of presence (8–9). The burden of the argument of the essay rests with these generalized traits. They are traits constitutive of intelligibility as such. They are in the nature of "conditions of possibility." Only by placing oneself on the level of this generalization is it possible to assess the inevitable and not less generalizable consequences that these traits have for intelligibility itself. Finally, Searle's "Reply" does not take into consideration the horizon of the problematics within which Austin's speech act theory is discussed in Derrida's essay. The major focus of "Signature Event Context" is with the notion of event. As pointed out by Derrida in "Limited Inc a b c . . . ," "what the *Reply* never takes into account is that the most insistent question ['Signature Event Context'] seeks to discover what an event—which, in the case of a speech act, is supposed to take place—might be, and whether or not the structure of such an event leaves room for certitude or for evidence" (37). Austin's theory on performatives is discussed not simply on its own grounds, although speech act theory is in fact a theory of certain kind of events, but with a view toward eliciting the fundamental structures of an event as such. This concern with the event brings a very specific angle to Derrida's treatment of Austin and prompts his inquiry to be, above all, as we shall see, an inquiry into the structures of locution, or the locutionary act, in advance, thus of the various distinctions that Austin makes with respect to such acts of speech as illocutionary and perlocutionary acts. Searle's "Response" is unmindful of this concern of Derrida's.

I now turn to Derrida's answer to Searle's "Reply." First, I wish to point out that Derrida recalls, in response to Searle's contention that he has misread Austin and Searle's self-assured passing of sentences in the name of truth, that in his essay he had underscored the fact that one of the reasons why Austin interested him was that "Austin was obliged to free the analysis of the performative from the authority of the truth *value*, from the true/false opposition, at least in its classical form" (42) and that, consequently, he himself might have been "*doing something other*" than stating the truth in "Signature Event Context." (43). Derrida writes that he might have proposed a text, a writing, and signatures "whose *performance* (structure, event, context, etc.) defies at every moment the oppositions of concepts or of values, the rigor of those oppositional limits that speech act theory endorses by virtue of its very axiomatics; offering the performance of a text which, by raising in passing the question of truth (beyond Austin's intermittent impulses in this direction) does not *simply* succumb to its jurisdiction and remains, at this point, qua textual performance, irreducible to 'verdictive' sentences (as Austin might say)" (43; trans. mod.). If then "Signature Event Context" has been written in such a way that its utterances undercut possible identification by way of the categories and categorial oppositions of speech act theory, Searle's lack of attention to the structure of utterances in the essay is not only not serious for a speech act theoretician, but it suggests as well an unwillingness to accept the very possibility of a position other than one's own and thus violates from the start the basic rules of debate.

Second, in "Limited Inc a b c . . ." Derrida repeats the main arguments that he had advanced in the early essay, reformulating them once more and expounding upon them in greater detail. Given Searle's misreading, this restatement serves to draw attention to what would have had to be discussed if a debate about "Signature Event Context" had taken place. The restatement thus serves to relaunch the "improbable" debate (33). Although "Limited Inc a b c . . ." does not offer any new insight, the theses of "Signature Event Context," because they are reiterated, are presented differently. As the early essay had tried to do something other than state the truth, Derrida's response to Searle does something other, too, and does it in yet another way. With this emphasis on the performative nature of both texts, that is on their act- or, rather, event-character, it is suggested that any debate about what "Signature Event Context" says and does— and, for that matter, any utterance in general—must also take into account the singular nature of these theoretical discourses. This is especially urgent when discourses or texts are parts of a debate. Furthermore, if this debate concerns speech act theory, one needs to ask, while applying and reapplying all the questions and categories accredited by the theory of speech acts, "whether or not they are performatives, in what measure and aspect they depend upon the per- or illocutionary, whether they are serious or not, normal or not, void or not, parasitic or not, fictional or not, literary, philosophical, theatrical, oratorical, prophetical or not, etc." (39). In other words, the unavoidable in a debate about speech act theory is whether the fundamental categories of this theory are capable of doing justice to the singular performative nature of any of the texts that contribute to the debate. True to this exigency, intent on inquiring into what he is doing in his response, Derrida considers Searle's "Reply" as an "example" of an event.

Third, although Searle's reading of "Signature Event Context" does not meet any of the exigencies that a debate with another's position would have required, even if that position were exclusively theoretical, and thus falls short of engaging a debate to begin with, Derrida does not simply dismiss it as a nonreading. In spite of his biting critique and caustic humor, and in spite of the combative and discursive violence to which Derrida has recourse in the exchange (113), "Limited Inc a b c . . ." raises the "Reply" to the status worthy of an opponent in a debate. This takes place at the precise moment when Derrida, after having evoked Searle's acknowledgment that he had discussed his reply to Derrida with Dagmar Searle and Hubert Dreyfus, decides "to give the presumed and collective author of the *Reply* the French name 'Société à responsabilité limitée'—literally, 'Society with Limited Responsibility' (or Limited Liability)—which is normally abbreviated to *Sarl*" (36). Undoubtedly, there are several reasons for thus recasting the name in a text that among other things takes up again the question of the signature. But if, indeed, "Limited Inc a b c . . ." engages a debate in a strict sense, it is only with an opponent named Sarl. Rather than diminishing the stature of the opponent, this renaming elevates the author (or authors) of the "Reply" to the status of a worthy opponent. Derrida writes that "Sarl has, in fact, very well understood the *Sec*-effect. . . . Sarl did indeed understand ['Signature Event Context']. No question here of the essentials being misunderstood. Or rather, if 'understanding' is still a notion dominated by the allegedly constative regime of theory or of philosophy, let us not use the word 'understood,' let us say instead that Sarl was touched" (41).[6] Derrida's observes at the outset of his response that he was struck by what he "read in 'Reiterating the Differences: A Reply to Derrida'" "as being very familiar," and of having a "strange, uncanny familiarity" (29), leaving no doubt that the opponent he is to engage under the name of Sarl is metaphysics itself. Indeed, later in the text it is made clear that what is so familiar in the "Reply" is not only the basic assumptions of metaphysics, but also a set of gestures by which metaphysics obstructs all inquiry that goes beyond a certain limit and by which it thus limits its own responsibilities. In other words, what takes place in thus renaming the author of the "Reply" is nothing less than what Heidegger has shown to be the essential condition for any *Auseinandersetzung*, namely that the argument of the opponent be construed with respect to his strongest position.[7] This is the minimal ethical requirement needed for a debate to be possible in the first place.

Fourth, before beginning the detailed rebuttal of Searle's arguments in the "Reply," Derrida, "in order to clarify the discussion . . . adopt[s] certain technical procedures and proposes[s] several conventions" (44). Two technical conventions secure the integrity of the text to be discussed (the "Reply"), and the reader's ability to verify the well-groundedness of any claim made. In distinction to Searle's decision to focus only on what he deems most important in Derrida's text, "Limited Inc a b c . . ." decides to take into consideration the whole text, not only the context in which statements are made, but also everything that may seem marginal to the arguments. In further distinction to Searle, Derrida decides to extensively quote so as to respect the reader's capacity of judgment. He acknowledges that the reader or interlocutor whom he has "neither the means nor the desire to consult on this matter, can always decide not to subscribe" to these conventions and even to interrupt his reading; and he asks: "But in proposing conventions that I deem to be *reasonable*, haven't I already consulted and involved him a bit, inasmuch as I impute a certain degree of reason to him, and even a certain amount of good faith?" (44). However, whether the participants of the debate will perform according to this consensus, which credits them with the ability of (at least) minimal reasoning, "remains forever in doubt" (44). In fact, as Derrida demonstrates throughout the essay, without this possibility of not observing the rules, a debate would not be a debate.

A further convention concerns a limit on the number of the arguments that Derrida proposes to make. Having ordered his arguments alphabetically, he writes under the entry *K*: "I will have to limit my arguments in number to eighteen. One of the conventions of this debate (and, says *Sec*, not the least determining, in the final analysis) is that it should take place, if it takes place, in a graphic element of a type that is phonetic, and more precisely, alphabetical. This is not without a certain arbitrariness. Its effect: henceforth I will have at my disposal only 18 letters or 18 blows and I will have to make the best of them" (45). Let it be borne in mind that "Signature Event Context" advances the argument that all communication, including communications at conferences and debates, has a "general graphematic structure" (19). If one generalizes the trait traditionally bestowed upon writing according to which it is the repetition of an oral utterance, the iterability constitutive of the sign, whether oral or written (in the common sense of "writing"), can be said to make every sign into a kind of writing mark. The debate with Searle was to take place in writing, in a language whose graphic element is not only phonetic, but also alphabetical. Undoubtedly, this convention limits arbitrarily in fact the exchange to one medium. But in order not to forget, and thus to be able to take into account, that the acts of speech that make up the debate with Searle "are *written*, and that this opens up possibilities and problems which are not negligible" (114)—a major issue of contention in the debate with Searle—Derrida submits his argumentation to the set of characters of written language. The customary and artificial alphabetical order of the arguments in "Limited Inc a b c . . ." enables Derrida to point not only to the graphematic structure of all speech acts, but also to the fact that this graphematic structure, and the iterability it implies, brings with it alteration and, consequently, an inevitable possibility of arbitrariness. Limiting his arguments to the number of letters of the alphabet that are left, Derrida, therefore, meets an ethical demand required by discussion: to acknowledge, and take responsibility for, the possibility that all speech acts are capable of becoming nonserious because of their general graphematic structure. He thus inscribes a certain limit into his response due to the fact that acts of speech cannot be prevented from becoming parasitized and parasitic, in recognition of the proposition that this must at all times be taken into account.[8]

Fifth, submitting himself "to the most demanding norms of classical philosophical discussion" (114), Derrida engages in a discursive critique of the arguments advanced by the "Reply" in which these arguments (and the positions that they articulate) are shown to be theoretically untenable. In essence, Derrida argues that given the presuppositions concerning the nature of speech acts, which are recognized in principle by Austin and Searle (iterability, in particular), it is illegitimate and impossible to seek, were it only for reasons of convenience, that is, to provisionally isolate pure acts of speech (the so-called standard, normal, serious speech acts), because this would be tantamount to excluding from those acts that which makes them speech acts to begin with. Derrida writes: "Iterability prohibits *a priori* (and in principle) the full and rigorous attainment of the ideal plenitude such exclusions purport to isolate. These hypothetical exclusions cannot be formed. They are illegitimate and impossible inasmuch as they suppose the self-identity of an isolated element which iterability—i.e., an element constitutive of the hypothesis—divides at once" (63). As already demonstrated in "Signature Event Context," the argument in "Limited Inc a b c . . ." consists in showing that because of speech act theory's fundamental assumptions about what constitutes an act of speech, it is impossible for structural reasons, that is, not justifiable even for methodological or strategic purposes, to engineer idealizations by excluding the necessary possibility constitutive of speech acts, namely, that they can become (because they are necessarily iterable) impure. To do so would mean to root out "the very roots of what one purports to analyze. For these roots are two-fold: you cannot root out the 'parasite' without rooting out the 'standard' at the same time" (90). By drawing all the possible consequences that follow from certain assumptions at the very core of speech act theory, consequences that the theoreticians of this theory have not themselves lived up to, Derrida thus abides with the rule of rigor in philosophical argumentation. His rigor consists in taking the implications of the assumptions into account in their entirety and in following them up to their logical end. He takes the theoretical risk that the theoreticians of speech act theory have so far shunned (72). This risk is above all one of uncompromising responsibility for what comes with certain assumptions.

That this critical vigilance and responsibility is more than theoretical is already manifest in the fact that in contrast to the "Reply," which permits itself a number of liberties and on more than one occasion indulges in imprecision, vagueness, and thoughtlessness, "Limited Inc a b c . . ."

neither seeks shortcuts nor takes the easy way out; it does not advance anything that remains ungrounded or not entirely thought through. The response to the "Reply" takes responsibility for every single move it makes, and everything it says, and does so by forcing itself to remain accountable at every moment. This critical vigilance, however, is not restricted to excluding from the discussion anything that has not fully been thought through and to giving all the implications that derive from the fundamental insight into the iterability of the speech act their full due. The vigilance in question applies especially to the performative nature of the discussion. There are at least three different ways in which this critical awareness impacts on the way a discussion is carried out. This vigilance concerns the enunciatory character of every speech act and the normative axiomatics that instruct its act insofar as something is done in performing it; it serves to actively further the argument (to make a point, or demonstrate, *in actu*, by producing in the course of theoretical demonstration an example of what is stated); and finally, it brings to bear the theoretical implications that come with the insight into the iterability of acts of speech on any act that is performed. The first aspect of the vigilance in question is fairly obvious. Resisting the traditional inclination to abstract and idealize, it is instrumental in actualizing the performative dimension of all theoretical utterances and in bringing to light the values that shape theory's categories and moves. But what about the second facet of this vigilance? Subsequent to the observation in "Afterward: Toward an Ethic of Discussion" that in "Limited Inc a b c . . ." he tried to respond to Searle point by point, Derrida writes: "In so doing I multiply statements, discursive gestures, forms of writing, the structure of which reinforces my demonstration in something like a practical manner: that is, by providing instances of 'speech acts' which by themselves render impracticable and theoretically insufficient the conceptual oppositions upon which speech act theory in general, and Searle's version in particular, relies." Here, the enactment of critical vigilance aims at "exemplify[ing] in the *practice* of speech *acts*" the propositions that are "demonstrate[d] on the theoretical level" (114). For example, the speech act itself that seeks to expose the limits of the categories of speech act theory is cast in a form that resists interpretation by these very categories. Finally, in "Limited Inc a b c . . . ," Derrida seeks to draw for the practice of argumentation itself the consequences that follow from the fact that all acts of speech are structurally inhabited by the possibility of corruption. As a result of the critical vigilance pertaining to the performative aspect of argumentation, not one single argument is advanced that does not at the same time inscribe within itself the limit that devolves from this possibility of infelicitous corruption. "Limited Inc a b c . . ." ("Signature Event Context" as well, as the "example" of the signature demonstrates) is a text that, in writing, takes seriously the a priori looming possibility of nonseriousness. In short, it is a text that, in its writing, accounts at all levels for "the '-bility' " (78) of the corruptibility (the possibility, and not actuality of corruption) of all acts of writing insofar as they must be possibly iterable in order to be such acts to begin with.

II.

As said before, "Signature Event Context" is an inquiry that in classical terms would have to be labeled "transcendental." Undoubtedly, while discussing iterability in "Limited Inc a b c . . ." Derrida warns against taking the latter as a "transcendental condition of possibility," because iterability at the same time as it introduces the relation by which something becomes a conditioned effect of a pure source radically distinct from the conditioned, also breaches such a relation (100). Even though one must thus speak of this inquiry as quasi-transcendental, the qualification, however modalized, is indicative of the specific level on which the essay unfolds its arguments. "Signature Event Context" speaks of an " 'effect' of transcendentality [that] is linked necessarily to the *possibility* of writing" (8; emphasis added). Generally speaking, Derrida can be shown to be concerned in the essay with possibilities that are constitutive of speech acts, possibilities, therefore, without which there would be no speech act. In fact, the reference to "possibility" in the essay is entirely reserved for "possibility" in this sense. Hence, Derrida makes the distinction here between "possibility" and "eventuality" (16). As is recalled in "Limited Inc a b c . . . ," "the possibility or fact that performatives can always be cited . . . is not the same as the *eventuality,* that is the fact that such possible events . . . do indeed happen, occur" (86–87). In distinction to the possibility that can always befall a speech act, which therefore is an essential part of it, "eventuality" only designates the factual occurrence of these possibilities. Derrida avers: "What makes the (eventual) possibility possible is what makes it happen even before it happens as an actual event (in the standard sense) or what prevents such an event from ever entirely, fully taking place" (57). "Signature Event Context" is primarily about what Derrida calls "structural possibilities," or "necessary possibilities" (57). These serve to explain what it is "in the structural functioning of the mark" that renders empirical events of "accidents" of speech acts possible. When discussing the structure of the linguistic mark, and the possible absence of the referent, including the signified meaning, Derrida observes that this possibility "constructs the mark; and the potential presence of the referent at the moment it is designated does not modify in the slightest the structure of the mark, which implies that the mark can do without the referent" (10). To further clarify this one example of a possibility that is a necessary possibility rather than an "empirical eventuality" (10), Derrida turns to Husserl's analyses in the *Logical Investigations* where the intelligibility of utterances is shown to remain intact even in the absence of the eventual presence of the referent. While discussing the case of an utterance such as "The sky is blue," which remains intelligible or legible even when no sky is in view, Derrida observes that "the structure of possibility of this utterance includes the capability to be formed and to function as a reference that is empty or cut off from its referent. Without this possibility, which is also that of iterability in general, 'generable,' and generative of all marks, there would be no utterance" (11). Instead of providing further examples (citationality would be another), let me follow up on the hint here that all the possibilities that necessarily can befall a mark, or an utterance, can be retraced to what is called iterability, not to the factual occurrence of repetitions, but to the constituting possibility of being repeated, more precisely, iterated. If these examples of necessary possibilities are "examples" of iterability in general, they cannot, of course, simply be the same as iterability "itself."

In the part of "Signature Event Context" devoted to Austin's theory of speech acts, Derrida recalls that the latter excludes from his analysis all utterances that consist in the citation of serious acts of speech because he is interested in establishing what constitutes the illocutionary force of ordinary, normal, standard acts of speech, or in Jürgen Habermas' words, what makes these acts effective as actions (*handlungswirksam*). Having emphasized that, according to Austin, all acts of speech are by definition capable of being repeated and that iterability is thus an intrinsic feature of the speech act per se, Derrida asks whether "*citation* (on stage, in a poem, or a soliloquy) is [not] the determined modification of a general citationality—or rather, a general iterability—without which there would not even be a 'successful' performative?" (17). Citationality is the possibility of an act of utterance being cited, and as such, it is a modification of the general iterability that Austin had acknowledged to be constitutive of speech acts. But if so, on what grounds can Austin deliberately ignore this possibility of citation when analyzing so-called standard acts of speech? How can a concern with the pragmatic effectivity of ordinary speech acts leave out of account that speech acts are such acts only if they are also iterable, for instance, by being cited? For Derrida, such exclusion is impossible, in fact, illegitimate, on the very basis of what Austin himself has said about the nature of the speech act.

How is one to interpret this inconsistency? The most plausible explanation for Austin's failure to recognize that such exclusion is not permissible would be that the theoretician of speech acts (and Searle as well) has not drawn the full consequences of his insight into the necessity for speech acts to be repeatable. Clearly, this insight has not in speech act theory the status of a transcendental, or rather quasi-transcendental truth, as it has in Derrida. Speech act theory has not unfolded the full range of what is implied by the acknowledged iterability of utterances. Above all, it has failed to address the fact that if an utterance is citable (and were this to occur only once), this possibility is "*always* inscribed, hence *necessarily* inscribed, *as possibility* in the functioning or the functional structure" of the utterance (48). Neither Austin nor Searle have given thought to the structural necessity of what is always possible, nor have they elaborated on the necessity of what they admit to be necessary for speech acts to be such acts in the first place, their iterability. Only when all the implications that follow from the iterability of acts of speech have been copresented, can the universality and necessity of the structure of iterability no longer be ignored (70). On this condition alone can iterability acquire the status of a "law." Yet Austin (and Searle too) has not been theoretically consequential, or consistent, and has not undertaken this step. In singling out a region of so-called normal and pragmatically effective acts of speech he (like Searle) has closed his eyes to what he himself had recognized. But one must ask why.

While calling the structure of iterability a law, Derrida takes up the question of the status of this law to remark that to give it the title of a law is not to say "that this law has the simplicity of a logical or transcendental principle. One cannot even speak of it being fundamental or radical in the traditional philosophical sense" (92). This is the point at which one can perhaps surmise for what reasons Austin (as well as speech act theoreticians after him) does not follow up on what his very insight means and what follows from it. Unfolded in all its consequences, iterability puts into question the possibility of pure, simple distinctions. It thwarts the possibility of construing an ideal object such as "ordinary language" radically distinct from non-ordinary ways of speaking. Heeded according to what necessarily follows from it, the insight into the necessary iterability of speech act would have prevented Austin from separating out an idealized realm in which utterances are univocal, the total context is present to the self, the intentions are transparent, and meaning is present to the absolutely singular uniqueness of the speech act (17). Indeed, without this possibility of pure distinctions, and the idealization of its object, no *theory* in the strict sense is possible. In speech act theory, the case we are dealing with, theory rests on the eventual exclusion of all nonserious acts of speech as parasites from its realm of competence. This methodological exclusion is the condition as well for the basic logical operations characteristic of a *theory*, and above all for the operation that consists in deriving the secondary from the logically prior.

In the last instance, the resistance of speech act theory—a resistance thus owed to its nature as a *theory*—to drawing all the conclusions and corollaries from its own discovery that speech acts are necessarily iterable has to be explained by the fact that iterability, if taken seriously, is not a transcendental, but a quasi-transcendental. Transcendentals are easily accommodated by any *theory*. The transcendental, as a pure constituting condition of possibility, obeys and commands at once the demand for ideality (hence of clearly cut distinctions) characteristic of theory. But the universal and necessary structure of iterability has not the simplicity of a transcendental a priori. Thought to its logical end, iterability is a "non-simplicity which makes possible *and* limits at one and the same time" (92). If iterability is the necessary condition of possibility for all ideality (including that of ordinary language and its acts of speech), it is also that which limits this ideality insofar as the possibility of iteration inscribes virtual impurities, and the possibility of corruptibility, into the ideality that it makes possible. Indeed, iterability implies a necessary possibility of alteration. As an ideality itself, iterability thus also houses a limit to its own ideality. For this reason, it has not the purity of a transcendental, and it is simply no longer conceivable in terms of a constituting ideality.

Iterability as a double limit, a limit that makes acts of speech possible but at the same time prevents them from achieving complete purity, would have required the speech act theoretician to recognize that the possibility of parasitizing, rather than being something that causes the perdition of language, is "its internal and positive condition of possibility" (17). It would have required the speech act theoreticians to admit that without a so-called negativity—an absence, impurity, or nonseriousness—even ordinary language, their object of predilection, would not be able to function effectively. This refusal of the theory to acknowledge the constitutive character of the nonserious and to admit that "a successful performative is necessarily an 'impure' performative" (17) brings to light the full extent of speech act theory's prescriptive axiomatics. In this resistance, nothing less is at stake than what speech act theory has decided speech acts *ought* to be. Paradoxically stated, they should be acts distinct from those that really occur, acts that, in reality, never take place. Indeed, speech act theory defines "ordinary" language by way of excluding from it "the very law of language" (17). It decrees certain linguistic forms as mere derivatives and abnormalities, without which no act of speech would have the value of a speech act.

In "Signature Event Context," the iteration that structures acts of speech is described in terms of a dehiscence. Derrida comments: "As in the realm of botany, from which it draws its metaphorical value, the word marks emphatically that the divided opening, in the growth of a plant, is also what, in a *positive* sense, makes production, reproduction, development possible. Dehiscence (like iterability) limits what it makes possible, while rendering its rigor and purity impossible" (59). Given this "two-fold root" of iterability, which bars it from playing "the role of philosophical radicality" (92), full recognition of what iterability entails would have stifled the speech act theoreticians' aim at developing a rigorous *theory*. But notwithstanding the difficulties that consideration of the full implications of iterability would have had for a theory of speech acts in the strict sense, this does not at all foreclose a rigorous discursive account of the law of language.

This then is the point where we need to introduce the question of the "general theory" that Austin alludes to in *How to Do Things with Words*, but which he never develops. Citing this work, "Signature Event Context" offers two examples of Austin's postponement of a "general account" or "general doctrine" regarding the ills that can infect all utterances (16). But in "Limited Inc a b c . . . ," while discussing Searle's suggestion in the "Reply" that it is he who after Austin has developed the general speech act theory "which Austin did not live long enough to develop himself," Derrida remarks that like Searle he "also believes[s] that Austin had, in an implicit state, a general theory. It was presupposed . . . and it cannot be the effect of an extension or accumulation of results or analyses of details. But this general theory did not permit him—and has never permitted anyone—to integrate what it started out by excluding, even strategically, in the name of those metaphysical concepts, values, and axioms upon which this theory was constructed qua general theory" (95). It follows that the general, but only implicit, theory that Austin is credited with is a theory that in fact inhibits the speech act theoretician from providing the "general account" of the ills that can beset all utterances. Though unspoken, the general theory presupposed by Austin's individual analyses, for instance, of pretending or excusing, is not the "general doctrine" that, in Derrida's words, "would have to entail a reelaboration of the axiomatics or of the premises" of speech act theory itself (85). Consequently, the "general theory" that, according to the 1971 essay Austin never developed and which Derrida in this essay proceeds to formulate, is evidently a "theory" in a wholly *other* sense than the theory Austin is said to have advanced implicitly. Even though Derrida elaborates the general theory by following up on the consequences that derive from Austin's recognition that all speech acts are necessarily prone to ills, the theory in question is neither a simple linear continuation of what Austin had already begun (since the very axioms of Austin's implicit general doctrine barred all possibility of taking these ills seriously) nor a theory in the narrow strict sense, despite its concern with generality. It is a "general theory" that Austin could not have had, either implicitly or explicitly, as long as he remained a theoretician of speech acts.[9]

To make this point more pointedly, let us bear in mind that the discussion of Austin's theory of performatives in "Signature Event Context" is framed by the overall problematic of the essay. This problematic, upon which to my knowledge no commentator on the essay, or, for that matter, on the Derrida-Searle debate, has found it necessary to pause, concerns the structure of the event—that is, the eventhood of the event. In the section "Writing and Telecommunication" that precedes the discussion of Austin's work, Derrida has been concerned with the structure of the mark and the necessity of a certain absence in presence for presence to be what it is. The section of the essay devoted to speech act theory opens with the explicit remark that this section intends "to elaborate a bit further this question with special attention to [*en prenant appui sur*]—but in order, as well, to pass beyond [*pour la traverser aussi bien*]—the problematic of the *performative*" (13). As the whole discussion on the performative demonstrates, this additional elaboration on the structure of the mark that constitutes presence concerns the very values of act and event at the core of speech act theory. However, if the question of what makes an event is the guiding question, the whole discussion of speech act theory will be geared toward certain defined issues in this theory. Indeed, the whole analysis carried out in the section "Parasites. Iter, of Writing: That It Perhaps Does Not Exist" concerns nothing less than the structure of the locutionary act itself. In advance of all the major differentiations relative to the specific acts of speech, Derrida broaches in this section "a general and systematic elaboration of the structure of locution" (15), an analysis that, as he recalls, Austin does not provide. He writes: "Austin has not taken account of what—in the structure of *locution* (thus before any illocutory or perlocutory determination)—already entails that system of predicates I call *graphematic in general* and consequently blurs all the oppositions which follow, oppositions whose pertinence, purity, and rigor Austin has unsuccessfully attempted to establish" (14). By focussing on the locutionary act itself— the act, or performance, of "saying something," which qua act constitutes an event—Derrida seeks to bring to light "a certain conventionality intrinsic to what constitutes locution itself " (in addition to "the conventionality constituting the *circumstance* of the utterance," which Austin considers when he discusses the locutionary act) (15; trans. mod.). With locution in the spotlight, the structures required for the performative in general, that is, for an event such as an act of utterance to be possible, can be brought to the fore. Only the general and systematic exposition of these structures of locution itself can provide the "general theory" that Austin, according to Derrida, did not develop.

To inquire into the structure of the locutionary act is, according to "Signature Event Context," to probe "the status of events in general, of events of speech or by speech, of the strange logic they entail and that often passes unseen" (18). Even though Austin admits that no performative is pure, the value of the "act" of the speech act, of its character as an event, is not made subject to systematic questioning, and implies "as in the entire philosophical tradition that supports it, [the value] of presence" (58), which the first section of "Signature Event Context" had begun to put into question. The concern with locution itself concerns precisely the purity of the singular event of a performative. Derrida asks: "Would a performative utterance be possible if a citational doubling did not come to split and dissociate from itself the pure singularity of the event?" (17). Indeed, if the allegedly present and singular event of an utterance, or speech act, must entail the possibility of this utterance's repetition, or citation, the question becomes one that touches on "the status of 'occurrence' or the eventhood of an event" (17). If the very successfulness of a performative utterance must "repeat a 'coded' or iterable utterance," an utterance "*conforming* with an iterable model," one that is identifiable, as it were, as a "citation" (18), the utterance as event can no longer be understood to signify an event that would be self-present, unique, or singular. In order for a locution to occur, to be an act of speech, "a general iterability" must break into "the allegedly rigorous purity of every event of discourse or of every *speech act*" (18). To have event character, the event of an act of speech must be iterable. Iterability in this general sense is not only what makes the event as such possible, it is also, as Derrida puts it in "Limited Inc a b c . . . ," "what prevents such an event from ever entirely, fully taking place (in the standard sense)" (57).

With this focus on the structure of locution, "the value of the kind of event that supports the entire theory of speech acts" (58) is thus put in question. "Signature Event Context" proposes "another kind of graphics of the event in general" (57) by which the value of presence that dominates the notion of the performative in speech act theory is shown to hinge on a general iterability and to be, for this reason, eminently, or structurally, parasitic. It is not a question of torpedoing the category of presence altogether but of showing that without being inhabited by a general iterability, it cannot possibly account for the *first time* of the event, and the event's eventhood. As Derrida writes in "Qual Quelle": "Here we are in need of a paradoxical logic of the event as a *source which cannot present itself, happen to itself*. The value of the event is perhaps indissociable from that of presence; it remains rigorously incompatible with that of self-presence."[10] In its last part titled "Signatures," "Signature Event Context" performs an operation, an event: the seemingly most singular act of signing with one's proper name. The performance of this singular act not only betokens the presupposition of iterability insofar as it is not possible without an at least implicit recourse to the law, but also that it is potentially subject to forgery and fraud, since "the test of authentification is part of the very structure of the signature" (133). As Derrida suggests, no category of speech act theory could hope to account for that act in all its complexity.

III.

With the focus on the act of locution, prior to the major distinctions characteristic of speech act theory, including the distinction between the constative and the performative, Derrida's discussion has sought to lay bare the system of graphematic predicates characteristic of the event, or, what he calls, in "Two Words for Joyce," "the law enounced [*qui s'énonce*] in the performative dimension."[11] This law concerns the conditions in advance of any existing rules and established norms, under which a performative act, or a singular event, can occur. With this a novel concept of the performative is established that is implied not only in all constatives, but also in all performative utterances as defined by speech act theory.[12] If the notion of the performative in Austin's work emerges, first and foremost, in opposition to the theoretical constative and serves to unseat the unique privilege that the latter enjoys in philosophy, particularly in logical positivism, this novel notion of the performative cannot be defined by way of opposition to acts of statement, or description. It is not simply because ultimately such acts would also imply a performative dimension (in the Austinean sense). If the "performative," as understood by Derrida, foregrounds the opposition with which speech act theory begins, it is because this performative concerns nothing less than "the *performative* logic of the event" of any utterance, or speech act whatever its kind. From what we have seen so far, this logic "inscribes a lack (*manque*) into the operation of performance."[13] A first consequence of this is that the performative in question undercuts the possibility (though not the need) of making the absolutely clear-cut distinctions on which speech act theory rests. As a result, this new notion of the performative cannot be defined in terms of the categories that speech act theory provides. It is not the outcome of a generalization of what Austin or Searle call a performative. Let us also recall that within the framework of Austin's theory "a performative must be a *sentence*, a sentence sufficiently endowed with meaning in itself, in a given conventional context."[14] But the performative that the general and systematic elaboration of the structure of locution yields is not of the order of a phrase. As the law of eventhood, this "performative" cannot be described according to the "classical philosophical code [as] the transcendental condition of any performative dimensions."[15] But mindful of what the performative means in speech act theory, and what the transcendental means in philosophy, this performative is neither performative nor transcendental even though it is presupposed by all performativity and all transcendentality.[16]

This novel conception of the performative accounts for the fact that a successful performative must be impure. For a performative to be felicitous, it is necessary that it come with the possibility of being insincere, unserious, abnormal, perverted, and so forth. It must also include the possibility of ambiguity as to its own specificity. A certain confusion with respect to the nature of the act is indispensable for it to be effective. A case in point is the act by which a group of people declares its independence. As Derrida has argued in a brief analysis of the Declaration of Independence, "one cannot decide—and that is the interesting thing, the force and the coup of force of such a declarative act—whether independence is stated or produced by this utterance." Rather than a deficiency, this undecidability is necessary. "This obscurity, this undecidability between let's say, a performative structure and a constative structure, is *required* in order to produce the sought-after effect."[17] The very lack of the possibility of being able to decide, whether the people state their emancipation or perform it by the act of declaration, is essential for this declaration to found and constitute a constitution or a state. Without a certain "performative contradiction," no successful performative can be achieved.

In the debate with Austin and Searle, the performative logic of the event is discussed primarily from the iterability to which all utterances must be able to lend themselves. As we have suggested, the recognition that all acts of speech must be capable of corruption, that without this possibility acts of speech would not be what they intend to be, makes it illegitimate to bring to the analysis of acts of speech norms and values (such as purity, normality, seriousness, and so forth), whose role can only be to pejoratively evaluate, and to exclude deviation from these norms. Considering what iterability entails, all discussion of acts of speech, therefore, have to be not only critically aware of the axiomatics that rules their distinctive criteria, but also responsive and responsible to and for the infelicities that must be able to befall from within any serious act of speech, even were it that of a promise. Without giving the possibility its due, that a determined act of speech can turn into something other—a promise into a menace— without taking into account that any utterance inevitably carries with it the possibility of evil, acts of speech are not adequately discussed.

In the aftermath of the debate with speech act theory, Derrida has refined this performative logic of the event. On the occasion of the discussion of the status of the *yes* in "Ulysses Gramophone," all utterance is shown to imply a coextensive *yes*, that is to say, a *yes* that affirms the address to, and by, an other—a *yes* in search of a *yes* of the other, a *yes* in response to a prior *yes*.[18] What follows from the recognition of this "minimal primary *yes*" as the "transcendental condition of all performative dimensions" is an obligation in all utterances to respond to the other in his or her otherness to which the utterance, qua utterance, is directed, and to whom it remains indebted as far as its own singularity is concerned. Derrida began the previously mentioned discussion of the constitutive undecidability of instituting language by recalling that a performance such as the act of a declaration of independence requires a signer to engage him- or herself. At the same time, this signer (the independent people) does not exist before the act in question, if it is, indeed, an act of emancipation. It follows from this that "the signature invents the signer." Derrida writes: "It opens *for itself* a line of credit, *its* own credit, for itself *to* itself. The *self* surges up here in all cases (nominative, dative, accusative) as soon as a signature gives or extends credit to itself."[19] But as the Declaration also demonstrates, such self-constitution requires a countersignature, the signature in the name of God, that is, the name for the ultimate signature. In other words, all self-constitution continues to refer to the authenticating countersignature of an other. As Derrida notes, what is true of the Declaration is true of everyday occurrences. The analysis thus stipulates that any act of utterance not only engages the author, or signer, but an other whom the author or signer is to engage responsibly, insofar as his signature remains a "function" of the latter.

Elaborating on the performative of the promise—a speech act to which Austin and Searle have devoted much of their attention—a further feature of the performative logic of the event, and thus of ethical responsibility, comes to light. As in the case of the Declaration of Independence, and the *yes*, so here too I will only sketch out this feature and the obligations that it brings with it, in very broad strokes. For Derrida, the promise is not just one speech act among others. As he remarks in "Avances," "The theoretical and ontological discourse on promise belongs to what it is about; from the start this discourse is overreached or outflanked (*débordé*) by the performative of the promise which remains its element, and which, implicitly or explicitly, confers upon it its general form."[20] However, if the performative of the promise antedates eventual acts of promise, as well as the theoretical discourse on promise, including that of speech act theory, it is because this performative is presupposed in all discursive acts insofar as they are acts of speech. To conceive of this performative of the promise, is, therefore, to think "the before in the before, the abyss of antecedence, the absolute or immemorial anteriority of the principle of promise."[21] If the principle of promise has this anteriority, it is because a promise is made with each utterance, whatever its kind. Derrida remarks: "Each time I open my mouth, each time I speak or write, I *promise*. Whether I like it or not; here, the fatal precipitation of the promise must be dissociated from the values of the will, intention, or meaning-to-say that are reasonably attached to it. The performative of this promise is not one speech act among others. It is implied by any other performative, and this promise heralds the uniqueness of a language to come."[22] In classical philosophical terms, the promise of this "still-unheard-of language" made in any utterance is the promise of a universal language. But at the same time, the promise in question, which in advance gathers together any language into the singularity of an idiom, is that of the "one" language, of "the monolanguage *of* the other. The *of* signifies not so much property as provenance: language is for the other, coming from the other, *the* coming of the other."[23] With this promise that in advance structures all acts of speech, a responsibility for a language beyond my own idiom and intelligible to the other, as well as to the language of the other in all its singularity, is inextricably bound up with all language. It is a responsibility for a language other than my own (hence impossible), a language to come, but without which I could not possibly speak. The performative logic of the event, which we have seen to inexorably imply ethical responsibility, thus also requires taking into account, not only theoretically, but practically as well, in fact, in a manner in which the theoretical and the practical become confounded, the promise coextensive with language of a language to come.

PART II

THEORY

6

Under the Heading of Theory

The generic use of the term "theory"—simply put and specified no further—suggests that those critical ventures that explicitly lay claim to this title are at the very least homogeneous. Yet, no field is less unified than "theoretical" studies. For example: those critics who, in the name of theory apply the insights from various other disciplines in the humanities such as sociology, linguistics, or psychoanalysis to literary texts have little, except the umbrella term "theory," in common with the rhetorical and tropological brand of deconstruction. Moreover, this "theory" is a regional commodity, "a purely North American *artifact*, which only takes on sense from its place of emergence in certain departments of literature" in the United States, to quote Jacques Derrida.[1] Undoubtedly, "theory" has acquired prominence for a variety of reasons, in particular the need to counter a tradition of pragmatically oriented, or thematic, literary criticism. Still, this shared regional or functional origin fails to provide the multifarious phenomenon of theory with any viable common denominator. One might be tempted to conclude that the term "theory" itself is of little use, that it could be discarded, and that other concepts might be more appropriate to the phenomenon in question. Indeed, anyone familiar with what is called "theory" at the present time in the literary departments in the United States must be sensitive to the fact that "deconstructive" criticism at least, whether of a de Manean or more Derridean variety, has nothing whatsoever to do with what one commonly calls "theory." For "theory" in the specific sense in which it is used in North American literary departments, corresponds neither to the philosophical nor to the scientific concept of theory.[2] It must, of course, be noted, that the literature department theoreticians do not pretend to address those cognitive processes that constitute the theoretical point of view in science or philosophy. In light of this disinterest in *episteme,* much of what has been leveled against theory simply misses the point. If one understands theory as do Steven Knapp and Walter Benn Michaels in *Against Theory* as a discourse that seeks to control the practice of literary interpretation by constructing a general account of interpretation, then what the critique of theory implicates can only be the mode in which methods and themes from diverse "scientific" discourses of the humanities—what the French call *sciences humaines*—have been applied to the discourse on literature. But, as Jonathan Culler has aptly remarked, "that excludes most of the writing that gets read as theory."[3] What insists it is or gets read as "theory" is, indeed, not very theoretical to the extent that it excludes epistemological concerns or conceptual reflection, both of which, by contrast, constitute what in France, and especially in the journal *Tel Quel,* came to be known as "theory." Theory, under this heading, aimed largely at achieving a degree of scientificity in literary studies similar to that to which structuralist linguistics or anthropology could lay claim. For these, but for other reasons as well, Derrida has argued not only that the term "theory" cannot be used to totalize the contemporary theoretical phenomenon, but that the phenomenon itself "cannot, does not, and must not want to claim the title of a science or a philosophy," in short, the very title of "theory."[4] Considering what theory *strictu sensu* means, to call the ventures in question "theoretical" would stabilize and domesticate what in them exceeds the theoretical, or, in Derrida's own words, the theoretical "jetty."[5] And yet the investment by the adherents of "theory" in the notion of "theory" cannot be ignored. It is, I hold, crucial. The very desire (and necessity) to practice a new approach to the literary text, one that is not pragmatic, thematic, moralizing, ideological, and so forth—a desire that is motivated by institutional reasons as much as by the nature of the text itself—has literally given rise to a theoretical cathexis. The theoretical movement in literary studies today is intimately linked with the effort to treat works of literature on their own terms, in light of the specific logic they display, rather than from extraliterary points of view. It is, therefore, most unlikely that the current "theoretical" challenge to the more traditional approaches in the field of literary studies could simply renounce the title of "theory."

Given the impossibility of subjecting what is called "theory" in the United States to any identity that would be gained by means of a totalizing, that is, theoretical glance, Derrida is right to say that "theory" in the United States is not *a* theory, but rather a "theoretical monster."[6] But it is, notwithstanding, a *theoretical* monster, that is to say, still theory. In spite of its monstrosity—a monstrosity that stems as much from a lack of rigor, an eclecticism or outright idiosyncrasy than from its opening up of a space of "ultra-disciplinary approaches, which, up to now, met nowhere, in no department, in no area of any discipline"[7]—its claim to be theory inevitably produces certain effects. The very pretension to be theory does unite and totalize the often very different directions that "theory" takes. It does also, despite contemporary theory's own lack of interest in epistemology, endow its diverse manifestations with a certain epistemological thrust. Indeed, by claiming to be "theory," and in particular Theory (theory with a capital T), the multiple theoretical discourses that have developed in literature departments are not simply indulging in an easily revocable misperception of their own undertaking. For this very claim also links them, knowingly or not, with a quite specific, even lofty, tradition—the movement of early German Romanticism.

In the following, I would like to explore this connection in some detail in the hope that it will shed a light on the nature of contemporary "theory," its "epistemological" ambitions and philosophical implications. However, before I turn to the early Romantics' conception of theory, I must evoke at least briefly, but with a particular emphasis, the first major formulation of theory as such in the history of Western thought. The theoretical attitude is of Greek origin. Anything that would call itself "theory" must confront what emerged in Greece as *theoria* in the fifth century B.C. The early Romantics, we shall see, measured themselves against that heritage. But the thesis that I would like to advance here is that contemporary (literary) theory, knowlingly or not, does so as well. Indeed, the thrust of this essay is to construe contemporary "theory" as an extreme recasting of *theoria*. If the "theoretical monster" that haunts departments of literature in the United States deserves our attention, it is precisely, and only, because of its extreme position. What then did the Greeks understand by *theoria*?

Traces of the idea of *theoria* can be found in Pythagoras. But it is with Plato's *Theaetetus* or *Philebos*, and in particular with Aristotle, that *theoria* effectively becomes a concept (almost) synonymous with philosophy. Let me note from the outset that the pristine religious connotations of the notion of *theoria* continue to shape the meaning of the term in philosophy. *Theoria* originally named both the festive embassy sent by the states to the holy games staged at the sacred places, the *theatron* on which the *theoi*, the gods, were celebrated under visible shapes, and the act itself of viewing the divine gods at these games.[8] With Plato and Aristotle, the notion of *theoria* becomes the spiritual contemplation characteristic of philosophy, the sort of contemplation that takes place for its own sake, detached from the immediate and bare necessities of life, and which, consequently, is *free*. As Joachim Ritter has argued, the fundamental reason that Plato and Aristotle called the philosopher's contemplation theoretical is that, essentially, it is the contemplation of the divine. As *theoria*, philosophy is primarily theology, and it is in the divine that philosophy finds its ground as a free knowing. What this means is that philosophy as a theoretical science does not have its ultimate foundation in the aims and concerns of humanity, but rather in the divine object of contemplation. Indeed, if philosophy as *theoria* has its purpose in itself, this purpose becomes exclusively the bringing into view of what is (the whole of nature as that which points toward God as its divine cause), and as it shows itself in itself, that is, without the interference of utilitarian purposes, this is because philosophical contemplation comes closest to the absolute vision that constitutes the divine itself. Aristotle goes so far as to suggest that theoretical contemplation has all the allures of being that are denied to man, that is, of a being that is the exclusive attribute of God alone. Ritter writes: "This belonging to God is fundamental for the Aristotelean meaning of theory. Aristotle determines theory as the kind of cognition that God has 'first and foremost' himself; in theory, God turns to the whole of the world and what is as the divine, as a consequence of which, Aristotle deduces and understands the essence of theoretical science from the essence of divine theory."[9] In other words, God is the first and most intensive realization of *theoria*. In *theoria*, as an *actus purus* of the spirit, God freely, that is, without any exterior end except the end of pure contemplation, looks at and enjoys himself in the pure bliss of absolute contemplation. Philosophical theory, undoubtedly, has this absolute vision for its ultimate object. Its possibility, however, is grounded in God's self-theorization. It is imperative to note with Ritter that this theological foundation of theory does not merely represent a historical doctrine of merely historical interest. Indeed, it would be easy to show that Western thought from Plotinus to Hegel consistently takes off from this high point of Aristotelean theology.[10] Following Ritter, this theological legitimation of theory is "the very ground that must be presupposed if free science as an aim in itself is to belong to human existence and to human culture."[11] Without such theological grounding, the autonomy of theory (and in the same breath, the idea of freedom) becomes impossible. Without it man slides back into a praxis dominated by the needs and necessities of his life as a natural being.

Keeping in mind the theological dimension both of *theoria* in its original sense and of the "theoretical" insofar as it constitutes the science of philosophy in general, I now proceed to evoke the specific concept of theory that is, I believe, the forerunner of the contemporary use of "theory" in literary criticism. Without denying that there are capital differences between them, I hold that without reference to Aristotle's theological notion of *theoria* as it is reformulated in early German Romanticism, in particular in the early writings of Friedrich Schlegel, it is hardly possible to understand what "theory" means today.

The early German Romantics' comprehensive discussion of the foundation of criticism, philology, and of literary studies in general, as well as the essentially comparative scope of their undertakings, produced the very concept of a science of literature of which certain trends in contemporary literary studies seem to represent the fulfilling realization. I cannot, of course, here retrace the phases of this complex genealogy. I must limit myself to delineating the concept of theory shared by both the early Romantics and the theoretical ambitions of that criticism currently en vogue, that, as Philippe Lacoue-Labarthe and Jean-Luc Nancy have asserted, "merely recall[s] and elaborate[s] in the contemporary context everything that was at stake in the Romantic idea of *criticism*."[12] And, as these authors emphasize at the beginning of their study, the type of investigation that takes place in literature today in which literature "devotes itself exclusively to the search for its own identity, taking with it all or part of philosophy and several sciences (curiously referred to as the *humanities*) and charting the space of what we now refer to . . . [calls itself after] a word of which the Romantics were particularly fond, as 'theory.' "[13] In their writings, indeed, "theory" is given an emphasis not unlike the one it receives nowadays. It is used in a substantive way, seemingly without any further qualification.

What, then, does Friedrich Schlegel say about Theory (with a capital T)? Theory, he writes, is "the piety (*Andacht*) of philosophers," "pure contemplation (*reine Anschauung*) of the divinity, calm and gay in silence. Spinoza is the ideal of the species."[14] Theory as a contemplation of divinity, that is, of the infinite, or the whole, is religious in essence.[15] In "Ideas," Schlegel writes: "every relation of man to the infinite is religion."[16] However, to correctly understand the sort of contemplation that constitutes theory according to Schlegel it is necessary to invoke *Athenaeum* Fragment Nr. 76. In German, it reads: "*Die intellektuale Anschaung is der kategorische Imperativ der Theorie,*" that is, "Intellectual intuition is the categorical imperative of any theory."[17] All theory, then, must yield to this necessary and absolute law of intellectual intuition. Yet to yield to the unconditional law of intellectual intuition, theory must think and perceive synthetically. It must make the whole, totality, all, its object. Not only that, the imperative in question also requires that theory itself be one, that it be *the* theory. Theory, for Schlegel, is relation to the whole in a mode of relating that is itself *ganzheitlich*, holistic, to the extent that its mode of cognition is that of the originary cognitive synthesis of intellectual perception. It fixes the whole, in a mode of perception that is at once sensible and intellectual (*sinnlich geistig zu schauen*).[18] This Schlegelian concept of theory seems thus to have all the attributes of the Aristotelean theological understanding of the term. Is there thus no difference between the theological concept of theory and Schlegel's celebration of the theoretical contemplation of the divine? My account of Schlegel's conception of theory would seem to support such a conclusion. Yet before making any hasty decision, let me present the following fragment from "Ideas": "The thinking of a religious person is etymological; it traces all concepts back to the original insight (*auf die ursprüngliche Anschauung*), to whatever is characteristic (*auf das Eigentümliche*)."[19] Religious thinking is theoretical thinking to the extent that it relates to the whole. It traces and leads all concepts, that is, all merely *intellectual* syntheses, back to their originary *intuition*, to the singular and empirical contingency of their first sensible beholding. This fragment, undoubtedly, confirms what we had established about intellectual intuition as being the categorical imperative of theory. But it also tells us decisively that this unitary approach of theory is achieved only as, or by means of, singularizing, individualizing concepts, or intellectual syntheses. Indeed, for Schlegel, theory achieves its aim of thinking the whole only in terms of the sensible. It brings the universal, the whole, into view in the shape of an individuality. At this point, I cite in full a fragment earlier referred to: "Every relation of man to the infinite is religion; that is, [of] man in the entire plenitude of his humanity. When a mathematician calculates what the infinitely great number is, that, of course, is not religion. The infinite conceived of in such plenitude is God."[20] In other words, only on condition that the human being who relates to the infinite is a whole, that is, both an intellectual and sensible human being—and that the infinite he or she relates to in the mode of thinking and presentation becomes "affected" by man's finite being—is there human contemplation and theorization to begin with. What this implies—and with this the essential difference between Aristotle's and Schlegel's concept of theory also becomes manifest—is that theory is in essence aesthetic. Aesthetic does not refer here to aestheticism, of course. Rather, as I hope to show hereafter, it is to be taken in the sense of a sensible presentation and, by the same token, historical realization of the infinite. For the early Romantics, theory, a notion traditionally linked to the representation of an unconditionally valid law, has thus also become "critique;" more precisely, it has become indissoluble from aesthetics in a broad sense. Rather than a sign of confusion, the Romantics' indiscriminate use of the terms "theory" and "critique" is intimately tied to their conception of an essential interrelatedness of universality and individuality, and the necessity to assess the adequacy of all individualization of the universal.

No wonder then that theory, for Friedrich Schlegel, is also, and primarily, aesthetics in the narrow sense of a philosophical foundation of the arts. Indeed, when Schlegel speaks of theory, theory without further specification, most of time he means "philosophical theory of poetry," "aesthetic theory," or "theory of genres" of poetry (29, 90). [21] Yet, as Schlegel's statements in "Dialogue on Poetry" on the theory of the novel demonstrate, in each case it is theory "in the original sense of the word: a spiritual contemplation [*geistige Anschauung*, i.e., an intuiting that is both sensible and spiritual] of the object in a tranquil, serenely whole state of mind as is, indeed, proper for the contemplation of the eminent play of divine images in festive joy." Moreover, what Schlegel advances in this context, namely that "such a theory of the novel would have to be itself a novel," holds true for the philosophical theory of poetry as a whole.[22] At the beginning of the "Dialogue on Poetry," Schlegel contends that "one cannot really speak of poetry except in the language of poetry" (474).[23] Let me also consider the following: "The law as such [*das reine Gesetz*] is empty," writes Friedrich Schlegel in the famous essay *On the Study of Greek Poetry*, and he continues: "In order that it be *fulfilled* and its actual application be possible, it requires an intuition [*Anschauung*] within which it visibly appears in harmonious completion [*in welcher es in gleichmässiger Vollständigkeit gleichsam sichbar erscheine*]—that is, an ultimate *aesthetic prototype* [*eines höchsten ästhetischen Urbildes*]" (47). It follows that for the Romantics, theory, or the contemplation of the divine, is intimately linked to presentation (*Darstellung*). Indeed, Romantic theory is inseparable from the question of the presentation of the law, the universal, the whole. It is an implicit recognition that the universal, totality, the One, can be thought only each time in a finite, more precisely, individual shape. As is now to be seen, Romantic theory, therefore, is not only necessarily aesthetic (in the broad sense of the term), but historical as well.

To elaborate on this double finitization of theory, I shall turn to an analysis of some aspects of Friedrich Schlegel's early essay *On the Study of Greek Poetry*.[24] In this essay, he argues that a theory of poetry is a recent arrival in the history of poetry. Greek poetry, for instance, was never determined by theoretical considerations. "The aesthetic development (*Bildung*) of the Greeks in Athens as well as in Alexandria," Schlegel remarks, "was never artificial in the sense that the understanding [*Verstand*] would have organized the entire mass, directed all the forces, determined the aim and direction of its course. On the contrary, Greek theory was not in any way associated with the practice of the artist" (66). Greek poetry, with its objectivity and beauty, is a function of natural *Bildung*, in other words, of a *Bildung* that concerns "the evolution of all humanity," rather than just one of its essential components (25). This natural *Bildung* takes effect, Schlegel adds, through "the laws of public taste" to which the individual artist yields without further mediation (86). However, the natural *Bildung* of a whole nation's humanity is only the result of "a vague longing" and an impure drive in whose legislating power "something alien is at work," an animal component (25–26). Although, the drive that guided the whole of Greek culture is "in fact, a powerful motivator [it is also] a blind leader," Schlegel concludes (26; see also 71). By contrast, Schlegel describes modern poetry as the result of artifical (*künstliche*) *Bildung*, in short, a *Bildung* that no longer rests on an undetermined longing, but that instead is a function of a determined purpose originating in understanding (*Verstand*) and its dominating concepts. With modern poetry emerges theory (24–26). In such a *Bildung*, which, unlike Greek natural *Bildung,* no longer fosters the development of mankind as a whole, but merely one among its essential parts—the intellectual faculties in particular—man is said to determine him- or herself after concepts of understanding. With their help, man brings order into the given material and determines the direction of his or her force. Since such an act of submitting to concepts is essentially a free act of the mind, the determining impulse of artificial *Bildung* has justly to be attributed to freedom. In sum, if artificial *Bildung* is the realm of theory, modern poetry shall depend as well on theory's legislating power. As Schlegel remarks: "The *legislative power* of the aesthetic development [*Bildung*] of the moderns . . . is already established. It is theory: for understanding was from the beginning the guiding principle of culturation [*Bildung*]" (46). But even though theory is the guiding principle of modern poetry, this does not mean that theory as it exists would already be a match for its task. Modern poetry stands under the legislating power of theory from the start, but theory, for Schlegel, is still a thing of the future. Theory, he claims, has not yet begun to realize "its great objective (*ihre grosse Bestimmung*)"—that is, its grand destination (28).

Modern poetry, according to Schlegel, lacks the objectivity and beauty of Greek poetry. What dominates modern poetry, on the contrary, is the characteristic and the interesting, in other words, "the presentation of the individual" (99). The interesting is what is new, and thus one sees modern poetry bound up in "the *restless, insatiable striving after something new; piquant, and striking* despite which, however, longing persists unappeased" (24). If only because of this obstinate concern with the interesting, modern poetry is in a state of what Schlegel calls "aesthetic anarchy" (21). Confusion reigns supreme as it conveys a sense of purposelessness and a total lack of binding rules. As the following passage reveals, in modern poetry all frontiers, all limits are confused: "Philosophy poeticizes and poetry philosophizes: history is treated as poetry and poetry is treated as history. Even the types of poetry exchange their definitions [*Bestimmung*]" (18). Considered as a whole, modern poetry reminds one of "an ocean of struggling, where the parts of the dissipated beauty, the fragments of shattered art, move confusedly through one another in a lugubrious mixture. One could call it a *chaos* of everything sublime, beautiful, and charming . . ." (21).

This utter confusion is precisely an outcome of modern poetry's concern with the interesting. Let me briefly address Schlegel's recasting of this crucial eighteenth-century concept of aesthetics.

The strict opposite to beautiful art—an art that is "the universal object of a disinterested pleasure," rooted as it is in "a free play without determined goal," and associated by Schlegel with Greek art—is *darstellende Kunst*, representational art (31). Representational art, for Schlegel, is an art involved with cognition, hence, an art that is philosophical. Such art presents individualities, he claims, that is, entities fully determined, consequently, fully *known*. It is, therefore, involved, primarily, with the characteristic and the interesting. If, indeed, modern art, as a representational art, caters to the faculty of understanding and is involved in cognizing processes, Schlegel, who here historicizes system-concepts of Kantian origin, is, of course, correct: artificial *Bildung* is theoretical. The achievement of representational art, the art of modernity, is nothing less than the presentation of "the individual and general, of conditioned and unconditioned knowledge [*Erkenntnisse*]," findings that are philosophically interesting (31). All of modern poetry, as its label "interesting" reveals, yields to concepts of understanding and is taken in by the theoretical. But even though the prevalence of concepts in modern poetry reveals, in contrast to the instinctive ordering of beautiful art in natural *Bildung*, that this poetry is an art of freedom, this art also suffers from anarchy. The wild chaos and the aesthetic anarchy that rules poetry's realm to such a degree that theory "appears to despair utterly of [finding] a *fixed point* in the endless flux," stems, precisely, from its theoretical bent (19). "Skepticism is the result of [modern poetry's] theory," Schlegel writes (20). But, at this juncture, it also becomes clear that the last word of theory has not yet been spoken. Theory must be set free from its concern with the interesting that has led to the anarchic scattering of poetry and concentrate instead on the whole of poetry. Its purpose must be to make sense of the profuse mess and to seek what modern poetry's manifold manifestations have in common. It must totalize poetry's appearances in order to determine the law of its progression and, with that, the "grand destination" of theory itself. In short, theory is not yet engaged in the theoretical gesture par excellence, the gesture of totalization. Since in *On the Study of Greek Poetry*, Schlegel sets out to do for modern poetry what Winckelmann had done for Greek art, namely to glimpse its interconnected and total shape, to bring order into the manifold of modern poetry is, undoubtedly, one realization of theory's essential and still outstanding task. But let me recall that this theory is to theorize poetic manifestations that are already theoretical *in nuce*. Theory is thus to theorize theory. It is to become a theory of theory. A couple of remarks may further clarify this Romantic conception of theory.

First, modern poetry wants an organizing theory because unlike Greek works, which blindly and instinctively realized public and universal taste, modern poetry yields from the start to man's freedom. Modern poetry is theoretical in essence, and thus requires that theory serve as its unifying principle. Only because modern poetry is already eminently theoretical can theory think its completion and set guidelines for its development toward that goal.

Second, the philosophical theory of poetry, the theory of modern poetry's representational art in all its manifold forms, must be a theory of modern poetry's representational mode. The grand destiny of theory is to theorize representation and to discover in this investigation the law that unifies all of its singular representations.

Third, if theory has a grand destination, it has of necessity a history. As we have seen, for Schlegel, theory is certainly a result of a history. But, theory itself also has a destiny. For as a theory of theory it must bring order into its manifestations and hence foster man's full self-determination or freedom. The fulfillment of this destiny, however, remains for the future. At the present time, Schlegel writes, theory is twofold: "It is, namely, in part a true reflection of modern taste, the distilled concept of an incorrect praxis, the rule of barbarism, and in part the commendable, constant striving for a universally valid science" (28). Restricted to the reproducing of the bad taste of the age, modern theory is "practical theory," "the spirit of an infelicitous history" (19). It looks for the purpose of art in stimulating charm (*Reiz*), correctness, or truth. Such a theory is static. The theory of theory, by contrast, strives in a continuous effort to realize, more precisely, to approximate, its grand destination, namely "universality—which is the object of all its efforts [*Strebens*]." In seeking universality, it strives as well toward achieving "the rank of a truly public power" in the modern age (28–29). Romantic theory is hence dynamic. It attempts to achieve its destiny in the temporal process of endless approximation that the notion of striving (*Streben*) demonstrates. It is thus historical in an essential way. This conclusion is obvious from Schlegel's comments on the three periods that characterize modern poetry and the role that theory plays in each one.

Modernity, Schlegel ascertains, has already passed through the first two of its three possible phases and "now it finds itself in the beginning of the third period" (88–89). While the theoretical instinct manifests itself during the first period in merely "pragmatic preliminary exercises" (90), in the second period theory becomes scientific, taking the shape of the dogmatic systems of rational and empirical aesthetics. However, the anarchy of individual manner, subjective theories, and the various imitations of the ancients trigger "the crisis of the transition from the second to the third period" (89), that is, from subjective to objective theory. Yet, according to Schlegel, objective theory has thus far been achieved only "*in isolated parts*" (89) of the whole of the *Bildung* that characterizes this last stage of modernity. What has already been achieved is, at best, "the brink of a great phase" (90). "*The time is ripe* for an important revolution in aesthetic development [*Bildung*]," Schlegel writes (89). Such a revolution of aesthetic *Bildung*, that is, of theory, would result in a "*thorough predominance of the objective over the entire mass*" of contemporary *Bildung* (91). With it, objective beauty would return at the hands of objective theory— a beauty that, Schlegel stresses, shall surpass that of Greek poetry if only because it will have been brought about in artificial *Bildung*, in other words, freely and willingly.

The final stage of modernity is thus to culminate in a public objectivity, in a universality of taste not unlike that which prevailed in Greece but with the significant difference that rather than being the product of an undetermined longing, it is brought about freely and in full consciousness. In the third stage of modernity, then, theory's grand destination, "universality— which is the object of all its efforts," is finally to take form. At the end of his essay, Schlegel announces that this great destination of objective theory and poetry is to be realized in Germany. What at first sight may look like a chauvinistic nationalism (and needless to say, is, to some extent), is, however, implicated in the Romantic notion of theory itself. As seen, for the Romantics the universal can only be realized (intuited, thought, or represented) in the finite shape of an individualizing representation. It follows, thus, that the great destination of poetry and objective theory can only be historically objectified in one singular nation, Germany, in this case. The theory and the beauty in question are not to be realized as such—for this would be a principial impossibility—but rather in the individual shape of one nation and in a form in which theory or beauty would only be approximated. But such an individualizing realization of universality is furthermore the most appropriate mode of its representation. Thanks to the approximate realization of universality to occur in the third and, in principle, the last period of artificial *Bildung*, the theoretical instinct and its striving remain unimpaired. This follows from the very object striven for, namely, universality.

I circle back to the question of the double finitization of theory spoken of earlier. Objective theory, Theory (with a capital T), is to accomplish "a complete transformation, the total reversal of a revolution" (45) of modern poetry, a transformation that is to foster a return of the objective and the beautiful. However, before theory will be capable of this task, it must fulfill certain requirements. Theory must first of all be objective itself, Schlegel remarks, and "in perfect and free agreement with itself," it must "provide its laws the most well-grounded reputation" (47). Only as a free science—free of all particular interest, and in a self-determined identity—can it achieve the objectivity of a "true public force" (47). But, as Schlegel notes, pure objective aesthetic theory is still "*empty*—just as experience would be confused, without sense or purpose" (47). "Pure Science," or theory, he continues, implicitly alluding to certain statements in Kant's First Critique, "only determines the organization of the experience, the pigeonholes for the contents of intuition" (47). In order to revolutionize the interesting, then, theory must fulfill a second requirement. "The law as such is empty. In order that it be *fulfilled* and its actual application be possible, it requires an intuition [*Anschauung*] within which it visibly appears in harmonious completion—that is, an ultimate *aesthetic prototype*," Schlegel writes (47). In short, if theory is to become objective, it must let itself be presented in a "*perfect intuition*" (47), an exemplary intuition, but an intuition first and foremost. Aesthetic *theory* must become *aesthetic* theory, that is, a theory that presents itself in a sensible fashion so as to be able to perform its task of revolutionizing the interesting. This theory must, indeed, combine concept and intuition. This is the reasoning behind Schlegel's and the Romantics' contention that a theory of modern poetry, a theory that expounds the theoretical already at the heart of modern poetry, must be a poetic theory, poetry itself. Without its presentation in aesthetic fashion it remains abstract, failing to accomplish what it is purported to achieve. Yet, such a theory, in itself poetic, that recaptures the beautiful for modernity and thus overcomes, overturns modern poetry, is a different genre from modern poetry itself. It corresponds to what Schlegel in *Fragments* shall call "a progressive, universal poetry," a poetry in becoming (*im Werden*).[25]

Theory, then, must be presented in an intuition, and such presentation, we are told, must also be exemplary. The intuition that theory requires in order to be theory *tout court* has to be a supreme aesthetic archetype. Significantly, Schlegel discovers such a perfect *aesthetic* intuition that would "be perfect [*vollkommen*] and legislative," in a "*perfect history*" (48, 47). More precisely, the aesthetic intuition required by theory is the intuition of a complete (positive) history of the aesthetic in the modern sense of art. Schlegel writes: "Science [or theory] needs the experience of an art that would be a completely perfect example of its type, art *kat'exochen*, whose exceptional history would be the *general natural history of art*" (47). Such a history of art par excellence would be the elemental and transcendental presentation of the pure law of art, an aesthetic presentation of that law without which theory could not hope to achieve the objectivity required for bringing about a revolution of modern poetry. Without such fulfillment by an archetypal history of art, the theory of art would remain empty, abstract, and without practical application.

Schlegel discovers this absolute history of art in which theory is to present itself in the "general natural history" of Greek art. Greek art, according to Schlegel, reached "the highest peak of ideality (the complete self-determination of art) and beauty that is possible in any natural culturation (*Bildung*) of any sort," during its Golden Age (48). What distinguishes Greek art, and makes it capable of becoming the complete and legislating intuition for the theory that is to revolutionize modernity, is that independently of sensibility or reason its concern is exclusively with "free art," the beautiful. And yet, in spite of the fact that it is nothing less than the history "of a nobler, purer humanity" (53), Greek art is *only* the universal *natural* history of art. In short, then, theory presents itself by dint of an intuition that is merely natural, an intuition of freedom that results from a blind force. It follows thus that the finitization of theory derives only in part from the need to present it aesthetically, by dint of the intuition of a complete history, but also from the fact that such an intuition is *only* the intuition of a natural, that is, instinctive and blind, realization of the concept of art. The specific discrepancy between the concept, or rather, the idea of art, and the exemplary yet only natural history of art that characterizes theory shows theory itself to be inhabited by an essential approximation and limit. Theory does not present itself as such; rather it finds its realization in necessarily limited figurations. It is not only finite, say, fragmentary, not only because it must present the universal, the whole, in an aesthetic and historical manner—as an individuality—but also because the intuition of the universal that serves to present it is only the intuition of a natural, that is limited, excellency of art.

In conclusion, I note that Schlegel's theory remains indebted to all the attributes that distinguished Aristotle's concept of theory as theological. But, unlike its Aristotelian determination, theory, like what it purports to theorize, has become an idea in the Kantian sense, realized only in a finite mode and in infinite approximation. Perhaps, at this point, one can understand what Schlegel meant when he claimed that intellectual intuition is the categorical imperative of all theory. The holistic glance of theory as well as the whole that it seeks to bring into view have indeed become *practical* concerns. No longer self-evident in a dogmatic sense, the synthetic mode of knowing and the divine totality to be beheld in the realm of phenomena have, for Schlegel, turned into ideas without which there cannot be any theory, but ideas that can always only be realized in finite form, as individualities, as fragments, and in a process of infinite, endless approximation.

At the beginning of this chapter, I suggested that the contemporary notion of theory as it dominates a certain type of literary criticism, in particular, rhetorical and tropological deconstruction, belongs to an already constituted tradition. But the reader may indeed wonder what the connection is, apart from the obvious fact that both speak of "theory" in an equally accented fashion. Undoubtedly, a significant shift has taken place between the Romantics of Jena and their understanding of theory and the way it is used by our contemporaries in the literary field. Despite their shared interest in theory itself, they seem to diverge entirely as far as the object of their theories is concerned. Indeed, theory today has for its object something that the Romantics may have anticipated, but that they vehemently barred from theoretical consideration. In both the Schlegel brothers' writings, and in Schiller as well, one finds, indeed, a rather forceful rejection of a position about art that is primarily interested in the parts and the matter of the work of art. The position in question, in Friedrich Schlegel's own terms, is that of the "critical anatomist," or the "passionate adherents of correctness" (75–76).[26] Although distinct from the contemporary critics'

roundly skeptical stance on the possibility of truth as adequation, and holding that the literary work is precisely a case in point, the critical approach
taken by the "adherents of correctness" to the artwork proceeds along lines
similar to those of the contemporary literary theoretician. Referring to
older French and English critics, but without naming anyone in particular,
Schlegel wonders whether the work of Gotthold Ephraim Lessing is not
at times reminiscent of that kind of criticism. In any event, the critical
anatomist focuses on what Schlegel calls the artwork's, the poem's, for
instance, *elementarische Masse*, that is, its elementary, unformed, shapeless
body of raw material, intending to extrapolate or calculate (*herausrechnen*)
"the presence of inner contradictions" (75). Yet, as Schlegel holds, this elementary raw material and the contradictions that it yields can only come
into view once "the critical anatomist destroys the beautiful organization
of a work of art" (75). But in this case, the "proudly reach[ed] conclusions"
of the critical effort in question are inessential, Schlegel remarks. He
writes: "Inner contradictions that *do not appear* do not harm the technical
truth; poetically they do not exist" (75). Even though Schlegel's reasoning
is clearly linked to a conception of the artwork as a sensible presentation of
an idea, it may well be valid for an appreciation of art that, though no
longer aesthetic in a strict sense, is still concerned with the singularity of
the work of art insofar as it is an artwork. Indeed, "everything that does not
appear is situated beyond the *horizon of aesthetics*," Schlegel concludes (76).
August Wilhelm Schlegel, for his part, in an attack aimed at "the calculating prosaic intelligence (*Verstand*)" of the critics in question, notes that
"improbability found only after a dissection, and that does not lie in the
area of representation itself," is *not* an improbability.[27] Concern with such
inner contradictions reveals, in Friedrich Schiller's words, a "responsiveness for the crude element." In *On the Aesthetic Education of Man*, he remarks that to argue for the formlessness of a work of art, "if it makes its
effect solely through its content," shows "evidence of a lack of form in the
observer," rather than in the work of art itself. And Schiller continues: "If
he is either too tense or too languid, if he is accustomed to read either with
his intellect alone or with his senses alone, he will get no further than the
parts even with the most felicitous whole, and no further than the matter
even with the most beautiful form. Being responsive only to the crude
element, he must first shatter the aesthetic organization of a work before
he finds enjoyment in it, and carefully disinter the particular qualities

which the master with infinite art has caused to vanish in the harmony of the whole."[28] This interest in the work of art that is not only a sign of "crude taste," Schiller ascertains, is not aesthetic to begin with. It is an interest either moral or solely *physical*.[29] Friedrich Schlegel echoes this verdict when he speaks of these critics' "physical experiments" with the manifold elements of a poem's raw material found after the destruction of its beautiful organization (75). The Romantics' concern with works of art is, by contrast, aesthetic. It is an interest in the sensible appearing of the idea or the whole, and requires, therefore, a kind of intuition that is sensible and intellectual at the same time. When they invoke theory they do not mean theory in the sense of a technical theory of art, as did some of their predecessors, such as Johann Georg Sulzer, Johann August Eberhard, Johann Joachim Eschenburg, and others.[30] In addition, by theory the Romantics certainly did not mean the exhibition of inner contradictions of artworks. Theory, for them, is primarily *theoria*, philosophy of art, or doctrine of the arts, that is, the theory of the (sensible) appearance of the whole.

By contrast, much of contemporary theory in North American literary departments aims precisely at bringing out literature's contradictions, antinomies, aporias of all sorts and on all imaginable levels, from the logical order to the materiality of the letter. The contradictions thus exhumed are said to interrupt, cancel out, or deconstruct what each of these levels individually purports to achieve—reference and meaning in the first instance. In other words, what the Romantics called insignificant, since it had no bearing on the aesthetic nature of a work of art, turns out to be the ultimate object of theory for the contemporary theoretician. This concern with the contradictions of the artwork marks a shift that clearly presupposes an approach to the work of art that is no longer aesthetic, but not, for that matter, physical or moral as the Romantics in the aftermath of Kant understood these terms. Undoubtedly, theory has become suspicious of art's claim to present and represent the idea of the whole in however fragmentary a fashion. If the sensible, traditionally associated with the empirical manifold, became for the Romantics the very possibility for the appearance of the Absolute in an enlivening individual shape, individualizing representation becomes for the new theoretician the very reason why all appearing of the Absolute is aborted from the start. Differently put, if Theory for the Romantics consisted in bringing together what refuses to come together—the Absolute and sensible appearing, the individual and the universal—"aporetic intensity," once a sign of the power of thinking and of the formidable problems that a thinker again and again must try to resolve, has now turned into a sign of failure.[31] If this is so, it is because for the theoreticians of literature, the sensible has undergone a transmutation. From what makes the Absolute real (*wirklich*) under the form of an individuality, that is, an intelligible sensible whole, the sensible has lost its ability to be permeated with intelligibility. It has become an opaque, crude element, the elementary, formless material of the signifier or textual web, so "singular" as to no longer allow for any "natural" (symbolic) or even conventional relation to an intended whole. Individualization, formerly a condition of possibility for the appearing of the beautiful whole, has now become the condition of impossibility for the Absolute to present itself.

The fundamental difference between Romantic theory and the theoretical phenomenon that has taken root in departments of literature, should not, however, make us overlook the equally fundamental continuity between the two conceptions of theory. The Romantics' emphasis on the individualizing power of the aesthetic as constitutive of the universal and the moderns' stress on the disruptive force of the materiality of the letter show them to partake in the same tradition. The same holds for their appreciation of the nature of the aporetic—the difference being only the success or the failure of philosophical thought in general, or more narrowly of the philosophical in the shape of a philosophy of art. But the new theorists' affiliation with the Romantics does not stop here.

Needless to say, if theory in the contemporary sense is to prolong the tradition that leads from Aristotle to the early Romantics, it too must be animated by a totalizing glance. Moreover, theory's glance must have a cognitive thrust of sorts. Yet, in view of both the anti-totalizing and anti-epistemological rhetoric that accompanies much of what is said in the name of theory in the literary fields, it might be difficult to make this point. Even though many theoretical approaches to literature seem to continue the New Criticist assumption about the self-referentiality and self-containment of the text and, hence, clearly attest to a desire for totalizing the object under investigation, other approaches under the heading of "theory" would seem radically to explode all philological, hermeneutical, or even New Criticist conception of the text. I think in particular of a theoretical approach to texts that, in the aftermath of Paul de Man's work has come to be known as *readings*.[32] Undoubtedly, on many occasions, these readings still proceed within the safeguards set by New Criticism. But in the more extreme and, that is, original readings, either the linkage of the semantic layers of one singular text to the material stratum of its language is shown to carry away in its wake the unifying power of meaning, or one particular text is shown to abyssally bottom out through its embeddedness in a web of chiasmatic referrals to and inversions of other texts. It is thus hardly possible to suspect these advocates of theory to contemplate, as did the Romantics, the whole as it appears in the inevitably individualizing and fragmentary realm of art or history. Even so, I would hold that the theory of reading is essentially, to varying degrees of course, a totalizing enterprise and, moreover, involved in cognitive processes even though, in de Man's words, they yield only "negative knowledge."[33] By seeking to demonstrate, sometimes with impressive virtuosity, that *all* elements of a text, or of a network of texts, stand in a bipolar relation to their respective opposites so as to cancel themselves out, the elements of a text, or set of texts mutually reading each other, present themselves as very particular wholes. Each text or textual element—whether linguistic, performative, or thematic—nudges the other, "*um eben dieser Entgegensetzung willen,*" as Hegel might have said, that is, merely for the sake of opposition, in the direction of a totality of reciprocally self-annulling elements. Yet the mode in which this process occurs is far from the Hegelian spirit according to which, in order to *become* what it is, everything "must first become an 'other' to its own self."[34] For in the case of contemporary theoretical readings, each entity is believed (more in a Platonic vein) to stand always already in a relation of opposition to its entirely other. Borrowing from the language of the Idealist philosophers, one might say that the text is explained in terms of a "thorough going mutual restriction, that is, reduction to nullity."[35] But although a text of this kind seems to climax in a complete devouring of everything and the abolishment of all result (in a movement reminiscent of negative dialectics), the text itself is not null. On the contrary, in giving priority to the relations of mutual restriction and cancellation rather than to what is nudged into relation, the text manifests itself as a totality, a dense whole of interlocked relations that cancel out what any isolated instance would purport to achieve. However abyssal, the wholes that are thus actively woven (rather than contemplated) in theoretical readings are wholes nonetheless, even if they achieve totality only by approximation. Infinitely bottoming out, these wholes, rather than dismantling totality itself, are in continuity with the Romantic problematic of the fragment as a mode of fulfillment or completion.

Now, although "theory" in the above sense constructs its wholes more often than not by bringing themes, motives, images, metaphors, or statements into relations of contradiction, this theory, at its best, its most radical, zeroes in on what the Romantics had called the work of art's elementary raw material. The wholes woven from the material and literal properties of language, from the merely mechanical rules of language as well as its performative acts, are wholes made up of thoroughly blind entities or instances, singular and arbitrary to the point of being meaningless in themselves. In this extreme calculation or experimentation performed on the raw material of a dissected artwork, the whole woven of the elements stripped of all signification, tends to collapse, or implode, into a single and singular point, so to speak. Indeed, if the different material levels of a text or work are arbitrary without exception, that is, without any natural or symbolic relation to what they are believed to mean or signify, then they become as much dispersed among one another even as they collapse for lack of interrelation. Yet, whether a whole in the form of a chaos of atoms or a black hole, this whole, with its sheer crudeness and formlessness, is said to stand in a binary relation of contradiction, and hence of annihilation, to the semantic stratum of a work. Since only arbitrariness is supposed to reign between the material, formless, mechanical substratum of an artwork and the meaning attributed to or imposed on it, the very lack of relation between the poles is interpreted to imply their mutual cancellation.

With this I return to the question of the continuity between theory in the current and the Romantic sense. If for the Romantics individuality was the very condition under which an otherwise ideal whole could appear and take on reality now the singularity of the crude element of the art work—the material whole of all presignifying elements that make up a work—enters into a relation of derealization with the idea of the whole. What "theory" shows is no longer the dependence of the whole on the beautiful, a dependence manifest in the form of manifold individualities, but on an absolute singularity, on the singular whole of the arbitrary elements and instances of language.[36] If for the Romantics the idea's dependence on aesthetic appearance leads to a fragmentation of the whole, for the contemporary theorist, the dependence of the whole on the material substratum of artworks ruins the idea of the whole altogether. Still, the very emphasis on the whole's relation to material singularity shows "theory" to be a variation of the Romantic conception of the work of art and its insight into the importance of the sensible and aesthetic for the becoming real of the ideal.

Throughout this chapter, I have stressed the theological dimension of theory from Aristotle to Schlegel. For Aristotle, *theoria* is, to quote *Metaphysics*, "the most divine science," divine in two ways: first, divine (*theia*) in the sense that it is the one that "would be most meet for God to have," and then divine in the sense that it is a "science that deals with divine objects."[37] For Schlegel, theory is contemplation of the divine in the beauty of its individual, or fragmentary representations. But what about the wholes woven by the contemporary literary critics? These wholes are formed of the material substratum of a work, a substratum that no longer lets itself be permeated by sense and whose extreme singularity makes all universality forever impossible. This effect derives from the pure materiality of the signifier and from the interconnections of the textual web that no longer have any (natural) or symbolic relation to an intended meaning. This is by needs an entirely arbitrary whole. But is this radical absence of a relation between the totality of a text and a possible meaning of it not indicative, precisely, of a *certain* divinity of that totality? Absence of all relation, total arbitrariness, is undoubtedly a qualification of the absent God, of the *deus absconditus* whose act of creation separates him infinitely, as the totally arbitrary positing power, from whatever he has given birth to. Thinking the absolutely singular—what is absolutely cut off from all universality and meaning—a task that characterizes in my view what contemporary theory is up to when at its best, is indeed a powerful reenactment of negative theology.[38]

If, then, there is continuity between the early German Romantic conception of theory and much of what happens today under the title of theory in literary studies—and not a superficial continuity, but one on a categorial level—it would be important to assess the accentuation and sharpening that the problem of individuality under form of the singular (and hence of representation) has taken in contemporary theory. It is a sharpening that is itself singular, so singular as to appear frivolous to many. Georg Lukacs, in the Preface to *Soul and Form*, analyzing the fate of the genre of the essay, in other words, of critique at the end of the nineteenth century, writes: "The problematic of the situation has become accentuated almost to the point of demanding a necessary frivolity of thought and expression, and this, for most critics, has become their life-mood."[39] Indeed, today as well, the frivolity of theory has become necessary. It is necessary, first, because it pursues a possibility that Romantic theory acknowledged, and that Schlegel tried to ward off when he declared inner contradictions to be insignificant to the work as an aesthetic whole. It remains of course to be seen whether theory today is simply a critique of aesthetic ideology or whether its anti-aesthetic stand also brings out an aspect of the work of art that traditional, and in particular Romantic aesthetics could not conceptualize. The frivolity of theory is necessary as well, as I have suggested by discussing contemporary theory in the history of its concept, because what is called theory today seems to be an inevitable consequence of the increasing concern with the problem of the (re)presentation of the universal. And finally, theory's frivolity is necessary because only by excessively pointing up and sharpening what has become problematic for it—the representation of the universal in an aesthetic form—can the limits of theory itself be constructively overcome. Theory, indeed, may no longer be an adequate "theoretical" response to what today we experience and understand by art.

7

Comparatively Theoretical

Compared to disciplines that study national literatures, the self-understanding of comparative literature has been highly volatile since its institutionalization early in the nineteenth century as a branch of learning in the university. Not that definitions of comparative literature have been hard to come by or that they have lacked clarity and rigor. The opposite has been true. Indeed, each of the various schools that emerged in each of the countries in which comparative literature had become an academic discipline formulated its own very definite concept of what this branch of learning comprised. Comparative literature was seen variously as the study of themes, motives, myths, or legends common either to a set or to literature as a whole, of their migration across national literatures, of the factual relationships between writers, of national illusions, and so forth. As a result of this national differentiation, manuals devoted to a presentation of comparative literature and its method must still break its idea down according to its different developments in different countries. But, as the history of the discipline shows, even within one national context, no unified understanding presides over its evolution. In the absence of such a unified conception, theories about the nature of comparative literature are thus in abundance. Yet, as if this plurality were not enough, a new way of thinking about the nature of comparative literature has lately arisen, especially in North America, which sees comparative literature as theory itself, not a theory, but theory period. As I shall argue in the following, this new definition is indeed not just one more theory. Rather, it is a conception whose eventual appearance was inevitable and which harbors, moreover, the possibility of understanding comparative literature in a more essential way, and thus also hints in the direction of its possible future.

René Wellek, in his review of the different trends in comparative literature up to the sixties, concludes that there is still no end in sight to the discipline's notorious crisis. Pointing to the factualism and historical relativism that, according to his analysis, make up most of what is called comparative literature, Wellek holds that the discipline "still has not been able to establish a distinct subject matter and a specific methodology."[1] Intent to lay to rest the dispute over what defines comparative literature, Wellek proposes a definition. This definition, some will undoubtedly argue, is just one more attempt, this time from the perspective of New Criticism and Russian formalism, to give meaning and substance to a field of research that in itself is hopelessly vague and malleable. But although Wellek's affiliations with the trends in literary theory just mentioned are not insignificant, it must first be noted that his definition of the discipline, task and method, follows from an appraisal of what is implied by the concept of comparative literature itself. Wellek writes that although "the method of comparison is not peculiar to comparative literature," and although it does not proceed by the method of comparison alone, but reproduces, analyzes, interprets, evokes, evaluates, and generalizes as well, it must first and foremost be understood from its comparatist orientation.[2] The fact, then, is that if it is to be comparative, as its title suggests, that all by itself contains the discipline's program, a program, as we shall see, with a very precise goal, methodology, thrust, and so forth. To delineate the implications of the title "comparative literature" is thus the urgent task upon which the possibility of a rigorous definition of this type of study of literature depends. That this is, indeed, Wellek's goal throughout all his essays on the subject is obvious from his inquiries into the history of the name and the concept of comparative literature. But that his analysis proceeds from the idea of comparison itself is, as we shall see, most evident in his understanding of comparative literature as the study of the universal foundations of all literature, which, like art and humanity, is fundamentally "one."[3]

Undoubtedly, some in academia would prefer that the quest for a definition of comparative literature remain inconclusive. If it is often accused of poaching in other territories, it is because it is seen to violate nothing less than the ownership rights of the institutions of the singular philologies to what they consider their sole property and heritage. It is thus in the interest of comparative literature as an institution to define itself, to resist conceptual vagueness and fragmentation by reflecting on what its own conception prescribes as a branch of study. It must overcome its crisis, come to know itself, and, in this manner, come into its own. Yet if the reflection on its concept begun by Wellek is crucial for the discipline to have a secure place in academia, such a reflection is even more important for comparative literature's own development and future potential.

Although considered by many as a new, and even intensified symptom of the crisis of comparative literature, "theory," I claim, answers the discipline's demand for an unshakable definition. If what J. Hillis Miller calls the "triumph of theory" in comparative literature (as well as in literary studies in general throughout North America) has indeed taken place,[4] it is not merely for local reasons. With comparative literature departments understanding themselves increasingly as departments of theory, the search for a self-definition of the discipline seems to have reached an end. In "theory," it has found both its method, subject matter, and the specificity of the kind and range of the claims that it seeks to make.

Yet, what justifies such a claim, one will ask? Is the still lingering influence of New Criticism, with its openness to theory in criticism, in departments of comparative literature (and English), as well as the impact of contemporary French thought on literary studies since the late sixties, not sufficient explanation for this turn to theory? What evidence suggests that there are more positive, that is, intrinsic, reasons that derive from comparative literature's comparative orientation that have caused the discipline to become more and more theoretical? And finally, on what grounds can one make the assertion that, with theory, comparative literature has finally found itself and overcome the crisis that has plagued it hitherto? These are the questions to which I shall begin sketching a response.

The poetology of early German Romanticism, it is said, and rightly so, anticipated many of the artistic values and devices that indeed have become dominant in modern and contemporary poetry and literature. Suffice it to mention the form of the fragment, self-reflection, *mise en abyme*, and irony, which find their first articulation with the early German Romantics. It is equally correct to claim that, notwithstanding the absence of a continuous history of influence of the early Romantics on the development of literary criticism and theory, early German Romanticism anticipated to a large extent the concepts dominant in twentieth-century and contemporary trends in literary criticism, the concept of criticism included. Further, it is also the case that early German Romanticism developed, in however embryonic form, the matrix of what, in the wake of Wellek's definition of it, we understand "today" by comparative literature. In what follows I will then try to show that the Schlegel brothers (but, undoubtedly, Novalis too) paved the way for the passage from comparative literature as the study of the universal foundations of all literature to its definition as "theory."

For reasons that will become clear hereafter, I shall frame my analysis of the turn to theory with a discussion of two passages from Gottfried Wilhelm Friedrich Hegel's *Aesthetics: Lectures on Fine Art*. The first is from the section on symbolic art. Toward the end of his elaborations on the symbolic art form, that is, on that sort of art in which the ideal is still in a relation of exteriority to the medium of its expression, which Hegel therefore characterizes as pre-art, he embarks on an analysis of what he terms the "conscious symbolism of the comparative art-form." This form of symbolic art is the final figure of symbolic art, and it follows upon the moments of "unconscious symbolism," and the "symbolism of the sublime," as the figure of the dissolution of symbolic art. Indeed, although this third realm of symbolic art based on conscious symbolism and comparison ought to be regarded "as a unification of the two previous stages, in that it comprises both the separation between meaning and external reality (which was the basis of the sublime) and also a concrete phenomenon's hinting at a related universal meaning (which we saw emerging in the symbol proper) . . . this unification is not a higher form of art at all but rather a clear but superficial (mode of) treatment which, limited in its content and more or less prosaic in its form, deserts the mysteriously fermenting depth of the symbol proper, and strays down from the height of sublimity into common consciousness," Hegel writes. And he concludes by saying that the symbolization that characterizes this final phase of the art form in question "remains a subordinate species."[5] Yet, what is the reason for such a derogatory evaluation of this terminal art form?

Let me first recall that the idea that gives rise to symbolic art is, as Hegel puts it in the "Introduction," itself "still in its indeterminacy and obscurity, or in bad and untrue determinacy" (76). Not yet fully determined, it is only the idea of the individualized, hence fully determined, idea that makes up true, that is, classical, art. Lacking adequation with itself, the idea in the sphere of symbolic art stands as well in a relation of inadequacy to the sensuous material in which it takes shape. In symbolic art, meaning and expression remain separate. Yet, although meaning or the universal "tower above individual reality" in this art form, their separation is not an absence of relation altogether. In the two moments preceding the comparative art form, meaning and expression stand indeed in "an essential and necessary kind" of relation. It is a relation of abstract determinedness in which the foreignness, or incommensurability of the idea with natural phenomena is made conscious. Expressing the idea of the idea, a negative relation must thus prevail between the abstract idea and natural objects in this sphere of art. In these first two forms of symbolic art "the two sides have [thus] not yet become external to one another in the strict sense of the word 'external.'" Yet the externality that, in spite of the however unfulfilled relation that persists in the non-correspondence between meaning and expression in symbolism, is implicit (*an sich*) in this art form must emerge as such, and express itself in a radical form. According to Hegel, this is what happens in the comparative art form. It is characterized by complete externality, and hence by a total lack of relation between the universal and its expression. In this final phase of the first sphere of art, meaning is "*expressly* posited as different from the external way in which it is represented," Hegel argues. Consequently, the mode of linkage of meaning and expression amounts here to not much more than "a more or less accidental concatenation produced by the subjective activity of the poet, by the immersion of his spirit in an external existent, by his wit and his invention in general" (378). Since, in this form of art, form and content are juxtaposed on the basis of an alleged similarity, or analogy between both, it is, following Hegel, comparative in nature. Yet, as he notes, the mere possibility of such concatenating similarity implies that the content of the comparative art form is no longer the Absolute. Indeed, with the Absolute becoming comparable to something other, it has become finite. The content of expiring symbolic art, therefore, is no longer "the Absolute, the one Lord," "but only some determinate and restricted meaning," with which "the sublime relation altogether disappears" (379). The comparative art form is thus not merely the final dissolving phase of symbolic art, but in it art ceases to exist as well.

Classical art, which follows upon the symbolic art form and which realizes the concept of art itself in that in it form and content enter into an adequate configuration, is itself superseded by Romantic art. In Romantic art, the free totality in which meaning and shape harmoniously related to one another dissolves again. Indeed, if, as Hegel holds, Romantic art be-gins with Christian art, the content of art and its medium of expression separate again. Since the content of art has now turned infinite and be-come absolute subjectivity, the true exteriority of that content cannot any longer be found in the sensuous shape of the human body in which the classical principle of art embodied itself, but in the absolute subjectivity's own spiritual medium alone. The principle of Romantic art therefore be-comes juxtaposed in this art form to sensuous and prosaic reality, thus an-ticipating its liberation from the medium of art altogether and its final sublation into philosophy. For all these reasons, Romantic art must be viewed as a return to symbolic art. In the "Introduction," after having de-scribed Romantic art in which inward feeling (*Innerlichkeit*) celebrates its triumph over the outer world (and which for this reason is still art), Hegel acknowledges that owing to this negative relation of the idea to outward-ness (which is not an absence of relation either), "the separation of Idea and shape, their indifference and inadequacy to each other, come to the fore again, as in symbolic art, but [since the idea is no longer indistinct and obscure] with this essential difference, that, in Romantic art, the Idea, the deficiency of which in the symbol brought with it deficiency of shape, now has to appear *perfected* in itself as spirit and heart. Because of this higher perfection it is not susceptible of an adequate union with the external, since its true reality and manifestation it can see and achieve only within itself " (81). What is more, the last and final phase, the one before art ex-pires as such and makes room for philosophy, corresponds in many regards to the ultimate phase of symbolic art just discussed. Indeed, in the last stages of Romantic art in which the implicit dissolution of the classical ideal manifests itself "clearly in fact as dissolution," an artform emerges not unlike the symbolic comparative art form, in which "the complete con-tingency and externality of the material which artistic activity grasps and shapes," prevails (549). In this last phase, art has become purely descrip-tive, or portraitlike through and through, yet, since this art emphasizes primarily the means of portraiture, it aims at the portrayal of the artist himself. "The artist's subjective conception and execution of the work of art, the aspect of the individual talent," is its true content (596). With "the stark subjectivity of the artist himself," or, "the productive artist," at the center of art, it has, according to Hegel, become an "art of caprice and humor" (600). Humor, indeed, characterizes Romantic art's last stages.

Yet, since the true humor "requires great depth and wealth of spirit in order to raise the purely subjective appearance into what is actually expressive, and to make what is substantial emerge out of contingency, out of mere motion" (602), art in this phase of art's expiration seems to have been abandoned by the spiritual wealth of the artist's personality. Although there are exceptions such as Theodor Gottlieb von Hippel and Lawrence Sterne, where humor that "consists in destroying and dissolving everything that proposes to make itself objective and win shape for itself in reality," or what seems already to have taken on shape in the external world, reveals a spiritual integrity of the artistic subject (601), in the majority of cases, this humor is mere subjective wit and expressive of a subject that in itself lacks the kernel and support of a mind filled with true objectivity (602). Although Hegel does not explicitly describe this final form of art as comparative art, in it form and content are likewise juxtaposed on the basis of similarity. As his elaborations on Jean Paul stress, such concatenation is a mere function of the artist's subjectivity, as had already been the case with art in the final stages of symbolism. In the same way as in conscious symbolism, the Absolute has fled this art too.

As should already be apparent, the final phase of Romantic art of which Hegel is speaking is the art of his time, in particular, German Romanticism. His descriptions fit especially well to what we know today under the title "early German Romanticism." And yet, with his emphasis on humor rather than on irony and wit, Hegel seems to clearly valorize the second generation of Romanticism, that of Jean Paul, in his characterization of the end of Romantic art and art in general. Owing to his allergy to Friedrich Schlegel and his denial of spiritual integrity to the latter, Jena Romanticism becomes eclipsed, and stripped even of the status of art. Still, to anyone less prejudiced it should be obvious that Hegel's characterization of the final stages of art exemplify early Romanticism. As proof, one would only have to refer to Friedrich Schlegel's statements about the subjectivity of the artist. However, for my purposes, I wish to make this point in a different manner. The last period of symbolic art—comparative art—distinguishes itself from all previous symbolic art forms through very specific artistic forms. These are, according to Hegel, the fable, parable, riddle, allegory, metaphor, image, and simile, to name a few. Yet these distinctly comparative art forms reemerge with early Romanticism, that is, according to Hegel's scheme, with the final stage of Romanticism in which the relating and connecting of material that has been gathered from the reality of all regions of the world leads back to symbolism where meaning and shape lie apart as well. These distinctive comparative forms return not only as the forms of the art of a fading Romantic art, but also, and in particular, as the "forms of reflection" on art (and literature).

Having expounded "the dissolution of the romantic form of art" in a chapter thus titled, Hegel adds still another chapter: "The End of the Romantic Form of Art." He writes: "Contrasted with the time in which the artist owing to his nationality and his period stands with the substance of his being within a specific world-view and its content and forms of portrayal, we find an altogether opposed view" characterizing contemporary art. Indeed, it is a view distinguished by reflection. With the reflective mode that in Hegel's eyes dominates the art of his time, the artist raises himself above the totality of the artistically consecrated forms and configurations of the past, with the effect that "no content, no form, is any longer immediately identical with inwardness, the nature, the unconscious substantial essence of the artist" (605). What then is the content of such self-reflective art? It is, Hegel holds, humanity, or the human in general. In reflective art, the *humanus* has become "the holy of holies." As "the appearance and activity of imperishable humanity in its many sided significance and endless all-round development," this art has thus a "universal" content (608). Yet, since the reflection that characterizes this final art form is rooted in the artist's self-inspection and withdrawal into self, its content is also entirely "contingent." Hegel sums up the diagnosis of this stage in which art returns to symbolism, more precisely to symbolism's comparative form, one that, moreover, has become reflective, by saying that what the artist expresses in this ultimate form of art in general, is "what is purely universal or quite accidental" (605). If this art based on reflection and universality is the final form of art, it is because in contradistinction to symbolism as pre-art, it is an art after art, the art of the end of art. With its emphasis on the "humanus," on what is "universally" human, this art has already deserted art in the sphere of art. It has turned not into philosophy but into Theory, into theory in anticipation of philosophy.

As is well known, early Romanticism not only sought to recover literary forms that Hegel had determined as the comparative art forms of symbolism, but it did so with the intent of raising art beyond all its distinct and canonical forms and genres as well. Their project is based on reflection, and its content is universal in thrust. This content is, as Benjamin has shown, the idea of art, art as the medium of reflection.[6] Although the Jena Romantics do not call their project one of comparative literature, they refer to it by the name of "theory"—theory of poetry, theory of the genres of poetry, aesthetic theory, and more often than not, simply, "Theory." What Hegel has thus described throughout his analyses of what constitutes the end forms of Romantic art, and art in general, coincides with the early Romantics' conception of an art that has art as its object. Moreover, they were also the originators of a new discipline about literature whose scope and method is comparative and whose aim is what is universal in humanity as well. Yet, rather than making broad statements, let me make my point in a more developed fashion.

What is the relation between early German Romanticism and comparative literature? Does the discipline not arise at a much later date, and without the direct influence of the early Romantics, even the enthusiastically received lectures of August Wilhelm and Friedrich Schlegel at the University of Vienna in 1808 and 1812, respectively? Comparative literature arises as a distinct discipline only later in the nineteenth century after the study of national literatures had been philologically secured[7] and in the face of their increasingly academic entrenchment, resuscitating the universalist understanding of literature that, from the Middle Ages to the end of the eighteenth century, had dominated the study of literature. Even so, the early Romantics' reflections on poetry and literature not only form a significant part of the prehistory of the discipline, they can in a certain way be said to have laid the foundations for the discipline as such. In the wake of Johann Gottfried Herder, and in resistance to the Enlightenment's universalist leveling of all cultural and national literatures, the early Romantics were certainly among the first to reemphasize the national heritage of literature in the form of the national languages and folk poetry, which they were among the first to systematically collect. But while fervently revalorizing national literatures against Enlightenment conceptions and rationalistic poetics, they conceived of all these singular literatures as partaking in one great orchestrated whole of poetry, for which Johann Wolfgang Goethe had coined the term "world literature." According to Friedrich Schlegel, for instance, literature is "a great, completely coherent and evenly organized whole, comprehending in its unity many worlds of art and itself forming a peculiar work of art."[8] While it is undoubtedly the case that the Romantics' reflections on literature did not have a direct influence on the establishment of comparative literature as a discipline—indeed after

Friedrich Schlegel's death in 1829, Hegelian and later, positivistic conceptions prevailed in the German and French universities—the poetics and comparative ventures of the early Romantics represent the cradle of the developments that have shaped what many now, and in particular in North America, understand by comparative literature, from the emergence around 1870 of the hermeneutically oriented *Geisteswissenschaften*, and the subsequent rediscovery of the period of the *Athenaeum*, to contemporary concerns in a variety of comparative literature departments. Indeed, if Wellek can claim that the Romantics' concept of literature "seems to me still true and meaningful in spite of the deficiencies of their information, the limitations of their taste, and the bias of their nationalism,"[9] it is not merely because this concept is rooted in a comparative approach to literature that transcends national and linguistic boundaries, but especially because the early Romantic comparative approach to literature realized the exigencies implicit to the very idea of a "comparative" study of literature in the first place. The thesis, then, that I would like to advance here is that the Jena Romantics developed the matrix for a science of literature (*Literaturwissenschaft*), which, although remaining largely at a programmatic stage, puts to work in a most rigorous manner the comparative method that flows from the concept of comparison itself. What then does the idea of comparison bring with it?

The notion of comparison has its origin in the ancient sciences. Yet, whether the comparative method first emerged in Aristotelian biology, as Wilhelm Dilthey holds, or according to Karl Reinhardt, in Posidonian geography is of little concern here.[10] But, what is of interest for what follows is that only with the introduction of comparative concepts into the natural sciences can one begin to speak of them as "sciences" at all. In contradistinction to merely classificatory concepts, comparative concepts are, indeed, as far as their informative content is concerned, richer and consequently much more flexible in their formulation of scientific laws. If classificatory concepts serve to attribute a property to an object, comparative ones say something about the relation of one thing to another. They provide information about the degree to which a thing possesses a property as compared to another. As Nelly Tsouyopoulos has demonstrated, by introducing comparative concepts to account for motion, Aristotle, in *Physics*, was able to formulate a law that represents the first attempt in the history of science of scientifically treating the kinetic nature of movement.

Considering Aristotle's otherwise overwhelmingly classificatory approach to objects of nature, this law of motion is, according to Tsouyopoulos, the sole example of scientificity in the latter's work. She writes: "systems that have not been able to produce such [comparative] concepts . . . have faltered in general in the development of science."[11] Yet, we ask, how does comparison achieve such scientificity in the humanities (*Geisteswissenschaften*), in particular in a science of literature with a general and comparative scope? Putting aside an intriguing limit to the comparatist project pointed out by Ernest Robert Curtius, namely that if the quantity of the material (historical facts, for instance, for history-writing) becomes too vast, the comparative method loses its scientific potential and must make room for a fictionalizing and poeticizing technique,[12] let us remark that the comparability of different literary works, or different national literatures, implies an alikeness of what is to be compared and, hence, an identity under which they are to be subsumed. Through comparison, to cite Hegel, a purification of the material "from its crudity and barbarity" is achieved in that with it the connections and relations between works of art, or singular literatures comes into view, the whole of which signifies "the growth of the universality of thought." As a mode of reflection, comparison invests its material with formal or "*abstract universality*."[13] The whole of the relations and connections that emerges in a comparison of works of art, or singular literatures, is not only the subject matter particular to the method of comparison alone, it also has a status of its own. On it, and not on philological accuracy or any other positivistic criteria, hinges the scientificity of the comparative method in the study of literature.

For the early Romantics, this universal object that arises through comparison has two facets. From the comparatist vista, from its totalizing and universalizing perspective, the differences between individual works become negligible compared to what they have in common, *in specie*—either the human or the poetic substratum, the temporal and logical unfolding of which accounts for the manifold of national literatures, periods, or the structure of individual works. The object of comparative studies for the Jena Romantics, whether of the order of the human or the poetic substratum, is hence as much a historical as a systematic one. The historical and systematic studies of literature thus emerge as two complementary types of comparison in the comparative ventures of the early Romantics. I shall discuss the first type by taking off from August Wilhelm Schlegel's influential *Vorlesungen über dramatische Kunst und Literatur* (but could as well have begun with Friedrich Schlegel's essay *On the Study of Greek Poetry*, to which August Wilhelm owes indeed a great deal).

August Wilhelm Schlegel starts off his lectures, which are to embrace the whole development from Greek dramatic art to Schiller and Goethe, with a reflection on the methodological and critical principles that guide his presentation. His aim is to "combine the theory of dramatic art with its history." As we are told, a general philosophical theory of poetry and all other arts establishes the fundamental laws of the beautiful. It is a theory that proceeds from an analysis of the human being's ability to experience beauty and to take pleasure in it. Important for the thinker, such a theory, however, is not a sufficient guide in the creation of art, Schlegel notes. A more narrow kind of theory is required for that purpose. Yet this theory, useful to the artist, is not attractive "to those friends of art who only want to enjoy the productions of exquisite minds." The theory in question is one of a particular art, and its aim is "to teach the limits, difficulties and means of a particular art." In seeking to combine the theory of dramatic art with its history, Schlegel seems to conceive theory as merely the theory of a particular art. Still, this theory, concerned "with the rules and models of that [particular] art," combines as well with general theory's elaborations on the beautiful. Schlegel consequently holds that "the *history* of fine arts tells us what has been achieved, the *theory* what should be achieved." The theory of dramatic art is prescriptive. It contains the rules according to which a specific art such as drama should proceed in order to yield to the universal laws of the beautiful in general. Theory and history are thus two entirely different things, and it is hard to see how they could be combined. Indeed, "they remain separate and inadequate unless a connecting central element (*Mittelglied*) is found," Schlegel contends. This element between theory and history is critique. He writes: "It is critique that illuminates the history of the arts, and renders their theory fruitful. Comparison and judgement of given productions of the human mind must furnish the conditions required for the formation of specific and significant works of art."[14] For Schlegel, then, comparison is an essential characteristic of critique, which itself permits the combination of theory and history in a presentation of the developments of a singular art form. Yet, what does the concept and the practice of comparison imply for Schlegel? A comparison of art works presupposes, first, that "each one is great and worthy of being marvelled at in its own way although each one is, and should be, something entirely different." In other words, comparability entails identity in difference, that is, equality of value of what is distinct. Comparison thus makes it possible to distinguish a common substratum of the variegated works of art. Now, says Schlegel, although "in its foundation human nature is simple . . . there is no fundamental force in the whole of nature that would be so simple as to prevent self-division, and not separate into opposite directions. The whole play of living movement is based on agreement and opposition. Why would this phenomenon not repeat itself on a grander scale in the history of mankind?"[15] What follows from this is that a comparatist critique of art works is necessarily historical. Its historicity, moreover, is based on a principle of opposition and contradiction. An identical subject matter, a substratum of formal, that is, simple, universality divides into opposite moments whose main titles in the history of art are those of the "ancients" and "moderns." However, their comparison, as sketched out by Schlegel in his lectures, is not without a constant reference to their common ground and is intended to bring this ground into relief. Finally, comparison of artworks rests on what Schlegel terms "the universality of the genuine critic."[16] Such a critic must be able "to block out his personal predilections and blind habits in order to transpose himself into the singularities of other peoples and ages, and to experience them from their center as it were."[17] In short, for August Wilhelm Schlegel, comparison of the individual works of art of various peoples and ages weaves a whole of relations in which the universal substratum of art in general, or rather, of the dramatic genre, articulates itself in a historical manner, that is, according to a logic of opposition.

But critique based on comparison is not limited to establishing the formal and universal substrate of a manifold of works of art. Comparison also serves to bring into view the inner unity, that is, the whole of relations that makes up an individual artwork. Friedrich Schlegel uses the term "comparison" in this sense. In *Literary Notebooks 1797–1801*, Schlegel remarks: "Critique is in principle nothing else than a comparison of the spirit and the letter of a work that is being treated as something *infinite*, absolute, and as an individual."[18] Or: "a critique compares a work with its own ideal."[19] What Schlegel means by "letter" and "spirit" would require a careful analysis of all the respective references in the *Notebooks*. For our purposes, the following aphorism must serve as an indication: "The letter of each work is poetry, the spirit philosophy."[20] A critique of a particular work, then, aims at bringing its unity into view. As a whole of connections, this unity emerges into light through a comparison between the letter of the work and its "*individual* ideal" (rather than general ideal), and this comparison also makes possible a critical judgment about that singular work.[21] Just as for August Wilhelm, critique has, for Friedrich Schlegel, a mediating role. It must combine the theory of the art of poetry, that is, the theory that deduces and determines the ideal of poetry, as well as the maxims for its production. Based on comparison, this kind of critique, however, establishes the common ground—the universal substratum—of both the letter and the spirit of only individual artworks. In addition, the whole of relations that such comparison exhibits as the makeup of individual works remains, despite its universality, couched in singularity. Rather than unfolding historically, it presents itself as an aesthetic individuality. Indeed, comparison is as necessarily aesthetical as it is historical. The Schlegel brothers merely formulated complementary facets of a critique for which comparison is the method.

Romantic criticism, founded on a comparison of the manifold aspects of its subject matter be they of the entirety of an art form or of the elements that make up an individual work of art and intending a historical or aesthetic presentation of the interconnections in question on both a formal and universal level, is an imminently theoretical enterprise. Indeed, theory proceeds by gathering the manifold in a totalizing glance achieved by exhibiting precisely what the elements of the manifold have in common and hence makes them comparable. That which a manifold of elements, above and beyond their obvious material differences, hold in common and which permits their unification is of the order of formal universality, also called the universally human by the early Romantics. It thus comes as no surprise that the Romantics, Friedrich Schlegel in particular, conceived of comparative criticism as theory and theory period, as do many today. My claim, then, is that "theory" in literary studies today, especially in comparative literature, is the fulfillment of what the early German Romantics had begun. With their conception of a criticism based on comparison, they developed a matrix for literary studies' increasing turn to the theoretical. I hold further that this turn has been inevitable given the comparative, or interdisciplinary, approach of the discipline in question, despite the fact that "theory" has taken on the allure of a discipline independent of literatures. Yet, such completion of the Romantic heritage in comparative literature's turn to theory, and the bringing to full fruition of the consequences and implications of the concept of 'comparative' literature, is nothing to be deplored. No new thematism or historicism can put this turn into question. Indeed, these reemerging trends are rarely so naive as to entirely exclude what they seek to challenge. The only thing that can bring the tendency to theory to a stop is the completion of the theoretical project itself. Such completion is achieved at the very moment the formal characteristics of "theory" have been fully spelled out. In the theoretical project's future closure, the limits of theory come into view, and with them a chance presents itself, perhaps, for a new and different approach in comparative literature. But it should also be clear that for comparative literature this cannot mean a return to factualism, thematism, or historicism, old or new.

If I have framed my discussion of the early Romantics' concept of comparative criticism, and thus also my answer to the question, what is comparative literature? by a presentation of Hegel's critique of the comparative art forms of symbolic and Romantic art, it is precisely because of Hegel's critical assessment and circumscription of the comparative method. Undoubtedly, Hegel's critical delimitation of the realm of comparison derives from the speculative thrust of his philosophy, and one ought to show (as, unfortunately, I cannot here) that it is Immanuel Kant's definition of comparison as a form of reflection, and as of the order of understanding (although it represents an exigency of reason), that compels Hegel to assume a critical position on comparison. Yet although Hegel's debate with the comparative nature of the art forms of symbolic and Romantic art is speculative, it is important here because, unlike the usual denunciations of comparative literature with which we are so familiar, it is not only largely free of affects (except, of course, for his invectives against Friedrich Schlegel), but also deals with the very presuppositions and characteristics of comparison as such, rather than with some of its epiphenomenal effects. It is certainly true that the speculative nature of the criticism of comparison, that is, Hegel's denunciation of its achievement as merely abstract, falling short of a concrete unity among the various arts and literatures, may arouse suspicion. But it remains a criticism that measures the comparative method up against its own concept and thus does at least minimal justice to it. It is thus that Hegel's treatment of the problematic of comparison has perhaps the potential to open up a limit other than that of the speculative.

Before returning to Hegel's specific objections to comparison, and his critical situating (and hence, limiting) of its method, we should recall that comparison is a reflective concept. Reflection (*reflexio*), according to the rationalist tradition from Christian Freiherr von Wolff through Alexander Gottfried Baumgarten and Kant, which significantly shaped early Romantic thought, is that activity of the mind through which one arrives at universal concepts. And reflection proceeds essentially through comparison. In comparing, my attention is directed on the representation of the whole. I either weigh the parts against one another in a whole (Baumgarten), or I hold my thoughts together in order to simultaneously represent the whole in all its parts (Georg Friedrich Meier).[22] As Alfred Baeumler has put it, the reflective concept for a manifold produced through comparison is "the universal in the form of totality."[23] It represents the unity with respect to which the elements of a manifold are comparable with one another. Yet, according to Hegel's elaborations in the Greater Logic, the reflective concept of comparison yields only a concept of the universal in the form of a whole that remains exterior to the compared elements. The reason that Hegel advances for this is that in the reflective comparison of two elements, these elements are not made to relate to one another, but only to a third term.[24] This third term, the concept of the whole, remains therefore abstract and alienated from the manifold that it is supposed to unite. In comparing, one merely computes a universal invariable that remains without a living relation to the manifold parts that it is supposed to embrace, and these parts, therefore, remain unconnected among one another as well, lacking systematic interconnection. In art, this absence of relation between the manifold and the universal in the form of totality is called symbolic, according to Hegel's terminology in *Aesthetics: Lectures on Fine Arts*. As we have seen, the similarity on the basis of which meaning and expression become juxtaposed in the symbolic artworks in the mode of the comparative art form is entirely accidental. But, as Hegel suggests, such contingent juxtaposition occurs as well in the recurrence of symbolic art in the last stages of Romantic art. If humanity becomes the universal content of the singular works of art, or if humanity is shown to unfold through the history of art or literature, then this universal content no longer has any intrinsic relation either to the works themselves in which it is expressed or to the history of the particular figure of spiritual activity that is poetry or the arts. The concept of the whole that a singular work expresses, or that unfolds through the history of the arts, remains, at the end of art, cut off from its base in the work of art.

Of comparative literature, Hegel would have probably said the same. Through comparison, it yields a concept of world history, or of a universal poetic substratum. But that is all it achieves. The individual works of art are not mediated by this universal, or the other way around. Comparative literature is therefore theoretical. It merely produces a concept that, although universal, does not make it concrete. In order to achieve a mediation between the universal and the individual works of art, in order thus to overcome the symbolic relation that holds between them and that appears as the crux of comparative literature, comparative literature, according to Hegel, would have to renounce its comparative method. It would have to become philosophy, speculative philosophy, more precisely.

Yet, is this imperative that theory raise itself to (speculative) philosophy the solution to the problems that haunt the discipline of comparative literature? Let us first remark that the definition that results from the eminently Socratean gesture of inquiry into what comparative literature is in general, like Hegel's solution to the mere formal and abstract nature of that concept, may strike many as unsatisfactory. Indeed, all talk of universality—formal or concrete—is considered offensive by many. Universality, totality, substratum, and the like are thought to suppress the real diversity of texts, and literatures, or at the very least impede access to the dynamic relations between the texts or literatures themselves. Yet, without universality, totality, or a common substratum, there is no similarity, or alikeness, hence, nothing to be compared. As Edmund Husserl has put it in *Logical Investigation*, "if one is not allowed to speak of the identity of the Species, of the respect in which there is 'alikeness,' talk of 'alikeness' loses its whole basis."[25] At first sight, it may be tempting to save comparative literature by replacing the intention to a Species with a reference to groups of only a few exact similars, or to groups made up contingently for a singular demonstration. But apart from the fact that such similarities, as well as the comparisons they might render possible, would only yield results of limited bearing, it is its inability to secure the individuality, singularity, or diversity of its subject matter that would be the downfall of this approach to comparative studies in literature. It is not enough merely to posit and insist on the diversity of texts or literatures among one another and within themselves. If diversity and singularity are to be constitutive marks of the texts or the literatures, they must be seized as such. Yet any securing of the individual, the singular, the diverse, presupposes nothing less than the identity of the Species. One cannot relativize universality without at the same time sacrificing the irreducibility of what is singular. The notion of a universal common substratum not only allows for the comparability of texts and literatures, but also renders possible any relation to the nonidentical, diverse, or singular that is able to recognize nonidentity as such, that is, as the irreducible mark proper of a singularity.[26] And yet, it must also be recognized that the universal has a suppressive function. Whether this is construed as abstractness, emptiness, ideality, power, imperialism, eurocentrism, or the like, what is at stake is the universal's appropriation or outright exclusion of the different, or the particular. One can, of course, always argue that such suppression of the particular by the universal is a function of the determined shape that this thought has assumed at specific historical junctures and that the time has come to embrace a more liberal, more open, more accommodating universal. But qua universal, even the most liberal universal remains reductive. Still, although no broader universal can ultimately resolve the universal's suppressive function (which is of course not to say that one should give up opening the universal's extension), all diversity, difference, singularity requires, for it to be intrinsically diverse, different, or singular, the identity of an ideal substratum. What does this mean for comparative literature, especially in its form as "theory"? Rather than attempting, and thus falling prey to, the seductive Hegelian option of turning theory into philosophy, that is, the attempt to mediate between those two contradictory exigencies, theory must maintain their contradiction as an "unsolvable" paradox. Comparative literature has a future only to the extent that it faces the tension between the universality that it must, for essential reasons, presuppose and seek to establish between individual artworks or national literature and the plurality or singularity of the works and literatures whose irreducible uniqueness is as much a function of an ideal Species as it is betrayed by it. The future of theory lies in the infinite negotiation of the contradictory demands of universality and singularity—the negotiation between world literature, or textuality, on the one hand, and, on the other, national literatures and all the ("regional") literatures that contest from within the priority of national literatures as well as that between the texts themselves and what in them is so singular as to evade classification.

As a conclusion, I wish to briefly take up Martin Heidegger's discussion, in his lectures in 1944–45, *Einleitung in die Philosophie. Denken und Dichten*, of what he calls "authentic comparison (*Das eigentliche Vergleichen*)." Although the comparative method enjoys a distinct privilege in human thinking, Heidegger wonders if we know what comparing is. In comparing two things, we assume in advance, and usually in indeterminate and confused fashion, that they have something in common. "But in comparing it is almost as if the sameness in question would only serve as the background against which to emphasize the difference," Heidegger notes.[27] Without reflecting on the sameness that the two things to be compared share, comparing amounts to nothing more than establishing an identity and a difference and thus becomes formally unlimited. Yet because of this sameness that is implicitly or explicitly acknowledged in comparing, "authentic comparison is always more than a comparing." As Heidegger remarks, "in genuine comparison we seek to catch sight of the different through the same, and through the different of what is identical, the specific nature (*das jeweils eigene Wesen*) of what is compared."[28] Authentic comparison, then, is a mode of thinking in which sameness serves first and foremost to bring the things to be compared into their own. Genuine comparisons are entirely directed to establishing the distinctness and peculiarity of what stands in a comparison. Yet rather than securing the individuality and singularity of the compared items in a merely general mode, it brings that singularity about in such a way that the circumstances of the comparison are honored in their contingency. The task of comparison is to establish the proper nature of what is compared as it obtains on the basis of the specific conditions in which the comparison takes place.

In short, then, if theory is to negotiate the contradictory demands of universality and singularity and do so without succumbing to the dialectical temptation of mediation, it must do so by realizing the unique singularity of what is compared both through comparison and a reflection on the sameness that it presupposes. Comparative theory harbors the possibility of passing beyond both mere formal universality and its speculative resolution and to thereby elicit and establish what each individual work, or each singular literature, is in its own right. Yet without reference to universality, or the identity of the species, theory cannot pledge such respect to the singular.

8

Theatrum Theoreticum

In 1826, Thomas Drummond's invention of limelight made it possible for theaters "to generate, in combination with concave mirrors, lighting 'effects'" which by sheer quantity of directed light surpassed the rather timid previous attempts at staged lighting found, for instance, in sixteenth- and seventeenth-century painting. With this he set the stage for opening up, in Hans Blumenberg's words, "new possibilities for an accentuating approach to vision, one that always takes as its point of departure the dark as *the 'natural' state*." "This manipulation is the result of a long process," he adds. The discovery that light could be manipulated and directed preceded the sometimes-violent development of technical devices that put this knowledge into practice. Indeed, as Blumenberg has shown, this discovery coincides with the origins of modernity, that is, of the conception that truth can only be methodologically secured. According to Blumenberg, the idea of method as it emerges with Bacon and Descartes rests on the presumption that phenomena lie in the dark and that only "a focused and measured ray of 'direct lighting'" aimed at them at a certain angle and from a certain perspective is capable of wresting their truth from them. The new concept of "seeing" manifested throughout modernity and at the heart of modern "theory" assumes, as its very foundation, that light is at the disposal of human beings, or that the modern subject is that light itself. Only the mastery of light can force the fetters of ignorance and pierce the darkness surrounding all things.[1]

Is it a coincidence if this conception of seeing and theory find in the realm of the theater the most powerful corollaries to their own central notions of "illumination" and magnification of sensory perception? Does theory, and the seeing that it implies, have a natural affinity, as it were, with the theatrical stage? To argue such a point might appear to be an arduous task. Given that theory is notorious for its concern with the immobile and the invariant, how could it entertain any relations worth our attention with a medium and an institution as fleeting and inessential as the theater? The Platonic reservations concerning the theater in the *Republic*, and elsewhere, have shaped philosophy's judgment of the theater up to J. L. Austin's description of stage recitation as a parasitic or nonserious use of language. Accordingly, the theater appears to be one of philosophical theory's others. It must seek to radically distinguish itself from, and must have no traffic with, the theater. Undoubtedly, it has been precisely the theater's otherness, its fleeting and transient nature, which appealed to those thinkers in the sixties and early seventies in France, who, seeking to overthrow metaphysics through an inversion of Platonism, discovered "the theater of thinking." I think of Gilles Deleuze, in particular, but also Michel Foucault. As Foucault writes in "Theatrum Philosophicum," a review article of two of Deleuze's books, philosophy must no longer be understood as thought, "but as theater: as a mime theater with multiple scenes that are fleeting and instantaneous, and where gestures, without being seen, make signs to one another."[2] But by merely exchanging the defining characteristics of theater and theory, the question concerning a possible intrinsic relation between them remains as improbable as before.[3] Nevertheless, if it should prove possible, if not necessary, to link theory and theater, the questions of representation and artificial redoubling, of spatial and temporal situatedness and of narrativity would seem to bear on theory and to have a much less superficial or extraneous relation to it than is commonly assumed. Indeed, if the theater is an other of theory, from which it needs to rigorously demarcate itself in order to secure a specificity of its own, the trace of the theater must inhabit theory's innermost core. To evoke, then, the theater in regard to theory suggests that theory occurs on some stage, that it has a plot, that it takes on a worldly appearance in which it shows itself to spectators, and so forth. But although theory, no doubt, has to do with seeing, it is still far from clear at this point why it requires a theatrical apparatus, or to be seen in the first place.

The near homophony of theory and theater is certainly not accidental. As is well established, the two terms derive from the same root: the Greek notion of *thea*, spectacle, contemplation. Still, however suggestive such etymologies are, they cannot serve—lest one indulges in a substantialist metaphysics of etymology, or a naive *Begriffsplatonismus*—to affirm some intrinsic relation between theory and theater. Rather, if we are to establish any intimate rapport between them, their difference about which theory has been quite eloquent should not be effaced by simply assigning them a common ground. Further, and just as importantly, the recourse to a common root does not itself provide one with a sense of the specific material ways in which theory and theater may be entangled. Besides the allure of the etymological shortcut, all attempts to clarify the relation between theory and theater face a set of what I wish to call strictly necessary temptations. These are the temptations of theory itself, possibilities to whose enticement theory must respond if it is to be what it is. By extension, these temptations belong to any effort to theoretically establish the relation between theater and theory. We can and must ask: In the event that, independently of their origin in a common root, theory and theater are drawn together, is it because theory must take on visible, tangible shape? Is the theater theory's inevitable aesthetic complement? Does theoretical vision require that vision take place within a theatrical space, that is, within a space in which that which is seen stages its own appearance? And in which seeing is thus necessarily a kind of spectatorship of that which exposes itself to its gaze? Finally, could it be that the theater as a locus of visualization and offering to view is precisely that space in which the theoretical gaze seeks to see what it looks like, what its looks look like, in short, to see itself? Is the theater mainly the setting and the event in which theory can find an answer to itself? However necessary these questions may be, they also tend to submit the space of theater to the theoretical, and hence to blur again their difference. Still, only by asking these questions can the theater be seen to make, perhaps, a difference with respect to theory.

In the following I intend to discuss these issues with reference to Blumenberg's *Das Lachen der Thrakerin: Eine Urgeschichte der Theorie*.[4] Blumenberg construes the story of Thales as recounted in the *Theaetetus* as the archetypal illustration of the antique ideal of *theoria*. In this archeology of theory, Blumenberg investigates the transformations, deformations, and extensions of this single anecdote throughout the history of the West.

Before I take up this anecdote itself, and especially its status as an archetype of theory, some very brief remarks concerning the "theoretical" (or philosophical) underpinnings of Blumenberg's own investigation are certainly in order. For his study of the various transformations that the anecdote has undergone, Blumenberg borrows the notion of a history of reception from Hans Robert Jauss, although he uses it in a sense more suited to his own purposes and at one further remove from what Hans-Georg Gadamer has termed "effective history." Through the analysis of the history of reception of the anecdote, Blumenberg seeks to establish what theory is about. In the entry "Theory" from *Begriffe in Geschichten*, we are told that "one can learn more through intuition and free variation, which brings the hard core of the meaning of a concept into view. One can assume that the history of 'theory' has already accomplished a good deal of free variation-work. All that remains to be done is to look at the model."[5] This is precisely the task Blumenberg has set for himself in *Das Lachen der Thrakerin*. In contrast to effective history, which "unfolds the potential of an originary invention unattainable in itself, and which is actualized in always new expressions [or turns]" (89), a history of reception is primarily concerned with the structural "frame for positions (*Stellenrahmen*)" within the originary configuration of the anecdote, which can be infinitely reshuffled or recast (108). From the perspective of a history of reception, "the anecdote [of Thales] becomes endowed with the function of standing for something that could never ever be exhausted either by itself [that is to say, the anecdote], nor by its reception" (108). Consequently, it is not so much the anecdote *itself* that is of interest in a history of reception, however originary it may be, but, more essentially, the anecdote's "imaginative (*imaginatives*) potential, one that anticipates deformations, and even the recasting of its stock figures" (109). Compared to effective history, in which continuity (tradition) is a function of the repeated innovative actualization of an identical semantic nucleus (of what Gadamer calls *die Sache*), a history of reception, as understood by Blumenberg, is discontinuous, a function of an identical model, pattern, or scheme (*Muster*, or *Typus*) whose nodal points, or positions, can be infinitely recast. For a theory of reception, the anecdote in question is important in that it, in Blumenberg's own words, literally "prefigures," in exemplary fashion, "a model that one cannot shake off in a history of theory" (45). This attentiveness to the structural elements in the model that the Thales anecdote illustrates (though it is only one possible, however exemplary, version of it) allows the history of reception to focus on the discontinuity in the variations of the model, rather than on the continuity of the tradition that all effective history presupposes, even (or especially) when the latter laments the alienation from the tradition. In a reception theory, the aim is not to "diagnose in the disturbed gaze (*in dem befremdeten Blick*) upon theory something like a preliminary stage of the alienated gaze of theory itself" (44–45), Blumenberg explains. This history of the reception of the Thales anecdote is not simply discontinuous; however, a meticulous analysis of all the deformations (*Verformungen*), distortions (*Entstellungen*), dissemblances (*Verstellungen*), perversions (*Verkehrungen*), and reversals (*Umkehrungen*) of the anecdote would be required to make out the internal logic according to which the history of its reception unfolds.

Since I do not propose to carry out this analysis but merely to maintain that a logic does support Blumenberg's exposition of the anecdote's historical variations, I will limit myself to calling up his discussion, toward the end of his study, of Martin Heidegger's interpretation of Thales' story. Occurring against the backdrop of a destruction of the history of metaphysics, Heidegger's treatment of the anecdote is, according to Blumenberg, a reversal (*Umkehrung*). Rather than interpreting the philosopher's fall as an essential consequence of the philosopher's neglect of the life-world, Heidegger, Blumenberg argues, interprets it as the very criterion of philosophical thinking (and in this continues a way of looking at the anecdote that began with Friedrich Nietzsche). The fall into the well is not a sign of the philosopher's shortcomings or of his inevitable downfall but a testimony to the superiority of philosophical thought. The servant maid's laughter reveals not only total incomprehension but also intrinsically lacks any critical bearing whatsoever. Heidegger can thus interpret it as an all out vindication of philosophy rather than as a critical voice from the life-world. Without further lingering on specifics, let me only mention that with this reversal, Heidegger, for Blumenberg, has not only cut all ties to modernity and the Enlightenment and severed philosophical thought from the horizon of the life-world, but he has, especially, freed philosophical thought, or theory, from the need to seek "agreement and consensus" (158). Although Blumenberg does not conceptualize this reversal as an alienation from the history of the reception of the anecdote, Heidegger's treatment of the anecdote seems to suggest the endpoint of a development in which the imaginative potential of the anecdote, and along with it the potential of a structural grid of intelligibility in the history of ideas and concepts, has come to an end.[6] Implicitly, this reversal in the interpretation of the anecdote also amounts to an end of theory, the end, thus, of what Blumenberg, in the wake of Edmund Husserl, continues to understand as the unifying telos of European culture.

Although the anecdote in question can be retraced back to one of Aesop's fables, only, as Blumenberg persuasively argues, in the Platonic reconfiguration of that story are the anonymous Aesopean protagonists of the fable identified in such a way that the original *epimythion*, or moral, of the anecdote fits the philosopher and theoretician, making it into the successful archetype of theory. The anecdote as told by Socrates in the *Theaetetus* only takes two sentences. It is "the story of the Thracian maidservant who exercised her wit at the expense of Thales, when he was looking up to study the stars and tumbled down a well. She scoffed at him for being so eager to know what was happening in the sky that he could not see what lay at his feet."[7] The context in which the anecdote is evoked, and which I will take up in moment, leaves no doubt that in fact not Thales, but Socrates, is the real referent of the story. Yet even so, it is not by happenstance that Plato has recourse to Aesop's fable about the astronomer and the well. As Plato holds in *Timaeus*, philosophy derives from the contemplation of the heavens and is the greatest good that "ever was or will be given by the gods to mortal man." Indeed, for the Greeks, star-gazing amounts to contemplating "the courses of intelligence in the heaven." The cyclical revolutions of the planets in the nightly skies, reveals to the astronomer the unperturbed, lasting, and steady presence of the gods. And philosophy, or *theoria*, which is first and foremost the sight of that which remains unchanged—the divine—contemplates those courses of intelligence in the heavens, according to Plato, in order "to apply to the courses of our own intelligence which are akin to them . . . and that we, learning them and partaking of the natural truth of reason, might imitate the absolutely unerring courses of God and regulate our own vagaries."[8] Thales of Miletus' prediction of the total solar eclipse in A.D. 585, which provided the Greeks with a spectacular demonstration of the effectiveness of theory, makes him, therefore, the proto-theoretician, or proto-philosopher. What befalls him befalls as well Socrates, the philosopher, and by extension philosophy and theory in general. Concern with theory in the shape of

Thales' astronomy only exposes the theoretician to mockery of his oblivion to the lower realities under his nose, his helplessness, clumsiness, and constant embarrassment by situations in the real world. His lack of realism, in short, draws the laughter of the uncomprehending yet very pragmatic and down to earth maid. But the projection of the anecdote upon the Platonic Socrates brings out something else: the true source of the onlooker's laughter in the mistrust, contempt, and eventually the hatred of theory on the part of the onlooking community. As Blumenberg remarks, "in the two centuries since Thales, it became clearer what was actually so ridiculous about theory. Precisely because Socrates abandoned the interest in nature which had dominated his youth and turned to questions concerning human action and life, it became clear that the spatial distance and unattainability of the objects of the starry heaven, compared to the proximity of the pitfalls of practical existence, did not constitute the strangeness of the theoretician, but was only a representation of it" (16). Indeed, the way the philosopher applies himself to issues of practical life shows him to be even more alienated from life and the point of view of his contemporaries than when he deals with the philosophy of nature. Socrates says in the *Theaetetus* that "whoever gives his life to philosophy . . . is unaware what his next-door neighbor is doing, hardly knows, indeed, whether the creature is a man at all; he spends all his pains on the question, what is man, and what powers and properties distinguish such a nature from another."[9] Blumenberg remarks, as if responding to this statement: "The philosopher of the Socratic type, in busying himself, and because he busies himself, with the essence of the human being, does not recognize the human being in the neighbor" (17). Like the astronomer, Socrates' aim is also to achieve wisdom and excellence. By determining the question of virtue in terms of knowledge, however, the philosopher sets a trap for himself. The very generality of the problem of how the knowledge is possible on which virtue is to rest drives him, in Blumenberg's words, "away again from the proximity of human things that he had sought by turning away from the phenomena of nature" (23). As a result, the object of theory, and its gaze—the true reality—rather than being sought in the sublunar realm of the human world, is located beyond everything that can be sensibly experienced, indeed, beyond the stars that punctuate the night sky (29). Riveted on the ideas in an intelligible *topos ouranios*, the philosopher not only looks stranger than ever; he now also shows himself to be an asocial being, disdainful of the human being's daily, practical concerns, and inattentive towards the polis and its citizens' political activities and obligations.[10] At this point, theory no longer provokes the laughter of a simplistic, though realistic maid, but, as Socrates' tragic end demonstrates, the distrust, and even hatred of the community. The confrontation between theory and (in Blumenberg's Husserlian terminology), the life-world in general, has taken a form that transcends the implications of the anecdote. In fact, the story of Socrates is the first variation on the encounter between the protophilosopher and the Thracian maid who witnesses his fall into a well, that is to say, the first variation on "the most lasting prefiguration of all the tensions and mis-understandings between the life-world and theory" (11). This variation (even more than its Aesopean predecessor or original) has determined the-ory's inexorable history, a history whose different phases are made up by the innumerable variations, transformations, deformations, and reversals, of the anecdote.

But what has this history of the archetype of theory to do with the theater or theatricality? If one were to assume that the title of the dialogue in which the anecdote is narrated would permit a clue, one would certainly be mistaken. The name "Theaetetus," according to Liddel and Scott, means "obtained from God," and thus derives from another root than "theater." Yet, if the title of the dialogue offers no clue, could the dialogue itself contain hints at an intrinsic relation of theory to the theater? Barbara Herrnstein Smith has pointed out that as a text about philosophical instruction—one in which the young Theaetetus, by witnessing the self-refutation of the doctrines to which he adheres, is delivered to a better understanding of the nature of knowledge—the *Theaetetus* stands out by its theatricality. She writes: "The archetypal, exemplary self-refutation, is, of course, dramatically scripted, and theatricality remains central to its re-productions. The dramatis personae are certainly among the most com-pelling in cultural history: the callow, showy, scoffing, hubristic truth-denier; the seasoned, gently ironic, ultimately martyred truth-deliverer; plus, as crucial parties to the scene, the mixed chorus of disciples and occasional interlocutors and, not insignificantly, the audience itself, motley representatives of the community at large."[11] Unquestionably, a certain theatricality promotes the search for truth, especially when the search has a pedagogical aim. But does this already indicate any deeper connection of the theoretical to the theater? After all, theatricality could here be understood as merely instrumental to the learning of theory, as something that helps to carry it out, but ultimately remains exterior to it. By contrast, I would like to inquire whether there is an essential link between theory *itself* and the theater. Does theory always, and necessarily, require to be staged? Must it always perform in front of spectators?

In order to further elaborate on this last question, I return to Blumenberg's *Das Lachen der Thrakerin*. What is this archeology of theory, if not the history of the different ways in which theory shows itself on the basis of the permutations that one visual archetype, the anecdote of Thales and the Thracian maid, makes possible. Theory, Blumenberg notes, is "something that one does not see. Although the theoretical attitude consists in actions that submit to intentional rules and lead to complexes of propositions in rule-governed connections, these actions are only visible on their exterior, and under the form of their 'performances, or proceedings (*Verrichtungen*).' To someone who has not been initiated into their intentionality, and who perhaps does not even suspect that these acts are a specimen of 'theory,' they must remain enigmatic, and may look offensive, or even ridiculous" (9). The seeing performed by theoreticians is not itself visible, but the acts that they must perform for the purpose of theorizing can be seen. To the spectator, theory offers the sight of its doings. It comes into an appearance by way of the acts of seeing, and these acts offer the sight of an exotic ritual. According to Blumenberg, the anecdote about the Milesian astronomer/philosopher and the Thracian maid is the first figuration (*Verbildlichung*) of theory, in other words, the archetypal image in which it shows itself to a spectator. The archetype of theory proposes as "the configuration of theory" a "scene," in a theatrical sense, that is "archaic" both in the sense that it is originary and ancient (116). In its originary figuration, theory shows itself on stage for a spectator. Blumenberg describes the anecdote as "the Milesian primal scene of theory" (120). The story of Thales is thus the première of theory, its opening night, as it were. Moreover, the spectacle that it offers on this occasion is a comedy. Thales, the type of the ancient theoretician, "the ancestor of the modern manufacturer of the product 'theory' " (1), is a comical figure. But as Diogenes Laertius reports, Thales' last fall was fatal. Blumenberg therefore concludes that "with theory the possibility of tragedy is also posited" (39). If this is not an accidental possibility, it is precisely because theory shows itself theatrically. Already in the first variation of the archetypal scene—that is, in its Platonic reconfiguration—the comedy at the edge of the well is replaced by the tragedy before the people's court, where the collision of worlds and concepts of reality, and their mutual incomprehensibility becomes deadly (14). In *Das Lachen der Thrakerin*, Blumenberg takes the position of a historian contemplating the "view(s) offered by theory of its own distance—in terms of worlds and times—from the *imago* of its beginning" (11). Like on a stage, in fact, these different scenes in which theory makes a show of itself parade before him, before Blumenberg, the spectator, while he, equipped with the theoretician's gaze, looks at what remains constant, in spite of all the transformations of all these sights, until, in the end, he makes the curtain fall when he is faced with a variation of the sight of theory, that, it would seem, has done away with theatricality, hence with theory, altogether. Still, one needs to keep in mind that the transformative potential of the anecdote is in principle infinite. Heidegger's reversal of it, therefore, may merely signify a provisional end of theory. Indeed, the question to be asked is whether the staged reversal, which eliminates the theatricality of theory, does not only presuppose (*ordine inverso*) the theater of theory, but is itself inherently theatrical as well. In any event, Blumenberg's archeology of theory, as a history of scenes in which theory offers itself to view, suggests a much deeper internal connection of theory and theater than is commonly assumed. One is even led to surmise that this whole archeology rests on the presupposition of a theater of theory, in other words, on the assumption that the theater has a constitutive role in the theoretical.

Because he distinguishes between the intentionality of theory and its subsequent scenic manifestations, Blumenberg could be seen to relegate the theatrical elements of theory to a merely superficial sphere, to make them seem mere theatrics. But although theory's intentionality cannot become visible itself, and for all to see, theory cannot avoid showing something of itself. Indeed, it must come into an appearance, offer a view of itself, give itself to be seen. In order to theorize, the theoreticians must perform certain acts, the chores of theory, as it were. If theory's intentionality cannot avoid appearing, one must infer some internal necessity for giving itself to see. Asking why theory must, precisely, show itself theatrically, or why it must make a spectacle of itself, perhaps makes it possible to clarify the necessity in question. Blumenberg distinguishes between the intentionality of theory and theory's doings. With this he hints already at an explanation as to why theory, as long as it remains theory, inescapably offers not only a view of itself, but one that is made up of gestures. Theory has the character of an act. To achieve what it intends, it must perform. Further, by appearing, and taking on an appearance, it necessarily appears to a spectator. In sum, if theory must take on a worldly appearance, one can assume that becoming seen, rather than remaining invisible, is essential to it. As Blumenberg demonstrates when he assesses Heidegger's reversal of the Thales anecdote theory by cutting all ties to the life world not only renders itself invisible again but thereby also sacrifices (or escapes) its ability to foster agreement and consensus (or dissent). As I hope to show hereafter, theoretical vision must become visible in order to accomplish what it strives for.

Theory achieves visibility in a theater of sorts, but it is not clear at all why the theoretician's doings and the spectator's observation of them are elements of a theater to begin with. What is it about theory that causes it to manifest itself scenically, on stage? The sight of the protophilosopher is the sight of one who stares at the heavens, rather than at what is at his feet. According to Blumenberg, "for the Thracian maid who observes the Milesian walking at night in this inappropriate manner, it is possible to surmise that she has caught him in worshiping his gods. In that case he did well to fall, since his gods were the wrong gods" (12). But whether or not his gods are the right ones, does the protophilosopher's bearing not derive precisely from him setting his eyes on the divine? Blumenberg reminds us of something the Greeks knew very well, that the divine produces incomprehensible behavior (12). Could it possibly be that, because theory sets itself the goal of viewing the divine, it cannot but offer a sight of itself that is fundamentally theatrical?

In the prospect of a possible answer to this question, I turn to an examination of the context of the story of Thales and the Thracian maid and of its precise role in the *Theaetetus*. In this dialogue Socrates engineers the self-refutation of three different determinations of knowledge directly after Theodorus has effusively praised Theaetetus, describing him not only as remarkably talented, but also as having a quaint physical resemblance (*homoios*) to Socrates himself. Socrates carries out the refutation in a dialogue before an audience, then, under the pretext of studying his own appearance as it is supposedly manifested in Theaetetus' performance. Theodorus is not a painter but, aside from being an expert in geometry,

calculation, music, and the liberal arts, he is, significantly enough, an astronomer. Socrates holds that Theodorus, in speaking of their resemblance, could only have noticed a similarity of the mind, rather than a
physical likeness between the two. Therefore, and in order to gain certitude
about such a similarity, Socrates invites Theaetetus to perform for him,
and to give him a display of what he is capable of (*soi men epideiknunai*),
while he will watch, contemplate, examine him (*emoi de skopeisthai*).[12]
Although the verb *skopeo*, to behold or contemplate, is generally used only
with respect to particulars, rather than to universals, for whose contemplation *theoreo* is the verb more commonly used, it is nonetheless clear that
with this the whole ensuing debate in the *Theaetetus* is set in a space of
visibility of performers and onlookers.[13] Since Socrates is not concerned
with physical likeness, this space, with its performers and onlookers, is certainly not a theatrical space in the ordinary sense, and yet resembles such
a space. In spite of Socrates' obvious irony concerning Theaetetus' alleged
similarity to him, Socrates' desire to test the young man's intellectual
abilities does not stem from an intention of reeducating him by refuting
sophistry. Rather, it concerns the philosopher himself, Socrates as a per-
sonification of theory. The philosopher wants to see himself, what he is
like, how he presents himself, and to what extent the figure he cuts corresponds to himself; theory wants to see itself, what it is like, how it appears,
and to what extent the appearance corresponds to its true nature. Here we
can begin to surmise a reason for theory's inextricable relation to the theatrical, which goes beyond, though it is related to, theory's preoccupation
with the divine. To be what it is and to secure this resemblance to itself,
theory must seek out the stage. Indeed, one may wish to ask why Socrates,
who rarely attended the theater, felt compelled to witness the mockery
that Aristophanes made of him in *The Clouds*.

It is a standard practice in hasty discussions of theory to recall that
the term derives from the Greek *thea*, seeing, looking at. But, particularly
when seeing is taken to be a mode of comportment in which one seizes an
object in the sense of taking power over it, such an explanation does not
do much to clarify the Greek sense of theory. To cite Gadamer, "*theoria*,
in its Greek sense, refers to observation, for example, of celestial constella-
tions, to being a spectator at, for example, a play, or a participant in a del-
egation to a sacred festival. It does not refer to a mere 'seeing' which
establishes what is present-at-hand or stores information. *Contemplatio*

does not linger with a determinable being, but in a region. *Theoria* is not so much the individual, momentary act as it is a comportment, a state and condition in which one holds oneself."[14] Even more significantly, the kind of vision specific to *theoria* in its Platonic sense—that is, *theoria* understood as knowledge (*episteme*)—carries the assumption that such seeing, or contemplation, is the highest and most perfect mode of cognition. Indeed, contemplation is the highest and most complete mode of knowledge because it maintains a relation to Being itself, to that which is originary, the ever present originary forms, in other words, the divine order of the world.[15] As a way of seeing, *theoria* derives its specificity from contemplative contact with the divine, from *theos*, even though the etymological root of *theoria* may be *thea*. Because of theory's prime concern with the divine, antiquity speculated already about *theoria*'s possible, though etymologically questionable, derivation from *theos*. Summing up the extensive philological research on the origin of the term, Hannelore Rausch distinguishes two main uses of the Greek word *theoria*. On the one hand, *theoria* refers to looking at, or watching in general, a meaning that permits *theoria* to refer to the phenomenon of the feast or festival. In this context *theoria* means spectacle, game, or theater; the viewing or watching of games, or spectacles; or, further, the sending of state-ambassadors to these festive events. On the other hand, *theoria* evokes the gaze of the mind, and, accordingly, signifies observation, speculation, intuition, contemplation, and so forth. The two meanings, Rausch notes, cannot easily be accounted for on the basis of one single etymon. According to most philologists, the Greek root *theoros* holds the greatest promise for unifying the two different series of meaning of *theoria*. Since the research into the notion of *theoros* has shown the impossibility of unequivocally deciding whether *theoros* derives from *thea*, sight, or looking, or from *theos*, god, this root *theos* must also be given due consideration in attempting to understand *theoria*.[16] In short, in attempting to come to grips with the meaning of *theoria*, and by extension, with the archetypal scene in which it shows itself in the *Theaetetus*, one cannot ignore this essential connection of the theoretical gaze to the divine. But how are *thea*, seeing, and *theos*, god, interrelated? To answer this question, a brief detour through the pre-philosophical and, as we will see, sacral meaning of *theoria*, is necessary.

Basing herself on Karl Kenrényi's interpretation of Greek religion as a religion of *Schau* (show, seeing), Rausch argues that a pre-philosophical interconnection between seeing and the divine is manifest in the Greek conception of the religious or sacred feast. The feast, she holds, is the spiritual occasion and place "in which the inner filiation of the two basic meanings of *theoros* that are under investigation, that of seeing and that of the divine, becomes clearly visible."[17] Following Kerényi, Rausch defines the religious festival as the moment at which the ever-present gods show themselves (in human form) and in which humans associate with the divine. The *theoroi*, the official envoys from the Greek city states, constituted the theoric delegations, the *theoriai*, that traveled to the great pan-Hellenic festivals. These envoys either performed an act of worship at the festive sites in their own name or participated in the feasts organized by their hosts as observers.[18] The *theoroi*, then, relate to the gods present at the festival. They partake of the divinity that takes on visible and determinate shape, figure, or form on the occasion of these sacred feasts in the capacity of spectators, in essence, by way of looking. Rausch, therefore, concludes: "For the Greeks, festivity and the point of view of the spectator are inextricably connected, and we now understand that in the Greek feast this situation of *thea*, of seeing, is always repeated as one in which the gods and the human beings come together."[19] Now for everything that concerns us here, it is important to emphasize that the chief place where this viewing takes place is the theater, whose name Plutarch conjectured—in a derivation that is doubtless extremely questionable, but nonetheless revealing—was, like *theorein*, taken from the *theoi*.[20] But the entire festive world also makes up a *theatron* in which the gods are both viewed and viewers themselves.[21] As Kerényi has remarked, the gods, too, "come festally, come as *theoroi*," to the festive shows, to be spectators of the holy games, dances, and other events.[22] Kerényi describes the fundamental situation of Greek religion as a "a reciprocal, active and passive, vision, a spectacle in which men are both viewers and viewed."[23] In the festive world, Greek religion found its accomplishment. When the gods take on visible shapes during the sacred festivals, they do so on stage, certainly, but they also participate in the festivities as divine onlookers. In the theater the seers are also seen, men and gods included. In the theater those who come to see the gods are the objects themselves of a divine gaze. Finally, considering that, in *The Peace*, Aristophanes brings the feast itself, personified as *theoria*, onto the stage, one can presume, that in this theater of *theorein*, the theater not only is a space of seeing and being seen, but that it is also the locus and the time in which theatrical space and time offers itself to view.

This pre-philosophical interconnection between seeing and the divine glance in the phenomenon of the sacred feast, still pervades the philosophical understanding of *theoria*. I mentioned the Platonic conception of *theoria* as a contemplation of the eternal, and divine, order of the world. One could as well evoke Aristotle, who derives the possibility of the highest science, the science concerned with the first causes and principles, from divine *theoria*, from god's own gazing at the world and at himself in joyful bliss. Yet, if *theoria* in the philosophical sense of contemplation implies a contact with the gods, it also reveals the sense of festivity characteristic of the pre-philosophical and sacral meaning of the term. It further follows from this prime concern of *theoria* with the divine that the world itself is like the festive world, in Rausch's words, "a *theatron*, a place of seeing for gods and men, and in which the philosopher accomplishes, in the face of god, that of which the human being is capable."[24] Yet, it is also a fact that for the Greek philosophers the human capacity in relation to the divine is limited, and that, furthermore, the divine is no longer present for them in the way it had been in pre-philosophical Greece. We must therefore assume that theoretical vision's approximation of divine vision has intrinsic limits. These limits will certainly affect theory's theatricality, but they will not abolish it. On the contrary, they will, as we shall see, endow theory with a new sense of the theatrical, a theatricality so pervasive that it will affect the nature of its glance.

For the time being, however, let me linger a while longer on the close link between theory and theater. I will do this by taking up the attempt made by Jacques Taminiaux, for instance, to critically unseat the philosophical privilege that Plato has accorded to the *bios theoretikos*. So far we have seen theatricality to have been the intrinsic medium in which theoretical contemplation of the divine order takes place. In order to resist theory's contemplative thrust in view of cementing the practical nature of theory, Taminiaux, too, must, significantly enough, stress the intimate connection of *theoria* to the phenomenon of the theater. Thus in *The Thracian Maid and the Professional Thinker: Arendt and Heidegger*, while opposing, along with Hannah Arendt, the Aristotelian conception of the *bios politikos* to the *bios theoretikos*, Taminiaux recalls that the *bios politikos* originates in the pre-philosophical meaning of *theoria* as being related to the theater. He writes: "Before the Platonic invention of *bios theoretikos*, the only *theoria* corresponding to the isonomic city consisted in the gaze of the spectators at the theater: the spectators attending a performance could cast their gaze upon human affairs not in order to detach themselves from the world of appearing so as to reach a higher region of contemplation but rather in order to find the means [in the sense of *phronesis*] of judging in the company of others, at the heart of plurality."[25] Practical life, a life in which thinking is secondary, and the pursuit of immortality in the public domain are governed by "another *theoria* than that of the philosophers absorbed in the contemplation of *physis*," Taminiaux remarks.[26] Since this *theoria*, according to Taminiaux, is "the tragic *theoria* echoed by Aristotle in his *Poetics*" and ultimately reaches back to "the prepolitical experience of action recounted in the Homeric legends—legends which inspired the playwrights of the tragic theater," it owes no less to the theater than theoretical contemplation does.[27] But the *theoria* of the philosopher, Taminiaux concludes, is only a metamorphosis of the originary glance that the spectators cast at the theater over the much more fragile reality of human life. Whether recourse is made to the pre-philosophical meaning of *theoria* to allow one to argue that theory's intrinsic relation to the theater determines it as the contemplation of a transcendent, and solidly unchanging, order, or whether it allows one to argue that the connection to the theater proves theory's deep affinity to the unstable realm of human affairs, *theoria* clearly cannot be thought without the theater. Both interpretations of the role of the theater for theory contain the assumption that theory is impossible without a lighted space in which showing and seeing can occur.

In modernity theory directs a focused beam of light upon objects under investigation in order to dissipate the darkness that surrounds it, and the lighting effects in the theater made possible by the invention of calcium light highlights this conception of theory. By contrast, Blumenberg reminds us, *theoria* rests on the Greek assumption that brightness fills the cosmos like a medium, that everything is already in the light and hence offers itself to a gaze to be seen.[28] The world is a theater because light is everywhere. Everything shows itself (by itself), and the natural attitude of the protagonists—gods and human beings both—consists in the contemplation, in theoretical bliss, of the appearing that accrues to them. The birth of modern theory, by contrast, is contemporaneous with the transition (as analyzed by Richard Alewyn) of the worldly parade, the *trionfo*, which during the Middle Ages and the early Renaissance took place under the open sky, in the unlimited public space of the streets, followed by fireworks of a magnitude that turned the night into the day, into the closed space of the theater hall, a transition that takes place at the end of the Renaissance.[29] The modern theater is surrounded by darkness, and one only sees what is in the spotlight, in the coerced optics owing to a directed beam of illuminating light.

At all times, both in the ancient and the modern conception of theory, an intimate connection between theory and theater obtains. From everything we have established so far, the theatricality of theory is tied to the seeing that characterizes it. But is this theatricality of a theory of the divine exhausted by the festivity that comes with the contact of gazes, in which those who see are seen? This question is all the more important since for Plato, and the Greek philosophers as a whole, the divine no longer enjoys the immediate presence that it had previously. With theophany no longer a self-evident given, the theatricality of philosophical *theoria* can no more presuppose the immediacy of seeing and being seen achieved in the festival. In what sense then must we conceive of the relation between theater and theory in philosophical *theoria*? To understand the theatricality of philosophical theory, let us first inquire into how the gazes that constitute theory are structured such that they may be said to have a theatrical dimension. More precisely, what is it that puts theater into this theater of gazes? With these questions, I return to the *Theaetetus*.

The inquiry into whether wisdom is related to the good or the useful is interrupted with a digression upon the kind of speech that distinguishes philosophical investigations. After having remarked that "one theory after another is coming upon us . . . and [that] the last is [always] more important than the one before," Socrates returns to the question of resemblance raised at the beginning of the dialogue by inquiring into what those men who spend their time in philosophical studies look like. Testimony to the strict inner logic of the dialogue (and perhaps also to a much tighter connection with the ongoing argument than some scholars have tended to believe), this question conjures up the sight that the philosopher offers to an assembly of men of law. It is natural, Socrates holds, that philosophers "should look ridiculous when they appear as speakers in a court of law."[30] What distinguishes the philosopher from the orators in court is, first, his freedom from his own discourses. As Theodoros remarks, "we are not the servants of the argument, which stand and wait for the moment when we choose to pursue this or that topic to a conclusion. We are not in a court under the judge's eye, nor in the theater with an audience to criticize our philosophical evolutions."[31] In contrast to those "men who have knocked about from their youth up in law courts and such places"[32] and who are slaves to their speeches, the philosopher is free, for example, to interrupt his argument and digress. Unlike the orators or the poets, the philosopher, it would seem, does not perform for an audience. The philosophers' doings are not addressed to spectators (and their expectations). Not only that, "from their youth up they have never known the way to market place or law court or Council Chamber or any other place of public assembly."[33] The philosopher does not perform for a court, or theatrical audience in the strict sense, but only for a select assembly of thinkers and disciples, where, in the *Theaetetus*, a young, and promising disciple can display his intellectual abilities before Socrates. In such a display, however, the philosopher cannot avoid making a show of himself, a show, in fact, that has all the characteristics of a theater play. As the anecdote about Thales and his maid makes plain, the philosopher makes a fool of himself during this performance. But he does so even more "on a public occasion or in private company, in a law court or anywhere else . . . [when] he is forced to talk about what lies at his feet or is before his eyes. [Then] the whole rabble will join the maidservants in laughing at him, as from inexperience he walks blindly and stumbles into every pitfall."[34] Resembling none of his fellowmen, the theoretician, consequently, offers the spectacle of one who is quite different, who is, indeed, other. His oddness derives from the fact that in addition to performing for those who like him seek the truth, he is a player on still another scene, this time, with other, non-human, spectators. As Socrates explains, only the philosopher's body "sojourns in his city, while his thought, disdaining all such things as worthless, takes wing, as Pindar says, 'beyond the sky, beneath the earth,' searching the heavens and measuring the plains, everywhere seeking the true nature of everything as a whole, never sinking to what lies close at hand."[35] Keeping his "eyes fixed on the whole," or thinking "of the earth as a whole,"[36] the philosopher, according to Socrates, "take(s) flight from this world to the other, and that means becoming like (*homoiosis*) the divine so far as we can."[37] The theoretician not only seeks to contemplate the divine. His act consists in emulating the way of looking that pertains to the gods, hence, of playing their role for them to view on the stage of this world. With them in sight, and performing under their glance, the theoretician, or philosopher perfects righteousness through knowledge—a knowledge based in seeing—nothing being "more like the divine." The theater of theory, though played on several scenes, is suspended from this glance of the divine onlookers. Its very theatricality, in a sense still to be specified, lies in the encounter, or, rather, non-encounter, as we will see, of seeing and being seen.

Seeing, whether by the theoretician, the gods, or the public, requires the medium of visibility, but that alone does not yet make seeing necessarily theatrical. A certain theatricality, however, comes already into play where the brightness of light allows things to present themselves to a gaze, in other words, to stage themselves for an observer. Yet, as soon as this observer, in turn, becomes seen, and even steps forth into the light to be beheld, seeing becomes theatrical. Seeing's theatricality is clearly a function of seeing being seen, of a play between the gazes that suggests no limit. Seeing, here, is seen abysmally, without end in sight. But with the agent of the theoretical glance offering a view not only to spectators such as the Thracian maids, or even other philosophers and disciples, but to the gods whom he has made the object of his contemplation, theoretical vision aims at bringing the infinite exchange of the gazes to a stop, and, thus, at neutralizing the theatrical space of theory. The divine look at the theoretician should, indeed, bring the infinity of perspectives to a halt. But even this dream of theory does not do without some theater.

Through the anecdote about Thales and the servant maid, theory, or philosophy, first stages its own worldly insignificance. It makes itself look silly. Against the backstage of this first play, theory stages itself for the disciples of theory, and, ultimately, in order to become the object of the "redeeming" glance of the gods. The theoretician's glance seeks out the sight of the gods, whose divine *theoria* he emulates. He needs divine onlookers not merely so that someone may witness his emulation of the gods but, ultimately, so that he may see himself in their gaze, so that he may witness his own emulation of the god's vision. As seen, *theoria* is *homoiosis theo*. The philosopher, because he is trying to resemble the gods who see him seeing, also emulates their vision of himself. As a result, theoretical vision hopes to see itself by itself. Under the eyes of the gods, it thereby hopes to see itself independently of the divine audience whose embracing gaze at itself it makes its own. Here it becomes evident why theory must show itself, and why it cannot but stage itself in such a manner as to be seen. But also the meaning of theory's theatricality becomes tangible here. The theatricality of theory derives from its impossibility to speculatively complete the closure of seeing's being seen by itself. Theatricality names theory's impossibility of achieving a reciprocity between seeing and being seen, one that would secure the possibility that it would see itself. To the maid, of whose look the theoretician pretends to be unaware, the theoretician only offers a silly sight. Being seen by her serves as the necessary backdrop for a seeing in which he aspires to recognize himself. But in the theater of theory the gods' look cannot be confounded with that of the man of theory. Of him Plato admits that he vies with their gaze only so far as he can. The asymmetry between their gaze and that of the theoretician directed at them remains irreducible. For Plato, the theoretical gaze can no longer be certain that it is seen and, therefore, is divine vision itself. Theory is no longer the direct and immediate vision of the divine itself. It is, to use a Platonic formula, only the next best way of beholding the divine. The theater has turned from the provider of a space of immediate commerce between the human gaze and that of the gods to the internal limit of the human gaze. But this limitation does not therefore invalidate the gaze in question. It is still the next best way, the only way for the human.

The maid's appraisal of the philosopher's gaze fails to see what the philosopher sees. But neither is his own gaze at the immortals rendered, or restored, to him in order for him to see himself. This asymmetry in the staging of the theoretical gaze designates a theatricality in theory that both opens, but also immediately closes the possibility that seeing could ever see itself. This asymmetry is owed to the impossibility that, in spite of all attempts at emulating divine vision, the gaze pertaining to the gods could ever be converted into the gaze directed at them. Since it is the gods' privilege to (actively) see seeing in the act of seeing, the theatrical dimension of theory indicates a prevalence of the moment of passively being seen (seeing) in the human theoretical gaze. The asymmetry between the gazes that constitutes the theatricality of theory also concerns a disparity in nature of the two moments. Theatricality names the inescapable necessity with which theory, of which Blumenberg held that it itself could not be seen, cannot but turn itself into a spectacle in which it can be seen, however, without ever being able to assimilate the audience's gaze directed at itself. The acts (*Verrichtungen*) in which it must engage, and which make it visible, are a function of the asymmetrical assembling of the spectators who witness a seeing that strives to become seen seeing. But to say that, therefore, there is an intrinsic theatricality of theory, is also to suggest that theory redoubles, multiplies, and transforms itself without end in sight. Indeed, thanks to the failure of theory to witness its own seeing, there is a history of theory, a world theater of theory, in which even the possibility of the "optics of prefabrication" and the subsequent "coerced vision" that arise with the technology of the manipulation of light is not an accident that befalls theory from the outside.[38] Rather, it is a possibility with which theory goes pregnant from the very beginning. Thanks to theory's theatricality, this is a history that includes the possibility of a loss, or end, of theory, of its entire theatricality, that is, of its performance for a public. Blumenberg deplores this loss at the end of his book on the Thracian maid, since it is nothing less than the loss of theory itself. But such loss can be tragic or comic. With the asymmetry of the gazes, theory is also exposed to the constant threat of becoming empty and futile. The threat of being turned into a comedy of itself, and even the temptation of turning itself into a comedy by itself, are real possibilities of theory, ones that are not accidental either. They too derive from theory's constitutive relation to the theater and is testimony to the fact that even the end of theory is still played out in the theater. It is a theoretical end—a theatrical end.

PART III

PHILOSOPHY

9

Something Like an Archaeology

As Eugen Fink reports in "Das Problem der Phänomenologie"—an essay from 1934—"Husserl always regretted that a positive science had already appropriated an expression which truly captured the essence of philosophy, the expression: archaeology."[1] Indeed, conceived as a radical turning back (*Zurückwendung*) to the beginning of all knowledge of what is, that is, to what Fink names the "primitive state of the human accessions to being (*Urstand der menschlichen Seinszugänge*)," phenomenological philosophy is not only characterized by what Tadashi Ogawa calls an "archaeological *Zug*," that is, trait, propensity, or even, pull: qua philosophy, phenomenology is, first and foremost, an archaeology, since the meaning of philosophy itself—its *Sinn*—is, according to Husserl, the study of the beginnings of knowledge as such, and of the attempt to reactivate that beginning.[2] Rather than naming the study of classical antiquity, or more generally of all historical or prehistoric cultures, that is, the study of particular knowledge formations, the term "archaeology," by referring to the beginning of the logos itself, should thus, by right, have been applied to phenomenological thought. Only as a title for phenomenological philosophy does "archaeology" truly acquire a proper meaning. One could even go as far as to say that, compared to what "archae" and "logos" imply from a philosophical point of view, positive, or rather positivistic, archaeology, that is, classical archaeology, has arrogated to itself a title to which as a science it does not live up. Since the stated aim of phenomenological archaeology is to reconnect the singular sciences to the reactivated origins of knowledge, the true meaning of the positive science of archaeology can thus, in principle, only be assessed in the light of phenomenological archaeology. Compared to the latter's inquiry into the origins of reason and all figures of rationality, an inquiry that reanimates this beginning and brings it to bear on all existing knowledge—rendering it (again) more originary through a movement that Fink calls *Verursprünglichung*—the positive science of archaeology is not only restricted to the exploration of particular knowledge formations: its aim is also only historical in the narrow positivistic sense. But even though Husserl deplored the appropriation of the title in question by a positive science, on one occasion at least he effectively reclaims the title and speaks explicitly of archaeology as the true name of philosophy, that is, of the universal science "about, and based on, the originary" sought by phenomenological thought. He writes in *Erste Philosophie (1923–24)*, "that a science entitled 'first philosophy' is warranted, which as an 'archeology' that truly merits its name, would explore in systematic fashion the ultimately originary, and that which contains within itself all origins of being and truth. Furthermore, this science would teach us how, on the basis of this originary source of all opinions and validities, any cognition can be provided with the highest and final form of reason."[3] This passage substantiates what has been said so far about the affinity of the phenomenological inquiry to the name "archaeology." But the context in which Husserl identifies phenomenology with an archaeology, whose aim is to ground all knowledge in a more originary fashion and which consequently has a teleological pull as well, also makes it clear that such a novel science and philosophy does not yet exist. As a result of the insight into the insufficiency of all positivistic sciences, and of a philosophy based on them, the need for a radical inquiry into the origins of knowledge is only deeply felt, and thus such an archaeology is a science that is only anticipated. In Husserl's words, it has only become "the highest purposive idea of all cognitive efforts."[4] In short, phenomenological archaeology/teleology is still a project, the *telos*—the aim, the purpose—of all epistemological inquiry. Archaeology, then, not only thematizes the beginnings of the logos, it is also concerned with what this beginning commands—namely, that this beginning be the horizon within which the logos unfold, and that, hence, the development of an archaeology be only the necessary consequence of what the beginning promised.

I.

In a response from 1971 to a review article in the *New York Times Book Review* on Michel Foucault's just published *Archaeology of Knowledge*— in which George Steiner questioned the originality of such an enterprise and where he held Sigmund Freud to have been Foucault's predecessor in this respect—Foucault rather caustically observes that "Mr. Steiner does not know that Kant used this word in order to designate the history of that which renders necessary a certain form of thought."[5] Indeed, Immanuel Kant has spoken on several occasions of an "archaeology of nature." But a footnote by the editors to the reprint of this response in *Dits et Ecrits* suggests that Foucault was thinking of a passage by Kant in what is called "Lose Blätter zu den Fortschritten der Metaphysik" in which Kant writes: "A philosophical history of philosophy is not itself historical or empirical, but rational, that is, a priori possible. Even though such a history presents facts of reason, it does not take these from historical narration, but draws them, in the capacity of a philosophical archaeology, from the nature of human reason."[6] The context of the reflections in "Lose Blätter" clearly situates this evocation of a philosophical archaeology in the context of the question of whether a philosophical history of philosophy is a priori possible. This archaeology is thus concerned with the conditions of possibility of such a history. As Kant writes, a philosophical history of philosophy "is of such a peculiar kind that in it nothing of what has happened can be recounted without the prior knowledge of what should have happened, and consequently, also of what can happen."[7] A rational history of philosophy would thus be one that presents history according to its necessity. Furthermore, such a history would allow for an evaluation of whether philosophy has made progress, and to speculate about "what its future destiny might be."[8] To the question of whether it is possible to "outline an a priori schema for the history of philosophy," and hence, for a rational history of philosophy, Kant answers that, yes, such an outline is possible "if, indeed, the idea of a metaphysics imposes itself with necessity on human reason and if the latter feels the need to develop this science which is marked out (*vorgezeichnet*) in the soul in its entirety though only in embryonic fashion."[9] Kant's philosophical archaeology is an inquiry into this embryonic design—the schema, in short—in the very nature of human reason, of such a philosophical history of philosophy. Now, as Kant holds, the interest taken in metaphysics throughout the history of mankind is not to be explained by philosophy's "analysis of concepts and judgments that can be applied to the objects of sense, but primarily because of the supersensible insofar as practical ideas are founded on it."[10] And he asks: "What has motivated the thinkers among human beings to reason about the beginning, the aim (*Ziel*), and the end of things in the world . . . [if not] the purpose of mankind itself?"[11] Philosophical archaeology thus discovers in the nature of human reason this concern with the purpose, end, or telos of mankind. In the depth of human reason, this archaeology locates the schema for the philosophical history of philosophy in question, that is, for a rational history in which necessity and progress toward that end can be assessed, and he discovers it in the purposive idea of an end of mankind. It is difficult see, I contend, what Foucault's archaeology of knowledge has to do with a philosophical archaeology that intends to develop, not an empirical history, but one of facts of reason, that is, of historical philosophies interpreted in view of an end, or purpose, of mankind in itself. If anything, Foucault's archaeology does not wish to be understood as a teleology.

Reading *The Archaeology of Knowledge*, one is surprised, as Maurice Blanchot has noted, by many "formulas of negative theology, given that Foucault puts all his talent to the task of describing in sublime sentences what he rejects: 'it is not . . . ,' "it is neither . . . ,' "it is even less . . . ,' and this to such an extent that he has almost nothing to say anymore" when it comes to defining his subject.[12] Indeed, it is primarily by taking his distances that, in this work, Foucault has, as he puts it himself in the introduction, "tried to define this blank space from which [he] speak[s]" (*AK*, 17).[13] Among the many things from which Foucault seeks to demarcate his own enterprise are various methodologies and philosophical or historical disciplines. Hermeneutics, the history of ideas, the analysis of the sciences, Kantian criticism, Hegelian speculative dialectics, historical materialism, and so forth are among the approaches from which Foucault repeatedly seeks to distance his own take on discursive formations. Transcendental phenomenology is another such type of analysis from which Foucault wishes to distinguish his own enterprise. But as is also evident from *The Archaeology of Knowledge*, transcendental phenomenology is not just one approach among others that Foucault seeks to keep at bay. Indeed the mantra of denunciations directed against phenomenology, the constant affirmations of a basic difference between archaeological description and phenomenology, make one wonder, on the contrary, about how close in the end the two disciplines might be. Could it be that what motivates the author's almost obsessive effort in *The Archaeology of Knowledge* to set himself apart from phenomenology is the fact that archaeology, rather than indebted to Kant as Foucault suggests, is, in truth, intimately connected to its phenomenological use, and more generally to phenomenology as a whole?[14] Indeed, Foucault's statements that archaeological description wishes "to dispense with 'things'; to 'depresentify' them"; to do without "any reference to the living plenitude of experience"; to no longer relate to "a horizon of ideality"; to abandon all search of an "absolute origin"; and to reject all "transcendental subjectivity" and "transcendental constitution" demonstrate that the attempt to separate archaeology off from phenomenology is an unrelenting concern in the work in question (*AK*, 47, 48, 62, 146, 122). In the final chapter titled "Conclusion," after having said that "the essential task was to free the history of thought from its subjection to transcendence" and the qualification of such subjection as "transcendental narcissism," Foucault invokes the name of Husserl (together with Kant and Maurice Merleau-Ponty) and argues that archaeology is not to be understood as "as a search for the origin, for formal *a prioris*, for founding acts, in short, as a sort of historical phenomenology." And he adds: "on the contrary, its aim is to free history from the grip of phenomenology" (*AK*, 203). Perhaps, the very meaning of archaeology is tied up with phenomenological thought to such a degree that any appropriation of the term remains indebted to phenomenology, and that, therefore, Foucault must ceaselessly decree his difference from the latter. In any case, *The Archaeology of Knowledge* claims to have extricated itself from the phenomenological appropriation of the term.

In his "On the Archaeology of the Sciences. Response to the Epistemology Circle," from 1968 in *Cahiers pour l'Analyse*—that is, a year before the publication of *The Archaeology of Knowledge*—Foucault writes: "To analyze the facts of discourse in the general element of the archive is to consider them, not at all as *documents* (of a concealed significance or a rule of construction), but as *monuments*; it is—leaving aside every geological metaphor, without assigning any origin, without the least gesture toward the beginnings of an *arche*—to do what the rules of the etymological game (*selon les droits ludiques de l'étymologie*) allow us to call something like an *archaeology*."[15] Discourse analysis, as Foucault understands it, is not an archaeology properly speaking, but still, it is something resembling "something like an archaeology." It is certainly not an archaeology if the latter is viewed as an inquiry into beginnings, origins, or an *archae*. This refusal of all reference to a beginning also includes the refusal of "every geological metaphor." This is further evidence of Foucault's wish to demarcate his archaeology from an archaeology in the phenomenological sense. Indeed, the mention of the "geological metaphor" does not refer to archaeology as the positive science that goes by that name, but to phenomenological archaeology, which discovers origins by systematically clearing what, in the context of the analysis in *Ideas I* of the noematic structures, are called the sedimentations of meaning that as so many layers have covered over these origins. But in what sense then is Foucault's analysis after all still something like an archaeology?

At this point, undoubtedly, some clarifications are warranted. What is archaeology in the first place? Liddel and Scott define the originary Greek meaning of *archaiologia*, to which the term has to be retraced, as "antiquarian lore, ancient legends or history." However, even though archaeology thus names the inquiry into all forms of the past, the title is intimately associated with the study of classical antiquity. Before archaeology becomes a positive science in the wake of nineteenth- and twentieth-century excavations, which led to the development of specializations and various auxiliary sciences that were required in order to take geographical, ethnological, linguistic, and other factors into account, archaeology is primarily motivated by the attempt to revive classical, that is, Greek and Roman, antiquity as that kind of past that is significant to the Western world and its culture insofar as it represents the very beginning of this world. Prior to becoming a science that is no longer concerned with finding and resurrecting the traces of a past that concerns the Western world in an immediate fashion, and that, consequently, also branches out into the study of the past of other cultures, archaeology is the study of the beginnings of Europe's cultural and political beginnings in antiquity. Now, given that Foucault claims that his understanding of archaeology is not dependent on the meaning of *archae*, understood as beginning, or origin, we must in particular consult the various meanings of that term. The Greek dictionary translates *archae* as beginning, origin, first principle, element, as well as first place, or power, authority, and command. *Archae* designates, on the one hand, a spatial or temporal beginning, and, on the other hand, a rule, dominion, or sway of power. Indeed, as Derrida has recalled, in *Archive Fever: A Freudian Impression*, the Greek notion in question seems to tie two different meanings into one. He writes: "*Arkhe* . . . names at once the *commencement* and the *commandment.* This name apparently coordinates two principles into one: the principle according to nature or history, *there* where things *commence*—physical, historical, or ontological principle—but also the principle according to the law, *there* where men and gods *command, there* where authority, social order are exercised, *in this place* from which *order is given*–nomological principle." The concept of the *archae* thus contains two principles, or "two orders of order," one *sequential,* the other *jussive*"—the meaning of *archae* as physical, historical, or ontological beginning, or origin, just being one of its two inextricably interlinked possible meanings.[16]

As Foucault has admitted in an interview following the publication of *The Archaeology of Knowledge*, he "has used this word [archaeology] at first a bit blindly in order to designate a form of analysis that would not simply be a history . . . and that would neither be an epistemology."[17] Since Foucault was led to redefine the notion of archaeology that at the beginning he seemingly had made use of without giving it too much thought, this is not unlike what happened to the notion of deconstruction, which, Jacques Derrida, at first, had only used in relation to Martin Heidegger's notion of *Destruktion* and which he subsequently recast in response to the attention that this term drew. In the interview, he remarks that "this word 'archaeology' bothers me somewhat, because it covers two themes that are not exactly mine. First, the theme of the beginning (*archae* in Greek means beginning) . . . And then the idea of excavation bothers me as well." Yet, he adds, "retrospectively, it seems to me that chance had not guided me too badly: after all, this word 'archaeology,' can mean, at the price of some approximation, for which I hope I will be excused: description of the *archive.*"[18] However, before seeking to understand this peculiar definition of archaeology as a description of the archive, let me linger for a moment on how in *The Archaeology of Knowledge* the name "archaeology" is bestowed on discourse analysis. At the beginning of the work, Foucault remarks that "there was a time when archaeology, as a discipline devoted to silent monuments, inert traces, objects without context, and things left by the past, aspired to the condition of history, and attained meaning only through the restitution of a historical discourse; it might be said, to play on words a little, that in our time history aspires to the condition of archaeology, to the intrinsic description of the monument" (*AK*, 7). As Foucault contends, to call discourse analysis an archaeology of some sort is justified by a right to play with the true, or original, meanings of words. Precisely because the term (as he understands it) "does not imply the search for a beginning [and] it does not relate analysis to geological excavation," he evokes "the right of words—which is not that of the philologists," to authorize the application of the title "archaeology" to the type of research that he pursues (*AK*, 131). But if the philologists' understanding of the meaning of words is disregarded, would this not seem to suggest that the term "archaeology" is used in a merely playful way? However, if it is not employed in any serious way, could the application of the word "archaeology" to discourse analysis, or as "a name given to a part of our contemporary theoretical conjuncture" (*AK*, 208), not also be called frivolous? Indeed, Foucault concedes that baptizing discourse analysis in this manner is a "jeu peut-être bien solennel," that is, a rather solemn play (*AK*, 135).[19] Not only does such naming use the name of the dignified science of archaeology for an analysis that does not concern the originary and the origins and through which also, and inevitably, some of the prestige of this venerable science is sought for discourse analysis, but such naming takes its liberties as well with the original meaning of the name. Undoubtedly, by claiming that archaeology is a name fitted to describe what *prima philosophia* is truly about, Husserl also reinterpreted *archaiologia* in a way that made use of the "right to play." But contrary to Foucault's conception of archaeology, archaeology in the Husserlian sense continues to refer to an origin. Since this origin is understood as that of knowledge, or *logos*, Husserl can therefore claim that his interpretation of the word is more fundamental than the one that governs its meaning as a title for one positive science among many. Furthermore, this more fundamental interpretation of archaeology also retains the two meanings of the Greek notion of *archae*, its meanings of beginning and rule. The question therefore arises whether by conceiving of archaeology as an approach that is no longer concerned with beginnings and origins, Foucault's exploitation of the term has also left behind the other meaning of *archae*, namely, its meaning of commandment, rule, or law. If not, Foucault's talk of archaeology is perhaps "playful" only to the extent that it one-sidedly privileges one of the traditional meanings of the Greek notion. As a result, the demarcation of discourse analysis from the traditional understanding of archaeology, as well as from phenomenological archaeology, would not be as clear-cut as claimed. Indeed, although Foucault no longer understands *archae* in "archaeology" as its traditional meaning of origin, or beginning, is his definition of archaeology as a description of the archive not tributary to, precisely, the second intrinsic meaning of *archae*, that is, *archae* as commandment? Even though Foucault does not take "archive" in its usual sense as the repository of public records, the word "archive" derives from *archaeon*, the town hall, or residence of chief magistrates, a word that itself relates to *archae* in the sense of government. Leaving Foucault's recast notion of archive still at abeyance, archaeology in the Foucauldian sense is indeed the description of discourses in light of that that commands them, *archae* being taken to refer to the rules of the formation of the *logoi*. *Logos*, furthermore, is no longer understood to mean science. *Logos* is description of the *logoi* in terms of the rules of their formation. However, this redefinition of archaeology does not radically break with the term's traditional use. All it does is only to put, in a one-sided fashion, the second meaning of *archae* as commandment, rule, or law to work in understanding the term. With this, no doubt, a new concept of archaeology emerges, which, like the Husserlian one, is based, it would seem, on a reactivation of the etymological meaning of its constitutive terms. As much at odds with that of the philologists' understanding of archaeology as the study of antiquity, as with Husserl's appropriation of the term, it is then not simply "playful." It draws on the authority of etymology to establish its new meaning. But given that the two meanings of *archae*—its sequential and jussive meanings— are intimately interwoven in that notion, is it possible to entirely avoid, as Foucault would like to have it, the meaning of *archae* as beginning and origin?

    Before I pursue these questions, I return to the contention that it is the right of words that permits baptizing the research into discursive formations as an archaeology. Foucault makes this claim after having asserted that "the never completed, never wholly achieved uncovering of the archive forms the general horizon to which the description of discursive formations, the analysis of positivities, the mapping of the enunciative field belong" (*AK*, 131). The appropriation of the title "archaeology" for discourse analysis is thus not simply based on interpreting the *archae* as what commands, rather than as a beginning or origin, but on Foucault's understanding of "archive." Even though the notion of "archive" can be retraced to *archae* in the sense of commandment, Foucault's interpretation of this term entirely disregards its etymological roots. Indeed, the right of words, of which Foucault authorizes himself, is not the right to choose one etymon over another, but to disregard etymology altogether and to make words mean what they never meant before. Indeed, as Foucault writes, "The archive is not that which, despite its immediate escape, safeguards the event of the statement, and preserves for future memories, its status as an escapee. . . . Nor is the archive that which collects the dust of statements that have become inert once more, and which may make possible the miracle of their resurrection" (*AK*, 129). On the contrary, archive, for Foucault, refers to the systems that within discursive practices—that is, within the ensemble of rules that define the conditions for the operation of the enunciative function within a given epoch—condition the event- and thing-character of statements. In short—we will come back to this definition—the archive concerns the singular existence and actuality of statements and groups of statements. Since the uncovering of the archive is said to be "the general horizon to which the description of discursive formations, the analysis of positivities, the mapping of the enunciative field belong," and thus the very background against which all this research becomes meaningful, Foucault claims the title "archaeology" for all the investigations in question. When one understands "archaeology" from the notion of archive, rather than from that of *archae*, archaeology comes to "designate the general theme of a description that questions the already-said at the level of its existence: of the enunciative function that operates within it, of the discursive formation, and the general archive system to which it belongs. Archaeology describes discourses as practices specified in the element of the archive" (*AK*, 131). The archive being understood in terms of the existence of the already-said, archaeology comes to mean the description of the system of the laws that command the apparition, and the becoming events and things of statements, and of the regularities to which they give rise. The right of words of which Foucault avails himself leads to a definition of archaeology from which the meaning of beginning and origin has been eliminated, but which concerns the commanding function that the archive has with respect to the enunciative function. If, admittedly, this redefinition of archaeology is playful, if not even frivolous, it is because the archive is made to mean something that it never meant, more precisely, something that it never meant before Claude Lévi-Strauss, in *The Savage Mind*, said of "the archives [that they] are the embodiment of eventhood (*l'être incarné de l'événementialité*)."[20]

In the conclusion to *The Archaeology of Knowledge*, Foucault underlines that he has "never presented archaeology as a science, or even as the beginnings of a future science." He adds: "The word archaeology is not supposed to carry any suggestion of anticipation" (*AK*, 206). It is neither a science in the sense of a positive science, nor the anticipated science of a rigorous philosophy that constitutes the telos of Husserl's investigations. Recast as a description of the laws, or rules of formation, that is, of discourses—*logos* being interpreted as discourse—archaeology, rather than the beginning of a future science, points to a mode of analysis and description of discourse that Foucault had put to work in his earlier works in a variety of ways, which he seeks to refine and expand in *The Archaeology of Knowledge*. But as Gilles Deleuze has also noted in his review article of the book in question, "perhaps, in this archaeology, Foucault offers us less a discourse on his method than the poem of his previous works, and reaches the point where philosophy is necessarily poetry, the severe poetry of what is said, which subsumes both nonsense and the greatest profundities."[21] Writing the poem of his earlier work, rather than providing a rigorous discourse about the method pursued in *Madness and Civilization, The Birth of the Clinic*, and *The Order of Things*, Foucault may thus also have poetically rewritten the word "archaeology," turning it into the poetic name for a philosophical poem.

Foucault characterizes archaeology as "a coherent domain of description" (*AK*, 114). It is, he holds, "a vast field," but what does it consist of? From the start, let us note that the archaeological discovery of this domain does not simply invalidate all the "unquestioned continuities [the work, the book, for example] by which we organize, in advance, the discourse that we are to analyze." However, since these continuities cover up the domain in question, they need to be "disconnected (*mettre hors circuit*)" (*AK*, 25). Now, the field that comes into view, once all the traditional unities of discourse are bracketed, is "made up of the totality of all effective statements (whether spoken or written), in their dispersion as events and in the occurrence that is proper to them" (*AK*, 26–27). Once "we renounce all those themes whose function is to ensure the infinite continuity of discourse," "every moment of discourse [can be received] in its sudden irruption; in that punctuality in which it appears, and in that temporal dispersion that enables it to be repeated, known, forgotten, transformed, utterly erased, and hidden, far from all view, in the dust of books" (*AK*, 25). By putting in brackets all the ready-made syntheses, the archaeological gaze faces thus "in the first instance . . . only a population of dispersed events" (*AK*, 22). The specific and autonomous domain of archaeological description, then, is the discourses, and the statements by which they are made up, not as documents that refer to a deeper meaning, but as monuments, that is, in their quality of empirical events, and existing items to be analyzed in terms that primarily concern the modalities of their emergence into being and existence. As the analysis of discursive formations, and, particularly, of the statements (*énoncés*, enunciations, utterances) by which they are made up, archaeology homes in on a domain beyond linguistics and logic, that is, beyond the inquiry into the rules that permit the formation of an infinitude of phrases, and the inquiry into the conditions of validity of propositions, in order to bring into view the presence of statements and discursive formations, in short, what I like to call the ontological thickness, or density, of signifying ensembles. The archaeological analysis of statements, which "does not replace a logical analysis of propositions, a grammatical analysis of sentences, a psychological or contextual analysis of formulations," proposes a different attack on verbal performances, one that inquires into their conditions of existence and continued actuality (*AK*, 108).

This, then, is also the moment to take up in some greater detail the question of the archive. As we have seen, Foucault conceives of the archive as the general horizon within which all the various archaeological descriptions of the modes of being of statements, and their conditions of existence, take place. Rather than a monotonous and endless plain, the domain of statements, all of which are characterized by the thickness of their existence, not only possesses a complex volume, but also features "systems that establish statements as events (with their own conditions and domain of appearance) and things (with their own possibility and field of use). They are all these systems of statements (whether events or things) that [Foucault] propose[s] to call *archive*" (*AK*, 128). The archive thus names the systems of rules that, within the discursive practices peculiar to individual epochs, turn statements into events and things. According to Foucault, "archive" is the system that, within a discursive positivity, instantiates statements as unique happenings and monuments, which, consequently, bestows the singularity and contingency of events upon statements and gives them physical existence.[22] As the system of the law that transforms the existence of statements into events and existing things, the archive itself is a law. It is above all the law that causes statements to become singular events and things. "The archive is first the law of what can be said, the system that governs the appearance of statements as unique events. But the archive is also that which determines that all these things said do not accumulate endlessly in an amorphous mass, nor are they inscribed in an unbroken linearity, nor do they disappear at the mercy of chance external accidents; but that they are grouped together in distinct figures" (*AK*, 129). The archive is thus also the law that causes statement-events to link up with other such events in finite sets and to share one and the same form of positivity. Foucault can thus hold that the archive "is that which, at the very root of the statement-event, and in that which embodies it, defines at the outset *the system of its enunciability*" (*AK*, 129). The archive codifies the rules for a statement becoming an event (and a thing) that is part of a larger group of events (and things). This archival law thus also determines the life of statement-events and statement-things, or monuments, that is, the way they become, are, and remain effective. It names the conditions under which a statement-event, once it has happened, and a statement-thing, once it has become monument, continue to be actual and to enjoy effective reality within the group within which they have come into existence. The archive, Foucault writes, "is *the system of [their] functioning*" (*AK*, 129). Finally, the archive comprises the law for the manipulation and transformation of the statement-events and statement-things within the group to which they belong. It concerns "a practice that causes a multiplicity of statements to emerge as so many regular events, as so many things to be dealt with and manipulated." In sum, then, the archive "reveals the rules of a practice that enables statements both to survive and to undergo regular modifications. It is *the general system of the formation and transformation of statements*" (*AK*, 130). On top of the domain of existence and the mode of being that characterizes statements in general, the archive names a distinct domain of existence of statements that concerns the possibility of their eventhood and monumentality. This particular domain of the actuality of statements and their effective reality is the general horizon against the backdrop of which all archaeological inquiry into discursive formations and the analysis of positivities takes place. It orients the research into the enunciative field, that is, into the ontological thickness of statements. It is primarily in light of the possibility of becoming effective that enunciative existence is made thematic in this archaeology.

But let us now look at the way the laws that pertain to statements in general are characterized. As we have already seen, Foucault's archaeology "designates the general theme of a description that questions the already-said at the level of its existence" (*AK*, 131). It is "the project of a *pure description of discursive events*," that is, of these events according to categories of existence, in an inquiry into why, for instance, one discursive fact appeared rather than another (*AK*, 27). Even though, in order to lay bare its domain, this archaeology must bracket all the handed-down unities of discourse, its basic concern with the existence of statements shows it to no longer be in need of clearing away sedimentations or geological layers that cover over a beginning or *archae*. Indeed, the domain of the statements beyond linguistics and logic "is not, for all that, a restored transcendence, nor a way that has been reopened in the direction of an inaccessible origin" (*AK*, 113). With its exclusive interest in statements (*énoncés*) as events, or "in the sudden appearance of a sentence, the flash of meaning, the brusque gesture of the index finger of designation" (*AK*, 112), Foucault's archaeology wishes only to "grasp the statement in the exact specificity of its occurrence (*dans l'étroitesse et la singularité de son événement*); to determine its conditions of existence" (*AK*, 28). Its object is the discursive practices, more precisely, the *fact* that they exist, the *fact* that they are given. Now, archaeology considers the discursive formations, and the statements that constitute them, "in themselves," as Foucault repeatedly writes, that is, without seeking "at a deeper level, some secret or some root of language that they have omitted" (*AK*, 112). Even though archaeology seeks to answer the question, how is it that one particular statement appeared rather than another? It is not by way of a hidden ground, foundation, or origin that it attempts to account for the appearance of a statement (*AK*, 27). Foucault writes: "We shall try to render visible, and analyzable, that immediate transparency that constitutes the element of their possibility"(*AK*, 112). Foucault's emphasis on the statements, or discursive formations, "in themselves" indicates that his archaeology does not look for the rules that govern their historical emergence outside and in advance of them but somehow within them, and within the relations in which they stand to one another. And yet, although these rules "remain within the dimension of discourse," they are neither simply internal nor immanent to the statements or discursive formations (*AK*, 76). "Discursive relations are not . . . internal to discourse: they do not connect concepts or words with one another; they do not establish a deductive or rhetorical structure between propositions or sentences. Yet they are not relations exterior to discourse, relations that might limit it, or impose certain forms upon it, or force it, in certain circumstances, to state certain things. They are, in a sense, at the limit of discourse" (*AK*, 46). And: "Neither hidden, nor visible, the enunciative level is at the limit of language: it is not, in itself, a group of characteristics that are presented, even in an unsystematic way, to immediate experience; but neither is it the enigmatic, silent remainder that it does not translate. It defines the modality of its appearance: its periphery rather than its internal organization, its surface rather than its content" (*AK*, 112). These rules, or systems of rules, that "in the density (*épaisseur*) of discursive practices" make up the "conditions of reality for statements" and thus also for discourse formations, which represent groupings of statements, are "*historical* [rather than formal] *a prioris*," that is, "purely empirical figures" at the limit of discourse (*AK*, 127–128). What Foucault terms the "archive," that is, what "at the very root of the statement-event, and in that which embodies it, defines at the outset *the system of its enunciability*," rather than, as one would expect, what "despite its immediate escape, safeguards the event of the statement, and preserves, for future memories, its status as an escapee," "involves a privileged region: at once close to us, and different from our present existence, it is the border of time that surrounds our presence, which overhangs it, and which indicates it in its otherness; it is that which, outside ourselves, delimits us" (*AK*, 129–130). In short, the object of Foucault's archaeology clearly is not of the order of an absolute origin or a foundation, a formal, or transcendental, principle of possibility, a critical condition of validity (of judgments), for it is neither on this side of what it makes possible nor indicative of a founding subjectivity. The rules that archaeology investigates have the paradoxical status of being at the limit of discourse and yet being very close, being conditions of reality and yet empirical, neither hidden nor visible, and so forth. However, even though the rules of discourse formation that Foucault aims at do not originate in a constituting transcendental subjectivity, but "break the thread of transcendental teleologies" and are "situated at the level of the 'it is said'" (*AK*, 131,

122), has, I ask, archaeology truly cut all ties to phenomenological archaeology, and in particular to the latter's concern with beginnings and ends, as radically as Foucault makes us believe? Undoubtedly, *The Archaeology of Knowledge* consistently assures the reader of the uniqueness of its enterprise. However, is it possible at all to redefine archaeology in such a way as to avoid all its traditional implications and, in particular, those that follow from its fundamental reassessment in phenomenological thought?

For the present purpose, a few schematic remarks must suffice. First, since the rules that Foucauldian archaeology exhibits are invisible even though they are not hidden, this archaeology admittedly requires "a certain change of viewpoint and attitude to be recognized and examined in itself," one that disconnects, or, to speak with Husserl, suspends, or brackets, all the ready-made syntheses so that it can lay bare its proper domain (*AK*, 111). As is well known, such a change of attitude is also at the very heart of the phenomenological approach. Second, methodologically speaking, Foucauldian archaeology shares with phenomenology at least its descriptive approach to phenomena. Richard Rorty already pointed out that although Foucault "mocks Husserl's enterprise of 'pure description' . . . he sounds much like Husserl when he talks of a 'project of a *pure description* of discursive events as the horizon for the search for the unities that form within it.' "[23] Third, in the discussion of "the interior hierarchies within enunciative regularities," Foucault observes that even though the rules that are put into operation by any statement "are never given in a formulation . . . certain groups of statements put these rules into operation in their most general and most widely applicable form." In short, notwithstanding the fact that the rules that statements and enunciative regularities obey are not axioms, the groups of statements in question can serve as the "starting-point" to show how other statements "may be formed on the basis of rules that are less general and whose domain of application is more specified" (*AK*, 146–147). Indeed, one of the "principle themes" of Foucault's archaeology is to "constitute the tree of derivation of a discourse. . . . It will place at the root, as *governing statements*, those that concern the definition of observable structures and the field of possible objects, those that prescribe the forms of description and the perceptual codes that it can use, those that reveal the most general possibilities of characterization, and thus open up a whole domain of concepts to be constructed, and lastly, those that, while constituting a strategic choice leave room for the greatest number of subsequent options. And it will find, at the end of the branches, or at various places in the whole (*dans le parcours de tout un buissonement*), a burgeoning of 'discoveries' . . . conceptual transformations . . . the emergence of new notions . . . technical improvements." This derivation, which is distinct from a deduction from an undemonstrable axiom, according to Foucault, is neither "the germination of a general idea, or a philosophical nucleus whose significance emerges gradually in experience or precise conceptualizations" nor "the psychological genesis based on a discovery whose consequences and possibilities gradually develop and unfold" (*AK*, 147). And he adds that one should not "demand of archaeological derivation that it reproduce the order of time or reveal a deductive schema" (*AK*, 148). But as its form is concerned, is this derivation for that matter distinct from the derivation that an eidetical kernel, intuited in absolute evidence, in an attitude that radically breaks with the natural attitude, makes possible? Furthermore, Foucault's recourse to terms and phrases such as a "root" and a "tree of derivation" make one wonder to what extent his archaeology is beyond origins and teleologies.

As we have seen, phenomenological archaeology is the search for the beginning of knowledge. Is it thus just by coincidence that Foucault's inquiry into the discursive formations and their laws conceives itself as an archaeology of knowledge as well? As Foucault acknowledges, all the examples of *The Archaeology of Knowledge* belong "without exception to a very small domain": the order of the scientific discourses and, hence, scientific knowledge formation (*AK*, 178). However, as Foucault asserts, his investigation does not concern the forms of cognition (*connaissance*), whether in the critical sense of a priori necessary conditions or in the sense of what at one historical moment are considered scientifically established findings. Making a distinction between cognition (*connaissance*) and knowledge (*savoir*)—a distinction that the English translation does not clearly bring out—Foucault suggests that even though the archaeological inquiry has until now focused exclusively on the sciences, it is not its cognitive achievements that archaeology is interested in, but what he calls the knowledge that makes the sciences possible. Pondering the question whether, apart from the archaeology of the scientific discourses, other archaeologies are conceivable, Foucault responds that archaeologies of the ethical, aesthetical, and political discourses are not only conceivable, but also that in each case these investigations concern knowledge. He writes: "What archaeology tries to describe is not the specific structure of science, but the very different domain of *knowledge*. Moreover, although it is concerned with knowledge in its relation to epistemological figures and the sciences, it may also question knowledge in a different direction and describe it in a different set of relations. The orientation toward the episteme has been the only one to be explored so far" (*AK*, 195). Whether dealing with the discourses of the sciences or with those on sexual behavior, the arts, or politics, in all cases the object of archaeology is knowledge. But what is knowledge for Foucault, if it is not cognition? It is the "group of elements, formed in a regular manner by a discursive practice, and which are indispensable to the constitution of a science, although they are not necessarily destined to give rise to one," Foucault writes (*AK*, 182). And he explains that the analysis of the anonymous rules, which govern the discursive practices that constitute positivities, show how these practices have formed groups of objects, enunciations, concepts, and theoretical, or strategical, choices. These elements and their relations characteristic of a definite discursive practice are what Foucault defines as knowledge. "They are that on the basis of which coherent (or incoherent) propositions built up, more or less exact descriptions developed, verifications carried out, theories deployed. They form the precondition of what is later revealed and which later functions as an item of knowledge (*connaissance*) or illusion, an accepted truth or an exposed error, a definite acquisition or an obstacle surmounted" (*AK*, 182).[24] In short, then, "archaeology finds the point of balance of its analysis in *savoir* (knowledge)," that is, Foucault explains, "in a domain in which the subject is necessarily situated and dependent, and can never figure as a titular (either as a transcendental activity, or as empirical consciousness)" (*AK*, 183).

This, then, is also the point where we can return to our assessment of the proximity and distance between Foucauldian archaeology and phenomenological archaeology. Although conceived as an archaeology of knowledge, Foucault insists on the fact that the knowledge investigated by his archaeology is the knowledge of neither an empirical nor transcendental subject. As the "the space in which the subject may take up a position and speak of the objects with which he deals in his discourse" and, hence, as the precondition of cognition and illusion, knowledge is not "a *donnée*, a lived experience, still implicated in the imagination or in perception, which mankind in the course of its history took up again in the form of a rationality, or which each individual must undergo on his own account if he wishes to rediscover the ideal meanings that are contained or concealed within it. It is not a pre-knowledge or an archaic state in the movement that leads from immediate knowledge to apodicticity" (*AK*, 182). What Foucault asserts of the rules of the formation of concepts, namely that "they operate not only in the mind or consciousness of individuals, but in discourse itself; they operate therefore, according to a sort of anonymity, on all individuals who undertake to speak in [a] discursive field," is valid of all the elements formed in a discursive practice and, consequently, of the knowledge formed by a particular practice (*AK*, 63). Knowledge, in Foucault's sense, is anonymous; it is not attributable to any subject, transcendental or not. It possesses "an anonymity on which no transcendental constitution [imposes] the form of the subject" (*AK*, 203). Furthermore, in a statement that is unmistakably aimed at Husserl, Foucault stresses that knowledge cannot be placed "at the level of lived experience (on this earth, which is given, irregular and fragmented, before all geometry; in the heaven that glitters through the grid of all astronomies)" (*AK*, 191). It is not "that which must have been lived, or must be lived, if the intention of ideality proper to [science, for example] is to be established; but . . . which must have been said—or must be said—if a discourse is to exist that complies, if necessary, with the experimental or formal criteria of scientificity" (*AK*, 182). The archaeology of the knowledge presupposed for a science to come into existence is thus not the knowledge of a subject. Let us recall that in order to lay bare the immense field of all effective statements in their dispersion as events, the archaeological gaze required the disconnection of all ready-made syntheses. However, as we have seen, this "dust of facts" is not the final purpose of the operation. Rather, the aim is "to be able to grasp other forms of regularity, other types of relations," in short, other unities, that is, syntheses (*AK*, 28–29). All syntheses, according to Kant, are functions of subjectivity, in particular of transcendental subjectivity. Yet, the syntheses of the archaeology of knowledge are anonymous. No subject, empirical or transcendental, can claim responsibility for them. Consequently, the syntheses of knowledge, and of knowledge *as* a synthesis, are clearly akin to the passive, or originary, syntheses (in particular, of inner time consciousness) that, Husserl has shown, underlie all active, that is, conscious, constitution and predicative syntheses as accomplishments of the ego. Knowledge, in the Foucauldian sense, is obviously a passive synthesis required for the coming into existence, especially, of the sciences, and for providing the places from which subjects can speak within discursive fields. Undoubtedly, apart from the fact that the passive synthesis of knowledge is, in Foucault, always only the finite knowledge produced by a singular discursive practice and not constitutive of discursive practice as such, what in particular seems to distinguish knowledge from Husserlian passive syntheses is that knowledge is not lived by a subject. But the anonymity, which for Foucault is the criteria for holding the syntheses of knowledge to be nonsubjective, is also a dominant trait of Husserlian passive synthesis as well. The passive syntheses of time-consciousness, "in which the ego constitutes itself as temporal and becomes aware as a stream of consciousness" at the bottommost level, endows, at first, the transcendental ego with only an "absolutely anonymous [ontic] sense."[25] In the same way, as the transcendental ego, which cannot bring this anonymous sense in its original performance before its reflective gaze, *is* nonetheless constituted by this sense, so the anonymity of knowledge does not per se prevent this knowledge to become that of, possibly, an absolute subject. Indeed, from a purely conceptual perspective, it is difficult to see how knowledge, however redefined, could at all be disconnected from a subject to begin with. Let us also point out that even though Foucault insists that knowledge in the archaeological sense is not akin to the preconceptual and prepredicative experience of Husserl's *Lebenswelt*, it remains that *The Archaeology of Knowledge* manifests some obvious stress in the attempt to prevent the level on which archaeology operates from resembling a kind of *preconceptual* level.[26] More importantly, by calling "knowledge" the elements that must have been formed in a discursive practice before it possibly leads to scientific knowledge, the specter of phenomenology cannot but continue to haunt this archaeology.

II.

But if Foucault's archaeology of knowledge may not succeed in cutting all ties to phenomenological archaeology and may therefore be permeated by the specters of origins and ends, phenomenological archaeology, for its part, may be plagued as well by a specter of its own that prevents it from fully achieving its goal. In a review of Fink's book, *Studien zur Phänomenologie*, which features the essay in which Fink recounts that

Husserl deplored not being able to use the title "archaeology" for phenomenological philosophy, Derrida points out that Fink's interpretation of
Husserlian thought is remarkable in that, despite the faithfulness of his
reading, "something in it began to make phenomenology tremble." Evoking
the capital phenomenological problem of the relation of presentation
and representation, Derrida argues that Fink "goes straight to the enigma:
what about that which in the movement of temporalization cannot be
determined as either presentation or representation, but somehow as *de-
presentation (Entgegenwärtigung)*? What about retention, protention, and
appresentation which do not belong to the sphere of the originary in the
strict sense, nor to the sphere of secondary reproduction?"[27] As Derrida's
review thus suggests—and this, from *Speech and Phenomenon* on, is a
major point that Derrida continues to make in his interpretation of
Husserl—the Husserlian conception of the beginning of knowledge in
the originary evidence of the presence, in which the thing itself is given to
intuition, brings to light a whole domain of non-originary structures that
are intimately woven into the originary. In other words, phenomenological archaeology, while exhibiting the beginnings of knowledge, also brings
to light a non-originary stratum constitutive of the originary, a stratum,
that in view of the fundamentality of the origin, deserves being called
"frivolous."

In the following pages, I argue that Derrida's text, *The Archeology of
the Frivolous*,[28] which in French was published together with the 1973 reed-
ition of Etienne Bonnot de Condillac's *Essay on the Origin of Human
Knowledge*,[29] is a critique not only of Foucault's attempt to constitute an
archaeology of knowledge, but also, albeit largely implicitly, of the Husserlian project of recovering the originary source of knowledge in general.
In such a context, my giving attention to a thinker such as Condillac may
seem frivolous. Indeed, at first glance, this Enlightenment thinker, who
countered the rationalists of the previous century by striving to make good
on and develop the problematic of Locke's empiricism, seems to have little
in common with the founder of phenomenological thought. It is nonetheless the case that the acknowledged goal of the *Essay* concerns the origins
and genesis of knowledge. Condillac aspires to nothing less than "the discovery of a primary experience that no one can cast doubt on and that
is sufficient to explain all other experience. It ought to point clearly to the
source of our knowledge."[30] Going back to perception, to the simple

thoughts or ideas to which this first operation of the soul gives rise, Condillac discovers the unique principle of the genesis of human knowledge in the "constant experience" of the connection of ideas ("either with the sign or between the ideas"). What predisposes sensations to serve as originary material and the connection of ideas as the basic operation of our knowledge is, on the one hand, the clear and distinct nature of the ideas that, in their simplicity,[31] are contained by perceptions and, on the other, the luminosity of the simplest principles as found in the very connection of ideas.[32] Because a simple idea does not have parts, it gives rise to no misunderstanding concerning its contents.[33] In the case of simple ideas that come to us immediately from the senses, the meaning of signs, or words, that designate the ideas and that allow for their connections is obvious. "[It] is known at once; its objects cannot be imagined realities, since it refers directly to simple perceptions, which are in fact in the mind just as they appear there."[34] With this return to a primary experience and to a principle of evidence or certainty to explain the genesis of knowledge, the *Essay* certainly bears a certain resemblance to archaeology, to a science of the origins of knowledge. We can note as well that, since Condillac's project is carried out not only with the aim of discovering the origin of knowledge and of explaining its progress, but also with an eye toward future scientific progress, this archaeology necessarily implies a teleology. By returning to a first experience known to all, it is, in effect, a matter of aiding what has germinated at the origin and of assuring its full realization.

Yet is it possible that Condillac's *Essay* is not only an archaeology in the literal sense, insofar as it explores the origins of logos, but also an archaeology in the phenomenological sense? Let us first consider the question of the name of the new science that the *Essay* puts forward. Derrida remarks from the very first page of the *Archeology of the Frivolous* that Condillac struggled to find a name for the science outlined in the *Essay*, namely "a *general* science ending nowhere (*à aucune région*) and utilizing a universal analysis, an analysis that leads us back in all fields of knowledge to the simplest, most elementary ideas and that also defines their laws of connection, combination, complication, substitution, repetition . . . [as well as] their laws of generation" (*AF*, 33–34)—but for which he finds no other name than that of "metaphysics," even though it was not supposed to be a metaphysics at all. This recalls the difficulty Husserl had, according to Fink, in finding an appropriate name for the phenomenological project.

Furthermore, when Condillac considers the possibility of calling this science "psychology" because it is aimed not only at breaking down combinations into simple elements but also at retracing their genesis and reactivating the chain of psychic operations that had brought them into being, the reserve that he expresses on this matter recalls the Husserlian critique of psychology and the difficulties concerning the parallelism between phenomenology and psychology. Condillac writes, "I would call it psychology, if I knew any good work under this title" (*AF*, 40). However, when Derrida characterizes the new science of the *Essay* as "a metaphysics of phenomena and relations ("connections") . . . a metaphysics of the open—we could say a phenomenology of the things themselves—and a critical science of limits . . . 'only trying to see things as they in fact are' " (*AF*, 33), there is no longer any doubt that Derrida understands it as a proto-phenomenology, or a phenomenology *avant la lettre*. We can see, as well, that in the introductory text called *The Archeology of the Frivolous*, Condillac's new science, which deals with the "given phenomenon," is said to be a "philosophy of consciousness, [a] philosophy of perception" (*AF*, 34, 96). Having established that, notwithstanding the Husserlian conception of phenomenology as first philosophy, the return in phenomenology to the most originary meaning (of geometry, for example) can be accomplished only after the fact—after the fact of the event of meaning (that is, after "geometry was *in fact* born and [after] it had in fact been given to me")—the assertion by Derrida that the new science of origins and of true beginnings proposed by the *Essay* is not a first but a second philosophy continues to foster the resemblance between the two enterprises.[35] Just as with phenomenology, the general theory of the *Essay* "comes *after* the development or acquisition of knowledge . . . [and] presupposes the scientific *fact*" (*AF*, 39). Echoing the theses concerning the factuality of the fact and the meaning of the fact as he had developed them in his introduction to the *Origin of Geometry*, Derrida writes, "Consequently, the new metaphysics will be second only by returning to the principle's true generation, to its actual production. The new metaphysics will surely resemble empiricism . . . [and] by progressing as second philosophy, [it] will methodically reconstitute the generative principles, the primordial production of the general starting from real singularities" (*AF*, 35), even if this means breaking down first philosophy. We should not forget, moreover, that this principled deferral with respect to an operation of knowledge and its fact—a deferral that characterizes the analysis of ideas—does not concern only the uncovering of the originary as such. The very method of Condillac's new science presupposes the path historically taken first by John Locke and Isaac Newton and amounts to expanding the concept of method that they had developed. Yet does not this very deferral of method with respect to the fact suggest as well that Locke's *Essay Concerning Human Understanding* is to Condillac what Franz Brentano's empirical psychology was to Husserl?

Although all these points of intersection are far from exhausting the analogies between the thought of the *Essay* and the Husserlian enterprise, one can already presume that Condillac's proto-phenomenology will be led to acknowledge, just as Husserlian phenomenology had to, according to Derrida, the presence of the non-originary within the very origin of knowledge. But before pursuing this argument, let me emphasize that, in addition to the parallels that I have already pointed out, the genealogical return initiated by the new science of Condillac to sensation as the first matter from which all knowledge is derived is, for Derrida, a return to "an irreducible core of immediate presence" (*AF*, 46). As the archaeological return strives for—to cite Condillac—"the discovery of a primary experience that no one can cast doubt on and that is sufficient to explain all the other experience,"[36] the archaeological turn ends up at sensibility, which is to say, "a first property which knows itself and which does nothing then but modify itself " (*AF*, 81). This primary experience is thus subject to the ultimate call of the "principle of evidence which alone 'must exclude every kind of doubt' " (*AF*, 80). Prelinguistic, natural, and thus silent, does not this first experience that knows itself and is by that fact self-evident and the source of all other knowledge correspond in some way to the prelinguistic soliloquy in the solitary mental life discussed by Husserl in the first of the *Logical Investigations*? Freed from any function of indication and thus of the sign, meaning [*vouloir-dire*] or sense would precede language in a sort of self-certain auto-affection. If, on the one hand, in *Speech and Phenomena*, Derrida has demonstrated that despite all of Husserl's efforts to reduce the indicative function in the solitary expression of the phenomenological mental voice, this voice, as meaning [*vouloir-dire*], is always and necessarily inhabited by the possibility of the sign-being and if, on the other hand, he observes in *The Archeology of the Frivolous* that the sensualist metaphysics of Condillac is "also throughout a metaphysics of the sign and a philosophy of language" (*AF*, 46), then we can conclude that the problem is similar in the two different cases? If the sensualism of the *Essay* is developed into a semiotics, in accordance with a logic or analogic that Derrida explores in his text, this is so because "sensation is not only a simple element, but also a *germ*" (*AF*, 46). This generative power of the primary experience opens a whole series of questions regarding the *Essay* that are similar to those that Derrida addressed to Husserlian phenomenology, such as the question of the synthetic power between the terms "germ" and "development" or between "the generative and the combinative exigencies" (*AF*, 47), in short, between the oppositions of genesis and calculation, genesis and structure. But this question of the germinal power of sensation and, thus, of the idea, requires also that one understand how archaeology is tied to teleology, as well as what role is played by the frivolous in this context.

Let us start by recalling that although it is placed before the work by Condillac, the *Archeology of the Frivolous* is not for that matter an introduction to the *Essay*, if by "introduction" one understands the explication of a text to a given reader, a reading that saturates the text with a comprehensive reading. When, just before the end of the *Archeology of the Frivolous*, Derrida raises the question of the status of this text, he does so to point out that "this alleged Introduction, in short, has prohibited itself from saying anything about the *Essay*, about what we would want to find there as its own proper and ventral content" (*AF*, 108). The principal reason why this text of Derrida refrains from defining the content of the work by Condillac is that its reading of the *Essay* discovers a "rigorous abyss" rather than an identifiable content (*AF*, 108). But there is also the fact that Derrida here discusses Condillac's text "in the spider web of other texts" (*AF*, 108); those of Condillac (thus raising the question of an apparent evolution in his thought), but also those of others to whom, consciously or not, Condillac is indebted. Finally, if this presumed introduction avoids saying anything about the *Essay*, this is so for the added reason that in it Derrida retraces the history of readings of Condillac in France. This history, which begins with Maine de Biran in the nineteenth century and is taken up again in the twentieth, is that of a simplistic critique of Condillac's philosophy that accuses it of contradiction, hesitation, and systematic incoherence. As Derrida points out, in this reading, "what are innocently called misreadings" are in fact "violent and self-serving operations" (*AF*, 53) by which Condillac's corpus is ordered and made accessible, bringing out themes and statements that expose it to interpretive stratagems. According to Derrida, Foucault's interpretation of Condillac in *Birth of the Clinic* belongs to this same type of simplistic critique. After having claimed that clinical thought in the eighteenth century (in particular as concerns the structure of the symptom) "merely transposes, into the more laconic and often more confused vocabulary of practice, a conceptual configuration whose discursive form was freely available to Condillac," Foucault proceeds to a critique of Condillac's logic.[37] This philosopher, says Foucault, "never derived a universal logic from the element—whether this element was perceptual, linguistic, or calculable; he never ceased to hesitate between two logics of operations: of genesis and of calculation."[38] There would thus be a contradiction in Condillac between a generative exigency and a combinatory exigency. The absence of any agreement between the two operations or of a categorical overlapping of their internal opposition leads Foucault to speak of a "deficiency . . . in Condillac's logic [that] opens up the field to a number of epistemological myths that are intended to mask it."[39] Yet, aside from the fact that the "hesitation" that Condillac is accused of is, according to Derrida, a "confused notion which always marks a reading's empiricist limit" (*AF*, 58), "the impotent hesitation between two models (for example, the algebraic and the biological)—indeed, to us today, this seems to constitute the force and interest of such a text" (*AF*, 49). Indeed, the impression that there exists a contradiction, if not a deficiency, in Condillac's text, is formed "only in comparison with an old philosophical opposition which prohibits thinking these two exigencies other than according to the category of exclusion or (speculative) dialectical synthesis" (*AF*, 47). There is no doubt that the opposition at question operates within Condillac's text; however, for Derrida, in distinction from Foucault for whom the opposition in question is a specific character of the age of representation, it is a question here of an opposition that is "even older than any so-called classical '*episteme*'" (*AF*, 49), namely, a metaphysical one that is anterior to all the so-called *epistemes*. Yet, maintaining these *two exigencies* would perhaps offer a non-dialectical way of resisting "the metaphysical opposition of calculation and genesis" (*AF*, 47). Indeed, what also operates in Condillac's text is a "a lever of disorganization" that "works at destroying this alternative between genesis and calculation, at ruining the whole system with which the alternative is interrelated" (*AF*, 49). Yet, if that is the case, Condillac's text is taken away not only from its author but also, as it is emphasized in *The Archeology of the Frivolous*, "from the all-powerful constraint of a mythic *episteme*" (*AF*, 48). Let us recall Foucault's subtitle: "An Archeology of Medical Perception." The introduction to the *Essay* cites as well *The Order of Things: An Archeology of the Human Sciences*, and even if *The Archeology of Knowledge*, which appeared in 1969, is not mentioned, one can assume that the critique of the general theory of *epistemes* sketched in Derrida's text has in its sights the project of an archaeology in general, as it is formulated in a programmatic way in this work. Derrida writes, "The finite code involved in the *episteme* still belongs solely to the representation of a particular *episteme*. The general theory of *epistemes* takes for its terrain and condition of emergence the imaginary of a single episteme—of that episteme which has as its determining norm the table, the finite code, and taxonomy" (*AF*, 48). Consequently, such a theory remains irreducibly finite, being structurally incapable of reflecting its own conditions of emergence.

The problem of archaeology and of its internal link to teleology is not taken up in *The Archeology of the Frivolous* in general terms. It is with respect to the text—precisely, to that of Condillac on the origin of human knowledge—that the question of teleology is posed. However, before addressing this question, we will have first to turn to Condillac's highly accented notion of the frivolous and of its archaeological interpretation by Derrida.[40] Let us keep in mind that Condillac's metaphysics is both a sensualism and a semiotics. Still, "although semiotics occupies the whole scene or rather the proscenium of all his discourse, Condillac will never have affirmed that the sign is first in experience in general" (*AF*, 94). Rising above perceptions, the chain of signs comes precisely to organize and develop the primary matter that is sensation, laid bare in the archaeological return to the origins of knowledge. Let us recall as well that as primary experience, sensation is the evidence itself whose possibility of indefinite certainty and ideal reproduction must rest on the ideal form of the present; in other words, of presence that is a self-present presence.[41] An atemporal experience, the self-presence of sensation would expose itself to a sign only upon the emergence of time in the living present. "*At the very moment* the present object comes to be missing from perception—the moment perception is absent from itself—at that moment the space of signs, with the function of imagination, is opened. . . . In the order of experience and of the operations of the soul, the sign then is never (*posited*) at the beginning" (*AF*, 95).

In his own introduction to the *Essay*, Condillac declares that to develop his principle of the connection of ideas, not only did he have to go back to "perception, because it is the first operation of the soul that we notice" and the first to give rise to ideas, but, in order to understand "how we have acquired the habit of using signs" that serve to link ideas together, he had also to begin with "the language of action [that] produced all the arts that pertain to the expression of our thoughts."[42] If in the beginning there is perception (and the simple ideas that are drawn from it), the language of action that is itself at the origin of language does not need signs. Yet even if the language of action, which is a silent, prelinguistic, and presemiotic language, precedes and founds all language, it signifies and *makes us act* only to the degree that, already, it judges, analyzes, and knows.[43] For it to be a language of action and practical knowledge, it must already bring about a certain connection. "For there is idea, judgment, and analysis before any signification [understood as activity and activation]" (*AF*, 97). In other words, in the language of action, before the appearance of the sign, the very being of the sign—sign-being—is at work, operates already, and links together sensations, or simple ideas. "Before there is signification, sensation analyzes, judges, and knows, but in confusion and obscurity, in the natural light of instinct" (*AF*, 97). But what does this imply? First, it implies that despite the anteriority of the mute sensation with respect to the sign, any metaphysical determination or delimitation between, on the one hand, the sensation (or idea) qua principle of origin and, on the other, the order of signs or, furthermore, between action language and sign language, is, to cite Condillac, nothing other than a question of degree (and, as Derrida insists, a question of time). Even if the "difference of degree" accounts for a difference between the concepts in question, it does not follow that the concepts are opposed. Indeed—to come to the second implication—the sign is in the end nothing but a "supplying remark" of that which already operates within sensation and action language; as it repeats that which is already at work within sensation, its function is solely to reflect and to assure clarity in the ideas of sensation, and thus to assure the acquisition of theoretical knowledge. Yet if for Condillac the theoretical "is only a supplying remark of the practical" (*AF*, 99), as Derrida holds, this is the case for the additional reason that the order of signs on which theoretical knowledge rests comes to supplement a lack, a deficiency, in the very order of sensations and of the action that it remarks methodically and theoretically.

Derrida continues: "Wherever such an operation takes place—that is, every-where, when the present comes to present itself, to do away with itself in its time—this operation remarks the anteriority in fact, of the *fact* (in the beginning was action, practice: in the beginning, i.e., in nature) as the anteriority with respect to itself of that which comes to be lacking in itself (*antériorité sur soi-même de ce qui vient à manquer à soi*). The analogy (to itself) ties this anteriority to that lack. To supplement is, after having re-marked and "retraced" the origin of the lack, to add what *is necessary,* what *is missing* [*ce qu'il faut*]. But what *is necessary*—what is lacking—also presents itself as a surplus, an overabundance of value, a frivolous futility that would have to be subtracted, although it makes all commerce possible (as sign and value)" (*AF,* 100–101). If the sign is necessary—a third implication—the origin is lacking with respect to itself. The sign remarks that which in fact precedes it—the origin—as something whose deficiency is older than itself. But although the sign seeks to compensate for this deficiency, it is also superfluous; it comes too late and, consequently, in what is a decisive impli-cation, it is futile and possibly frivolous. What, then, are the consequences of this for Condillac's new science?

The *Essay on Human Knowledge* does not exclude only a semiolin-guistic interpretation; it excludes as well, according to Derrida, "a reading of history as the history of discourse, indeed as an autonomous history of discursive statements" (*AF,* 99–100). The stated goal of Condillac's ar-chaeology is not the same as that of Foucault, whose archaeology seeks to establish the laws of the emergence of discursive and epistemic configura-tions, or, in short, the archive of their coming into existence. The archae-ology of the *Essay,* however, retraces the origins of knowledge so as to be able to rework or restore the sciences that are poorly elaborated on account of their languages. Its task is thus to supplement the existing scientific dis-courses by reworking their languages in accordance with first principles. But the secondariness of this archaeology is not solely a consequence of the task that thus befalls it. It always comes *after the fact* because, if there is a prelinguistic and presemiotic stratum of knowledge, it can only develop the mute material of sensation and thus supplement primary experience, that is, the supposedly full presence and evidence that it is supposed to represent. However, in coming after the fact and being secondary in two different senses, the original or originary principle put forward by this sci-ence can no longer be rigorously distinguished from that to which it is supposed to give rise and in respect to which it is thereby said to be the *archae*. Moreover, in coming after the fact, this archaeology is threatened by frivolity and futility. Just as the effect of overabundance produced by that which supplements the lack within sensibility—which is to say, by the sign that, for Condillac, is the real cause of any progress of the imagination— leads to a proliferation of empty signs, so archaeology, understood as a necessary corrective to the existing sciences, runs the risk of turning into frivolous chatter. It would thus, as archaeology, be necessarily threatened with frivolity.

What, then, can be said of frivolity? Under what conditions is it possible? What does an "archeological interpretation of the frivolous" amount to (*AF*, 122), and what makes such an interpretation possible, if not necessary? For Condillac, for whom "frivolity" is an explicit theme that the *Essay* frequently takes up, frivolity "originates with the sign, or rather with the signifier which, no longer signifying, is no longer a signifier. The empty, void, frail, useless signifier" (*AF*, 118). Doubtless, the sign is that which assures the availability of the object in our presence and our mastery of it when it is absent; but the sign, "fragile and empty, frail and futile . . . can also, immediately, lose the idea, get lost far from the idea, this time, and not only from the thing, from sense and not only from the referent" (*AF*, 118). Rather than come to the sign from without, "frivolity arises with the very origin of the sign . . . as a kind of essential fate, structural destiny, or original sin" (*AF*, 124). It is "its congenital breach: the *archae*, beginning, commandment, its putting in motion and in order—if only, in deviating and splitting from itself, frivolity, the sign's availability, could ever be or be made present *itself*. Since its structure of deviation prohibits frivolity from being or having an origin, frivolity defies all archaeology, condemns it, we could say, to frivolity" (*AF*, 118–119). Sign-being implies the existence of a deviation or inner gap from (it)self. This structure of the gap is what makes a sign a sign, makes it capable of signifying, and at the same time, what threatens it with straying far from the referent.[44] Although it provides the signifier with its ideality, its identity, and thus its iterability, the inner gap can always give rise to a "drift in which the sign repeats itself and identifies with itself to signify nothing other than itself" (*AF*, 124). "Frivolity begins its work, or rather threatens the work of its work in repetition in general, i.e., in the fissure which, separating two repetitions, rends repetition in two" (*AF*, 127). If frivolity is born from within this deviation or gap, this is because the gap always makes possible the "folding back on itself in its closed and nonrepresentative identity" (*AF*, 128). Divided, the repetition of the absent referent to which the sign applies itself can thus always (which is to say, necessarily) repeat nothing at all, other than the empty sign. Yet as long as this gap or deviation (of the sign) is simultaneously the condition for the fully signifying sign and the empty sign, frivolity concerns the possibility of meaning. Interpreted in an archaeological vein, frivolity is the origin of signification. It is "properly" the *archae*, assuming it is possible to so name a divided origin, an origin without any properties of its own, and thus that is lacking with respect to itself, being deprived of all self-identity.

The serious archaeological discourse assumed by *Essay on the Origin of Human Knowledge* would thus be inextricably linked to an archaeology of the frivolous as to "its infinitely alike double" (*AF*, 119). And, indeed, Condillac's tireless recourse to the values of analogy, the same, and the identical, show him to be concerned with trying to preserve his discourse from a frivolous double that haunts him at every turn. But before pursuing further the question of the spectral presence of the archaeology of the frivolous in the search for the origin of knowledge, I address the question of the teleology of the text—in this case, of Condillac's text. As we shall see, this question is also one of (the reading, by Derrida, of the) rereading, which here means of Condillac's reading of himself, since this rereading is itself teleological in nature. Although in the introduction to his *Essay*, Condillac promotes a reading of his work in which part 2 would develop only one of several types of signs that are distinguished in part 1, and would thus be only a part of the whole found within part 1, the fact that the type of sign at question is that of the instituted sign, or arbitrary sign (the two other kinds being the accidental sign and the natural sign), shows that from the very start the whole process of the progress of knowledge is oriented teleologically toward the mastery of meaning that the instituted sign alone allows for and that this type of sign is thus, in fact, the only true sign. As one of Condillac's letters to Gabriel Cramer proves, it was only upon rereading his own text that Condillac develops this teleological understanding. Consequently, the teleological process in which the *Essay* describes the progress of knowledge is established in a "teleological deferred action [*après-coup*], which reveals in the end an order of clarification" (*AF*, 110). If the rereading suggests that Condillac "had *always already* said that the sign as such was *always already* destined for the arbitrary," it is still the case that the possibility of the sign thus controls the totality of progress only from the vantage of its *end* (*AF*, 112). After the fact, the first part of the *Essay* will thus have "been part of a whole defined in part II, so part II remains, as well, by itself alone, the whole" (*AF*, 113). Viewed in light of its own introduction to the *Essay on the Origin of Human Knowledge*, the archaeological investigation of part 1 totalizes the text as a whole; however, viewed from its end, it is the possibility of the arbitrary sign that will have dominated the text as a whole. Concerning what Derrida calls "an internal reading of the *Essay*" (*AF*, 117), archaeology and teleology in the end amount to the same thing. Tied together intrinsically, they both work to shape the text in accordance with the thesis and to assure, at the level of meaning, the semantic unity of the text, its identity, the evident nature of its meaning. But a reading of the text such as Derrida's that "busies itself round about [with] lines, grating, borders, ribs, architecture, after-cuts" (*AF*, 108), "instead of being an introduction—to such a circle—can only proceed, with some excess, by means of elliptical and frivolous gestures" (*AF*, 118). In the reading that Derrida gives of the *Essay*, it is a question at bottom of analyzing "the great machine of oppositions (including that of form and content) wherein a text displaces its program: what the text programs, what programs the text, and what on all sides *breaches* the program, limits it in its very opening, and unravels in advance its teleology, undecides its circle" (*AF*, 108). In its reading of Condillac's text, the frivolous and infinitely similar double of the *Essay* that is *The Archeology of the Frivolous* adds to the semantic and internal reading of the *Essay* that in opposition to which the *Essay* has been conceived and constructed. *The Archeology of the Frivolous* is a critique neither of archaeology nor of teleology; rather, it simply retraces the negativity, the absence of origin, the absence of meaning that any archaeology as such presupposes in a spectral manner and against which it erects itself by protecting itself from frivolousness. It is arch-originary to such a degree that it no longer has anything about it that is originary.

The discourse of the *Essay* is wholly organized in light of the decision between the useful and the futile. In it, method serves as the privileged instrument for guarding against the threat of the frivolous. But the discourse on the origin of knowledge is also tied to a semiotics that raises the arbitrary sign to the dignity of a fully realized sign, which is the ultimate goal of all progress. As frivolity emerges with the arbitrary sign, not only does the "philosophy of the sign—Condillac's—always threaten this decision [between the useful and the futile], it also exerts itself, doing its utmost to reduce the threat, always adding 'too many signs' in order to efface the gap or fraction" (*AF*, 119), thereby undoing the very teleology of the process of knowledge. As we have already seen, frivolity emerges at the heart of repetition itself, separating it from itself in such a way that there exists both a good, and a bad, repetition. "The repetition of the idea, the identity of ideas is not frivolous. . . . It is the difference between these two identities, thus between these two forces of repetition, that would justify the gap or deviation between the more and the less, the positive and negative in all its forms, and in particular between the serious and the frivolous." But Condillac has linked together the two forces of repetition. Against Locke, he wanted to mark that there was "no connection of ideas without the connection of signs" (*AF*, 127). Yet if there is no connection of ideas without a connection of signs, "we never escape the double or stand-in for the idea itself " and thereby undo from the start the whole archaeology on which the progress of knowledge rests. "This," writes Derrida, "is frivolity's first or last garment" (*AF*, 119). Summoning one another, so as to effectively push knowledge forward and disallow frivolity, archaeology and teleology destroy at the same time the possibility of a core of self-evident presence that would be capable of being repeated without a loss of identity. Thus, the archaeology-teleology of human knowledge belongs to the archaeology of the frivolous against which it had hoped to defend itself and thus differs from the latter only gradually.

As a proto-phenomenology, or phenomenology *avant la lettre*, Condillac's philosophy undergoes the effects of that which it will have unveiled. Just as with Husserl, where the discovery of the structure of time results in the disintegration of the basic concept of the living present on which the whole phenomenological project was to depend, the structure of time disintegrates Condillac's philosophy of conscience and perception, a philosophy that was meant to find its indubitable origin in the primary experience of sensibility. We can recall that according to the author of the *Essay*, all metaphysical determinations and delimitations are possible only in a gradual manner. Derrida writes, "There is difference in general only by degrees. This fundamental proposition propagates its effects over all of Condillac's discourse. . . . The degree, the gradual difference, ruins the identical proposition by dislocating the *is*. But, by the same token, the degree makes the identical proposition possible by giving it a synthetic value which advances knowledge and prohibits frivolity. Of frivolity, time, an element of degree, thus marks at once the possibility and the impossibility" (*AF*, 131–132). Indeed, the frivolity exposed by Condillac, a frivolity against which he constantly struggles and that he tries methodically to exclude, is inextricably linked to the time whose cadence both opens and disallows self-presence. More precisely, the question of the frivolous is the very question of this nothing that is time. Time is the gap or deviation, the absence of presence whose deficiency opens the space wherein the present can relate to itself as it unfolds and deploys itself. Time, understood as "the gap of the present relation to itself and no less the present's self-relation in iterability—will have named *at once* the root of sensibility and the instance of the frivolous" (*AF*, 128). Compared to sensibility's core of presence, the frivolous would be its mere shadow. Arising from the gap or deviation of the signifier (that also allows the present to relate to itself), as well as from the folding of the signifier onto itself that this gap makes possible (that causes the signifier to relate to itself alone), the frivolous is an inevitable effect of time. "The fragility, the frail structure of the frivolous *is nothing but* (the time of a) difference (of degree), the spacing that ontology, as such, simply could not be capable of" (*AF*, 132). However, if, as we have seen, the "gap or deviation of time (repetition and absence of the present perceptive to itself) opens the representative vector-ing within both the sign and the idea," and if "the sign announces itself before the sign" in the idea itself (*AF*, 132–133), and if, therefore, the sign not only constantly risks running up against the absence of ideas, but also suffers from the lack of the thing, the extension of the frivolous is such that without its possibility time could no longer be the condition of possibility of sensibility and of knowledge. This extension "completes" the archaeological interpretation of the frivolous. However, as scientific progress is suspended at the arbitrary becoming of the sign, this process also makes frivolity grow. "The extension of the frivolous which leaves the idea without the thing and the sign without the idea, which lets the term's identity fall far from its object—the identity of the idea—this extension increases with progress itself. This extension follows the teleological movement, and grows in proportion to what it disintegrates" (*AF*, 133). Frivolity, therefore, is not only originary, it gestures toward the future. It is not only a threat that grows alongside progress; it constantly risks becoming its full realization.

III.

That any archaeology is also necessarily a teleology does not require extensive demonstration. As we have seen, in the case of Husserl, the project of a phenomenological archaeology is motivated by the desire to tie cognition back to reactivated primitive sources of all human accessions to being; in the case of Condillac, the reason for returning to primitive experiences is to secure future progress in knowledge, as well as to rework poorly made sciences in accordance with first principles. But, more generally it is easy to see that the very concept of *archae* entails the concept of *telos*. The very idea of a beginning implies that something arose, or will arise, as a product, a result, or a consequence, something that is intelligible only on the basis of what brought it about. A beginning or origin makes sense only with respect to what it has engendered, or what it will give rise to in conformity with what Husserl calls the "foundation of meaning (*Sinnesfundament*)," or *intentio*, of the beginning.[45] By emptying the title "archaeology" of all reference to beginnings, or origins, and by rejecting any teleological orientation, Foucault would seem to have freed archaeology from the implications that come with the concept. If he were successful, this archaeology then would no longer be an archaeology, nor would it merit to be called by that name.

But is it possible for the name "archaeology" to no longer refer to "archaeology"? Foucault's archaeology remains indebted to phenomenological thought; even though he rests his interpretation of archaeology on the notion of the archive, it continues to communicate with the phenomenological conception of archaeology to the extent that the archive, in the Foucauldian sense, is a discursive law and thus resonates with the meaning of *archae* as rule or law. Is it possible then to extricate a concept from its received meaning to such a degree that it would cease completely to refer to it? As we have shown, the undisputable intellectual feat of Foucault's archaeology is to have opened up the domain beyond linguistics and the logic of statement-events and to have articulated the laws of the emergence into existence—the becoming monuments—of statements and discourses. But, by calling this inquiry into the already-said on the level of its existence "archaeology," does Foucault not also draw on the resources and implications of the philosophical conception of archaeology that he has dismissed? Undoubtedly, existence here does not mean full and immediate presence since Foucault speaks of a dispersed population of singular discursive events—nor does existence suppress contradiction and difference, which Foucault shows are constitutive of the ontological dust of statement-events. In contrast to what obtains in the case of philosophical or phenomenological archaeology, in which the telos of the implied teleology is that of full presence and the undivided, and transparent realization of the beginning, there is no parousia—nor any transparency and indivision—involved on the level of existence to be accounted for by Foucault's archaeology. The domain of existence in question, whose laws of emergence are described by archaeology, is one of raw factuality given in advance of all ready-made synthesis. This has led Friedrich A. Kittler to advance a thermodynamic information-theoretical, and, in particular, statistical, interpretation of the laws that regulate the statement-events.[46] But, even in this case, the question remains whether it is possible for the speech events to emerge into existence without the propensity of the law to bring forth these events. A teleological trait, or pull, however minimal, is inevitable as long as one speaks of the enunciability of statements, of the conditions of existence of statements, of the sudden coming into appearance, or of the occurrence, of discursive events. By the same token, the law that governs this coming into existence, though perhaps not an absolute origin, is also inevitably tied to a function of beginning.

Let us bring to mind again Derrida's main critique of Foucault's archaeology as a general theory of *epistemes*: all the constitutive features of an *episteme* in general are drawn from one particular *episteme*—the classical *episteme*—for which, indeed, the table, the finite code, and taxonomy are the determining norm. It is in light of one singular *episteme* that all other configurations of knowledge are characterized as *epistemes* and analyzed with respect to their laws of emergence. As a consequence, Foucault's archaeology not only misses out on the specificity of the laws that explain the coming-into-existence of the other *epistemes*, but it itself remains irreducibly finite and incapable of reflecting on its own emergence into existence. Furthermore, as Derrida's critique of Foucault's reading of Condillac demonstrates, Foucault's archaeology, which conceives of itself as an intrinsic description of documents transformed into monuments, rather than being "the questioning of the *document*" (*AK*, 6), is itself put into question by the document.

It is certainly a paradox that both Condillac's archaeological inquiry into the primitive experiences at the origin of all knowledge and Husserl's phenomenological archaeology let themselves be inhabited by an archaeo-logically interpreted frivolousness yet this very frivolousness contributes to their greatness. But, aside from the frivolity of playing with the title "archaeology," is there any constitutive frivolity of the Foucauldian inquiry into the archive that commands the emergence into existence of statement-events and discourse formation? As is obvious from what we have seen, the laws that account for the conditions of existence of statements and dis-courses are not of the order of originary evidences of presence in which the thing is given to intuition. Although these laws of knowledge are called roots and all of the aspects of a particular episteme can be derived from them, their analysis does not reveal any non-originary structures like those that come to light in Condillac's and Husserl's investigations, which force one to recognize the presence of a spectral archaeology of the frivolous in their archaeology. As Foucault writes, "I not only admit that my analysis is limited, I want it so; I have made it so" (*AK*, 158). The limitations that characterize his archaeology derive primarily from its confinement to the description of particular configurations rather than totalities—to the analy-sis of configurations that are always each only "one of the describable groups," and that consequently cannot lay claim to any privilege (*AK*, 159). What limits the laws of the positivities from being first principles is, thus, only a function of the contingent grouping of the discursive phenomena to be analyzed and of the irreducibly factual nature of the syntheses, rather than non-originary structures presupposed by self-evident and self-present principles, structures that make these principles both possible and impos-sible. Ultimately, then, what restricts Foucauldian archaeology from within is not any essential non-originariness, but simply the empirical manifold of discursive events. More precisely, as a scattering of elements whose primal characteristic is their factual existence, the dispersion from which the archaeological descriptions starts out "can never be reduced to a single system of differences"; the sole title that the archaeological syntheses can lay claim to is that of having *made* differences and to continually bringing about "differentiations" within the ensemble of the dispersed statement-events—that is, a solely factual or empirical title (*AK*, 205).[47] Consequently, since it rejects any "absolute axes of reference," Foucault's archaeology not only relinquishes the project of being "a recollection of the original or a memory of the truth," its also forfeits the possibility of exhibiting radical structures of non-originariness that serve to account for the coming into existence of such ideas and concepts as existence, presence, originarity (*AK*, 205–206).

Undoubtedly, Foucault also recognizes the importance of time for his archaeology. The discursive formations that are the object of an investigation that is "never completed, never wholly achieved" (*AK*, 131) are not timeless formations. They do "not play the role of a figure that arrests time and freezes it for decades or centuries; it determines a regularity proper to temporal processes; it presents the principle of articulation between a series of discursive events and other series of events, transformations, mutations, and processes. It is not an atemporal form, but a schema of correspondence between several temporal series" (*AK*, 74). These formations exist neither simultaneously nor in a linear succession—that is, they do not share a homogeneous medium of time. But their internal time structure is not homogeneous either. In each case it is made up of a singular complex of a number of distinct, if not unequal, temporal series. Foucault's archaeology does not seek to reduce the diversity of the discourses by imposing an atemporal unity on them. Rather, it divides up their diversity into distinct temporal figures. Furthermore, the basic elements of the discursive formations, discursive statements, which, as we have seen, enjoy in Foucault's archaeology the status of discursive events characterized by positive existence, are capable of repetition, although, as Foucault observes, "always in strict conditions." "Instead of being something said once and for all . . . the statement, as it emerges in its materiality, appears with a status, enters various networks and various fields of use, is subjected to transferences or modifications, is integrated into operations and strategies in which its identity is maintained or effaced" (*AK*, 105). In no way does Foucault wish to reduce the existential dust of the statement-events. But the conditions, however strict, that determine a statement's identical repetition or effacement do not seem to affect the statement-event from within. In fact, even though a statement-event can cease to exist, its temporal nature (its existence) is only at the mercy of time in a conjectural or contextual sense—that is, a function of empirical and historical networks and fields of use. Time, here, is not what permits a statement to be identically repeated or to deviate frivolously from itself. Foucault's archaeology is not frivolous enough and, hence, "truly" an archaeology. If there are conditions that determine the identical repetition and possible effacement of statements that have come into existence, these are not structural or essential conditions with respect to the very existence of these events. Rather, they are of the order of exterior modifications.

It is precisely because of this lack of frivolity that Foucault's archaeology may also only be a poem—the poetic rewriting of all his own archaeological endeavors, the strong poetry of what makes such an undertaking meaningful but also nonsensical, as Deleuze has suggested. It is frivolous solely insofar as the appropriation of the title "archaeology" for a type of investigation of the existence of statement-events and discursive formations is concerned—especially given that archaeology does not question the intrinsic non-originary structures of the emergence into existence of such events. Yet, although Foucault holds that his archaeology has never pretended to be a science, and especially not a *philosophia prote*, the persistent concern with knowledge throughout all of his great archaeological investigations causes phenomenological archaeology to remain the standard against which his own undertaking is to be measured. Indeed, despite his admission that other archaeologies are conceivable, his archaeology remains primarily one of knowledge, and unfolds, in a way similar to Husserlian phenomenology, in view of the acquisition of further knowledge about knowledge. Husserl's phenomenology, though, opened itself up, however reluctantly, to the thought of the non-originary—that is, to an essential frivolity.

10

Thinking Within Thought

Although commonly understood as a concern with the ultimate questions, philosophical thought has been just as much, if not even more essentially, about thinking itself—its beginnings, characteristic aspects, and aims. Apart from the necessary awareness, and full mastery, of philosophy's main issues and their acknowledged goals, this concern with thinking itself is nothing other than a concern with, and disquietude about, the enigma of philosophy itself. As with any philosopher of stature, Gilles Deleuze could not satisfy himself with the answers (including his own) to this question, and he never ceased to inquire into the nature of philosophical thought. Perhaps the most intriguing indication of this preoccupation with what constitutes philosophical thinking are the three chapters in three of his early works devoted to the "image of thought": "New Image of Thought" in *Nietzsche and Philosophy* (1962),[1] "Image of Thought" in *Proust and Signs* (1964),[2] and, finally, "The Image of Thought" in *Difference and Repetition* (1968).[3] Strikingly similar, at moments even repeating themselves verbatim, the chapters from the Nietzsche and Proust books reveal an almost obsessive effort to elucidate the new image of thought that makes its irruption with Nietzsche and Proust. Nietzsche, for instance, is said to set up "a new image of thought, freeing thought from the burdens which are crushing it" (*NP*, 195), whereas Proust is said to set up "an image of thought in opposition to that of philosophy" (*PS*, 94). But Deleuze's effort also consists in defining an image of thought from which the new image breaks away. Yet, since the new image of thought that emerges with Nietzsche and Proust marks a break with another, older image, the chapters are above all the attempt to articulate what characterizes genuine philosophical thinking as such. This is especially the case with the chapter "The Image of Thought," roughly situated in the middle of *Difference and Repetition*. Deleuze asserts there that "we do not speak of this or that image of thought, variable according to the philosophy in question, but of a single Image in general which constitutes the subjective presupposition of philosophy as a whole" (*DR*, 132). By subsequently advocating "a thought without image," *Difference and Repetition* is thus intent on demarcating true philosophical thought from any image of thought, old and new. *What Is Philosophy?* by contrast, seems to reconsider the previous condemnation of the image. Indeed, Deleuze's encounter with cinema, and his attempt to define its singular essence, leads him, in *What Is Philosophy?* co-written with Félix Guattari, to a reevaluation of the ontological status of the image.[4] He, now, no longer disapproves in the same way of the image of thought—indeed, in this work the image of thought is said to fully participate in "the plane of immanence of the concepts," or rather, it is equivalent to the plane of immanence, that is, to the opening for the settlement of the concepts produced by philosophy. It thus coincides with the image that "thought gives itself of what it means to think, to make use of thought, to find one's bearing in thought." But if Deleuze can thus reconsider the status of the image, is it not because the image of thought as "what thought claims by right" now characterizes all philosophy, old and new?[5] Is Deleuze not led to recognize in this later work that at least a minimal element of the nonphilosophical is essential to philosophical thought as such and that all philosophy thus comes with an image of thought?[6] Considering these different evaluations, it appears that the notion of an "image of thought," and, particularly, the notion of "image," is equivocal and needs some clarification.

In *What Is Philosophy?* a work that still resonates with many of the concerns of the three chapters on the image of thought, Deleuze and Guattari distinguish, in a way somewhat reminiscent of Foucauldian categorizations, between the classical and the modern image of thought.[7] The modern image of thought differs from its classical image, which stretches from its beginning in Platonismus to Kant, who according to Deleuze in *Nietzsche and Philosophy*, "is the last of the classical philosophers [because] he never questions the value of truth or the reasons for our subjection to it" (*NP*, 94).[8] Whereas the classical image of thought defines philosophy from its relation to truth, modern philosophical thought, Deleuze and Guattari argue, "does not consist in knowing and is not inspired by truth. Rather, it is categories like Interesting, Remarkable, or Important that determine success or failure."[9] If "there is no will to truth" in the modern image of thought, it is because for the latter image, "thought constitutes a simple 'possibility' of thinking without yet defining a thinker 'capable' of it and able to say 'I,' " and thus the determining feature of the modern image of thought is the question: "what violence must be exerted on thought for us to become capable of thinking; what violence of an infinite movement that, at the same time, takes from us our power to say 'I.' "[10] However, in *Difference and Repetition*, this concern with what makes thinking possible and puts thinking into thought, as it were, is a concern suspicious of any image of thought, thought having been subjected to an image from early on to the present. In the latter work—perhaps, Deleuze's most ambitious one—it is a question of freeing thought from the yoke of the image. Before probing any further the question of the image of thought, a brief and preliminary reflection on how "image" is to be understood in this context may be warranted. Such a reflection is all the more urgent as Deleuze himself does not, to my knowledge, give any explicit hint at how he wishes "image" to be understood. Right away, however, it needs to be emphasized that "image" here suggests a nonconceptual approach to thinking in which the latter is "enveloped in sentiment rather than concepts" (*DR*, 129; trans. mod.). Rather than grasping thinking from its essence as thought, that is, in terms of what can only be thought, the image rests thinking on feelings, and on concepts that are not truly concepts, because, continuing to refer to empirical beings, they are not pure.

The image of thought, it seems to me, is not a thought-image, that is, an actualization in a psychological present in a sense akin to what obtains in the case of Henri Bergson's recollection-images, or perception-images. Nor is the reference to Bergson's conception of a universe of images, according to which the image entails movement, matter, and light, helpful for understanding the notion of the image of thought in Deleuze's work up to, and including, *Difference and Repetition* (although that may well be different in the case of Deleuze's work after the cinema books). Rather than retracing the term "image" in *Difference and Repetition*, to

Bergson's *Matter and Memory*, or to *Creative Evolution*, I suggest two different avenues. First, does not the claim that the image of thought distorts thought, and, especially, the programmatic invocation of a thought without image in chapter 3 of the work from 1968, recall Immanuel Kant's remark in the third *Critique* that "perhaps there is no sublimer passage in the Jewish law than the command, 'Thou shalt not make to thyself any graven image, nor the likeness of anything which is in heaven or in the earth or under the earth'?"[11] The image of thought is, as we will see, a representation of thought, and as Deleuze remarks, "representation is a site of transcendental illusion. This illusion comes in several forms, four interrelated forms which correspond in particular to thought, sensibility, the Idea and being. In effect, thought is covered over by an 'image' made up of postulates which distort both its operation and its genesis. These postulates culminate in the position of an identical thinking subject" (*DR*, 265).[12] If the concept of a transcendental illusion refers to the deceptive nature of any cognition that transgresses the boundaries of experience, the image of thought is illusory not merely because it pretends to make something noumenal intuitable and subject to concepts, but above all because, according to Deleuze, representation distorts and denaturalizes thought.[13] The other lead for explaining how Deleuze conceives of the "image" in *Difference and Repetition* I take from Martin Heidegger. Even though Heidegger's conception of "image" in his discussion of *Weltbild* (world picture) may no longer be pertinent to what Deleuze establishes in the cinema books and his works thereafter about the image, it provides a decisive clue that helps demarcate the image of thought from any thought-image.[14] In "The Age of the World Picture," Heidegger notes that the world picture is not a copy of the world, "a painting . . . of what is as a whole . . . 'world picture' means more than this. We mean by it the world itself, the world as such, what is, in its entirety, just as it is normative and binding for us. 'Picture' here does not mean some imitation, but rather what sounds forth in the colloquial expression, 'We get the picture' [literally, we are in the picture] concerning something. This means the matter stands before us exactly as it stands with it for us." To this definition of the image as a representation, a *Vor-Stellung*, in which the matter has been arrested just as it stands with it for us, Heidegger adds what he terms "a decisive determinant in the essence of the picture. . . . 'We get the picture,' concerning something does not mean only that what is, is set before us, is represented to us, in general, but that what is stands before us—in all that belongs to it and all that stands together in it—as a system (*in all dem, was zu ihm gehört und in ihm zusammensteht, als System vor uns steht*)."[15] As concerns the image of thought, image does not, in this case, designate a copy of thinking. Rather, in the image of thought, thought is understood as image, that is, as a systematic entirety of postulates. The image of thought is the systematic complex of the postulates through which it norms and binds our thinking. The image of thought further suggests that, as all of it that stands together in it, thought "is set up by man, who represents and sets it forth (*durch den vorstellend-herstellenden Menschen gestellt ist*)."[16] The systematic nature is, indeed, a major feature of Deleuze's conception of the image of thought, a feature through which, according to *Difference and Repetition*, thought, from Platonism on, has become disfigured, and from which thought has to be liberated for thinking to occur in the first place.

If thought is to be liberated from its image, it is because the image projects a "distorting image of thought (*image déformante*)" (*DR*, 132), and thus "betray(s) the very essence of thought as pure thought" (*DR*, 133). It "crush[es] thought under an image which is that of the Same and the Similar in representation, but profoundly betrays what it means to think" (*DR*, 167). On several occasions, Deleuze describes the effect of the image on thought in terms of a denaturation. For example: "Thought is covered over by an 'image' made up of postulates which denature (*dénaturent*) both its operation and its genesis" (*DR*, 265; trans. mod.). In *Difference and Repetition*, Deleuze also remarks that, "according to this image, thought has an affinity with the true; it formally possesses the true and materially wants the true," and, since the true is in complicity with the good, he defines it as a "moral image" (*DR*, 131). To liberate thought from this moral image, be it "at the cost of the greatest destructions and the greatest demoralizations" (*DR*, 132), is "to break this unjust (*injuste*) bond" (*DR*, 269; trans. mod.), which subordinates thought to the true and the good and which "alone can ground the supposed affinity between thought and the True" (*DR*, 132). Following Nietzsche, Deleuze understands both values as offshoots of "an interpretation of force which is that of *ressentiment*," a ressentiment against life and existence found to be guilty. He writes: "The spirit of revenge is the genealogical element of *our* thought, the transcendental principle of *our* way of thinking" (*NP*, 34–35). The effort to free thought from the postulates, or the values of the "dogmatic, orthodox or moral image" (*DR*, 131)—values that "hide an extraordinary hatred, a hatred for life, a hatred for all that is active and affirmative in life" (*NP*, 122)—thus takes place against the existing morality that wrongs thought by covering it over, deforming, denaturing, and betraying it in regard to its very nature. To break this "unjust bond" of thought to the dogmatic, or moral, image is thus an attempt to do justice to thought. According to the distinction made between morality and ethics in *Nietzsche and Philosophy* (*NP*, 122), the task of liberating thought from the image, a task whose cost is destruction and demoralization, is, thus, for Deleuze, unmistakably, an ethical undertaking.

As long as thought remains subject to this image, thought has not yet begun. For philosophy to begin in a rigorous sense requires a radical demarcation from the pre-philosophical, that is, from nonphilosophical presuppositions of philosophical thinking. It comes, therefore, as no surprise that the struggle to free thought from this image is also the struggle for a radically presuppositionless beginning of philosophy. The chapter "The Image of Thought" in *Difference and Repetition* opens with the observation that although philosophy has laid claim to a beginning free of presuppositions, it succeeded only in avoiding all "objective presuppositions," that is to say, "concepts explicitly presupposed by a given concept" (*DR*, 129). But it "does not escape presuppositions of another kind—subjective or implicit presuppositions contained in opinions rather than concepts" (*DR*, 129). In short, the image of thought, made of these subjective or implicit presuppositions (later called the plane of immanence of the concepts), is what has prevented all philosophy hitherto from achieving the presuppositionless beginning that it claims. As the association of these presuppositions with feelings and opinions rather than concepts suggests, philosophy has until now not been able to extricate itself entirely from *doxa*. Deleuze writes: "As a result, the conditions of a philosophy which would be without any kind of presuppositions appear all the more clearly: instead of being supported by the moral Image of thought, it would take as its point of departure a radical critique of this image and the 'postulates' it implies. It would find its difference or its true beginning, not in an agreement with the pre-philosophical Image but in a rigorous struggle against this Image, which it would denounce as non-philosophical" (*DR*, 132). The attempt to free thought from the image is thus the very condition under which thought could make a beginning: "as though thought could begin to think, and continually begin again, only when liberated from the Image and its postulates" (*DR*, 132). As we shall see, this radical, if not absolute departure from *doxa*, which Deleuze advocates for philosophy to finally have the ability to make the presuppositionless beginning that it always promised, requires also a radical new conception of the *thaumazein*, of philosophical wonder, that is.

Aiming at making it possible for thought to occur by liberating it from what prevents thought from making a, if not *the*, difference from the image by which "difference is crucified" (*DR*, 138), Deleuze seeks to secure the purity of philosophical thought, "pure thought," that is. Indeed, the value and the concept of the pure is frequently invoked in *Difference and Repetition* as something, finally, to be accomplished by the philosophy of difference that this work pursues. As we have seen, purity from *doxa* is a requirement that comes with the call for a presuppositionless beginning. Undoubtedly, Deleuze also criticizes the philosophical conception of purity because under the yoke of the image of thought it has never been capable of radical purity. Although Kant is credited for having discovered "the prodigious domain of the transcendental" (*DR*, 135), according to Deleuze, he failed to secure the latter's radical difference from the order of the empirical facts and merely traced the transcendental structures, that is, the pure intuitions and concepts, from the empirical facts of psychological consciousness. What philosophy considers to be pure thought is only "the image of what dogmatic thought is by right (*l'image en droit de la pensée dogmatique*)" (*DR*, 149; trans. mod.). Pure thought, as philosophy knows it, is thus not simply copied from the empirical and the factual, as the frequent use in the chapter under discussion of the verbs *calquer, décalquer, copier*, and so forth seemingly suggests, but consists in extrapolating what thought is in principle, or by right, from certain facts of thought—facts that, moreover, are "particularly insignificant," if not simply childish (*DR*, 135). As Deleuze's discussion of Descartes' definition of thinking and Kant's transcendental philosophy shows, his is a critique of purity in the name of purity.[17] Thought will achieve purity solely if it radically draws the transcendental consequences of what thinking implies and if thought strictly determines itself in view of, and in terms of, "that which can only be thought" (*DR*, 142).

The contention in *Nietzsche and Philosophy* that "philosophy since Hegel appears as a bizarre mixture of ontology and anthropology,

metaphysics and humanism, theology and atheism, theology of bad consciousness and atheism of ressentiment" (*NP*, 183) shows that this attempt
to, at last, secure the purity of thought is coupled with a nostalgia of sorts,
a nostalgia of some lost purity of thought. Deleuze's characterization of
pre-Socratic philosophy and its continued echo in Plato's thought, where it
survives in the shape of a repentance, or remorse, are a case in point.[18] Furthermore, as Deleuze recalls, "Nietzsche called the philosophers and philosophy of his time 'the portrayal of all that has ever been believed.' He might
say the same of today's philosophy where Nietzscheanism, Hegelianism,
and Husserlianism are the scraps of the gaudily painted canvas of modern
thought (*nouvelle pensée bariolée*)" (*NP*, 194). Deleuze's attempt, then, "to
break with dangerous alliances" and escape from the "strange mixture"
(*NP*, 194) in question, clearly suggests that the struggle to eventually allow
philosophy to make a radical beginning is also a struggle against what philosophy, since the *Philebos*, denounced as mixture and to retrieve the purity
of philosophical thought.[19] This then is also the point where a second
requirement—one that is intimately linked to the demand for an outright
break with *doxa*—can be shown to bear on thinking, if thought, indeed, is
to be pure thought. Although in the end Kant's *Critiques* do not overturn
the image of thought, and thus fail the transcendental project, it is Kant
who again has explicitly thematized this requirement and has shown the
way in which it is to be met. Indeed, Kant's discovery of "illusion," that is
to say, of the illegitimate use of faculties in thought's natural state, a use
that needs to be corrected by critical philosophy, is the discovery that in
this state "thought confuses its interests and allows its various interests to
encroach upon one another" (*DR*, 137). For Deleuze, the fate of thought
hinges on taking Kant's doctrine of dialectical illusion seriously, that is, the
demand to avoid at all price any mixture, as well as any confusion, of levels. Drawing out its extreme consequence for thought, illegitimate mixing
and confusion of pure thought and *doxa* in general are shown to extend to
thought's natural, as well as to its philosophical, state: "The natural illusion . . . is in effect extended into a philosophical illusion" (*DR*, 159).
Whereas in natural illusion what is principial is copied from empirical and
puerile examples, in philosophical illusion, the essential, or the pure, is determined in terms of the form of the factual. Thought strictly begins only
where the rupture with *doxa* frees itself of all confusion, the latter being always a "celebration of monstrous nuptials" (*DR*, 136).

Before I broach a third requirement for thought to be nothing but thought, a brief discussion of the status of "representation" in Deleuze's work is warranted. Indeed, Deleuze's criticism of the image of thought, in *Difference and Repetition*, is intrinsically linked to the condemnation of representation, which "as a whole is the element of knowledge" (*DR*, 191). The concept of representation can refer either to the portrayal or depiction of something or someone or, in its sacral or legal sense, as standing in for or in the place of something or someone by delegated authority.[20] Since the "generality" of what is represented is also what causes all representation to be a representative, both meanings are, as we will see, thoroughly interlinked for Deleuze. In his first book, *Experience and Subjectivity,* Deleuze contends that "Hume's philosophy is a sharp critique of representation," representation being understood here as rationalism's failed attempt to present the ideas, in other words, what is given, sensed, or experienced. Rationalism, Deleuze claims, sought to absorb the ideas into reason, thus putting into the idea "something which cannot be constituted within experience or be given in an idea without contradiction: the generality of the idea, the existence of the object, and the content of the terms 'always,' 'universal,' 'necessary,' and 'true.' " Representation thus consists in rationalism's transferral of "mental determinations to external objects, taking away thereby from philosophy the meaning and the intelligibility of practice and of the subject."[21] From this early study on Hume on, this critique of representation is in essence an effort to dismiss "the general in order to reach the most singular as principle or as universal" (*DR*, 7). Indeed, the critique of representation has become associated in Deleuze with the critique of the assumption that the subject can be a knowing subject and has been carried out in the name of a certain empiricism for whom the subject is primarily "a practical subject for which all real ends belong to the moral, passionate, political, and economic order."[22] In contrast to the knowing subject, or subject of representation, who frequents only the world of generalities, the practical subject inhabits the world of singularity—singularity being that which, according to Deleuze, alone merits the title of universality.[23] No other statement, therefore, characterizes his evaluation of representation better than the following from *Nietzsche and Philosophy*: "the notion of representation poisons philosophy" (*NP*, 81), poisons it with the general and generalities.[24]

This emphasis on the general in representation (as opposed to the singular, i.e., the only universal) causes any picture, copy, or model—in

Kantian language, any *Vorstellung*—to be at the same time a proxy, a mouthpiece, or an organ of the general (*Repräsentation*). As demonstrated by the very form of the subjective or implicit presuppositions of philosophical thinking that make up the image of thought, which constitutes the world of representation and prevents thought from ever radically beginning in a presuppositionless way, the pre-philosophical evidences on which thinking in philosophy rest are evidences supposedly shared by all, more precisely, by the greatest number. Indeed, the form of these presuppositions is that of " 'Everybody knows' . . . *Everybody knows, no one can deny*, is the form of representation and the discourse of representation" (*DR*, 129–130). The presupposition in question, which amounts to the assumption that everybody naturally thinks and that thinking is of an upright nature and of good will, that is, the assumption of a common sense and a good sense, in short, allows the philosopher to "assume that the universality of his premises—will be universally understood" (*DR*, 130). By founding itself on these pre-philosophical evidences, the philosophical discourse (even though, on the surface, it sides with the *idiota*, the layman, who has no presuppositions regarding this or that) is, first and foremost, a discourse that represents the opinion of the majority. To represent something is defined as a "speaking *for others*" (*DR*, 52), that is, either in their place or in their name. Even though the philosopher is not the mouthpiece for this or that particular opinion, by not questioning the subjective or implicit presuppositions of philosophy, the philosopher yields to, and stands in for, the form of *doxa*—an opinion that is general solely because it concerns only the greatest number. Philosophy as a mode of representation is based on the assumption that everybody shares a basic knowledge and a natural predisposition to knowledge, in short, a *common sense* and a *good sense*, which together "constitute the two halves of *doxa*" (*DR*, 134). It follows from this that thought does not begin, because it only represents something that supposedly is common to all, and knowledge in such thought is restricted to the re-cognition of what everybody already knows implicitly.

According to Deleuze, "the prefix RE- in the word representation signifies [the] conceptual form of the identical which subordinates differences" (*DR*, 56). On the opening page of *Difference and Repetition*, he writes that "the primacy of identity, however conceived, defines the world of representation" (*DR*, xix). This principle of identity is the presupposition of all representation whether organic or orgiastic, finite or infinite.

Because of the primacy of identity, representational thought fails to capture difference, multiplicity, the immediate, and singularity. Indeed, by relating difference to a thought identity, or represented equality, difference "loses both its own concept [that is, the concept that permits to think difference in itself] and its own reality" (*DR*, 35). In "the distorted (*dénaturé*) world of representation" (*DR*, 117), or the general, real difference, that is, "free, wild, or untamed difference" (*DR*, 50), is submitted to a previously established identity and thus becomes mediated difference. This mediation in the world of representation is accomplished in four ways, which are "the requirements of the concept in general" (*DR*, 29). Representation, Deleuze holds, has a "necessarily quadripartite character" (*DR*, 34–35). Its four principle aspects—aspects that render it synonymous with "reason" itself— are: "identity, in the form of the *undetermined* concept; analogy, in the relation between ultimate *determinable* concepts; opposition, in the relation between *determinations* within concepts; resemblance, in the *determined* object of the concept itself. These forms are like the four heads or the four shackles of mediation. Difference is 'mediated' to the extent that it is subjected to the fourfold root of identity, opposition, analogy and resemblance" (*DR*, 29). Thanks to these four requirements of representation, "difference is, as it were, reconciled with the concept" (*DR*, 29), or more precisely, as mediated difference, it acquires the status of a "*reflexive concept*" (*DR*, 34).

Representational thought as the thought that "saves" difference by inscribing it within the concept in general concurs with the so-called "propitious moment—the Greek propitious moment (*l'heureux moment grec*)" (*DR*, 29). One of the prime aims of *Difference and Repetition* consists in drawing what Deleuze characterizes as "the arbitrary boundaries of the propitious moment" (DR, 34) in question. For the time being, let me only emphasize that by establishing the general and the concept in general as the medium to which all difference is to be related, and thus to be raised to the status of a reflexive concept, the Greek propitious moment—that is, the emergence of representational thought and the "world of representation"— coincides with the ascendance of good sense and common sense, in other words, of a way of thinking that can claim to be general (rather than universal) and is shared by everybody over thinking that "makes" a difference. However paradoxical it may sound, for Deleuze, the propitious Greek moment, rather than a suspension, is the triumph of *doxa*. Leaving a detailed discussion of the question of good sense and common sense for another occasion, let me only say at this point that according to Deleuze, the latter are intimately linked to the whole problematic of judgment in philosophical thought. The instance capable of proportioning the concept to difference is that of judgment. Deleuze writes: "For judgment has precisely two essential functions, and only two: distribution, which it ensures by the *partition* of concepts; and hierarchization, which it ensures by the *measuring* of subjects. To the former corresponds the faculty of judgment known as common sense; to the latter the faculty known as good sense (or first sense). Both constitute just measure or 'justice' as a value of judgment" (*DR*, 33). As a kind of thought that seeks to "save" difference, that is, to make it "both livable and thinkable," representational thought approaches what it has predetermined "as an evil in itself," in moral terms, asking "how far the difference can and must extend—how large? how small?—in order to remain within the limits of the concept, neither becoming lost within nor escaping beyond it" (*DR*, 29–30).

If representational thought as it emerges in the Greek propitious moment identifies difference, the task of modern philosophy, that is, the philosophy of difference, is to think difference itself by overturning Platonism, since "Platonism already represents the subordination of difference to the powers of the One, the Analogous, the Similar and even the Negative" (*DR*, 59). With this, a third basic requirement for thought to be pure thought comes into view. In addition to the need to radically break with *doxa* in order to make a presuppositionless beginning, and to avoid all confusion of levels, a reversal of all previous hierarchies and values is required to discover the true transcendental structures of thought. Representational thought, or the thought subject to the image of thought, is not only based on a confusion of genres; it also errs in the way it sets priorities. As Deleuze writes: "We always rediscover the necessity of reversing the supposed relations or divisions between the empirical and the transcendental" (*DR*, 167). Indeed, "without . . . reversal, the famous Copernican Revolution amounts to nothing" (*DR*, 162). The declared aim of this overturning is to exit completely from the world of representation and to rediscover the "world of pure difference" that it presupposes (*DR*, 125). As Deleuze holds, the "crucial experience of difference" (*DR*, 50), of real, nonmediated difference, that is, of difference as "pure presence" (*DR*, 69), consists in the "lived reality of a sub-representative domain" (*DR*, 69), namely, of a realm made up by "a swarm of differences, a pluralism of free, wild or untamed differences; a properly differential and original space and time; all of which persists alongside the simplifications of limitation and opposition" (*DR*, 50). Deleuze's "superior empiricism" (*DR*, 57) is the attempt not only to reconnect philosophy to the experience of such nonmediated difference, but also, as the second half of *Difference and Repetition* demonstrates, to exhaustively map the space-time of differential multiplicity. "*The fundamental principle of empiricism* [is] *the principle of difference*," Deleuze remarks in the book on Hume.[25] In *Nietzsche and Philosophy*, he states that "in fact, pluralism (otherwise known as empiricism) is almost indistinguishable from philosophy itself. Pluralism is the properly philosophical way of thinking, the one invented by philosophy; the only guarantor of freedom in the concrete spirit" (*NP*, 4).[26] As we have already seen, a thinking of difference itself is a thinking of what escapes the realm of the general: the real in the shape of quality, intensity, the remarkable, singularity, the event, and "our power of creation and decision" (*DR*, 268). If this is "the most important task" (*DR*, 268) that thinking has to pursue, thinking must not only free itself from "the four iron collars of representation," that is, "the four roots of the principle of reason" (*DR*, 262), which raise difference to the level of the general. Since to represent something is to speak in the name of the others, thinking must also liberate itself from representation as the mode of thinking characteristic of everyone. Indeed, "the representant says: 'Everyone recognizes that . . . ,' but there is always an unrepresented singularity who does not recognize precisely because it is not everyone or the universal. 'Everyone' recognizes the universal because it is itself the universal, but the profound sensitive conscience which is nevertheless presumed to bear the cost, the singular, does not recognize it" (*DR*, 52). Philosophy in a genuine sense, according to Deleuze, takes the side of the individual who "full of ill will" "does not manage to know what everybody knows" and who thus "neither allows himself to be represented nor wishes to represent anything' (*DR*, 130). In short, true philosophical thought arises from what is peculiar, singular, and private, as opposed to what is publicly established and what everyone knows and cannot deny.

As I have already suggested, the critique of the image of thought—of thought's representational mode—is an attempt to free at last thinking radically from *doxa*. The significance of Deleuze's work, I hold, rests on the attempt at radically accomplishing such a liberation of thinking from *doxa*, by taking serious the extreme consequences implied by this philosophical demand par excellence.[27] The guiding hypotheses for what follows is, therefore, that Deleuze's philosophy of difference seeks to renew and reform philosophical thought by radically following up on the *real* conditions of the philosophical spelled out at the origin of philosophy in Greece—that is, before the propitious moment in which thought becomes dominated by the principle of identity—first and foremost, the demand to break without compromise with *doxa*. As Deleuze's repeated critiques of the phenomenological notion of *Urdoxa* demonstrate, his effort is aimed at expelling not only all particular *doxa* from thinking, but *doxa* in all its forms, as well as, as we will see, in the form of the form of *doxa*, and thus to cut off thinking, ab-solutely, from this inferior type of knowledge.[28]

It is well known that the *pathos* of wonder with which philosophy is said to begin is, according to Aristotle, awakened by the realization that one does not know why something is as it is. Therefore, wonder makes room immediately for the search for the grounds and causes of the wonder in question. As Ute Guzzoni has argued, with this metamorphosis of the wonder that something is, and is such as it is, into the question of why it is, "a significant preliminary decision has taken place that, at least since Aristotle, has shaped all of metaphysical thinking." Guzzoni is thus led to ask "whether philosophy can only correspond to an experience of such radical wonder by asking the why-question, and by thus taking the road of foundation as a result of which the all-encompassing wonder becomes sublated."[29] It seems to me that Deleuze's philosophy of difference pursues a different road than the one prefigured by Aristotle, one on which philosophical wonder, and the difference that it makes, rather than being sublated into knowledge is conserved and perpetuated. Wonder qua difference not only opens up philosophy, but it is also what philosophy incessantly must reactivate, or repeat. Now it needs to be acknowledged that "wonder" is not a particularly prominent term in Deleuze's writing. Indeed, what incites thought, more precisely what forces thought to think, or what "engender[s] the act of thinking within thought itself" (*DR*, 114), is, for Deleuze, of the order of a different pathos. According to *Nietzsche and Philosophy*, the determined "use of philosophy is to *sadden*" (*NP*, 106). But the pathos that Deleuze primarily associates with the philosophical is one that is experienced in aggression, as a violent, terrifying, if not even cruel intrusion. Violence, however, is not an arbitrary substitution for wonder; in fact, as is to be seen, violence is what enables wonder to be wonder in the first place.

All the chapters devoted to the image of thought in *Nietzsche and Philosophy*, *Proust and Signs*, and *Difference and Repetition* concur in the assumption that "stupidity is a structure of thought as such" and that, in the average, it consists of "imbecile thoughts, imbecile discourses, that are made up entirely of truths; but these truths are base" (*NP*, 105). In *Nietzsche and Philosophy*, Deleuze asserts that "thinking is never the natural exercise of a faculty. Thought never thinks alone and by itself. . . . Thinking, as an activity, is always a second power of thought, not the natural exercise of a faculty, but an extraordinary event *in* thought itself, *for* thought itself. Thinking is the n-th power of thought. . . . But it will never attain this power if forces do not do violence to it. Violence must be done to it *as* thought, a power, *the force of thinking*, must throw it into a becoming-active" (*NP*, 108; trans. mod.). After the statement that "thought is nothing without something that forces and does violence to it," Deleuze writes in *Proust and Signs* that "the *leitmotiv* of Time regained is the word *force*: impressions that force us to look, encounters that force us to interpret, expressions that force us to think" (*PS*, 95). And, finally, after having approvingly invoked Heidegger's claim that though man possesses the possibility to think, there is no guarantee that we are in fact capable of thinking, he observes (in a passage omitted in the English translation of *Difference and Repetition*) that "thought thinks only when constrained and forced, in the presence of what 'gives to think,' of what is to be thought— and what is to be thought is also the unthinkable or non-thought, that is, the perpetual fact that 'we still do not think.' "[30] Now, what "gives to think" (though for Deleuze there is, strictly speaking, no *gift* involved here) are not ordinary things, the things that surround us, those that are easily available. In the Nietzsche book, Deleuze avers that "thinking depends on certain coordinates. . . . We are not going to think unless we are forced to go where the forces which give food for thought are, where the forces that make thought something active and affirmative are made use of. . . . It is up to us to go to extreme places, to extreme times, where the highest and the deepest truths live and rise up. The places of thought are the tropical zones frequented by the tropical man, not temporal zones or the moral, methodical or moderate man" (*NP*, 110). In *Proust and Signs*, where the places "in which are elaborated the effective forces that act on thought, [and] the determinations that *force* us to think," are called "dark regions" (*PS*, 95), Deleuze makes thinking dependent on the chance encounter of certain things. He writes: "Truth depends on an encounter with something that forces us to think and to seek the truth." Throughout *Proust and Signs*, the objects that impose upon us the need to think are what Deleuze calls "signs." "What forces us to think is the sign. The sign is the object of an encounter, but it is precisely the contingency that guarantees the necessity of what it leads us to think. The act of thinking does not proceed from a simple natural possibility; on the contrary, it is the only true creation. Creation is the genesis of the act of thinking within thought itself. This genesis implicates something that does violence to thought, which wrests it from its natural stupor and its merely abstract possibilities. To think is always to interpret—to explicate, to develop, to decipher, to translate a sign" (*PS*, 97). The chance encounter with a sign—the sign being defined as "a substance, an object, a being as if it emitted signs to be deciphered, interpreted" (*PS*, 4)—that, unprepared, overcomes us, and "impels us to a search" (*PS*, 15), forces thought upon us. Only because the thought thus provoked is the result of a violence or an encounter by which one is caught off guard is it a thought that, rather than being arbitrary, has genuine necessity. Indeed, "it is the fortuitousness of the contingency of the encounter which guarantees the necessity of that which it forces to be thought" (*DR*, 145). Solely a violent encounter that sets off thinking can endow its truths "with necessity and the mark [*la griffe*, that is, the claw] of necessity" (*PS*, 95). Only the violence that engenders it, guarantees its authenticity as a singular response to an unexpected event. Indeed, thinking is thinking on the condition only that it is engendered within thought as a "pure creation" (*PS*, 97), in an act of thinking that thus makes a difference within thought, or more precisely, within thought as abstract thought, thought in general, everybody's thought. The genesis of thinking, or "the *genitality* of thinking," that is, "that difference that thinking makes within thought" (*DR*, 266), amounts to the singular event in which an act of thinking is violently wrenched from the natural stupor of thought in a response to a chance encounter for which one was not prepared. Deleuze writes in *Proust and Signs*: "To think is to create and primarily to create the act of thinking within thought" (*PS*, 111). A reference, in the work on Proust, to a passage from the *Republic*, which Deleuze takes up again in *Difference and Repetition*, permits to further clarify the kinds of objects, or signs, that violently provoke thinking within thought. Plato's remark that "the experiences that do not provoke thought are those that do not at the same time issue in a contradictory perception. Those that do have that effect I set down as provocatives, when the perception no more manifests one thing than its contrary, alike whether its impact comes from nearby or afar,"[31] leads Deleuze to conclude that by demarcating the things that do not stir up thought from those that provoke it, "Plato offers us an image of thought under the sign of encounters and violences." He writes: "Plato distinguishes two sorts of things within the world: those that leave the mind inactive or give it only the pretext of an appearance of activity, and those that lead it to think. . . . The first are the objects of recognition; all the faculties are exercised upon these objects, but in a contingent exercise, which makes us say 'that is a finger,' that is an apple, that is a house and so on. Conversely, other things force us to think; no longer *recognizable* objects, but things that do violence, *encountered* signs. These are 'simultaneously contrary perceptions,' Plato states" (*PS*, 100–101). *Difference and Repetition* provides a more extensive commentary of the whole passage in question in which Plato also illustrates his point with the down-to-earth example of the three end fingers of one of our hands whose sight leaves no doubt that each is a finger, but whose qualities—their size, for example—lead to contradictory perception. Indeed, in the latter case, "what we see enables us to say that the finger is large, but also, and equally well, to say that it is small. So in these cases the mind is forced to reflect, and to come in to settle the problem."[32] Deleuze points out that in the face of recognized objects, "thought may busy itself thereby, but such employment and such activity have nothing to do with thinking" (*DR*, 138). Yet, the objects, by contrast, that force thinking upon us are not, therefore, objects that we would have difficulty recognizing, in short, objects that would be uncertain or doubtful. "Certainties force us to think no more than doubts," Deleuze remarks (*DR*, 139). In other words, only those objects that are entirely heterogeneous to the realm of the certain and the doubtful, that is, to the register of the recognizable, "giv[e] birth in thought to the act of thinking." Only those objects that escape the concept and the order of truth, "things that do violence, encountered signs" (*PS*, 101), are capable of giving rise to thought, for concepts, Deleuze asserts, "lack the claws of absolute necessity—in other words, of an original violence inflicted upon thought; the claws of a strangeness or an enmity which alone would awaken thought from its natural stupor or eternal possibility: there is only involuntary thought, aroused but constrained within thought, and all the more absolutely necessary for being born, illegitimately, of fortuitousness in the world. Thought is primarily trespass and violence, the enemy, and nothing presupposes philosophy: everything begins with misosophy. Do not count upon thought to ensure the relative necessity of what it thinks. Rather count upon the contingency of an encounter with that which forces thought to raise up and set up the absolute necessity of an act of thought or a passion to think" (*DR*, 139; trans. mod.). Thinking occurs within thought only by way of a violent break-in, triggered by something in the world that forces us to think, that is, something that is not an object of recognition by thought, "but of a fundamental *encounter*" (*DR*, 139). What thus forces thinking upon us is not the fact that the things in question are inexplicable, that we do not yet know *what* they are, or that we are surprised by the fact *that* they are, but these things' utter heterogeneity to thought, more precisely, their absolute difference from the image that thought has of itself. Yet, as Deleuze writes: "Thought must think difference, that absolutely different from thought which nevertheless gives it thought, gives to be thought" (*DR*, 227). The encounter of such things is per se a violent confrontation to which thought is forced to respond in an act as singular as the encounter is contingent.[33]

What causes thinking is thus not wonder about inexplicable phenomena or about bigger things such as the world or the universe. Rather, thinking is triggered by what makes wonder, wonder in the first place. Indeed, if one draws on the implicit conditions under which alone wonder, in conformity with its concept, can take place, wonder is genuinely wonder only if one becomes truly unsettled, violently shaken, and torn from one's everyday setting—*ent-setzt*, as Eugen Fink translates the Greek *thaumazein*.[34] Deleuze, in advancing that thinking emerges in thought only when violently provoked by a thing in the world (rather than by the awareness of "the" world itself, and thus by the concept as such of the world as distinct from what is in the world), does not arbitrarily replace one understanding of wonder with another. Rather, in the classical philosophical conception according to which philosophy arises from wonder, Deleuze singles out a necessary implication and pushes it to its extreme consequences. Deleuze makes his understanding of philosophical thinking dependent on the *thaumazein*'s ab-solutely unsettling effect on everyday thought. Undoubtedly, from its outset, philosophical thought has claimed to be radically distinct from common thought. Deleuze does not propose anything else (although it is no longer the same "object" that causes such wonder). His interpretation of thought only radicalizes this already radical claim; he pushes it to the extreme point of defining thought as the enemy of thinking.

In "The Vienna Lecture," while discussing the reorientation implicit in the *thaumazein* as a " 'theoretical' attitude, [one that] is not practical in any sense used so far" and that sharply distinguishes it from the mythical-practical attitude, however universal it may be, Edmund Husserl observes that what he is primarily interested in understanding is "the path of motivation, the path of the bestowal and creation of meaning which leads from the mere reorientation, from mere *thaumazein*, to *theoria*." He adds: "We must clarify the transformation from original *theoria*, the fully disinterested seeing of the world (following from the epoche of all practical interests, world-knowledge through pure, universal seeing) to the *theoria* of genuine science, the two being mediated through the contrast of *doxa* and *episteme*."[35] In distinction from Husserl, one could perhaps conjecture that Deleuze wishes to hold on to the *thaumazein*, preventing it from developing into "genuine science," the latter being precisely that in which, dominated by the image of thought, the *thaumazein*, and thus the difference that thinking makes, becomes domesticated. Indeed, in the chapter "The Image of Thought" in *Difference and Repetition*—the most elaborate of the three chapters devoted to this subject matter—Deleuze not only establishes in systematic fashion eight postulates that characterize the orthodox image of thought, but also he puts these postulates into question by "systematically" confronting them with all the implications, radicalized *à outrance*, of the origin of thought in the pathos of the *thaumazein*. What the radical critique of the image of thought seeks to achieve is the thorough activation and affirmative de-velopment of all the major implications of the fact that thinking is violently born from the encounter of unrecognized, and unrecognizable, things. Without pushing the implications in question to the utmost, philosophical thought, according to Deleuze, remains a shadow of itself.

The pre-philosophical presuppositions of philosophical thought that make up the image of thought are what Deleuze terms "postulates." He writes: "Postulates in philosophy are not propositions the acceptance of which the philosopher demands; but, on the contrary, propositional themes which remain implicit and are understood in a pre-philosophical manner. In this sense, conceptual philosophical thought has as its implicit presupposition a pre-philosophical and natural Image of thought, borrowed from the pure element of common sense" (*DR*, 131). These eight postulates are all interrelated, following from and incorporating one another without any one having priority over the others (though Deleuze's order of exposition of these postulates may also suggest a certain line of derivation). They spell out the different aspects of "the pure element of common sense," that is, what is essential about its form rather than this or that content. Each of these postulates "has two forms, because they are both natural and philosophical, appearing once in the arbitrariness of examples, once in the presuppositions of the essence" (*DR*, 167). They are thus constituted by a double transcendental illusion—a natural and a philosophical illusion. Indeed, upon analysis of the dogmatic image of thought, the postulates consistently reveal "the same confusion: elevating a simple empirical figure to the status of a transcendental, at the risk of allowing the real structures of the transcendental to fall into the empirical" (*DR*, 154). Furthermore, as Deleuze repeatedly remarks, the simple empirical figures (singled out in the natural transcendental illusion) are always based on the same puerile examples, whose form, or essence, is raised to the status of the transcendental in philosophical illusion. By espousing these postulates, thought remains stillborn from the outset. For thought to begin at last, it thus becomes necessary to dispel the confusion and to reverse the valorizations, radically drawing out the implications of what has become "crucified" in representational thought.

At the end of the chapter "The Image of Thought," after a lengthy and detailed discussion of the eight postulates, Deleuze provides us with their schematic list. Taking into account that each one of them has two forms, this list reads as follows:

(1) the postulate of the principle, or the *Cogitatio natura universalis* (good will of the thinker and good nature of thought); (2) the postulate of the ideal, or common sense (common sense or the *concordia facultatum* and good sense as the distribution which guarantees this concord); (3) the postulate of the model, or of recognition (recognition inviting all the faculties to exercise themselves upon an object supposedly the same, and the consequent possibility of error in the distribution when one faculty confuses one of its objects with a different object of another faculty); (4) the postulate of the element, or of representation (when difference is subordinated to the complementary dimensions of the Same and the Similar, the analogous and the Opposed); (5) the postulate of the negative, or of error (in which error expresses everything which can go wrong *in* thought, but only as the product of *external* mechanisms); (6) the postulate of logical function, or the proposition (designation is taken to be the locus of truth, sense being no more than the neutralized double or the infinite doubling of the proposition); (7) the postulate of modality, or solutions (problems being materially traced from

propositions or, indeed, formally defined by the possibility of their being solved); (8) the postulate of the end, or result, the postulate of knowledge (the subordination of learning to knowledge, and of culture to method). (*DR*, 167)

Rather than discussing each one of the eight postulates in detail, in conclusion, I wish, with Deleuze's basic tenets for a radical beginning of thought in mind—the radical break with "what everybody knows," utmost purity of the transcendental, and the reversal of established hierarchies—to briefly spell out, although quite schematically, how each of these postulates of the image of thought becomes an instance for extrapolating and radicalizing the implications of the "fact" that philosophical thought emerges within thinking only if it is forced upon thinking in a violent and unpredictable encounter with an object, or sign.

1. Although philosophy has always understood itself as pitted against *doxa*, it has never been consequential in following up on this demand; it has never severed itself without compromise from pre-philosophical assumptions. Only by freeing thought, not only from this or that opinion, but also from the very *form* of *doxa*, that is, from the assumption that everybody is naturally capable of thought and that thought is upright by nature, does philosophical thought begin without any presuppositions and thus make good on the demand, which, from its inception in Greece, defined philosophical thought.[36] Relinquishing the assumptions that everybody has a natural inclination to thinking and that thought has an affinity to truth is to disconnect thought from any love for truth and to have it begin with the individual, who is full of ill will.

2. Given that the image of thought raises common sense and good sense to the status of what thought is by right (rather than by fact), "it provides a philosophical concept for the presupposition of common sense" (*DR*, 133). As "the harmonious exercise of all the faculties upon a supposed same object," common sense and good sense "become philosophical" in that they are raised to the status of the "pure element" within which thinking operates (*DR*, 133). Though the image of thought "upholds no particular propositions of good sense or common sense . . . [it retains] the essential aspect of common sense—namely, the element" (*DR*, 134). For thought to begin, then, this pure element must be undone by radicalizing what is essential to each faculty and thereby elevating it to its transcendental form; by replacing the unity of the subject implied in the conception of the *concordia facultatum* with a fractured I, the illusory "distribution of the

empirical and the transcendental" (*DR*, 133) on which the image of thought rests is put into question.[37] The thought born within thinking, thought without image, will finally have to be serious about the transcendental and not allow any empirical reality, or the form thereof, to be raised to the level of the transcendental.

3. For thinking to be distinct from the stupor of ordinary thought, it is necessary to propose "a completely other model" (*DR*, 136) than the model of recognition, which is the "the instrument of every orthodoxy" (*DR*, 146). Given that in the model of recognition all the faculties that are grounded in a supposedly universal subject (that is, a formal abstraction from common sense) are exercised upon an identical object, the cognized is always only something that is knowable, or recognizable. Rather than basing itself on identical, or identifiable objects (objects that thus are formally known in advance), the entirely different model for thought is that of "a fundamental *encounter*" (*DR*, 139). Thought is free from the image of thought if it is a creative response, which nothing anticipates, not to recognizable and insignificant things but to things encountered that do violence to thought. Thinking must "seek its models among stranger and more compromising adventures" (*DR*, 135).

4. The postulate (or model) of recognition, with its quadripartite fetters, is itself only a function of the "much more general postulate of representation" (*DR*, 139). Since something becomes an object of representation always only on the basis of hypothetical truths (such as the identity, analogy, opposition, or similitude in relation to which it is viewed), "which presuppose all that is in question," the element of representation cannot give birth in thought to the act of thinking (*DR*, 139). No wonder, no encounter, strictly speaking, occurs in the element of representation. For thought to emerge within thinking, the tranquility of a thought voluntarily busying itself with objects that it already recognizes, which, therefore, do not put the image it has of itself into question, must be supplanted by the "passion to think" (*DR*, 139). Such a passion arises involuntarily from things that force themselves upon thinking, which, thereby, also thoroughly unsettle it. For thought to begin, the passionate character of philosophical wonder (the *pathein* of the *thaumazein*) must be realized to the extreme. If thinking in a genuine sense cannot be of the order of intellection (recognition, representation, conceptional identification), it is because, as the involuntary result of a violent encounter,

thinking (a) takes place in a mode in which the encountered object "can only be sensed" and in which the object "really gives rise [as if for the first time] to sensibility with regard to a given sense (*fait réellement naître la sensibilité dans le sens*)" (*DR*, 139); (b) unsettles the mind, "moves the soul, 'perplexes' it—in other words, forces it to pose a problem" (*DR*, 140), rather than allowing the mind to identify it according to "what everybody knows"; and thus (c) "forces thought to grasp that which can only be thought" (*DR*, 131). For thought to erupt into thinking, the encounter with the object must be such that each one of the faculties involved in the process is born in a unique fashion to begin with, by being unhinged from its form in common sense, and raised to its nth power.

5. Within the context of the image of thought, thinking knows only one misadventure of thought, namely, error, which is considered to be the sole "negative" of thought. If Deleuze emphasizes the need for multiplying (and radicalizing) the possible misadventures of thought, it is not simply to dethrone the privilege of truth with which thought is tied up, but in particular to point out that within thought itself more than one obstacle, and above all obstacles that are more recalcitrant than error, must be conquered for thought to arise. The landscape of the true transcendental structures of thinking is more animated than just by error, which is nothing but an arbitrary fact projected into the order of the transcendental. "Everything must therefore be inverted" (*DR*, 150): the structures of thought, which thought must overcome for it to arise, include "cowardice, cruelty, baseness and stupidity. The transcendental landscape comes to life: places for the tyrant, the slave and the imbecile must be found within it—without the place resembling the figure who occupies it, and without the transcendental ever being traced from the empirical figures which makes it possible" (*DR*, 151). With this, a foundation of an "unthought and unthinking" comes into view, which thought has to overcome, making it, like the object that brings it about, a contingent affair.

6. By establishing error as the only misadventure of thought, the image of thought privileges the function of designation (the logical form of recognition) and its propositional dimension of truth and falsity and limits its expressive function to being the indifferent condition (known by the philosopher as "sense") of both the truth and falsity. In the name of the non-propositional and pre-representational, Deleuze not only puts the privilege afforded to the proposition in the dogmatic image into question, he

also radicalizes the conception of the ground, or condition, as "that which is truly groundless" and the way that it affects what is grounded. It is sense that will carry the burden of this ground, which will effectively constitute the intrinsic genesis of the proposition's function of objective reference. Propositional truth being nothing but the empirical result of sense, the radicalization of sense amounts again to a lifting of the confusion by the dogmatic image of thought of a simple empirical figure with the real structures of the transcendental and the subsequent reversal of this relation. Indeed, rather than pertaining to answers, or solutions, to problems, truth and falsity affect primarily the element of sense. Sense, in the position of such a real structure of the transcendental, includes also the structural elements (the nonsense) that constitute sense (and is, therefore, akin to what Deleuze terms the "Ideas" in his text on Hume). "Nonsense, false sense and misconstrual [*contresens*]" are thus an intrinsic part of the element of sense (*DR*, 159). Furthermore, sense in the role of such an extra-propositional ground for propositions is construed as "the problem" with respect to which "propositions serve as elements of response and cases of solution" (*DR*, 157). Deleuze writes: "The problem or sense is at once both the site of an originary truth and the genesis of a derived truth" (*DR*, 159).

7. In the image of thought, propositions are considered answers to problems that become irrelevant, or neutralized, once they are solved. Problems are thus determined by their capability of being solved. More precisely, the truth of the problems is rendered dependent "upon the *logical possibility* of finding a solution" (*DR*, 160). Deleuze adds: "The new form of the illusion and its technical character comes this time from the fact that the form of the problem is modelled upon the *form of possibility* of propositions" (*DR*, 159–160). However, if one wishes to understand the genesis of the act of thought, "problems and questions must no longer be traced from the corresponding propositions which serve, or can serve, as responses" (*DR*, 157). Based on "the propositions of the common empirical consciousness," that is, on the "probable truth of a simple *doxa*," according to which problems and questions are dismembered and then reconstituted, the illusion that problems are a function of the extrinsic possibility of their solvability must be overturned. Problems are no longer to be considered as givens, but as "ideal 'objecticities' possessing their own sufficiency," whose "imperative internal element" is the site of the genesis of their truth or falsehood. Possibility (logical or transcendental possibility) is

thus replaced by a radicalized conception of foundation, namely, effective genesis, or the production of the true and the false, which already antici-pates Deleuze's later recourse to Bergson's concept of the virtual.

8. According to the image of thought, the structures of thinking have to be elicited not only from the solutions provided for questions, or problems, but, ultimately, from its end—knowledge (*savoir*)—which "designates . . . the generality of concepts or the calm possession of a rule enabling solutions" (*DR*, 164). Hence, to grasp the emergence of thinking within thought, "it is from 'learning,' not from knowledge, that the tran-scendental conditions of thought must be drawn" (*DR*, 166). Learning, then, is no longer to be conceived as an "intermediary between non-knowledge and knowledge" but, rather in a Platonic sense, as "the tran-scendental movement of the soul, irreducible as much to knowledge as to non-knowledge" (*DR*, 166). As Deleuze already points out in *Nietzsche and Philosophy*, "We are not going to think unless we are forced to go where the forces which give food for thought are. . . . Thought does not need a method but a paideia, a formation, a culture" (*NP*, 110). Considering "knowledge" to be no more than an empirical figure, this (final) reversal of the supposed relations and divisions between the empirical and the tran-scendental, introduces time into thinking, however, not as factual time, but as the "time of pure thought" (*DR*, 166). The discovery that the force of time constitutes thinking from the outset concludes the dismantling of the image of thought. It is not the discovery of the empirical fact that it takes time to think, but rather, in Deleuze's own words, that "time takes thought," in short, that, in the form of an in-principle condition (*DR*, 166), time effectively engenders thought and that thought, as understood by Deleuze, namely, as that which makes *the* difference, is the shape that time takes.

11

Saving the Honor of Thinking

Through all the distinct displacements undergone by Jean-François Lyotard's thought—from the philosophy of desire in *Discours, Figure,* and *Libidinal Economy*, to the pragmatic turn culminating in *The Differend*, and, finally, to the further inflexion of his thought on the differend in *The Inhuman* and his sudden interest in writing—one concern in particular not only has remained unchanged, but has progressively gained in importance and has with increasing urgency taken front stage.[1] This one concern is the concern of philosophy with thinking itself. The question regarding the nature of thinking, and especially philosophy's responsibility for thinking, is one of the central issues—or indeed, I would hold, *the* central issue—that Lyotard has relentlessly pursued in his later work. By way of evidence, I will limit myself to referring to *The Inhuman*, where Lyotard says quite unambiguously that "the philosopher asks only: 'What is thinking?' "[2] It is precisely this preoccupation with thinking that also leads him, in the preface to *The Differend* titled "Preface: Reading Dossier," to formulate the problem arising from the grounding assumption in his pragmatic approach to language that he has made his own in this work, namely, that "there is no language 'in general.' "[3] The sole object of Lyotardian pragmatics is what he calls the "phrase."[4] This notion is much broader than the linguistic act of speech; even though Lyotard's analysis of this notion in *The Differend* centers largely on articulated phrases, the notion of the "phrase" itself places the accent on the occurrence of an event in the kind of utterances under investigation.[5] Whether linguistic or not, phrases happen, and they "do" something. Their doing is a function of the instances that together constitute phrase universes—referent, sense, addressor, and addressee—instances that are "the pragmatic posts" of a phrase, and are somewhat akin to categories or genera that form nothing less than the event.[6] The same principle is valid for the rules of the phrase regimens, as well as for those of discourses. In all cases, these are pragmatic rules that constitute phrases as cognitive, descriptive, prescriptive, narrative, deictic, and so forth, or that derive from what a specific discourse seeks to accomplish. Understood as events, phrases "do" things. They have actual effects as well as side effects, and inadvertent effects, and therefore trigger other responses, other events that may clash with the initial phrase event. But there is a particular consequence of the fact that phrases come about according to heterogeneous rules (the rules of phrase regimens and genres of discourse) for which, in the absence of "a language 'in general,'" there can be no universal unifying rule. While Lyotard holds that linking onto a phrase that has happened is necessary, the follow-up to a phrase inevitably brings with it the risk of wronging the phrase event—the singular phrase—that has occurred, thus causing a differend. In a section titled "Problem," Lyotard therefore asks:

Given 1) the impossibility of avoiding conflicts (the impossibility of indifference) and 2) the absence of a universal genre of discourse to regulate them (or, if you prefer, the inevitable partiality of the judge): to find, if not what can legitimate judgment (the "good" linkage), then at least how to save the honor of thinking. (xii) [7]

As one can gather from the 1980 essay, "Discussions, or Phrasing 'After Auschwitz,'" Lyotard's turn to pragmatic linguistics sought first and foremost to secure a possibility for thought in the face of "the impossibility to think Auschwitz,"[8] that is, in the face of speculative thought's failure, including through negative dialectics, to continue to link onto this event. *The Differend*, published three years later, includes a modified version of this essay in "Result," a chapter on Hegelian dialectic. But within the context of the book, the attempt to secure a possibility for philosophical thinking has become aggravated by the fact that the very presuppositions of pragmatics tie phrasing up with an inevitable risk of wronging the event onto which it links, hence the concern with saving thinking and, more precisely, its honor.

As a maxim, however, the expression "to save the honor of thinking" may come across as oddly antiquated. In referring to the norm of honor, Lyotard seems to evoke a rather ambiguous ideal that lies at the heart of traditional social relations—based on a familial model in the Mediterranean countries or on social order and privilege in North and Middle Europe. Considering that honor has diminished its central normative role in egalitarian and democratic societies, the expression seems bound to provoke some irritation. We may ask whether Lyotard's evocation of honor is not involved in a dubious revalorization, if not even re-archaicization, of this outworn norm; a gesture that is all the more disquieting as the theme of honor is making a regressive comeback today, in the form of a mythicized national honor in eastern and southeastern European countries, as well as in the form of a resurgence of family and gender honor in Islamic fundamentalism.[9] From antiquity onward, the concept of honor has been primarily a social and cultural regulator, setting rules for the behavior of individuals, groups, or nations. Such behavior can also include the activity of thinking; Jean-Jacques Rousseau provides an example of this when he writes in *Emile*: "I am not simply a sensitive and passive being but an active and intelligent being; and whatever philosophy may say about it, I shall dare pretend to the honor of thinking (*l'honneur de penser*)."[10] Lyotard's gesture of linking honor and thinking is thus not without precedent. However, Lyotard no longer shares Rousseau's self-assurance; rather, for him the problem has become one of *saving*, and reclaiming, the honor of thinking—especially of thinking philosophically. Nevertheless, the call for saving philosophical thinking in the name of a value as atavistic as the exalted and ceremonial "honor" makes one wonder all the more why Lyotard would have resorted to this notion.

In an essay from 1982, "Answering the Question: What Is Postmodernism?" Lyotard speaks of the need "to save the honor [not of naming, but] of the name."[11] However, on the occasion of his "Postscript to Terror and the Sublime" (1985), published in *The Postmodern Explained, Correspondance 1982–1985*, he refers explicitly to the requisite of saving the honor of thinking as such. He writes: "The avant-gardes' unremitting work of anamnesis has, for a hundred years, saved the honor of thought, if not of humanity, without compromise and everywhere."[12] One can thus assume that what is at stake in the call to save the honor of thinking is not so much the honor of the thinker, but that of philosophical thought itself.

But does not such talk not amount to an intimation of anthropomorphism, and ironically in a work that systematically takes great pains to
avoid humanizing language and thinking? Lyotard is fully aware of the
threat in question. Given that phrases are heterogeneous and that there is
no universally valid rule for linking onto them, any and all such linking
can inevitably wrong a phrase. Indeed, Lyotard voices the following question in *The Differend*: "How can a phrase offend a phrase, or do it wrong?
Do phrases have honor, or pride? An anthropomorphism; now, it's your
turn? [*anthropomorphisme; à votre tour?*]." He then goes on to respond: "In
simple terms, you never know *what* the *Ereignis* is. A phrase, in which idiom? In which regimen? The wrong is still in anticipating it, that is, in pro-
hibiting it" (85). As Lyotard contends, it is necessary to link onto a phrase
that has happened; but that phrase is a singular event in a singular idiom,
and with its own regimen. Linking onto it implies anticipating the *what* of
something that, qua a singular event, defies cognitive appropriation. To
prejudge *what* the phrase presents—without which another phrase is not
possible—causes any linking phrase to deprive the prior phrase of its singularity as an event. The phrase in response to which another phrase arrives is missed or wronged necessarily because of the very nature of its
event quality. But not only does a responding phrase wrong the phrase
onto which it links, it also wrongs all other phrases that could have arrived
in its place. Lyotard asks: "In the absence of a phrase regimen or of a genre
of discourse that enjoys a universal authority to decide, does not the linkage (whichever one it is) necessarily wrong the regimens or genres whose
possible phrases remain unactualized?" (xii). Injustice (*adikia*), according
to Anaximander, has come about by the very fact that existing things have
come into existence in lieu of others, thus preventing those others from
manifesting themselves; the result of this injustice is that things need "to
give justice and make reparation to one another for their injustice, according to the arrangement of Time."[13] But just as this injustice is not to be
understood in a moral sense, so the wrong that the arriving phrase causes
to the phrase onto which it links, and to the phrases it ousts or represses, is
a sort of "objective"—or, more precisely, ontological—wrong. Although it
is still far from clear why the injustice in question damages an honor that
is specific to phrases, such honor cannot be understood as an anthropomorphism, but must, of necessity, be just as "objective" or ontological as the
wrong it suffers. Since one wrongs a phrase, necessarily and for ontological

reasons, by linking onto it, a phrase event must have, by extension, something of the order of an honor that calls to be saved. This much should already be obvious at this point: that similarly to the wrong that is done to a phrase, the honor of a phrase must be retraced to the phrase's character as an event.

If the traditional role of philosophical thought has always been one of establishing a universal genre capable of settling all disputes, the problematic broached by *The Differend*—precisely the kind of conflict for which no universal mediating genre exists—would seem to entail the outright abdication of philosophical thinking. The question with which *The Differend* is concerned is whether, given the impossibility of ever providing universal rules for "good" linkage, philosophical thought can still have a role to play. After the prevailing philosophical kind of thinking has proven its shortcomings, is there another task of thinking that only philosophical phrasing can fulfill? Even though no role will ever match philosophy's initial privilege, is there not still a way for philosophy to claim a task that is still honorable, or in other words, a task that compares favorably to philosophy's previous employment? And is this indeed the sense in which we have to understand the talk concerning the honor of thinking? Here, too, honor would refer to the integrity of thinking itself and would thus characterize the state of thinking. At this point, it may be appropriate to remark that if all linking onto a phrase inevitably wrongs that phrase, then philosophical thinking must uphold its honor in testifying to the differends that arise from this situation. But it is also obvious right from the outset of *The Differend* that there are ways of linking onto phrases, and hence there are differends, that are brought about by precisely thinking. The chapter titled "The Differend" opens with examples of situations in which thinking itself serves to cause and perpetuate injustice: historical revisionism, editorial rationality, and communist rhetoric. By providing the logically impeccable argumentational schemes that serve to wrong parties and plaintiffs, this employment of thinking actually disgraces thinking; but it also induces the call to save the honor of thinking, and demands that thinking testify to those differends for which thinking itself is responsible.

Before further elaborating on this response to thinking's self-disgrace, let me return again to the notion of honor that is linked, for Lyotard, to the very fate of philosophical thinking. In light of the archaic connotations of this term, and also of the marginalization of the notion of honor in modern society, one might have had reason to expect that Lyotard would speak of the dignity of thinking rather than of its honor. Indeed, whereas honor concerns identity in relation to institutionalized social roles and socially imposed norms, dignity refers to the intrinsic values that pertain to the self or individual as such, independent of any institutional context.[14] However, if honor, rather than dignity, is emphasized here, one can safely assume that this is not by accident. Could it perhaps be that in calling on the notion of honor, Lyotard is not gesturing at all toward the institutional codex of traditional societies, which serves to secure identity by way of social roles? What if he were not invoking honor in the sense of its Latin derivations, namely as implying an official recognition by a public institution, but were instead suggesting that honor in "the honor of thinking" would first have to be retraced to the Greek "time"? Unlike the Latin "honor," "time" signifies simply the recognition and respect shown, through words and deeds of fellow citizens, to someone who merits such esteem because of his excellence (*arete*). In distinction from *eudozia*, which refers to the fame or good reputation enjoyed by an outstanding person, "time" is the respect shown to someone whose reputation derives from outstanding services he has rendered for the well-being of the community. In the *Rhetoric*, Aristotle explains that "fame (*eudozia*) means being respected by everybody, or having some quality that is desired by all men, or by most, or by the good, or by the wise. Honour (*time*) is the token of a man's being famous for doing good."[15] Because "time" is "the end of political life," Aristotle labels it, in *Nichomachean Ethics*, "the greatest of external goods."[16] The public life of the polis, the life in common, provides the horizon within which the Greek conception of honor is properly situated. Understood in this sense, honor is the ultimate end and highest good for a life devoted to the state and the well-being of its citizens. In other words, honor is of the order of the *bios politikos*, and is, so to speak, a concept of practical reason.[17] By speaking of the honor of thinking, Lyotard therefore situates thinking immediately on the level of the practical and, more precisely, of the "political." If, according to Lyotard, the honor of thinking is at stake, it is because the involvement in public and political life of the thinker and especially of thinking itself is in jeopardy. When it is no longer evident that thinking intends what is just and good with respect to the life in common, then nothing less than the honor of thinking needs to be saved. Throughout the *The Differend*, this task—which is the task par excellence of thinking—is understood as a political task.

Nevertheless, as Lyotard remarks in *Just Gaming*, the "political" is something that needs to be redefined and completely overhauled in light of the point of departure of the pragmatic approach to language, according to which "all discourses [are to be conceived] as moves [*coups*] in language games."[18] As we know, *The Differend* inquires into the inevitable conflict that derives from the fact that phrases qua events are incommensurable and that a universal rule for regulating this conflict is lacking. Lyotard defines the "Stakes" set by this inquiry thusly: "By showing that the linking of one phrase onto another is problematic and that this problem is the problem of politics, to set up a philosophical politics apart from the politics of 'intellectuals' and of politicians" (xiii). What such a philosophical politics consists in—a politics intrinsically called upon by the pragmatic approach to "language" at work in *The Differend*—will become somewhat clearer hereafter.

This is an appropriate point at which to return to the question left in abeyance: the question concerning the need to save the honor of thinking from the disgraceful and dishonoring forms to which thinking lends itself. First, however, a brief detour is warranted through the last section of Adorno's *Negative Dialectics*, titled "Meditations on Metaphysics," and his lectures from the summer of 1965 when he was completing this last section. These lectures have been published under the title *Metaphysics: Concept and Problems*. The reasons for this detour are that not only are the "Meditations" a constant reference point throughout Lyotard's pragmatic turn, but also even the maxim "to save the honor of thinking" may refer back to Adorno. In *Negative Dialectics*, Adorno concludes a discussion of nihilism by remarking that "thought honors itself by defending what is damned as nihilism."[19] "Honor" is invoked at one point in *Metaphysics: Concepts and Problems* as well, when Adorno calls for saving the honor of the history of philosophy.[20] But most importantly, in connection with Lyotard, is the fact that "saving" (*retten, Rettung*) is a leading concept in Adorno's work. The "idea of rescue" in *Negative Dialectics* is linked to the conception that metaphysical thought "conserves," in transformed fashion, what it criticizes, and it is intrinsically bound up in the question of whether metaphysics is still a viable possibility.[21] In the face of the atrocities of Auschwitz that have irreparably damaged traditional metaphysical thought, Adorno's overall concern in *Negative Dialectics*—and furthermore in *Metaphysics*, where he unfolds the concept of saving in greater detail—is the attempt to foster "a respect for the possibility of the mind [*des Geistes*], despite everything, to raise itself however slightly [*um ein Geringes*] above that which is."[22] For Adorno, not only is thinking's ability to transcend the given the sole thing that merits respect; this ability is what secures the possibility of a new metaphysical experience, in spite of the irremediable ruin of traditional metaphysical thought.

"Saving," for Adorno, represents a constitutive moment of this ruined traditional metaphysical thought. As we shall see in a moment, despite the collapse of such thinking in consequence of Auschwitz, the effort to elicit a new metaphysical experience and a new kind of philosophical thought can also only be achieved by way of a "saving." First, however, we need to understand how traditional metaphysical thought and the "idea of saving" are intertwined. The first part of the lectures of the summer 1965 is devoted to Aristotle's *Metaphysics*, and Adorno holds here that the essence of metaphysics is constituted by the double intention of critique and rescue.[23] Metaphysics has "the dual character of the critical or, as is often said, the destructive, and of the apologetic and rescuing,"[24] or conservative moment.[25] Adorno assumes that the concepts of metaphysics, that is, concepts in general, are secularized phenomena, or abstractions of empirical intraworldly givens, but that these concepts are to have a pertinent relation to the empirical. Given this assumption, the inevitable rupture with the empirical, that is implicit in conceptual secularization and abstraction, needs constant mending. This takes place in the attempt to save the phenomena that have been critically overcome or destroyed by being transformed into concepts. Consequently, metaphysics is double:

On one hand metaphysics is always . . . rationalistic as a *critique* of a conception of true, essential being-in-itself which does not justify itself before reason; but, on the other hand, it is always also an attempt to *rescue* something which the philosopher's genius feels to be fading and vanishing. There is in fact no metaphysics, or very little, which is not an attempt to save—and to save by means of concepts—what appeared at the time to be threatened precisely by concepts, and was in the process of being disintegrated, or corroded, to use the more affective language of the ancient anti-Sophists.

Adorno thus concludes that "metaphysics can thus be defined as the exertion of thought to save what at the same time it destroys."[26] Metaphysics, he continues, "is always present where enlightened rationalism both criticizes traditional notions and ideas, ideas existing in themselves, as mythological, and at the same time—and not just out of an apologetic need, but out of a concern for truth—wants to save or restore these concepts, which reason has demolished, precisely through the application of reason, or even to produce them anew from within its own rational resources."[27] Saving is intimately linked to critique—the gesture by which thinking raises itself to the level of the concept—and is thus the conceptual answer to what metaphysical thought, as conceptual thought, must put into question, jeopardize, or squarely demolish in order to become conceptual. Although this concept of saving is an intrinsic feature of the traditional metaphysics that has become obsolete with Auschwitz, the different kind of metaphysical experience and a new mode of philosophizing that is to replace traditional metaphysical thought also form a mode of thinking that saves. Furthermore, this different mode of thinking saves precisely that remnant of metaphysics that has "passed through the portal of its death;" and this includes its ways of saving.[28] Against the backdrop of this Adornian notion, Lyotard's talk of "saving the honor of thinking" will reveal a further aspect, in addition to those which we have already teased out.

We have begun to see how by taking the phrase in a pragmatic sense as its starting point, *The Differend* is led to recognize an inevitable conflict between phrases, a conflict that admits of no arbitration. Because phrases arrive and it is necessary to link onto them by way of another phrase event, a wrong occurs with respect to the "first" phrase and all the phrases in lieu of which the "second" phrase comes into being. Given the absence of a universal genre of discourse to regulate the conflicts in question, the problem formulated in "Preface: Reading Dossier" is "to find, if not what can legitimate judgment (the 'good' linkage), then at least how to save the honor of thinking" (xii). Two tasks, therefore, need to be distinguished: two tasks that "bear witness to the differend" (xiii). The first task is to seek a "good" linkage, and this would consist in finding ways to address or voice the wrong that a phrase or party has incurred. The second task would seem to be much more modest, but at the same time it is an almost desperate one. It seeks to accomplish the minimal goal of saving the honor of thinking, but in the face of a wrong so radical that the task of bearing witness to it by providing a "good" linkage is at the limit of what is possible for thinking.[29] The two tasks are clearly distinct from one another. Notably, the second task, intent on saving the honor of thinking, is not to be

explained primarily, or exclusively, on the basis of the ontological differend caused by phrasing as such.

In an essay titled "Lyotard: Differend, Presence," Jacob Rogozinski has
distinguished "two figures of the wrong, two versions of silence, two modes
of necessity" in *The Differend*.[30] This distinction is between a restricted
wrong, and the "radical wrong designated by the name of Auschwitz;" in
other words, between a wrong that, in principle, can be repaired by other
phrases, and one in which the possibility of phrasing is threatened or even
destroyed. Rogozinski remarks:

One [regimen of the wrong] concerns only the choice of possible phrases, and another which strikes a blow at the *power to phrase*, at the "capacity to speak or to be
silent." The first case would be ontological. It designates the inevitable discarding
of the possible for the real, the impossibility of "saying everything," the *impossibility of possibilities*, their exhaustion. It is the pathos of finiteness. This case
pleads in the name of the multiple, of the profusion of possibilities sacrificed each
instant by an actualization of one of them. The second case would be an ethical
wrong. It would plead in the name of uniqueness, of a *power to phrase* each time
unique and threatened with interruption. It signifies the *possibility of the impossible*, that which cannot happen, in any case, and which happens nevertheless.
While the ontological wrong can be repaired, and can cease to be a wrong, the
ethical wrong would be radical, that is to say, beyond repair. It would not arise
from *every* sequence, but only when the very possibility of a linkage is menaced.[31]

This suggestive distinction seems, at first glance, to correspond to the
two tasks of thinking that Lyotard has distinguished; however Geoffrey
Bennington has criticized it, arguing that even a restricted wrong cannot
be repaired, because no later phrase can ever come close to being the very
phrase that was sacrificed for the benefit of the actualized phrase. I would
also add that it cannot be repaired because any phrase that links onto another one anticipates the *what* of the initial phrase and, thus, inescapably
wrongs it. Lyotard himself, significantly enough, also wonders whether
"the threat with interruption [Rogozinski referred to] could at all be thought
under the title of a wrong."[32] What is at stake in this question is the status of
Auschwitz in *The Differend*. Even though "Auschwitz appears in every chapter of the book" as the "principal example," and even though it may form its
very starting point, "Auschwitz seems to be a problem," Bennington remarks in *Lyotard: Writing the Event*. Indeed, he points out, "the *différend*
cannot describe Auschwitz," since as even Lyotard acknowledges in the

work in question: "Between the SS and the Jew there is not even a differ-end, because there is not even a common idiom (that of a tribunal) in which even damages could be formulated, be they in the place of a wrong" (106).[33] Auschwitz "itself," if one can put it this way, does not yield to the key concepts of "wrong" and "differend." In *The Differend,* Auschwitz is the name, par excellence, for the event; in other words, it names that which requires phrasing, and in the process of which radical wrongs occur—wrongs such as those that the revisionists inflict on the Holocaust survivors when they put into question *that* it happened. As Lyotard remarks in an interview with Elizabeth Weber, titled "Before the Law, After the Law": "Auschwitz preeminently belongs to the order of the event. It *is* the question: *Is it happening?* First of all, we never finish establishing that it did happen. . . . But above all, secondly Auschwitz is the event because we don't succeed (*arrive*) in establishing its *meaning.*"[34] Still, Rogozinski's distinction points to a real problem in *The Differend,* namely the absence of any systematic differentiation between types of differends. Such differentiation is a task that the pragmatic origin of the differend, and the action it requires, compels one to perform. Undoubtedly, there is the general ontological differend that is inherent to the very event character of all phrases. But if the name "Auschwitz" designates a wrong, it is not an irreparable wrong that would contrast the ontological differend—for the ontological differend cannot be repaired either—but a wrong, and not just any wrong, that has occurred for reasons other than ontological reasons. Indeed, in addition to the ontological differend, or against the backdrop of what explains it, there are a host of other kinds of differends; they derive from the specific rules for linking two phrases with heterogeneous regimens, a process by which the various genres of discourse submit phrases to a single finality. These genre-based rules alone are the reasons that cause "Auschwitz" to name an irreparable wrong and to be a paradigm of the differend.

There are many differends that derive from the "shift [of] the differend from the level of regimens to that of [the] ends" pursued by the genres of discourse (29). But among the various types of genre-based differends, Lyotard lingers in effect almost exclusively on the differend brought about by the cognitive discourse.[35] This is, as we will see, particularly palpable in the opening chapter of the *The Differend,* the chapter titled "The Differend"; but it is also evident in the subsequent chapters, which explore one after another the four instances that constitute phrases—the referent ("The Referent, The Name" and "Presentation"), meaning ("Result"), addressor, and addressee ("Obligation")—before taking on the issue of the genres themselves. As Alain Badiou has noted in his review of Lyotard's book, "For him everything that is of significance takes place in the question of the referent."[36] In what follows I will not take issue with this prioritization of the differend that arises from of the cognitive genre or question the degree to which it may affect the theory of the differend itself. I will only be interested in figuring out why the differend caused by the cognitive discourse presents such a challenge to thinking that it puts the honor of thinking itself into question. To put it differently, what will occupy me are the reasons why it is precisely the cognitive differend that causes Lyotard to invoke an honor of thinking and to call for its salvation.

The first chapter of *The Differend* opens with three examples of differends—the testimony of the Holocaust survivor faced with the revisionist historian Robert Faurisson's demand for proofs; the assertion that major works of art have remained unpublished and the professional editor's demand to name one such work; and the Ibanskian witness and the communist authorities. In each case, the differend is shown to be owed to the impossibility faced by the plaintiff of demonstrating the existence of what is in question. The kind of demands for verification that are made of him stifle the plaintiff's ability to furnish proof. To all appearances, these demands come with phrases that belong to the genre of discourse whose aim is cognition. However, let me state right away that it is entirely possible in all three examples that some other goal is at stake: that, as the text suggests, Faurisson "is 'playing' another genre of discourse, one in which conviction, or, the obtainment of a consensus over a defined reality is not at stake" (19); that the play of the editor is primarily one of "defending his or her profession" (4); and finally, that for the communist authorities the real issue is the maintenance of their monopoly over what is or is not to be accredited as real. But the differend that results from the possible manipulation or monopolization of the cognitive discourse by the revisionist historian, the professional editor, and the communist authorities is of another kind than the one demanded by the discursive genre of cognition itself; this forms already a third kind of differends, wrong, and silence. If the victim of the Holocaust is further victimized by Faurisson, it is not primarily because the latter may be playing another game, but it is a consequence of the preliminary discursive demands of cognition. Now the reason why the Holocaust survivor cannot furnish proof for the existence of what he or she reports is not the same as the reason why the Ibanskian witness cannot hope to sustain his testimony. In the latter case, the differend arises from reasons other than those that pertain to the case of the Holocaust victims, who would have to be dead in order to render their testimony credible. It is thus necessary to distinguish still further kinds of differends. In the case of the Ibanskian witness, the supplementary differend results from the demand for proof of the existence of what, by definition, is a nonobservable entity: the "idea of historical-political reason" called communist society. Lyotard writes: "As a general rule, an object which is thought under the category of the whole (or of the absolute) is not an object of cognition (whose reality could be subjected to a protocol, etc.). The principle affirming the contrary could be called totalitarianism. If the requirement of establishing the reality of a phrase's referent according to the protocol of cognition is extended to any given phrase, especially to those phrases that refer to the whole, then this requirement is totalitarian in its principle" (5). The differend here arises from the illicit application of one genre of discourse to a phrase whose regimen excludes cognitive verification. It is a differend that comes from a disregard for, or blindness to, the differences that distinguish phrase regimens and from the illegitimate extension of the expectations and competences of one genre of discourse to heterogeneous phrase regimens. But this differend that is due to an illicit extension of the scope of scientific cognitives has to be kept separate from the differend that arises as the result of legitimate applications of cognitive discursivity. Both, however, derive from the rules of cognitive rationality and have their origin in established discursive procedures. Similarly to the ontological differend inherent in the event character of phrases, these differends are "objective." They are rooted in the intrinsically heterogeneous nature of phrase regimens and of genres of discourse and come with the rules that constitute such genres of discourses.

If the plaintiffs in the three examples are wronged for reasons that, when they are owing to an investigator's or judge's oblique intentions, could certainly have been avoided,[37] it is precisely because their testimony is met by the demand to furnish evidence for what they assert—the existence of the gas chambers, unpublished major works of art, the existence or nonexistence of a communist society. As should already be evident by now, this demand is the distinctive trait of cognitive discourse. Indeed, as

Lyotard recalls, this discourse also obeys the rule that "reality is not what is 'given' to this or that 'subject,' it is the state of the referent (that about which one speaks) which results from the effectuation of establishment procedures defined by a unanimously agreed upon protocol, and from the possibility offered to anyone to recommence this effectuation as often as he or she wants" (4). It is thus not possible to contend that something exists because one has seen or experienced it, unless that contention is backed up by well-formed phrases whose operators have been clearly distinguished and rendered completely explicit and consists of unanimously agreed upon "effectible procedures whose reiterable effectuation authorizes the consensus between addressor and addressee" (17). Others must be able to verify or falsify the contention made, at a different time and a different space. Without following these established procedures, no cognitive claim can be made and upheld. If one ignores these rules, there is, as Lyotard remarks in the context of the Ibanskian witness, "no more credit to be accorded to [someone's] testimony than that of a human being who says he has communicated with Martians" (4). Now let us remind ourselves that this constitutive demand of the cognitive discourse—the demand to prove the existence or reality of the claim one makes according to established rules, so that they can be verified by others—is a very reasonable demand. Indeed, it is reason itself. Furthermore, as the Gorgias and Plato Notices will argue, it is the kind of thinking that came into being in early Greece and whose rules as a whole have changed little over time.[38] As Lyotard will say, this is "our way of thinking," the way *we* think since philosophy's inception in Greece (9). The expectations and rules of this thinking are manifest in paradigmatic fashion in the genre of the cognitive discourse; it requires, first and foremost, that any statement one makes (regarding, especially, the existence of something) be accounted for according to universally agreed-upon procedures—which means, in essence, publicly, in the open, for all to be able to agree or disagree about. This request for clarity, transparency, and public openness is at the heart of Western thinking. The Greeks called this demand to make oneself intelligible *logon didonai*. It is a request to which it is difficult to object.

From this characterization of "our way of thinking that reality is not a given, but an occasion to require that establishment procedures be effectuated in regard to it" (9), several things follow that need to be underlined. If reality is not to be thought of as a given, that is to say, as something that shows itself immediately to a subject without the latter's contribution, and that, consequently, could serve, as such, as the unquestioned foundation and reference point from which inferences and judgments are made and if, on the contrary, reality is discursive and rests on rational demonstration, then its assertion always puts the subject in the position of a plaintiff before a public court, of sorts. Lyotard writes that "reality is always the plaintiff's responsibility." "The one who says there is something is the plaintiff, it is up to him or her to bring forth a demonstration, by means of well-formed phrases and of procedures for establishing the existence of their referent" (8). If reality is discursive, then there can be no exception to this rule: "That is why it is [even] up to the victims of extermination camps to prove that extermination" (9); and furthermore, "the proof for the reality of gas chambers cannot be adduced if the rules adducing the proof are not respected" (16). Lyotard contrasts this in noting that, "for the defense, it is sufficient to refute the argumentation and to impugn the proof by a counter-example" (8–9). In our thinking, therefore, the discursive status of reality brings with it the further implication that even a successful plea for the reality of a referent can always only be temporary. It means merely that "until further notice it has not been falsified" (10). Reality is always potentially in suspense, or in dispute. Since it has not yet been refuted, it has always only been given credence until further provision is made.

The Notice on Gorgias follows Lyotard's analysis of the conditions under which a victim's silence—for example, before Faurisson's demand to give evidence about the existence of gas chambers—could be lifted. The Notice brings out additional presuppositions that underlie "our way of thinking." The text states that "the silence of the survivors does not necessarily testify in favor of the non-existence of gas chambers, as Faurisson believes or pretends to believe," and then it argues that in order to prove the existence of the gas chambers, the plaintiff's silent denials of the four instances that make up a phrase (referent, sense, addressor, and addressee) would have to be withdrawn (14). Having just called for new idioms to do justice to a victim's silence, this suggestion that to prove the existence of the gas chambers, it is necessary to lift the silence concerning the four instances in question, Lyotard seems to intimate that even the assessment of reality in the cognitive mode of thinking is a kind of phrasing that occurs only after a silence. The Notice on the sophist serves to sustain this point. Lyotard writes that "in its form, the argumentation establishing reality follows the nihilist reasoning of Gorgias in *On Not-Being*: 'Nothing is; and even if it is, it is unknowable; and even if it is knowable, it cannot be revealed to others'" (14). Analyzing Gorgias' "simultaneously nihilistic and logological standpoint" (16) regarding Being (that nothing happens), Lyotard points out that this argumentation rests on the concession granted to the opponent, in what he calls a "logical retreat," and in the process of which the four instances of a phrase universe are successively negated. Lyotard notes that "the logical retreat, absurd when it is isolated from the course of the prosecution's argumentation, unveils the rules for the family of cognitive phrases: determination of the referent . . . attribution of a predicate to the subject of the utterance . . . display of a case which proves conclusively" (15). The matrix of the establishment procedures that philosophical thinking adopts in arguing for reality correspond to the four steps that serve Gorgias' refutation of Being; the only difference is that in the cognitive discourse, the four silences induced by the sophist are to be withdrawn "in reverse order." If the reality of a referent is to be discursively established, it must be argumentatively ascertained that "there is someone to signify the referent and someone to understand the phrase that signifies it; the referent can be signified; it exists" (16). But what also becomes clear in the process is that although this procedure is not nihilistic, as in the case of Gorgias' refutation, it shares the sophist's denial of Being, in that it entails a fundamental doubt concerning existence. This doubt is the prime reason why, in Western thinking, anything that can be shown to exist can hold on to that claim only as long as it has not been invalidated by some counter proof. As a result, our way of thinking, the way that requires a discursive establishment of reality—and a way that is not to be surrendered easily—pays a price. It is fundamentally suspicious of the event. The discursive genre of cognition, which is largely responsible for shaping philosophical thought, is intrinsically skeptical of the "Does it happen?"—the "Arrive-t-il?"—and thus is bound to produce differends.[39]

But what about the third Notice in the chapter "The Differend"? The context in which this Notice on Plato is inserted concerns the suspicion that bad faith and prejudgment of the plaintiff may hamper any consensus over a defined reality. Given that rules of scientific cognitives are intended precisely to prevent prejudgment, the question that arises is whether those who establish these rules are not "prejudging their competence to establish them" in the first place (19). Lyotard recalls here that the proper rules "to allow a consensus between partners concerning a phrase that identifies its referent as it should" become instituted by Plato in response to "the loss or decline of the referent's reality" (22). This decline occurs by dint of the paralogical operations employed by those who seek to make weak arguments win over the stronger ones, as well as through mimetic poetics, all of which engage in operations that manipulate the instances in phrase universes. The Plato Notice inquires into the kind of discourse, within the dialectical genre, in which the rules of consensus become established. Since the quest for consensus is not the aim of eristics or of sophistics, or even of peirastics or of the dialectic of experimentation, consequently "the rules for forming and linking phrases and the adducing of proofs are far from established and far from being the object of a consensus even for those who seek the true through discussion" (23). As Lyotard shows, the Platonic solution to finding a consensus about the adducing of proofs concerning a referent is the living, and (in principle) infinite, dialogue between two, the *dialegesthai*. This Platonic solution to the problem is to "separate the *mathematikoi* from the *politikoi*";[40] and this means that the consensus about the rules for public discussion is sought out of sight of the public sphere. But instituting the rules in question within living dialogue is not only a matter of eliminating the third party—both the witness and the judge—at a remove from public places (23). This living dialogue is also selective (i.e., undemocratic) in that it admits as partners only those who agree to seek agreement and excludes idiots, infirm brutes, and anyone who is in bad faith. Ultimately, the living dialogue intent on producing the rules that are to govern phrases and their linkage takes place only among friends, and, to be entirely specific, between simulated interlocutors who, through simulation, have been made more civilized (as Plato says with respect to the materialists with whom he pretends to dialogue in the *Sophist*). In the Plato Notice, this narrative procedure of Plato's dialogues is thematized in terms of metalepsis. This is also the device by which we readers are kept at distance from the truth-seeking living dialogue, especially if, as Lyotard remarks, "we are incapable of coming to an agreement concerning the rules of the dialogue, whose principal rule is that the agreement concerning the referent ought to be obtained for ourselves by ourselves. We believe in the decision of the third party in matters of reality. We think that success in the eyes of the third party is the sign of the true. We believe in agonistics. We allow the lesser argument to prevail, under the right conditions" (25–26). What follows from this is that the genre of discourse that "seeks to institute the rules for what we call scientific discourse" (26)—that is, the rules for our prevailing mode of thinking in the West, whose values of clarity and public openness are not negotiable—is instituted at a remove from the public sphere and by exclusion of the third. Therefore, it is bound to produce still further inevitable wrongs. This attempt to establish the rules for cognitive phrases brings about the differend between, on the one hand, those who share the values of cognitive thinking and wish to arrive at a consensus about its rules by way of public discussion and via third parties and, on the other hand, the partisans of the living dialogue. This differend "between the partisans of agonistics and the partisans of dialogue" irreducibly inhabits the institution of the dialogue in which the rules in question are set forth. Lyotard concludes that none of Plato's attempts to defuse the threat of agonistics, and hence to reduce the differend caused by the dialogic approach to the rules, has been successful.[41]

So much for the necessary evils that beset from within the principal mode of "our" thinking. As we have seen, the demand to establish the reality of a phrase's referent according to unanimously agreed-upon procedures—a demand that in itself is rational and without which thinking (in its cognitive mode, at least) is not possible—can thus wrong a witness or plaintiff; in situations such as those that *The Differend* evokes, this demand can produce unsolvable conflicts, or radical differends. A wrong, according to Lyotard, is "a damage accompanied by the loss of the means to prove the damage" (5). It is thus a privation to which "there is added the impossibility to bring it to the knowledge of others, and in particular to the knowledge of a tribunal" (5). To make matters worse, and in addition to all the differends it causes, philosophical thought has supplied a mode of argumentation that manipulates the rules for the cognitive discourse, and it shuts up any victim of a differend that derives from the rules of cognitive phrases and who yet dares speak up. "Should the victim bypass this impossibility [of bringing the wrong it has incurred to the knowledge of a third party] and testify anyway to the wrong done to him or her, he or she comes up against the following argumentation: either the damages you complain about never took place, and your testimony is false; or else they took place, and since you are able to testify to them, it is not a wrong that has been done to you, but merely a damage, and your testimony is still false" (5). Lyotard formalizes this argument and then traces it back, in the Protagoras Notice, to this most important sophist, the friend of Pericles and Euripides, who was held in respect by Socrates and Plato. What is the role of this first Notice on Protagoras in the context of the chapter "The Differend"? It is to argue that the sophist's argument is also the philosopher's response to the differends that philosophy cannot fail to produce. Protagoras is both a sophist and a philosopher, but the mechanism of the *double bind* contained in the argument is also, as Lyotard argues, "a linchpin of Hegelian dialectical logic" (6), that is, of speculative thought (speculative dialectics). But this kind of response is not worthy of philosophical thinking. It is a mode of coping with thinking's inevitable shortfalls that, in seeking to attain legitimate goals, in fact disgraces thought. The demand to account in verifiable ways for the claims to reality cannot but produce inescapable wrongs, and philosophy's disgraceful response to these inevitable wrongs adds, as it were, insult to injury. In light of this situation, Lyotard's prime concern in *The Differend* becomes visible. Given that the established procedures for proving reality cannot be relinquished without condoning the worst, and given furthermore that an inevitable evil arises from the demands of rational thinking, and finally, given that speculative thought, for instance, covers up disgracefully the wrongs caused by thinking, the problem, as defined in "Preface: Reading Dossier," becomes indeed one of how "at least . . . to save the honor of thinking." The nature of the differends in question means precisely that the very honor of thinking itself is at stake. If thinking disgraces thinking, the good standing of thinking is in question. It is in a differend with itself, and though no solution offers itself, it must respond to this differend if it is not to lose face.

At this point, where the true stakes of the question of the honor of thinking come into view let me briefly circle back to Adorno. For Adorno, all major concepts of metaphysical thinking have become obsolete in the aftermath of the genocide of the Jews, and therefore the question concerning the possibility of metaphysical experience—that is, a transcendence of what he calls in *Negative Dialectics* "the closed system of immanence"—is a question of saving thinking from stupidity and the triumph of realized unreason.[42] Metaphysics, according to him, is characterized from its inception in Greece by a double movement: the movements of conceptual destruction and conceptual saving of what has thus been destroyed. To save the possibility of a metaphysical experience in the aftermath of Auschwitz, the traditional form of metaphysics must be surrendered unreservedly and in its entirety. A new metaphysical experience can be won only by metaphysics and on condition that metaphysics throw itself away (*Metaphysik möchte gewinnen allein, wenn sie sich wegwirft*).[43] "If rescue is the inmost impulse of any spirit," Adorno writes, "there is no hope but that of unreserved surrender: of that which is to be rescued as well as of the hopeful spirit."[44] In light of what happened in the extermination camps, it has become plain that within all venerable metaphysical concepts and values "the destruction of nonidentity is teleologically lurking."[45] According to Adorno, thinking "must measure itself against the ultimate, the absolutely unthinkable, to have any right to be thinking at all." It achieves this task by bringing to light the destructive potential inherent in all prior and current metaphysical conceptions. The form of thinking that survives the Holocaust is a thinking of uncompromising resistance to any affirmation, and that pushes "the process of de-mythologizing, or enlightenment, to the extreme"—indeed, to the point where thinking begins to "think against itself."[46] The *Negative Dialectics* insists that thinking must become "a thinking against itself."[47] Lyotard shares with Adorno the insight into the price attached to concept formation. Yet the two also differ, in that for Adorno the concept inevitably does injustice to what it conceptualizes, with the effect that thinking acquires the additional task of saving what has been condemned (or as he puts it in *Negative Dialectics*, what has "passed the portal of its death"),[48] including metaphysics as a whole, in the aftermath of Auschwitz when all metaphysical concepts have become exposed. However, Lyotard's pragmatic analysis of philosophical thinking displaces the question of saving onto an entirely different level.[49] For Adorno, the question is one of saving the possibility of metaphysical thinking by thinking against it; and although Lyotard agrees that concept formation comes with a high price, according to him, the rules that govern it are rules that cannot be rescinded for fear of the worst. For Lyotard, the task is not to save thinking by thinking toward a new metaphysical experience, but rather to thinkingly address the evils of thinking while allowing that no enlightening critique can ever hope to completely free thinking of its potential for the worst. The extreme against which thinking is staked, according to Lyotard, is the fact of the inevitable wrongs to which thinking itself subjects witnesses and plaintiffs—those who make existence claims that, according to the rules of the cognitive discourse, cannot be validated, or who phrase according to the rules of genres of discourse other than the cognitive discourse, and who are further victimized by the speculative thinking that robs them of the very power to speak. For Adorno, saving a minimal metaphysical experience for thinking is aimed at preventing the total closure of the system of immanence; for Lyotard, the question is one of responding, by thinking, to the worst in which thinking inevitably gets caught up when it seeks to avoid the worst, and thus it is a question that concerns the honor of thinking.[50]

In order to address this question, Lyotard must reconceive and reformulate the task of thinking. In *The Differend*, he asks: "What if the stakes of thought concerned differend rather than consensus?" (60). This task is distinct from what thinking has hitherto considered as its role, and it may thus also imply that with this new task, thinking is no longer thinking. Implicitly, Lyotard is asking here whether philosophical thought is intrinsically, or in truth, about consensus; about establishing universal rules to solve (dialogically, as Gadamer and Habermas would have it, falling into line with Plato) conflicts that are of the order of litigations between damaged and damaging parties. What if philosophical thought would not be true to its essence if it understood conflicts solely in terms of litigations, nor be faithful to its own task if it engaged in finding rules for solving them? Against the philosophers who understand philosophy "as the pursuit of conciliation or as obedience to its principle," Lyotard "pleads inconsistency [with respect to such a principle] which is not only the risk that thinking and writing runs, but the honor (honesty and probity) of thinking and writing."[51] As the analysis of the differend has shown, "at the far end of univocality, something announces itself (through feeling), which that 'unique voice' cannot phrase." (86) This feeling, according to Lyotard, signals that a differend must be put into phrases, though it cannot yet be done (13); and philosophical thought must link onto this feeling if the honor of thinking is to be saved. "To give the differend its due is to institute new addresses, new addressors, new significations, and new referents in order for the wrong to find an expression and for the plaintiff to cease being a victim. This requires new rules for the formation and linking of phrases. . . . Every wrong ought to be able to be put into phrases. A new competence (or 'prudence') must be found" (13). To give the differend its due requires finding ways of phrasing the wrong that a victim has incurred, and that inhibits the victim's overall power of doing things with words. Given that there are no universal rules for linking onto the silence to which the victim has been condemned, the competence Lyotard calls for can only be the practical wisdom of *phronesis*, which in Latin is called *prudentia*. What is required of any thinking that tries to save the honor of thinking by seeking to give the differend its due is not the theoretical elaboration of rules (not a *bios theoretikos*), for no differend is reducible to litigation, but a praxis, a *bios politikos*, on the level of linguistic pragmatics. Lyotard writes: "A lot of searching must be done to find new rules for forming and linking phrases that are able to express the differend disclosed by the feeling, unless one wants this differend to be smothered right away in a litigation and for the alarm sounded by the feeling to have been useless. What is at stake in a literature, in a philosophy, in a politics perhaps, is to bear witness to differends by finding idioms for them" (13). I would like to recall here Lyotard's definition of philosophy: the philosophical discourse, he says, "has as its rule to discover its rule: its *a priori* is what it has at stake. It is a matter of formulating this rule, which can only be done at the end, if there is an end" (60). If in philosophical thought "the links from phrase to phrase are not ruled by a rule but by the quest for a rule" (97), then the search for new rules—rules for forming the phrases that may link onto the silence caused in differends—is philosophy's task par excellence. Rather than proceeding according to established rules, thinking is properly thinking only in the absence of preestablished rules. Its fate, therefore, is necessarily linked to the differend—that is, to the task of phrasing what cannot be said.

A Stupid Passion

Any attempt to rehabilitate the philosophical category of the sublime runs the inevitable risk of the charge of aestheticism, an accusation that further implies apolitical romanticism and antirationalism. This is particularly the case when contemporary developments in the arts are enlisted to justify the reintroduction of this aesthetic category. Thus, by affixing "postmodern" to the "sublime," the intimation would seem to be clear: the postmodern is not merely an epochal break for the arts and aesthetic perception; but the developments in the arts confer on the very notion of the sublime the heightened actuality of a category of comprehension for what obtains today. Jean-François Lyotard's recourse to the sublime is certainly not immune to the charges in question, given that he has made the explicit connection between the postmodern avant-garde and the sublime. But rather than confirming standard prejudices, Lyotard's interest, if not passion, for the sublime may, at closer scrutiny, reveal a notion of the sublime that does not only contradict the charge of aestheticism, but also has not its like in the tradition. The significance of Barnett Baruch Newman's work in Lyotard's recourse to the notion of the sublime is beyond doubt. However, the assumption that an irreducibly aesthetic and immutable sublime thus categorizes contemporary developments in the arts and, by extension, aestheticizes other realms might need requestioning. Indeed, what is the significance in this context of Lyotard's insistence on stressing not only the fact that Newman read the texts on the sublime, but also that he is a Jewish painter, deeply steeped in the Jewish tradition? Furthermore, this Jewish painter was deeply inspired by the Indian earthworks he beheld in Akron, Ohio, from a source, consequently, that is non-Western, non-European, and foreign to the tradition of the sublime. Do these facts square with what one commonly understands as the sublime? These alone should have been sufficient reasons to make critics hesitate to simply take it for granted that the category of the sublime is, for Lyotard, an aesthetic category in the traditional sense. The fact that the notion of the sublime does not serve, first and foremost, to account for current trends in the arts should have led to even greater caution.

From the outset it needs to be underscored that Lyotard's concern with the sublime arises from philosophical questions. Indeed, the primary context for Lyotard's recourse to the notion of the sublime is his attempt in *The Differend* to rethink philosophical thinking. The question of how to save the honor of thinking motivates primarily Lyotard's interest in the sublime. Attention to this context might force one to reconceive what is meant by the sublime, and, ultimately, by the category of the aesthetic itself.

I recall that the first chapter of *The Differend* argues that for Western thought the reality of a referent is not a given but a predicate or property. The reality of referents is established in a genre of discourse called cognitive, one in which referents are, moreover, subordinated to strict establishment procedures. When those discursive exigencies cannot be met, discourse about referents and their reality is prone to differends. When the revisionist historians demand proof of the existence of the gas chambers at the extermination camps, they ask for proof that only victims of the gas chambers could provide. But one who has seen them with his or her own eyes, can no longer testify. From these wrongs that thinking itself—thinking in its cognitive mode—inflicts in certain cases where reality claims are made arises the specific task of philosophical thinking. It must testify to the wrongs done in the name of thinking to the silenced plaintiffs or witnesses lest it face the loss of its honor. Besides the differends that result from the establishment and verification procedures regarding the existence of referents, the second chapter—"The Referent, the Name"—inquires into a further set of differends caused by the way a sense is assigned to a referent. This second kind of differend devolves from the role that names inevitably have in the establishment and verification procedures concerning reality.

   In contrast to the common idea of reality, which is believed to have an existence independent of any witness, reality in scientific thinking is the result of a syllogistic conclusion. Furthermore, for the reality of something to be admitted, the asserted reality must be verified in the cognitive phrase universes by means of monstrative or ostensive phrases. Nevertheless, as Lyotard observes, the deictics, or designators of reality, operative in such phrases, do not suffice to make a referent real. He writes: "Reality is not established by ostensation alone (*TD*, 40)."[1] As the Notice on Antisthenes reveals, Saul Kripke's demonstration that all operations on referents must first fix the referent by means of rigid denominators brings to light a requirement as old as Western thinking itself. Before showing a referent as an example for which a cognitive phrase is true, names are called for to fix a referent and to assure that it remains one and the same within multiple contexts. Above all, names are warranted to secure identity of the referent in the case of ostensive phrases that serve as validation for cognitive phrases that assert its reality. Nothing but the empty rigidity of the pure mark of the designative function, the name itself does not endow the referent with any reality. But without the name acting as a "linchpin" (*TD*, 43) between phrases, reality claims are impossible. At the same time, this crucial role of the name as "an empty link" (*TD*, 46) in the conferral of reality on a referent introduces an element of contingency and uncertainty into the establishment of reality. Lyotard holds: "If the name can act as a linchpin between an ostensive phrase with its deictics and any given phrase with its sense or senses, it is because it is independent of the current showing and deprived of sense even though it has the twin capacity of designating and of being signified. But that it actually acts as a linchpin and endows its referent with a reality, that at least remains contingent. That is why reality is never certain" (*TD*, 43). Since in itself the name is empty, hence not determined by a specific sense (*Sinn*), attachment of sense to a name as a name of a referent "includes the possible in the constitution of reality" (*TD*, 45). In fact, it includes the possible in a double sense: first, in the sense of that which is no longer the case and, second, in the sense of what is not yet the case. As a result, Lyotard speaks of an inconsistency with regard to negation that is implied by all assertion of reality (*TD*, 45). Having recalled that in order to be able to assert that a referent is real, it is necessary that "the referent profits, so to speak, from the permanence of the name that names it," he remarks that "what is equally necessary for this assertion . . . is a property that appears to contradict the former: a named referent is real when it is also the possible case (the object of an ostensive phrase) of an unknown sense (presented by a not yet current phrase). In the assertion of reality, the persistence of the referent . . . is combined with the event of a sense" (*TD*, 47). In addition to serving as a fixed mark, the name, in order to be able to establish the reality of a referent, must also be susceptible to the assignment of multiple senses. As merely a rigid and empty designator, a name not only cuts across phrase universes, but also is associated with a host of different senses. Any real referent is " 'the case' of senses presented by phrases which have not yet taken place" (*TD*, 47) and that are, in principle, infinite. Indeed, since the name is not "by itself a designator of reality (for that to occur a sense and an ostensible referent need to be associated with it), the inflation of senses that can be attached to it is not bounded by the 'real' properties of its referent" (*TD*, 47). Lyotard, who speaks in this context of a "hollow" entailed by the named and shown referent, defines the negation as follows: "A 'swarm' of possible senses of indeterminate quantity and quality, inhabit this 'hollow' " (*TD*, 51).[2]

The consequences for the validation of reality, which follow from this plethora of possible senses of which a name signifying a referent must be capable in order to be an empty and fixed mark that can cut through different phrase universes, are plain and clear. Lyotard writes: " 'Validation' consists in showing cases of provisional nonfalsification. Reality is the referent of an ostensive phrase (and of a nominative one). This referent is cited . . . 1: as what refutes the sense contrary to the sense in question; 2: as what does not prohibit maintaining the latter until there is further information. The example presented to the tribunal of cognition does not, properly speaking, have any conclusive authority, it is permissive. . . . By naming and showing one eliminates. Proof is negative, in the sense of being refutable. . . . Reality is invoked by ostension and nomination as the prohibition to deny a sense. It allows for all the contrary senses to be placed in the position of possibilities" (*TD*, 54–55). The sense whose reality is invoked is thus a sense that takes the place of other eliminated senses. Its validation takes place at the expense of other senses associated with the name of the referent. Inevitably, these senses are wronged. As Lyotard remarks, "Phrases come to be attached to [a] name, which not only describe different senses for it . . . and not only place the name on different instances, but which also obey heterogeneous regimens and/or genres. This heterogeneity, for lack of a common idiom, makes consensus impossible." He can therefore conclude that "reality entails the differend" (*TD*, 55–56).

At this precise juncture, Lyotard comes to speak about the name "Auschwitz." In response to the revisionist historians' insistence on applying cognitive rules to establish and validate Auschwitz's reality, Lyotard remarks: "With Auschwitz something new has happened in history (which can only be a sign and not a fact), which is that the facts, the testimonies which bore the trace of *here's* and *now's*, the documents which indicated the sense or senses of the facts, and the names, finally the possibility of various kinds of phrases whose conjunction makes reality, all this has been destroyed as much as possible" (*TD*, 57). From a cognitive vantage point, it has therefore become excruciatingly difficult to establish the reality of the extermination camp in question. If one is to stick to the rules particular to the discursive genre of cognition, it is almost impossible to muster ostensive evidence in support of the sense or senses of the name "Auschwitz." A "silence is imposed on knowledge," if knowledge is not possible without strict adherence to these rules. Yet, as Lyotard maintains, this silence "does not impose the silence of forgetting, it imposes a feeling (*sentiment*)" (*TD*, 56). This is a "complex feeling . . . one aroused by the negative presentation of the indeterminate," in short, the feeling "that something which should be able to be put into phrases cannot be phrased in the accepted idioms" (*TD*, 56–57). Thus, a phrase such as the one that "*Auschwitz was the extermination camp*" is a phrase surrounded by silence because in addition to the millions who were exterminated, "the means to prove the crime or its quantity were also exterminated" (*TD*, 56). But this phrase, or silence, equally points at the possible senses, "the indetermination of meanings left in abeyance [*en souffrance*]" with respect to the name Auschwitz. "The shadow of negation hollowing out reality to the point of making it dissipate" signifies "that something remains to be phrased which is not, something which is not determined" (*TD*, 57). It is a call for "unknown phrases to link onto the name of Auschwitz" (*TD*, 57). Even though Auschwitz is a unique historical event, such a qualification does not imply that it was merely an accident that befell history, a fluke that will not happen again. Rather, Auschwitz is unique inasmuch as it reveals something about reality in general. Auschwitz, Lyotard remarks, is only "the most real of realities"—"the meta-reality that is the destruction of reality"—as it exemplifies, in the most horrid ways, that in all reality there is something "not presentable under the rules of knowledge." Hence, "every reality entails this exigency insofar as it entails possible unknown senses," the exigency, namely, to lend an ear "to what is not presentable under the rules of knowledge" (*TD*, 57–58).

As corollary of Lyotard's conclusion that all reality contains a differend because of the role that names play in the establishment of the reality of referents, it now appears that all reality, and any sense that reality validates, is accompanied by a sentiment that something remains unsaid, or muffled. This feeling that there is something undetermined and left to be phrased in all reality claims and that it has not been presented in the phrase universe proper to the claim amounts to the unpresentable's negative presentation. This sentiment that something unpresentable has been left in abeyance suggests a kinship to the feeling of the sublime. Kant associates the latter with the negative presentation of something unpresentable. Lyotard, for his part, alludes to a feeling that inevitably accompanies any validated sense, since the accredited sense must have excluded all the other possible senses that inhabit, or hollow out, the name required to fix a referent before its reality can be established. The feeling in question is thus one that is provoked by the elimination of all the senses of a name in the process of cognitively establishing the reality of a referent. These senses are wronged not only because they have been excluded for the benefit of one privileged sense, but also because the cognitive could not do them justice in the first place. This feeling of something unpresentable presented negatively is thus, first and foremost, an inevitable side effect of the cognitive genre. But as Lyotard also notes, phrases that become attached to a name obey heterogeneous regimens and/or genres regardless of consensus. Consequently, it would seem that the feeling in question structurally accompanies every phrase. It is a feeling congenital to phrasing.

This feeling that comes with all phrasing "does not arise from an experience felt by a subject. It can, moreover, not be felt" (*TD*, 57). This is not the "state of mind" of a subject; the sentiment in question is a function of the addressee in phrase universes where the referent, rather than displaying "significations validatable under the cognitive regimen," is in the situation of a "sign." In other words, it signals "something which should be able to be put into phrases [but] cannot be phrased in the accepted idioms" (*TD*, 56–57). Lyotard writes: "That, in a phrase universe, the referent be situated as a sign has as a corollary that in this same universe the addressee is situated like some one who is affected, and that the sense is situated like an unresolved problem, an enigma perhaps, a mystery, or a paradox" (*TD*, 57). The feeling that some undetermined meaning of the cognitively processed referent remains to be phrased is thus a feeling that affects the instance of the addressee in a phrase universe. It is not a feeling signifying a subjective urge for expression. An effect of the inner dynamic of the instances of phrase universes, the sentiment is a call for unknown phrases to link onto a name (such as Auschwitz). It designates the linkage of phrases "affected" by a referent in the situation of a sign. With Auschwitz in mind, Lyotard avers: "The indetermination of meanings left in abeyance, the extermination of what would allow them to be determined, the shadow of negation hollowing out reality to the point of making it dissipate, in a word, the wrong done to the victims that condemns them to silence—it is this, and not a state of mind, which calls upon unknown phrases to link on the name of Auschwitz" (*TD*, 57). This sentiment, like the sublime inasmuch as it is aroused by the negative presentation of something indeterminate, is thus an "objective" sentiment, as it were. Yet, in order to glimpse the exact reasons why Lyotard can suggest that this nonsubjective sentiment is of the order of the sublime, it is necessary to return to and reformulate in a more precise fashion what causes it.

While discussing the role of the name in the establishment and verification procedures of the real, I emphasized the elimination of the possible senses attached to the name (as an empty designator) in order to fix a referent in favor of one sense, for which the shown referent becomes the example. Now, Lyotard speaks of the senses and of their presentation in phrases as events. Even before engaging the specific way in which "presentation" is to be understood, the fact that senses happen compels us to remark that the differend concurrent with the establishment of reality—the differend innate to reality—results from the elimination of possible events. The feeling in question thus concerns cut-off events of sense and serves as a call to let them happen. At this point, I recall that when Lyotard held that with Auschwitz something new happened in history, he referred first and foremost to the systematic destruction by the Nazis of all evidence that could have served to prove the reality of what occurred in the death

camps. What makes Auschwitz unique in a sense is the destruction of reality. The terror wedded to its name not only signifies the extermination of
millions of human beings, but also the extermination of that extermination itself. The sentiment that links onto the name of Auschwitz does thus
not only consist in the demand to lift the silence that surrounds this name;
it also registers the fact that with Auschwitz the impossible proved possible. As Lyotard remarks in *The Differend*, linking onto phrases is necessary. In other words, it is impossible not to link, as even silence is a phrase.
Because phrases are events, the impossibility not to link signifies that it is
impossible that nothing occurs. With Auschwitz, the attempt has been
made to destroy all vestiges of what happened. With Auschwitz, the possibility arose that nothing happened, that the impossible was possible. But
then Auschwitz only brought to light something that pertains to reality in
general. Consequently, the feeling that, according to Lyotard, calls for
phrases to link with names surrounded by silence must also be understood
as a demand to phrase this possibility that the impossible is a possibility.
Indeed, this feeling emerges from the possibility that something worse
than the worst could happen—namely, nothing. This doubled feeling, one
that, as Lyotard suggests, is akin to the feeling of the sublime, thus clearly
concerns Being itself. The feeling is not only nonsubjective, but also it is
fundamentally ontological.

However, despite the unmistakable Kantian overtones that shape Lyotard's references to the sublime, the double sentiment that calls for linking with the unphrased that remains in the name and referent is not
Kantian. Lyotard's notion of the sublime cannot be illuminated through
recourse to the *Critique of Judgment*. By extension, to demonstrate that
Lyotard's reactualization of the notion of the sublime does not do justice
to the status of the sublime in the third *Critique* is of little relevance as
well. Even though we are here primarily interested in accounting for the
Lyotardian sublime as it is put to work in Lyotard's writings, in particular
in *The Differend*, a brief excursus on the relation of his notion of the sublime to Kant's is still appropriate. Considering the extensive discussion of
this notion in the *Lessons on the Analytic of the Sublime*, it is rather revealing that this exemplary analysis—indebted to the guiding thesis that the
problematic of the sublime has been preprogrammed by the "Analytic of
the Principles" in the first *Critique*, and, hence, of the highest philosophical interest—is of little help in coming to grips with Lyotard's own use of

this notion. Indirectly, however, some of the major theses that this book advances about the Kantian sublime provide clues to how Lyotard himself wishes this notion to be understood. What guides him through his reading of "Analytic of the Sublime" is the idea that this section that Kant had qualified as a mere appendage to the "Analytic of the Beautiful" is, in fact, "contra-final" to the project of unification (implicit in the analysis of the beautiful) of the two previous *Critiques*. It menaces this project, and, in fact, "breaks the proper order of the natural aesthetic and suspends the function it assumes in the project of unification."[3] Similar to "a meteor," the "Analytic of the Sublime," furthermore, drops into a work whose first part on beauty "allows one to hope for the advent of a subject as unity of the faculties, and for a legitimation of the agreement of real objects with the authentic destination of this subject, in the Idea of nature," putting an end to these hopes.[4] As Lyotard asserts, in a recourse to the second *Critique*, "there is [something] *frevelhaft* in the sublime." By "overwhelming not only the specific functioning of the imagination" and disorganizing "the very principle of practical reason, which is precisely the uncondi-tioned of the law and the regard owed to it," the sublime produces a crisis by which "the general economy of the faculties is affected."[5] The sublime thus interrupts all of Kant's attempts in the *Critique of Judgment* to secure a unity of the critical inquiry, of the faculties in the subject by practical reason, beginning with the unity of the mind and nature in the notion of beautiful form. As *The Inhuman* states quite unambiguously, the "aesthetic of the sublime which comes about through the distension of beautiful forms to the point of 'formlessness' . . . brings about the overturning, the destruction, of the aesthetics of the beautiful."[6] Yet whatever difficulties that from a systematic point of view regarding the matter of the sublime itself, arise so as to haunt the "Analytic of the Sublime," the Kantian sub-lime fails to disrupt the aesthetic of the beautiful. By contrast, it secures the possibility of purely aesthetic judgment in the face of absolute form-lessness, a possibility co-implied by beautiful form. By emphasizing the sublime's disruptive effects, Lyotard's take on the Kantian sublime, how-ever suggestive and illuminating, makes sense only in view of a sublime that takes Kant's sublime as at best a domesticated form.[7]

    In light of Lyotard's repeated reservations concerning the transcen-dental Kantian conception of the sublime, which evidence the differend he has with Kant regarding the notion of the sublime, critics have suggested that Lyotard falls back on the precritical, theological, and metaphysical notion of the sublime in order to recover some of the dimensions of philosophy that transcendental philosophy had to surrender.[8] Indeed, as his short outline of the history of the concept in both "Newman: The Instant" and "The Sublime and the Avant-Garde" demonstrates, it is Edmund Burke's elaboration on the sublime in *A Philosophical Enquiry into the Origin of Our Ideas of the Sublime and the Beautiful,* that bears the burden of the attempt to make the aesthetic category of the sublime fruitful, at least for an understanding of the contemporary arts. But before taking up his interest in Burke's sublime, it is necessary to explain what motivates Lyotard to construe avant-garde art as sublime to begin with. Only then will it become fully understandable why the recourse to Burke, rather than to Kant, is warranted. As the title "Newman: The Instant" indicates, Newman's art concerns time. But unlike much modern art, such as, for instance, the work of Marcel Duchamp, which represents events gone by or about to happen, time for Newman is, as Lyotard argues, "the picture itself" (*TI,* 78). He writes: "The purpose of a painting by Newman is not to show that duration is in excess of consciousness, but to be the occurrence, the moment which has arrived" (*TI,* 79). As a consequence, the plastic nudity of Newman's canvasses leaves the commentator dumbfounded, as it were. "The best gloss consists of the question: what can one say? Or of the exclamation 'Ah.' Of surprise: 'Look at that.' So many expressions of a feeling which does have a name in the modern aesthetic tradition (and in the work of Newman): the sublime. It is the feeling of 'there' (*Voilà*)" (*TI,* 80). Nothing is announced by these paintings; they are not expressions of a "non-representable annunciation" (*TI,* 79); they are the angel itself, the happening of annunciation, in short, nothing but the happening of the event itself. But why is work that is nothing but its own event indexed to a feeling of the sublime? If, moreover, it is the breaking-into-being, or presence, that triggers this feeling, what then does "sublime" here mean? For, indeed, within the tradition it would be hard to find evidence of such a definition of the sublime. But to answer these questions, we first need to pursue Lyotard's discussion of Newman's work.

Notwithstanding their abstraction, subject matter is not eliminated from Newman's paintings, Lyotard asserts. Thematically, they are about artistic creation itself, the symbol of divine creation, and the "(paradoxical) idea of *beginning*" (*TI,* 82). Newman's paintings are concerned with the event through which what is comes into being. Such breaking into Being, independent of what occurs in the flash of an occurrence, is to be grasped "in terms of [an event's] *quod* rather than its *quid*." And Lyotard adds: "Without this flash [of the event], there would be nothing, or there would be chaos. The flash (like the instant) is always there, and never there. The world never stops beginning. For Newman, creation is not an act performed by someone; it is what happens (this) in the midst of the indeterminate" (*TI*, 82). It follows from this that in creating objects (paintings) that convey nothing but their happening, and hence the flash without which there would be nothing, these objects respond to and activate the beginning that inaugurates the world. This is a beginning that must never stop happening if something rather than nothing is to be. As events through which something arrives into being, the paintings presuppose an addressee. Indeed, the arrival of something arrives for someone and comes with the instantaneous demand for acknowledgement. According to Lyotard, Newman's paintings transform the triadic structure of communicational space from the bottom up. His paintings are no longer the medium of an expressed message from the painter-subject to a recipient. Communicative space is reduced to two instances: the painting, which communicates nothing but its happening, and the addressee. But the very nature of the relation between art and its recipient is reduced as well. Indeed, if the message amounts to a *Here I am*, one whose immediate recipient is in the position of an addressee, a *You*, of whom it demands an immediate response, then the relation between the painting and its addressee is no longer communicative. For Lyotard, it has become a relation of obligation. When creations emphasize the *that* of their happening, they turn the spectator into a *You* who has to bear witness to the event. Indeed, if a painting presents only its presence—a *Here I am*—the " 'pragmatic' organization [between it and its addressee] is much closer to an ethics than to any aesthetics or poetics. Newman is concerned with giving colour, line or rhythm the force of an obligation within a face-to-face relationship, in the second person, and his model cannot be *Look at this* (*over there*); it must be *Look at me* or, to be more accurate, *Listen to me*" (*TI*, 81). The claimed spectator's feeling of sublimity is thus the immediate result of an address. It testifies to the addressee's concern with being rather than nothingness.

Even though in "Newman: The Instant" the event is already determined by the backdrop of the nothing from which it comes into presence, this dimension of the event is fully highlighted only in "The Sublime and the Avant-Garde." Inquiring into the meaning of Newman's *Now*—invoked by the titles of some of his paintings and writings—the temporal nature of the *quod* of the occurrence is refined here to the point of inscribing the reference to nothing into the very acknowledgment that something happens. Newman's *Now*, Lyotard ascertains, is neither a temporal moment constituted by consciousness nor "a matter of sense or reality bearing upon what happens or *what* this might mean," but rather it is the occurrences themselves that precede any determined presence, that is, any presence determined according to its meaning or in terms of the real. What something means is established in response to the question, *quid*? or, what is it? By contrast, the *Now* of the event denotes the *that* it happens (the *quod*) in advance of the question of what is it that happens (the *quid*). Lyotard writes: "Before asking questions about what it is and about its significance, before the *quid*, it must 'first' so to speak 'happen,' *quod*. That it happens 'precedes' so to speak, the question pertaining to what happens. Or rather, the question precedes itself, because 'that it happens' is the question as event, and it 'then' pertains to the event that has just happened. The event happens as a question mark 'before' happening as a question. *It happens* is rather 'in the first place' *is it happening, is this it, is it possible?*" (*TI*, 90; trans. mod.). Unmistakably, all happening is thus intrinsically tied to the question concerning happening itself. Rather than a given, or a fact, the event inscribes its own surprise, the marvel of its own possibility. The *quod* is intrinsically the event of the question of whether a happening has occurred. Because as event the event marks a difference with the nothing from which it bounces off, the event is marked by the possibility that it could not have taken place. This possibility leaves a question mark on the event. It leaves it forever problematic, forever wondrous for having occurred. Speaking from here of the *quod* in terms of a *Is it happening?* Lyotard thus brings to bear the fact that anything that occurs does so against the possibility that nothing might have occurred, on the very categories that capture "eventness."

In a further move, "The Sublime and the Avant-Garde" argues that traditional institutions and philosophical disciplines are unfit to deal with the notion of the event. Philosophy as a discipline is preoccupied with the determination of "something that hasn't yet been determined," but it does not reflect upon the fact that what it determines must first have emerged into existence. Furthermore, philosophy is oblivious to the evidence that the question of the *quid* is preceded by the event of the question and that, consequently, any *it happens* is a *Is it happening?* Philosophy, therefore, "forget[s] the possibility of nothing happening, of words, colours, forms or sounds not coming; of this sentence being the last of bread not coming daily" (*TI*, 91). Although the event, or occurrence, would seem to be "infinitely simple . . . this simplicity can only be approached through a state of privation [*dénuement*, poverty, bareness]," free of the tradition of philosophical thinking (*TI*, 90). What is required, Lyotard holds, is an approach that is sensitive to the negativity implied in the *that it is*. As this approach is preconceptual, such an address is thus closer to what is commonly called a feeling. As he remarks, "The possibility of nothing happening is often associated with a feeling of anxiety," but the "suspense can also be accompanied by pleasure, for instance pleasure in welcoming the unknown, and even by joy, to speak like Baruch Spinoza, the joy obtained by the intensification of being that the event brings with it" (*TI*, 92). The feeling that relates to the event is thus "probably a contradictory feeling. It is at the very least a sign, the question-mark itself, the way in which *it happens* is withheld and announced: *Is it happening?*" Lyotard concludes (*TI*, 92). Approached through a state of privation, the event is felt. It is the object of a contradictory feeling in that it is felt as "the question-mark itself." Reinvoking Newman's *Now*, Lyotard observes that "the mark of the question is 'now,' *now* like [*comme*, as is] the feeling that nothing might happen: the nothingness now" (*TI*, 92). Newman's *Now* would thus have to be understood as the sentiment that results from the improbability of the happening: marked by an interrogation point, it is the feeling of wonder that it happened and the anxiety that it might not have happened. It is the sentiment that the event of Being is fragile and constantly threatened by the nothingness from which it bounces off into presence. "This contradictory feeling," Lyotard avers, "was christened or re-christened by the name of the *sublime*" between the seventeenth and eighteenth centuries in Europe.[9]

In the subsequent discussion in the essay of the history of the sublime, Lyotard asserts that "the question of time, of the *Is it happening?* does not form part—at least not explicitly—of Kant's problematic" (*TI*, 99). With this statement, it is made plain that the Kantian notion of the sublime does not lend itself to capturing the feeling caused by works of avant-garde art. In fact, Kant is explicitly said to have "rejected" this problematic of time and eventness, which is at the heart of this conception of the sublime. Kant's characterization and condemnation of Edmund Burke's *Philosophical Inquiry into the Origin of Our Ideas of the Sublime and Beautiful*, in which, according to Lyotard, this question is central, is testimony that this question is dismissed in the transcendental account of the sublime, since Kant judges Burke's work to be merely empirically descriptive. Lyotard writes: "Kant may well reject Burke's thesis as empiricism and physiologism, he may well borrow from Burke the analysis of the characterizing contradiction of the feeling of the sublime, but he strips Burke's aesthetic of what I consider to be its major stake—to show that the sublime is kindled by the threat of nothing further happening" (*TI*, 99).[10] As he remarks in "Newman: The Instant," "certain 'objects' and certain 'sensations' are pregnant with a threat to our self-preservation, and Burke refers to that threat as *terror*: shadows, solitude, silence and the approach of death may be 'terrible' in that they announce that the gaze, the other, language or life will soon be extinguished" (*TI*, 84). But Burke's notion of terror—a feeling that in Burke is but a function of the individual's self-preservation—is broadened here so as to name the privation of Being altogether. In terror, Lyotard holds, "one feels that it is possible that soon nothing more will take place" (*TI*, 84). The threat that causes terror is thus interpreted as a threat to the ontico-ontological. Lyotard writes: "What is terrifying is that the *It happens that* does not happen, that it stops happening" (*TI*, 99). But when that threat is suspended, or kept at bay, the feeling of terror mixes with a kind of pleasure that is akin to relief. It is the pleasure of "delight"—a delight at the fact that the threat that nothing may happen anymore has been held back—that must combine with the feeling of terror for it to be a sublime feeling. "What is sublime is the feeling that something will happen, despite everything, within this threatening void, that something will take 'place' and will announce that everything is not over" (*TI*, 84).

This is not the place to discuss Lyotard's interpretation of Burke—of whether the terror Burke speaks of concerns the anxiety of nothing happening anymore and whether delight lets itself be interpreted as the relief that not everything is over yet. What needs to be highlighted, in contrast, is that this interpretation provides us with Lyotard's own conception of the sublime. The perceived threat is one that concerns the total cessation of "it happens." It is the threat that nothing may occur anymore, in short, the threat of an ontological disaster. With reference to Burke, Lyotard writes that this threat "strikes [the soul] with 'astonishment' (at lower intensities the soul is seized with admiration, veneration, respect). The soul is thus dumb (*stupide*), immobilized, as good as dead" (*TI*, 99–100). But if the possibility that the impossible may happen is held at bay, and the soul realizes that the world will continue to begin, delight sets in, the delight of the *Is it happening?* Undoubtedly, this conception of the sublime is not Kantian. But is it, for all that, a precritical concept of the sublime? Burke does not say *à la lettre* what Lyotard makes him say. Lyotard himself, after having linked the feeling of the sublime to the relief that something is happening rather than nothing, admits: "It's still the sublime in the sense that Burke and Kant described and yet it isn't their sublime anymore" (*TI*, 93). From a brief discussion of the short history of the sublime as sketched out in "The Sublime and the Avant-Garde," some points can perhaps be gleaned about how Lyotard's sublime relates to the precritical tradition of this aesthetic concept.

Lyotard begins this history with the publication of Boileau's translation of Longinus' *Peri tou hupsou*, "christened or re-christened" as *Du Sublime*, along with his own treaty on *L'Art poétique* in 1674. As he remarks, between the seventeenth and eighteenth centuries in Europe, the name "sublime" invoked "the destiny of classical poetics [namely, that it] was hazarded and lost; it is in this name that aesthetics asserted its critical rights over art, and that romanticism, in other words, modernity, triumphed" (*TI*, 92). Now, what is remarkable in Lyotard's account of Longinus' treaty, as well as of Nicolas Boileau's and Dominique Bouhours' commentaries and writings, is his contention that the discursive treatment of the sublime poses major obstacles to the didactic form of the *techne rhetorike*, to which, after all, the rhetorician Longinus was devoted. The sublime "destabilizes the text's didactic intentions" of the rhetorical or poetic genres, Lyotard asserts (*TI*, 94). It inflicts a "major blow" to didactics, especially when a discourse, in order to be sublime, "accommodates defects, lack of taste, and formal imperfections" (*TI*, 95). Undoubtedly, Lyotard's insistence on this disruptive effect of the sublime fits with his argument that the sublime destabilizes beautiful form in every respect. But what also appears to be of tantamount importance here is that the sublime subverts classical Greek and Roman modes of thinking and practice. A further reason for Lyotard's interest in the precritical and pre-Romantic conception of the sublime concerns the role that Longinus and Bouhours accord to silence as being expressive of the indeterminate. Lyotard notes that Longinus allows for "a sublimity of thought" that is recognizable by "the form of outright silence" in speech (*TI*, 94). Finally, Bouhours is recalled to have referred to the "Messieurs de Port Royal" in his polemic with Pierre Daniel Huet about "whether the Bible's *Fiat lux, et lux fuit* is sublime, as Longinus thought it was, because "the Jansenists are masters when it comes to matters of hidden meaning, of eloquent silence, of feeling that transcends all reason and finally of openness to the *Is it happening?*" (*TI*, 96). For the time being, I leave the question that links sublimity to the expression, or rather presentation, of the indeterminate in abeyance. However, it is important that the disruptive effects of the sublime are here linked to this notion's origin in a tradition different from the classical tradition. The notion of the sublime is not a Greek concept. The tradition from which it originates is circumscribed in terms of Christianity. Lyotard conjures "the influence of early Christianity on Longinus" (*TI*, 95). "The sublime which is introduced into Western thought by Longinus comes directly from the kind of thinking that is called Judeo-Christian. Half of the examples of Longinus stem from the Bible whose author at the time was Moses."[11] Elsewhere, the sublime is referred to "as a strange notion . . . that does not come to us from the Greeks but from the Jews and the Christians," which clearly suggests that this is a notion foreign to Greek thought, foreign in particular to "the *aisthesis*, to the pertinence of the beautiful."[12] It remains, however, that neither Longinus nor the theoreticians of classical French poetics have an explicitly ontological concept of the sublime that we find in Lyotard. Of Longinus, it is said that he had not the means to conceptualize the sublime.[13] Consequently, I do not agree with those critics who argue that Lyotard leaves the transcendental understanding of the sublime behind for a precritical, theological, and metaphysical concept. Although Lyotard turns away from Kant to Burke and Longinus, he aims at something else in advance, or on this side, of this precritical tradition, something that surfaces more in Longinus and Burke than in Kant, though none of them have given it its full due.

Within the context of his debate about contemporary art, two examples provide hints at what, precisely, it is that is thus at odds with the Greek legacy of beautiful form and, more generally, the institution of philosophical thinking. Even though Kant's sublime falls short with respect to the postmodern sublime, both essays—"Newman: The Instant" and "The Sublime and the Avant-Garde"—recognize that "avant-gardism is . . . present in germ in the Kantian aesthetic of the sublime." The imagination's painful failure to present Ideas, nevertheless, gives rise to a negative presentation of the Absolute in the sublime, which is accompanied by pleasure. With this notion of negative presentation, Kant, according to Lyotard, anticipates abstract and minimalist art. While discussing this concept of negative presentation, Kant, as Lyotard recalls, cites "the Jewish law banning images as an eminent example of negative presentation: optical pleasure when reduced to near nothingness promotes an infinite contemplation of infinity" (*TI*, 98). Like so many commentators on the "Analytic of the Sublime," Lyotard too ignores that Kant refers both to the Mosaic and the Islamic law. In his case, however, such an oversight may be a strategic neglect pointing at the antecedence of the Jewish law to both Christian and Islamic law. Be that as it may, this reference to the Mosaic law and its prohibition of making graven images links the sublime, as Lyotard conceives it, more intimately to the Jewish tradition. The idea's root in Jewish tradition opposes it to the Greek idiom and the beautiful.

I must underscore that Kant's anticipation of abstract and minimalist art comes only to full fruition with the sublime art of Newman. In "Newman: The Instant," right after having evoked Kant's reference to the Mosaic law, Newman's efforts to escape figurative space are described as intent on confounding "the event-bound time [with the] presentation of the pictorial object itself" (*TI*, 85). Lyotard continues: "It is chromatic matter alone, and its relationship with the material . . . and the lay-out . . . which must inspire the wonderful surprise, the wonder that there should be something rather than nothing. Chaos threatens, but the flash of the *Tzim-tzum*, the zip, takes place, divides the shadow, breaks down the light into colours like a prism, and arranges them across the surface like a universe" (*TI*, 85–86). By conceiving of the event that arises from, and in defiance of, the threatening chaos in terms unmistakably tributary to the cabalistic doctrine of the *Tzim-tzum*, the sublimity of Newman's paintings becomes explicitly linked to a problematic foreign to the Greek ideal of beautiful form.[14] But when further exploring the sense of time that defines Newman's work down to its very capillaries, Lyotard broadens the scope of this non-Greek problematic at the very heart of the sublime in a highly intriguing way. So far the sublime has been clearly associated with

the Jewish and Christian idiom. "The sublime is not pagan," he asserts.[15]
As yet, as "Newman: The Instant" recalls, the latter's enthusiasm for the
Miamisburg mounds, which he describes as "the greatest works of art on
the American continent . . . [if not] perhaps the greatest arts monuments
in the world," compared to which "the Mexican and Northwest Coast
totem poles are hysterical, overemphasized monsters" and the "Egyptian
pyramid . . . nothing but an ornament," stems from the sense that these
Indian earthworks also possess the simplicity, an eventfulness, in which
presence happens against the backdrop of chaos.[16] And when finally Newman, in a text intent on introducing the maquette of a synagogue he de-
signed and built together with Robert Murray, defines the place where the
Torah is read as "the mound where, under the tension of that 'Tzim-
Tzum' that created light and the world, [each man] can experience a total
sense of his own personality before the Torah and His Name," "Indian
space and Jewish space" become, as Lyotard emphasizes, condensed in "an
attempt to capture 'presence'" (TI, 86–87). The non-Greek, non-European problematic of the sublime is thus not merely wedded to the Jewish
heritage; it has its roots in a certain paganism as well. In no way, however,
is one to conclude from this that the notion of the sublime, as Lyotard sees
it, could simply be retraced to and nailed down as belonging to Jewish
and/or a certain pagan thought.[17] Both, perhaps, communicate in their
opposition to the Greek paradigm. In any case, we have not yet fully accounted for Lyotard's conception of the sublime.

Let's bear in mind that in the context of the discussion of the differend that arises from the specific ways Western thought secures the establishment and validation of reality, Lyotard suggests that all reality, and any
sense established according to these rules, travels with a sentiment that
something indeterminate has not been presented, or rather is only negatively presented. Because the notion of a negative presentation is Kantian,
and in Kant associated with a feeling of the sublime, we called the sentiment in question sublime, even though Lyotard himself did not do so explicitly. From what we have seen so far in the essays concerned with the
postmodern sublime, the sublime articulates above all the feeling of *Is it
happening?* But where then does the problem of the indeterminate, the unpresentable, come in? How is the question about the presentation of the
unpresentable linked to the question of the event that arrives and defeats
silence and nothingness?

While discussing Newman's assessment of Burke's *Inquiry* and his judgment of the latter as over-surrealist, Lyotard explains "surrealist" as "a pre-romantic or romantic approach to indeterminacy" (*TI*, 92). Newman, consequently, is critical of Romantic art, but does not "reject its fundamental task, that of bearing pictorial or otherwise expressive witness to the inexpressible" (*TI*, 92–93). And Lyotard specifies: "The inexpressible does not reside in an over there, in another world, or another time, but in this: in that (something) happens. In the determination of pictorial art, the indeterminate, the 'it happens' is the paint, the picture. The paint, the picture as occurrence or event, is not expressible, and it is to this that it has to witness" (*TI*, 93). In contrast to the Romantic conception of the undeterminable as a determined indeterminacy—suggested by the reference to an "over there"—the inexpressible that characterizes Newman's sublime is the happening of the event itself. In the novel concept of the sublime that Lyotard ascribes to Newman, the inexpressible concerns the event's occurrence, an occurrence that does not become manifest as such. By zeroing in on the event itself that does not show itself as such in what it makes possible, Newman testifies to the fact that what occurred could also not have occurred. The inexpressible, or unpresentable, to which witness is to be given, is thus thought of as the event of the coming into presence of being against the possibility of nothing happening at all or, anymore, a possibility co-implied in the very concept of the event. If "here and now there is this painting, rather than nothing, and that's what is sublime" (*TI*, 93), it is sublime because of the delight that something is happening and that, consequently, the threat that nothing might have happened has been suspended.

According to the *The Inhuman*, avant-garde painting enters the field opened by the aesthetics of the sublime via its concern with the activity of painting itself and its revelation of the invisible through the visual. If these paintings call forth sublime sentiments, it is because they "present that there is some absolute." They do not present the invisible, the absolute itself; by definition the absolute is the unpresentable. Rather, they testify to the fact that there is some absolute by way of what Kant called a "negative presentation." This question of the unpresentable is, Lyotard emphasizes, "the only one worthy of what is at stake in life and thought in the coming century" (*TI*, 127). In order to refine this non-Romantic notion of the unpresentable, which demands witnessing, I circle back to *The Differend* and the question of the indeterminate that makes itself felt whenever reality is asserted in conformity with the establishment and validation procedures characteristic of Western thinking. A short elucidation of the chapter "Presentation," in which the notion of the sublime is invoked for the first time, will allow us to grasp with greater precision the radically ontological dimension that distinguishes the Lyotardian sublime. Until here we have seen Lyotard to posit indeterminacy as a function of the possible senses that remain unactualized in all the attributions of sense and their validation by referents due to constraints of genre and temporal regimes. But with the presentation that occurs inherently in any and all phrases, a more fundamental indeterminacy comes to light. This is an indeterminacy that anchors the feeling of the sublime in the phrase-event itself.

Before embarking on a discussion of the concept of "presentation," and in order to avoid any misunderstandings, I recall that phrases are not propositions (*TD*, 65). "A wink, a shrugging of the shoulder, a tapping of the foot, a fleeting blush, or an attack of tachycardia can be phrases." A silence can also serve as a phrase (*TD*, 70). Phrases, first and foremost, are occurrences. They are events, before they are beholden to obey specific regimens, such as, for instance, the logical and cognitive regimen to which propositions belong. Viewed as occurrences, phrases are, in classical language, ultimates. To the extent that the sense of a phrase (or its reality) is an instance or quantity taken as a referent in a phrase universe, sense or reality is subject to doubt. Conversely, if we consider phrases as events, they escape universal doubt. Lyotard holds that they are "merely what happens, *what is occuring, ce qui arrive, das Fallende* [*sic*!]. You cannot doubt that something happens when you doubt: it happens that you doubt" (*TD*, 66–67).[18] Indeed, "when we are surprised that there is something rather than nothing, we are surprised that there is a phrase or that there are phrases rather than no phrases" (*TD*, 65). Understood as an occurrence, a phrase co-implies a non-phrase, or the abyss of the nothing. Being a "what" (a *quod*), "a phrase arises out of nothingness to link up with" another phrase (*TD*, 66). Because the phrase occurs—and there is no occurrence without a "something" to which this occurrence "relates" and by which it is called forth—a phrase always follows another phrase. In effect there is no first (and no last) phrase. This complicates the phrase's status as an ultimate as this paratactical structure is an intrinsic characteristic of the phrase. It emerges from nothingness, but always emerges in the form of an added other, as *And a phrase*. The nothingness that is consistently co-implied by any and all phrases is a nothingness that counters not the phrase itself (the phrase as such) but the phrase as intrinsically an additional phrase, the one that links onto another phrase. Lyotard avers: "Paratax thus connotes the abyss of Not-Being which opens between phrases, it stresses the surprise that something begins when what is said is said" (*TD*, 66).

And a phrase is thus the "ultimate" that escapes universal doubt. Although it implicates the abyss of non-Being from which it arises, to add itself to the prior phrase that calls it, it is impossible for there to be no phrase. "For there to be an *And a phrase* is necessary. It is necessary to make linkage." Lyotard adds: "This is not an obligation, a *Sollen* [an ought to], but a necessity, a *Müssen* [a must]" (*TD*, 66). Since the ultimate is defined as *And a phrase*, the phrase at its core implies the necessity of continuing linkages. To the extent that linking has the quality of an event, the linking of phrases is necessary. It cannot not be a possibility. Linkage is intimately tied to the question of the *quod*. Its necessity is ontological (*TD*, 66). Furthermore, the necessity in question "signifies that the absence of a phrase (a silence, etc.) or the absence of a linkage (the beginning, the end, disorder, nothingness, etc.) are also phrases" (*TD*, 68).

According to Lyotard, "a phrase presents at least one universe. No matter what regimen it obeys, it entails a *There is* [*Il y a*]. There is what is signified, what it is signified about, to whom and by whom it is signified; a universe" (*TD*, 70). The presentation of a universe through the phrase event should not be construed as something that is performed by a subject for another subject. "The universe presented by a phrase is not presented to something or to someone like a 'subject.' The universe is there as long as the phrase is the case. A 'subject' is situated in a universe presented by a phrase" (*TD*, 71). Subjects are merely instances in phrase universes, inasmuch as they make something happen or something happens to them. But how are we to understand "presentation" here? It should not be mistaken for, or conflated with, "representation." *The Inhuman* even refers to presentation as that "which is implied, and forgotten, in representation," namely, "the fact that something is *there now*" (*TI*, 111). More importantly, the "Notice on Kant: 1" in *The Differend* warns against confusing presentation defined as "the event of [a universe's] (inapprehensible) presence" (*TD*, 61), with Kant's problematic of *Darstellung*. Lyotard writes: "Despite the name it bears, the Kantian *Darstellung* is not at all the presentation of a phrase universe." *Darstellung* does not in any way articulate the question of the *There is* (*TD*, 65). If this Notice deserves special attention, it is because Lyotard's sharp demarcation of his notion of presentation from Kant's concept of *Darstellung* is further evidence of his attempt to argue that the question of the sublime that surfaces in precritical, and especially in critical, philosophy needs to be anchored in a dimension of "thought" foreign to Western thinking, even though it may be that it is (only) within Western thought that this foreign dimension can make itself manifest. In fact, the point made in the "Notice on Kant: 1" is that with the idea of the immediate given—a given to a subject—Kant both receives and censures the idea of a presentation. Rather than the presentation of a phase universe, Kant's *Darstellung* consists in building a bridge between the intuition of the given and our conception of it. *Darstellung* enables the subject to form a representation of what it beholds by allowing for links between heterogeneous faculties. Hence Lyotard can conclude that "with Kant, a *Darstellung* is not a presentation, it is a situating. The repression of presentation by representation (situation) is permitted and encouraged by the doctrine of the faculties and, finally, by the metaphysics of the 'subject' " (*TD*, 65). Thus, Lyotard's notion of presentation is not Kantian. Presentation, insofar as it denotes a phrase universe's character as event, its surge into presence, seems to be closer to what Heidegger terms *Anwesen*, presencing. The second Notice—on Aristotle—in the chapter "Presentation" confirms that much.

The excursus on Aristotle follows Lyotard's assertion that although phrases entail a presentation of universes, presentation cannot be presented itself in the universe that the phrase presents. However, it can be presented in the universe of another phrase that links onto it, as a preceding phrase. But what happens once presentation is grasped in the universe of another phrase? The linking phrase situates the presentation of the previous phrase as an entity or referent. The *There is* is no longer the *There is*: "now becomes the now, and it cannot be grasped as *what*, as (at) the time it happened" (*TD*, 74). Determined as the now, now undergoes "the inevitable alteration of diachrony" and thus yields to the temporality intrinsic to phrase universes, as the instances that constitute the universe are situated with respect to one another. "The 'current' or 'actual' presentation is impossible, the event is forgotten as such insofar as it is conserved (the after), anticipated (the before), or 'maintained' (the now)," when it is phrased in the universe of other phrases as a situated referent (*TD*, 74). But "the presentation-event (or occurrence) which as such is absolute (now)," is, according to Lyotard's interpretation of Aristotle, distinct from time. Consequently, Lyotard refers explicitly to Heideggerian concepts of temporality and ontology to underscore that "the *There is* takes place, it is an occurrence (*Ereignis*), but it does not present anything to anyone, it does not present itself, and it is not the present, nor is it presence. Insofar as it is phrasable (thinkable), a presentation falls short as an occurrence" (*TD*, 75).

Presentation itself being unpresentable, it follows that "the occurrence, the phrase, as a *what* that happens, does not at all stem from the question of time." Instead, Lyotard maintains that the occurrence is of the order of the more fundamental question of "Being/non-Being." Lyotard then provides his most comprehensive definition of presentation: "Presentation is not an act of giving (and above all not one coming from some *Es*, or some *It* and addressed to some us, to us human beings). Nor by presentation . . . do I understand the act of a *dunamis*, of a potency, or of a will of this potency, a desire of language to accomplish itself. But merely that something takes place. This something is a phrase, undoubtedly. Since a phrase presents a universe, for a phrase to take place is what I call presentation" (*TD*, 75). If the occurrence is a question of Being/non-Being, presentation co-implies its alternative; namely, that nothing takes place. As Lyotard specifies, the question of Being/non-Being "is called forth by a feeling: it is possible for nothing to happen. Silence not as a phrase in abeyance, but as a non-phrase, a non-*what*. This feeling is anxiety or surprise: here is something rather than nothing" (*TD*, 74–75). Any and all occurrences, presentations, or events are accompanied by the feeling that they may not have come into being at all and the subsequent wonder that there is something, anything, rather than nothing. With this focus on the event of presentation itself, prior to the significance (*quid*) of the event, it becomes clear that the possibility that "the impossible, nothingness would be possible" (*TD*, 79) is an inexorable possibility. Thought that illuminates the mere *that* of an occurrence cannot but also acknowledge the contingency, and extreme fragility, of any and all occurrences. What happened could just as well not have happened. For even though it is necessary to keep making links, no logical necessity (for logic is a question of *how* to link) commands the breaking into being of a phrase-event itself. The possibility of nonoccurrence, that the phrase may not have happened, is structurally implied by the presentation-event. From what we have seen thus far, *And a phrase* is necessary. But in determining the phrase event as event, we must concede "that the necessary is contingent. That linkage must be made, but that there won't be anything upon which to link. The 'and' with nothing to grab onto" (*TD*, 75). The possibility that there won't be anything induces a certain a sentiment—the sentiment of anxiety. But since "evidently" "it is not so" (*TD*, 79), this feeling is also one of surprise, and relief, that there is something rather than nothing. This, then, is also the precise context in which the notion of the sublime enters the ontological problematic of the presentation-event. In paragraph 126 of *The Differend*, Lyotard remarks that "with the notion of the sublime (and on condition that *Darstellung* be understood as we have here), Kant will always get the better of Hegel" (*TD*, 77), thus linking the question of the sublime to the impossibility of presenting the presentation inherent in phrase events in its absolute form. Because "it is only presentable as an existent, that is, as non-Being" in the phrase universes that situate it, presentation (which is thus given a Heideggerian twist), can only be negatively presented. And, indeed, in *The Inhuman*, Lyotard observes that "in a certain way the question of the sublime is closely linked to what Heidegger calls the retreat of Being, retreat of donation" (*TI*, 113).

Does the unpresentable, which provokes the feeling of anxiety and relief co-implied in all occurrences, refer only to the absoluteness of the event-character of an event that cannot lend itself to presentation? The sentiment that accompanies any happening is, as we have seen, a contradictory, or sublime, feeling. It is a feeling of anxiety, or terror, that nothing might occur, and the subsequent surprise that something has occurred. It follows that the unpresentability that this doubled feeling invokes must necessarily be more complex than the absoluteness of the event. We can glimpse the nature of the unpresentable in question from the following passage about contemporary art. Lyotard writes: "The task of art remains that of the immanent sublime, that of alluding to an unpresentable which has nothing edifying about it, but which is inscribed in the infinity of the transformations of 'realities'" (*TI*, 128). The unpresentable, witnessed in sublime sentiment, on the occasion of any and all events, is judged unedifying. Lacking the quality of edification, it must necessarily have the antonymous qualities of destruction and corruption. This aspect of the unpresentable to which the sublime feeling responds, is precisely the possibility of non-Being, of nothing happening anymore, of a last phrase. This possibility is tightly woven into the absoluteness of the presentation-event itself. This negative ontological possibility is an unpresentable that inhabits, and constantly threatens, the presentation event in its very absoluteness. It is as absolute as presentation, which accounts for the contradiction, tension, or paradox we feel in the sublime sentiment. Lyotard's understanding of the sublime is thus inseparable from his understanding of the ontological. Rather than referring to the question of the self-preservation of the individual, or the integrity and power of reason, Lyotard's sublime implicates the possibility of Being and the concomitant possibility of non-Being. The sense that there is something left unpresented, and unpresentable, in any and all presentation-events means that the sublime testifies to an indeterminate that escapes presentation, not by virtue of the absoluteness of the *There is*, but because it is the refusal and the destruction of any such absoluteness to begin with. It is unpresentable because it destroys all possible presentation. This unpresentable is unpresentable as such because it is of the order of the nothing.

Before further unpacking this notion of the unpresentable at the heart of the Lyotardian sublime, it needs to be noted that in elevating the sublime to the status of a feeling that accompanies the fulguration of Being and signals the unpresentable as a demand for further linking—this is a status that the sublime has never previously enjoyed—Lyotard reshapes what Heidegger has called the *Grundstimmung* at the outset of Western thought. Indeed, Lyotard links the feeling of wonder (*thaumazein*), which, according to Plato and Aristotle, consists in the realization that there is a world, to the feeling of anxiety or terror that nothing might have happened. Undoubtedly, even though the question of why there is anything at all, rather than nothing, was posed in these explicit terms only by Gottfried Wilhelm Leibniz in "Principes de la nature et de la grâce, fondés en raison," the wonder that there is something included this question from the very beginning. However, in conceiving of the *that* there is something in terms of *Is it happening?* Lyotard fundamentally transforms the question, as well as the pathos the question evokes. The feeling of wonder or surprise is joined by one of terror that nothing may have come to pass. What was true of wonder is also true of this novel doubled feeling. It sets thinking free and attunes it in all its aspects and at all its moments. But when the pathos of the sublime replaces that of wonder, such a replacement also signals a displacement of the task of thinking. Rather than inviting the determination of the *quid* that both the acknowledgment and the forgetting of the *quod* have made possible, thinking now turns to the indeterminate that shadows the *quod* and sees testifying to it as its task. Lyotard writes: "Being prepared to receive what thought is not prepared to think is what deserves the name of thinking" (*TI*, 73). What thought is not prepared to think is what escapes "the procedures for controlling time," which thus requires "a position of resistance" against such procedures (*TI*, 74). We must think the event of Being, Being being irreducible to time (*TD*, 75). As Lyotard observes: "In thinking, one accepts the occurrence for what it is: 'not yet' determined. One does not prejudge it" (*TI*, 74). To receive the event in thinking is, therefore, primarily, "to bear witness to the rest, to the untameable, to what is incommensurable with" thinking, the indeterminate, the unpresentable, in short (*TI*, 197).

In *The Differend* and elsewhere, this recast notion of the sublime feeling is linked to Jewish thinking. Jewish thought, as Lyotard emphasizes on several occasions, articulates itself in a genre of discourse that is placed "under [the regimen] of the *Is it happening?*" (*TD*, 106). Differently worded, with its openness, on the plane of affects, to the possibility that it also could not have happened—indeed, that the impossible is a (real) possibility—the Jewish idiom knows the doubled affects of anxiety and surprise. More precisely, the feeling of surprise is itself doubled here. Surprise is not simply the feeling of wonder known by the early Greek thinkers, but also shock that notwithstanding the persistent threat of nothingness, something occurs, and there is still something. Jean Améry points to this doubled nature of the affect of surprise, and the kind of (philosophical) thinking that it brings about, when he describes the refound power of intellectual articulation after having survived torture. "Thinking is almost nothing else but a great astonishment. Astonishment at the fact that you had endured it, that the tumult had not immediately led also to an explosion of the body, that you still have a forehead that you can stroke with your shackled hands, an eye that can be opened and closed, a mouth that would show the usual lines if you could see it now in a mirror." And: "If from the experience of torture any knowledge at all remains that goes beyond the plain nightmarish, it is that of a great amazement and a foreignness in the world that cannot be compensated by any sort of subsequent human communication. Amazed, the tortured person experienced that in this world there can be the other as absolute sovereign, and sovereignty revealed itself as the power to inflict suffering and to destroy."[19]

For Lyotard, Auschwitz not only enjoys the macabre privilege of a paradigm of reality because of the systematic effort on the parts of the Nazis to eradicate all evidence of the fact that it happened. But it also thus illustrates the possibility, that, indeed, non-Being could have been and is always possible. The Shoah is an attempt to mute, once and for all, the idiom of the *Is it happening?* Lyotard oberserves that by "exterminating the Jews, Nazism [sought to] eliminate a phrase regimen where the mark is on the addressee (*Listen, Israel*) and where identifying the addressor (the Lord) or the sense (what God wants to say) is a dishonorable and dangerous presumption" (*TD*, 106). With the attempt to smother this idiom, Nazism "assails the occurrence, the *Ereignis*" (*TD*, 106). Auschwitz, as Lyotard maintains in *Heidegger and "the Jews,"* is consequently a paradigm for the West's continued forgetting and sustained repression of the unpresentable affectively acknowledged by the Jewish idiom. Auschwitz represents the concerted effort to eradicate from Western thinking the non-Greek relation to the *Is it happening?* even though Nazism does not seek this elimination in the name of the Greek heritage but, as *The Differend* demonstrates, in the name of a genre of discourse—mythical and savage—that is placed under the regimen of the already there (*TD*, 105). In any event, Lyotard's argumentation clearly reveals that his redefinition of the sublime consists in an attempt to retrieve a notion of the sublime that is in no way Hellenic, that stands in contrast to that tradition.

Auschwitz, then, forces us to recognize that the Nazis wanted to destroy not just the Jews, but also the Judaic sublime, the affect of *Is it happening?* They endeavored to destroy a mode thought open to the contingency of the presentation event, a thinking that lets it be in its sublime indeterminateness—a mode of thought, therefore, that in its affect of anxiety or terror acknowledges the nothing that could have happened. This mode of thought that responds to the event, with its cargo of unpresentability, is the kind of thinking Lyotard characterizes as the most fundamental; it is the very task of thought. When we respond to the *Is it happening?* thinking is intrinsically tied up with the feeling of the sublime. This feeling of an ontological sublime that characterizes philosophical thinking at its most elemental thus has very little in common with the category of the sublime familiar from the history of aesthetics. Rather than suggesting an aestheticization of philosophical thinking, Lyotard's sublime is indication of philosophical thinking's elemental linkage to the affect of the possibility of non-Being. Auschwitz signifies the attempt to silence for good this kind of thinking in *The Differend*—a thinking that embodies thinking's most fundamental obligation. Despite this, thinking cannot for all that simply be equated with the Jewish idiom. The distinction that Lyotard makes in *Heidegger and "the Jews,"* between the Jews and "the Jews," evidences that such an equation is not warranted. Indeed, by being sensitive to the event and the unpresentable, the sublime of the Jewish idiom communicates also with a certain non-Greek paganism—even though this non-Greek element may be deeply buried within the Greek paradigm itself.

In conclusion let me then take up one more time the question of the unpresentable and the feeling of surprise it induces and in which the unpresentable is given its due. The unpresentable is also the untameable that resides in the very entrails of the familiar—the Greek, for example. The final essay of *The Inhuman* titled "Domus and the Megalopolis" inquires into the possibility of thinking in the aftermath of the ruin of the *domus*—the native place, the community of the family household, the home—at the hands of a world become one monad. Lyotard must ask this question because the task of thinking arises precisely in response to the unpresentable, and untamed, which haunts the *domus* in spite of the domination peculiar to it, and which threatens to interrupt its cycles and to disrupt its order. Lyotard conceives of this untameable element not only as a savagery and unbridled violence, but also as the senseless as such. Thinking is what gives witness to the evil that sleeps in the entrails of the *domus* and what is domesticated by way of legends, representations, and above all, Greek tragedy. It follows that if thinking is fundamentally a witnessing of the untameable, then, in order to remain thinking and to inhabit the inhabitable world of the city become megalopolis, thought must continue to relate in some way to the *domus* even after the latter has been lost for good. Lost without appeal, nostalgia being out of the question because the *domus* is anything but bucolic and cannot be construed as an alternative to the megalopolis, thinking must inscribe within itself the *domus* as an ineradicable absence, as an impossibility. Lyotard observes: "Thought cannot want its house. But the house haunts it. The house does not haunt contemporary thought in the way that it once pierced [*poignait*] the untameable, forcing it into the tragic mode. The untameable was tragic because it was lodged in the heart of the *domus*. The domestic schema resisted the violence of a timbre that was nonetheless irresistable" (*TI*, 202). However irresistible, savagery and the senseless in the entrails of the *domus* could be schematized, and thus made intelligible, by tragedy. Violence still belonged to the family dwelling; it was the untameable *of* the house. But, as Lyotard remarks, the house that must continue to haunt thinking in the world of the city become global cannot proceed by forcing the untameable into the tragic mode. Lyotard speaks of the incommensurable that smolders at the heart of the *domus* and is subsequently staged in the tragic mode as provoking "a bewilderment, a being taken aback [*un interdit*] amid the always already said: stupor. A stupid passion rises in the domestic dough. As though the god were dropping the share he took in the common bake" (*TI*, 202; trans. mod.). The untameable that appears in the *domus* incites stupor, or makes us completely dumbfounded. It gives rise to a feeling, or pathos, of stunned surprise (*passion stupide*). Stupor is a divine feeling: it is the wonder, or amazement, with which *theorein*, the kind of contemplation that, as Plato and Aristotle acknowledge, is the gods' proper lot, sets in. But in distinction from the Greek wonder in which the mind takes in the whole of what is, and sees what is as a whole, the stunned and dumbfounded surprise that Lyotard invokes concerns the senseless at the very core of the abode. Witnessing, in stupor, an untameable senselessness in the *domus* thus brings philosophical thought into its own. We cannot find this untameable, in all its irresistibleness, at the beginnings of Western thought. Lyotard remarks that, in fact, "this abandon, this bankruptcy [of the *domus*] can still be taken up by the *domus*, it represents them as tragedy. Untameable dominated, sublime held to the rules of the beautiful, outside-the-law redestined." The "sublime encounter" (*TI*, 202), in the stupor incited by the untameable, makes room for the tragic stage where the senseless is subjected, mastered by the rule of the beautiful. Philosophical thinking that emerges in the stuporous witnessing of the unpresentable also gets housebroken, domesticated. What "is accessible except to stupor"—the nothing, the uncultivated, the senseless—is, Lyotard suggests, fashioned into ideas that pave the way for the programmed processing of the untameable found in the megalopolis (*TI*, 201).

Although the *domus* must continue to haunt contemporary thinking, it cannot continue domesticating the senseless at the core of the abode. Schematizing the unpresentable into facile intelligibility cannot fulfill the task of thinking set by the stupor at the realization that non-Being could prevail. Thinking absolves its task of witnessing only if it encounters the unpresentable without resistence. The sublime feeling in which the impossible possible is acknowledged can therefore no longer be a sublime that plays by the rules of the beautiful. Rather, it must be a sublime that is no longer to be thought from its opposite, the beautiful. It must abandon aesthetic categories in favor of ontological ones. There is nothing edifying about it. The abyss of non-Being, of the nothing, and the senseless, is only truly and properly acknowledged in a feeling of sublime stupor. In such stupor alone, philosophical thinking is true to its task. At the same time, with this stuporous *Grundstimmung*—an attunement to the possibility, in advance of what is, of the nothing, or the senseless, placed at the outset of philosophical thought—philosophical thought has also been dislodged, displaced, from its initial Greek determination.

13

Aporetic Experience

Although philosophers of the continental and analytic schools cannot generally agree on much, they do tend to concur on one thing—namely, that Jacques Derrida's thought is self-contradictory, incoherent, or inconsistent. Sung in unison, this song reassures them that they share a common ethos in spite of all the unbridgeable chasms. One mode of formulating the imputation of inconsistency has been especially successful at consensus building. This is Jürgen Habermas' thesis that Derrida's writings are characterized by "pragmatic inconsistency" and revel in "performative contradictions."[1] Accusing Derrida of self-refutation, Habermas has recourse to what Barbara Herrnstein Smith wittily calls "the lone item in a traditionalist's logical toolbox." Herrnstein Smith reminds us that the archetypal—if not exemplary mise-en-scène of the charge of self-refutation occurs in the *Theaetetus* and she argues that this type of accusation is "the most ancient and probably most common of . . . logicist arguments" directed against positions that one cannot agree with simply because they diverge from one's own.[2] A performative contradiction is commonly understood to obtain where a discourse *in actu exercito*—in the act of philosophizing, for instance—effectuates something that it has *in thesi* refuted, and thus declared impossible. But in her examination of the "logical, rhetorical, psychological, and to some extent institutional" operations that characterize the charge of self-refutation, Herrnstein Smith points out that (already) in the *Theaetetus*, the argumentation that leads up to the conclusion that Protagoras contradicts himself hinges on a dubious paraphrase of his adversary's position as well as on a questionable inference. She writes: "For the self-refutation charge to have logical force (as officially measured), the mirror reversal it indicates must be exact: What the self-refuter explicitly, wittingly denies must be the same as what he unwittingly, implicitly affirms. Accordingly, the charge fails to go off properly, and the supposed demonstration is declared a trick or an error, if the restatement diverges too obviously or too crucially from the original or if the supposedly implied affirmation is itself questionable."[3] Occasionally, the logistic trick is played in the name of truth; it can, therefore, claim a legitimacy, however dubious, since it is a matter of bringing the truth-denier to his senses. This is certainly the case in the *Theaetetus*. More often than not, however, the aim of the self-refutation argument is simply to destroy one's opponent.

The allegation of self-refutation may thus be based on an illegitimate restatement of an adversary's position, but such a charge can also derive from a certain conception of language in which language is reduced to its semantic or differential organization and in which its pragmatic dimension is held to be entirely subservient to the formal structures and semantic organization of language.[4] This is the case in Habermas' notion of language. In Habermas, language is interpreted throughout within the orbit of a conception of the subject as self-consciousness—a subject potentially in control of himself and his language. Thus, the pragmatic dimension of language is reduced to representation. Such a reduction of the pragmatic aspect of language to the mere representation of what it effectuates underlies the charge of self-refutation when the latter is conceived as a *performative* contradiction or as pragmatic inconsistency. Indeed, any linguistic operation that is not reducible to the semantic level of language is then taken to be an obstacle to language's representative function. The fundamental asymmetry between what is said and saying as doing is not taken into account when language is understood from a semantic, syntactical, and narrow interpretation of the pragmatic level. A different dimension of doing—which is in excess of everything that is enunciated or expressed—comes to light when doing things with words is understood as presentation rather than representation, that is, when it is seen in terms of the effectuation of an event, for instance, the event of addressing someone. Indeed, in advance to anything it says, all discourse is allocutive. The presentation that occurs in the doing of language, or what Emmanuel Levinas calls "Saying," can never become the object of saying; it can never become what is said. We can see that this "Saying" implies a performative, pragmatic dimension of language, which escapes both speech act theory and the logic of contradiction. To put it differently, the asymmetric irreducibility of the "Saying," which is constitutive of all acts of speech, causes all acts of utterance to be marked in depth by an inevitable discrepancy. This inconsistency, however, is not one of logical contradiction.

Whatever the reasons for declaring a work of thought to be pragmatically inconsistent, or performatively contradictory, the charge in question seeks to contest the philosophical validity of Derrida's work. The flattest way in which the accusation is made with respect to Derrida is to argue that in his attempt to overcome the logocentric heritage, he has recourse to concepts that are still metaphysical. An ostensibly more sophisticated formulation of the contradiction in question goes as follows: Derrida's radical skepticism and total rejection of the metaphysical concepts of reason and truth are caught in a contradiction because his statements and assertions still make claims (rather than merely reveling in postmodern arbitrariness) and, hence, presuppose the rationality and truth that they seek to discredit. For Habermas, Derrida contradicts himself, and this contradiction leads to unsolvable aporias. In Habermas' own robust language, Derrida is said to be unable to escape "the aporetic structure of a truth-occurrence eviscerated (*entkernten*) of all truth-as-validity (*Wahrheitsgeltung*),"[5] and, consequently, he is denied the title of "philosopher." I do not intend here to take on in a critical or polemical fashion this characterization of Derrida's writings. To rebut it, one would first have to show that the accusation in question is based on a misreading of Derrida's "project." Indeed, metaphysics is not, for Derrida, a futile exercise or speculation. But, if this is so, using its language to overcome it cannot be a sign of self-contradiction. Derrida has made it amply clear that "the passage beyond philosophy does not consist in turning the page of philosophy (which usually amounts to philosophizing badly), but in continuing to read philosophers *in a certain way*."[6] Yet, if the aim of deconstruction does not consist in seeking a beyond of metaphysics in the sense of an absolute other of metaphysics, then the charge of a "performative contradiction" has no ground whatsoever. In any case, on two occasions at least, Derrida himself has taken issue with this misreading of his work by Habermas.[7] Other scholars as well—among them and in exemplary fashion, Philippe Forget, in an essay titled "Das 'Gerede' vom performativen

Widerspruch"—have shaken the "self-evidences" on which Habermas' argument is based.[8] I can thus dispense with refuting one more time the accusation that Derrida's "project" is aporetic.

Derrida himself has clearly laid claim to performative contradiction. Thus, an accusation of "performative contradiction"—in the particular form that Habermas and others have leveled against Derrida's thought—is irrelevant to such a degree that this misconception cannot even be said to unwittingly harbor a rational insight into Derrida's thought; the tone and ductus of the theoreticians of "performative contradiction" are sufficient proof for this, and it is made even more suspect in that it comes in a more general assertion of the inconsistency and incoherence of his writings. In *The Other Heading*, for instance, Derrida says that it is not only necessary "to accept but to claim this putting to the test (*revendiquer cette épreuve*) of the antinomy (in the forms, for example, of the double constraint, the undecidable, the performative contradiction, etc.)."[9] Furthermore, "contradiction" and "aporia" are at the heart of the deconstructive approach. They are not only a constant and dominant theme in Derrida's writings, they are also intrinsically tied to the possibility, the "topoi," and the style of deconstruction itself. To quote "Force of Law," "deconstruction finds its privileged site—or rather its privileged instability"—in "several aporias." There are two styles of deconstruction, Derrida adds here; the first consists in meticulous readings and interpretations of texts and the second, notably, "takes on the demonstrative and apparently ahistorical allure of logico-formal paradoxes."[10] Do these acknowledgments not give the lie to all the statements parrying the accusation that deconstruction is self-contradictory and inconsistent? Or could it be that what Derrida lays claim to differs essentially from what Habermas, for instance, understands by "performative self-contradiction," or by the aporias to which it supposedly leads?

Even though in *Aporias* Derrida holds that his interest in the notion of aporia goes back to his debate in "Ousia and Gramme" of Martin Heidegger's remarks in *Being and Time* on the Aristotelian concept of time in *Physics IV*, "where the word 'aporia' appears in person,"[11] "aporia" is granted a highly distinctive if not extraordinary role in Derrida's thought from the very beginning, even before the deconstructive turn—that is to say, already in *Le problème de la genèse dans la philosophie de Husserl*.[12] In this early work in which he seeks to respond with a truly (i.e., nonmundane) dialectical philosophy to the genetic demands of Husserlian phenomenology, while also seeking to avoid falling pray to the difficulties of a mundane genesis and a materialist dialectic à la Tran-Duc-Thao, Derrida writes:

All unilinear conception of genesis seems to result in an aporia from which dialectic comes out victorious since it determines this conception to the point of transforming it into its opposite without changing its real content which thus proves to be absent. But to say that the meaning of genesis is dialectical, is to say that it is not "pure" meaning; it is to say that "for us," genesis cannot present itself in the absoluteness of its meaning. It is thus not to propose a "solution" to the problem. It is simply to affirm that in a dialectic known as such, the aporia "understands itself " as "real" aporia. At that point we encounter perhaps philosophy (*Alors nous rencontrons peut-être la philosophie*).[13]

What clearly follows from this passage is that "aporia" and the concomitant impossibility of dialectically solving it, rather than representing a dead end, is viewed as the chance, or opportunity ("peut-être"), for philosophy itself. Instead of being taken as an obstacle to thought, the insolubility of aporias becomes the condition of possibility for an encounter with a kind of thinking that is distinct from all other modes of thought—namely, philosophical thinking. Even though after *La genèse* Derrida is no longer interested in dialectical philosophy, and though the concern with deconstructing metaphysical thinking has thoroughly displaced the early privilege accorded to philosophy as such, the continued role given to aporias in and by deconstruction, rather than being indicative of the alleged self-contradiction and inconsistency of deconstruction, is only testimony to a continual exploration of the relevance of aporia for thought itself. Deconstruction's unrelenting pursuit of aporias shows it to be in search of a mode of thinking, which is distinct, as we shall see, from the dialectical, but also from the sophist's treatment of aporia. Deconstruction is in search of a mode of thinking for which conceptual impasse, rather than the ruin of thought, is indeed the very possibility of thought itself.

But isn't making this point also to valorize something that is generally understood as an insurmountable contradiction in reasoning, a weakness of thought, and the very criterion of philosophical failure? Undoubtedly, this is the prevailing understanding of aporia, and it is partially responsible for the fact that deconstruction is often viewed, both by followers and detractors alike, as an obsession with flaws that, supposedly, undermine all texts. But has this always been the way philosophers have thought about aporia? Derrida, in *Aporias*, explains that "for many years now, the old, worn-out

Greek term *aporia*, this tired word of philosophy and of logic, has often imposed itself on [him] . . . and [that] recently it has done so even more often."[14] Should we not inquire then first into what that old Greek term means, before condemning deconstruction for the thematic and "methodological" use of aporia? Indeed, what does *aporia* mean? According to Liddell and Scott, *aporia* means being *aporos*, without passage, having no way in, out, or through, and it is said first of places that are difficult to pass through or definitely impassable, in particular of the sea and the waters. Faced with an aporia, one must find a *poros*, a way out of the difficult and intolerable situation. Yet, a *poros* is not just any way. As Sarah Kofman notes, "It is not to be confounded with *odos*, a general term that designates any kind of way, or route." One only speaks of *poros* "where it is a question of opening up a way where none existed before, and where no way in the proper sense can exist to begin with; where it is a question of crossing an uncrossable world, a world unknown, hostile, illimited, *apeiron*," as is the case with the most dangerous of all ways, the one in which one faces the dangers of the sea or the ocean. Kofman writes: "*Poros* is only a maritime route or waterway, the opening of a passage across a chaotic expanse that it thus transforms into a qualified and well-ordered space, by introducing different routes that make the diverse directions of space visible, and that thus orient a stretch of space that originally lacked all lay-out, all point of reference."[15] Thus understood, the *poros* that practices a way out of the impasse is never a given way. At all times, as with the waterways, the *poros* will have to be found and retraced each time anew.

But *aporia* refers as well to difficult questions or puzzles, more precisely to situations in which none of the mutually exclusive positions regarding a discursive or practical issue can claim any superiority over the others. In short, we have an aporia whenever we are faced with two equally valid, but mutually exclusive arguments. Now, it is important to remember that it was in no way an embarrassment for the Greeks to reach a conceptual and argumentative impasse. In lieu of a detailed discussion of Plato's, Aristotle's, and the skeptics' distinct conceptions of aporia, I offer the following brief remarks. Whereas the skeptics valorized aporia as the only possible outcome of all philosophical endeavors, the argumentative impasse or initial difficulty constitutes for Plato and Aristotle the heuristic point of departure of philosophy itself. For Plato, the aporia designates the situation in which the one who is ignorant becomes aware of his or her ignorance and is thereby set on the path to truth. Socrates' dialectical art of questioning consists precisely in trying to throw his interlocutor into an aporetic impasse so as to cause aporetic wonder and a motivation to seek its solution in philosophy. In Aristotle, the aporetic situation is systematically the methodological beginning of most of his investigations. By having to confront conflicting but equally valid arguments about an issue, the thinker is compelled to sharpen his understanding of the problem and to explore various routes (*diaporia*) so as to work out a solution (*euporia*) to what appeared to be an unsolvable dilemma. In all cases where it is not seen as the only possible end point and the final result of philosophical investigation, aporia has a heuristic, preparatory, propaedeutic function for philosophical thinking. And, needless to say, it is this conception of aporia that Derrida has in mind when he refers to it as a Greek word.[16]

But, even though aporia is not at all the bad thing that many philosophers believed it to be, their condemnation of aporia has its antecedent in Platonic philosophy as well. Undoubtedly, Socrates' custom of interlocutory discourse, which aims at confronting his interlocutor with equally valid but mutually exclusive arguments, valorizes aporia since it causes the speaker to recognize his ignorance. At the same time, Plato is also vehemently critical of aporia when, as with the sophists, it becomes a technique for its own sake, or even worse, a means of seduction of the ignorant. Plato's verdict, in the name of philosophical truth (*episteme*), on the sophist's (and the rhetor's) amazing power and professional skills (*techne*) at systemically exhibiting and creating aporias is without compromise. By juxtaposing contradictory theses and equalizing contrary arguments, the sophist's discourse disorganizes the *logos* and precipitates it into chaos; the aporetic marvels that such discourses reveal are condemned because of their primary appeal to man's sensible nature. They serve to dupe and imprison him in their webs. But above all, they attract and seduce the young, that is to say, those who, more than adults, are still prone to being affected by double-headed discourses and find pleasure in playing with language. In *Philebus*, Plato describes the threat of discursive aporetics as follows:

As soon as a young man gets wind of it, he is delighted as if he had discovered an intellectual gold mine; he is beside himself with delight, and loves to try every move in the game. First he rolls the stuff to one side and jumbles it into one; then he undoes it again and takes it to pieces, to the confusion first and foremost of himself, next of his neighbors at the moment, whether they be younger or older or of his own age. He has no mercy on his father or mother or anyone else listening to him—a little more, and he would victimize even animals, as well as human beings in general, including foreigners, to whom of course he would never show mercy provided he could get hold of an interpreter.[17]

As Sarah Kofman has noted, "the profound jubilation felt in eternally introducing, at every turn, trouble, disorder, chaos into the well-ordered world of adult reason," by way of the aporias of language, is a jubilation about one's "having booby trapped one's parents, and having succeeded in locking them up and imprisoning them in shackles similar to those that Hephaistos forged in order to catch by surprise Ares in Aphrodite's arms."[18] Even though Plato does not say so directly, for Kofman the delight in playing with language and creating aporias is, ultimately, a delight in the parricide of those who forbid such play.

In following Plato's statements about aporia one must distinguish between two kinds of aporia: a good one—that is to say, a philosophical kind of aporia—and a bad, sophist one. According to Kofman, this distinction is made along the *episteme/techne* divide, along the division between the disinterested contemplation of *theoria* and, as we shall see, a certain interpretation of the art of invention. Basing her argument on an analysis of the myth of the cave in the *Republic*, Kofman notes that for Plato there are two ways of being clouded, more precisely, "two symmetrical and inverse ways of falling into aporia. And yet they are not for Plato equivalent: one aporia is better than the other. There is a good and a bad one. The aporia to be feared is the one that stems from the soul's being clouded and offended by obscurity. If, by contrast, the soul is obfuscated by light, one must, he says, consider oneself fortunate to experience such trouble, to find oneself in a state of aporia."[19] The good, or philosophical, aporia is not, like the one of the sophist, an end in itself, a means of seduction, or of subversion of the *logos* and its order. Unlike the latter, it does not obstruct understanding. On the contrary, it summons us and is an incitement for us to find a solution, to invent a way out, and to get onto the right track. Philosophical aporia is a fertile impasse in that it forces one to seek a way out. Speaking of the prisoners in the cave, Kofman argues that it is the aporia alone into which the philosopher plunges them, that is "paradoxically capable of setting them free; of making them see the fetters of the pleasure and the sensible that chain their soul to their body and prevent it from thinking; of making them become conscious of the aporetic state in which they were initially immersed without their knowledge."[20] As the final aporias of *Protagoras* and *Theaetetus* demonstrate, aporia is a temporary, provisional state that calls for a resumption of the investigation. To find oneself caught in such a fruitful impasse means to be in transition, in a state of passing over, of being on the way to. It is, undoubtedly, a disquieting state of transition, but also one of wishing to give birth.[21] Kofman writes: "The aporia is simply a somber, provisional but necessary, passage, for the trouble that it creates forces us to seek a way out of the impasse: 'For my part . . . when I see the subject in such utter confusion I feel the liveliest desire to clear it up' " (*Protagoras,* 361). The desire to be delivered, to find a way out of an impasse, or to unravel a hopeless problem is only awakened by the aporetic confusion. Because it is untenable, the aporetic state rather than paralyzing, calls for research, gives rise to the invention of some *mechane*, of some *poros*, in order to find a way out. . . . For no one possesses the *poros*. . . . Each time, and on every occasion, it must 'be found.' "[22] Undoubtedly, the aporia compels the philosopher to resolve the difficult problem. But does such solving simply consist in inventing some *mechane*, in other words, some contrivance, expedient, or scheme, as Kofman suggests? Is the *poros* that the thinker must cut to find a way out of the impractical (*amechanon*) situation just a clever trick to escape from the conflicting constraints he faces? As we have seen, for Plato sophistry excels in producing aporias for their own sake. But since the sophist is also associated in Plato with the invention of deceitful contrivances, Kofman's insinuation that philosophical solutions to aporias are based on the invention of some *mechane* conflates *theoria*, or *episteme*, with the art of cunning characteristic of the sophist or rhetor. Yet, is this not to misrepresent the achievement of philosophical thought? Is it not also, and in particular, to misconstrue the very nature of the aporia? An aporia is only an aporia if it is *amechanon*, or thoroughly unpracticable—that is, if no trick, however cunning, will do to solve it.

Kofman argues that in spite of Plato's seemingly uncompromising denunciation of aporetic play, philosophy's commerce with aporia is, perhaps, not limited to the good aporia alone. Indeed, as she suggests, as a problem-solving discipline, philosophy may be heavily indebted to the same technical skills that it is quick to condemn in the sophists. To make her point, she recalls the myth invoked by Socrates in the *Symposium* of

Love's descent from a father called Poros, who is himself son of Metis, who is also philosophy's ancestor, according to Kofman. As Marcel Detienne and Jean-Pierre Vernant have argued in a beautiful book titled *Cunning Intelligence in Greek Culture and Society*, Metis, a female divinity and the daughter of Okeanus was Zeus' first wife, who, recently pregnant with Athena, was swallowed by the god (thus causing her mythological career to have been a very brief one). According to Detienne and Vernant, she personifies the art of practical know-how, more precisely, the kind of intelligence that the early Greeks associated with the "flair, wisdom, forethought, subtlety of mind, deception, resourcefulness, vigilance, opportunism" required by the practical arts, ranging from that of the navigator to the illusionism of the rhetors and sophists.[23] Highly obligated to Detienne and Vernant's work, Kofman concludes her analysis of Socrates' account of the myth in question as follows: "To emphasize this parental link between Love, Poros, and Metis is to hold that cunning intelligence, the intelligence full of expedients, which is at the origin of all *tekhne*, is also the ancestor of philosophy, the love of *sophia*."[24] This amounts, she continues, "to attributing to philosophy the same soteriological finality as we attribute to *tekhne*: to inventing *poroi* in order to help man out of aporias, of all kinds of difficult situations without a way out." In other words, this origin of philosophy blurs the classical division between *episteme* and *tekhne*, on whose basis philosophy as pure knowledge has sought to discredit all technical knowledge, particularly, the sophist *tekhne*. Technical knowledge is an intrinsic part of philosophy's search for truth. "It is, indeed, Metis, who makes it possible to clear a *poros*, a way, a trajectory through obstacles, to invent an expedient (*poros*) in order to find a way out (*poros*) of a situation without a way out, an aporetic situation."[25] Undoubtedly, assuming that Kofman is correct in equating Eros and philosophy, this filial descent of philosophy from Poros shows philosophy bent on finding solutions to aporetic situations. But according to Kofman, Poros' own descent from Metis also implies that such invention of answers to unsolvable problems proceeds essentially by means of *mechane* and *tekhnai*, in other words, with the help of "technical" traps, tricks, ruses, plots, or stratagems that resort even to aporias in order to accomplish the intended goal. In essence, then, there is no difference between philosophy and sophistry except that philosophy in its uncomparable hunger for power has been led to become even more "sophisticated" than the sophists. In other words, despite philosophy's antitechnical attitude, the solutions that it proposes to aporias would only be highly cogent tricks of an art of cunning dissimulating itself, in what amounts to one more stratagem, under the mask of *episteme*. If philosophy not only has been able to make the sophists' procedures its own, incorporating them and turning them successfully against the threat that they represented to its own sovereignty, but also has even been able to refine these procedures themselves to the point that they are indistinguishable from the procedures of *episteme*, it is simply because from the start philosophy has been affiliated with Metis.

At first glance, Kofman's analysis of the myth of the origin of philosophy would seem to be convincing. But if we reread Plato's text, what do we find? First, Kofman has not taken into account the precise status and function of that myth within a dialog—the *Symposium*—whose rhythm consists in incessantly deferring the disclosure of the secret of Eros. The myth in question (i.e., a myth attributed by Socrates to an inspired poet, the Mantinean woman called Diotima) is Socrates' subtly tailored answer to Agathon's mannered and inept elaborations on love, during which the latter has used and abused mythology. But rather than offending the ever-so-beautiful Agathon by tactlessly refuting him point by point, Socrates has recourse to a myth as well. Seemingly adopting Agathon's own level of pretense, he makes use of this myth to ironically subvert Agathon's innane make-believe. In recounting this myth, Socrates lets Diotima speak: her discourse is primarily intended to intervene on the level of mythology (and pretense) and to make a point within this domain alone.[26] It is a mythological response to mythology. In no way does this myth reveal any definite truth about the nature of love.

This myth certainly provides a (mythological) account of the origin of love (Eros), but does it also, as Kofman suggests, explain the origin of philosophy? According to Diotima's story, Eros is conceived when the beggar Penia lies down beside the sleeping and totally intoxicated Poros in the gardens of the gods who have been celebrating the birth of Aphrodite. From his father, Eros inherits the power of invention, from his mother, suffering and the condition of a beggar. Love, thus, is intrinsically unstable, made up of conflicting contrasts. Destitute, it must strive after beauty and immortality, and in this, it is also a "life long seeker of truth" (203 d), in other words: a philosopher. But Eros is not, therefore, *the* philosopher. Eros, as Diotima makes sufficiently plain, is but one among the philosophers. To

Socrates' question of who the seekers of truth are, "if they are neither the wise nor the ignorant," Diotima responds: "They are those that come between the two, and one of them is Love" (204 a–b). Undoubtedly, when Diotima claims of Eros that "he brings his father's resourcefulness to his designs upon the beautiful and the good, for he is gallant, impetuous, and energetic, a mighty hunter, and a master of device and artifice—at once desirous and full of wisdom, a lifelong seeker after truth, an adept in sorcery, enchantment, and seduction" (203 d), one could be tempted to conclude that seeking truth is just one more trick that Eros has in his bag.[27] But even if, in the case of Eros, the search for the good, the beautiful, and immortality were pursued by way of strategems, there is no evidence to suggest that this is *necessarily* the case. Nor does Eros' example imply that as an aporetic problem-solver, philosophy, in some essential way, would have to resort to cunning intelligence and hence to depend on the invention of expedients, which would ultimately be more-sophisticated sophist tricks.

If, as I have suggested, philosophical thinking is rooted in aporetic wonder, or starts with a seemingly hopeless difficulty for which it must invent a solution, do we not misrepresent philosophy's achievements in claiming that all it does is invent expedients to clear a way out of a hopelessly difficult situation? Is the aporetic wonder in which the ignorant comes face to face with a position that contradicts his own but that seems equally valid not rather an incentive to deepen his or her understanding of the issue, and to thus give him- or herself the means to solve the problem? Indeed, doesn't the single emphasis on cunning intelligence as a technique of finding a way out run the risk of understanding not only aporia but also philosophical reasoning too narrowly? Finally, if philosophy's struggle with sophistry becomes the prime example for its treatment of aporias, does this not create the biased impression that all that is at stake in this strife is philosophy's defense of its sovereignty and quest for power? To construe the status of the aporia in philosophy in this manner is to insinuate that there is no specific philosophical way of solving difficulties. As Kofman herself cannot but admit, the specifically philosophical way to find a *poros* out of aporias is dialectics. However, she hastily identifies it as a *tekhne*, as an art for inventing devices that, in the last resort, do not get beyond the aporia. But dialectic is not sophistry. As Hans-Georg Gadamer notes, this is precisely what Theaetetus learns in the "Sophist."[28] As I have already argued, the aporetic wonder is supposed to provoke a deepening of the difficulty itself. Such a more thorough understanding is concomitant with the opening onto the philosophical and the very background against which the invention of a solution, which is different from contrivance of evasion, becomes meaningful to begin with. It is, therefore, necessary to look for a more fundamental account of aporia in philosophy and for a more fundamental explication of philosophy's origin in theoretical impasses for which it must provide a way out. I find Heidegger's Marburg Lectures of 1924/1925 on Plato's *Sophist* to provide the necessary hints. Indeed, they contain (to my knowledge) Heidegger's most explicit elaborations on the notion of aporia.

Heidegger broaches the issue of aporia in the context of an elucidation of the Aristotelean concept of *sophia*. He wants to demonstrate that *sophia*—as the highest and most privileged mode in which Dasein relates to the good because it is merely "contemplative" or theoretical—is, in the same way as *poiesis*, an independent mode of being of Dasein. The two primary performative moments of Dasein—*thaumazein* (wonder) and *diaporein* (to be at loss, in doubt)—serve to substantiate this point. To wonder whether something is really the way it shows itself and to be taken aback by the possibility that one's familiar acquaintance with something might not suffice to understand it are, according to Heidegger, two primitive states of mind of Dasein from which *sophia* originates. As Aristotle remarks, "a man who is puzzled and wonders thinks himself ignorant."[29] Wonder in the sense of *thaumazein* consists, first and foremost, in the awareness that something is not right. Heidegger remarks: "*Thaumaston* is that which is not right (*was nicht stimmt*). 'Here something is not right.' While looking at things, something becomes astonishing, 'marvelous,' if one fails to come to grips (*durchkommen*) with the encountered fact by way of the understanding that one actually possesses. In this case, comprehension is disturbed by what shows itself to it."[30] Aristotle, according to Heidegger, beholds in this originary phenomenon of Dasein, a tendency to look at things simply for the sake of looking at them and the attempt to understand them simply for the mere sake of understanding them, in other words, the tendency to theorize. Heidegger writes: "In making this point, Aristotle uses a term that was quite common in philosophy at the time: *aporein*. *Aporos* is that which permits no passage, where one does not get through. Originally *poros* signifies the passage through a river in a shallow place. *Aporia* means: the contemplation of the world does not get through; it finds no way. One does not get through with the *aitia* one has at one's disposal, that is, with the available means of explanation. The way of going through in an explicating fashion is blocked. The way a thing really looks is barred by the way in which it actually shows itself."[31] In wonder, then, contemplation experiences an obstruction to its endeavor. It faces a situation without a way out. It finds itself stuck since it has not yet achieved any familiarity with the situation or matter in question. In the explicit realization of the *aporein*, contemplation becomes convinced that it does not yet know the situation or the matter under consideration. "Yet, to the extent that the one who is convinced of not being able to get through becomes aware of this predicament, and thus continues the *diaporein* by making efforts to come through, such *aporein* and *diaporein* contains the will to get through. . . . The one who continues the *aporein* and the *diaporein*, and seeks to get through, reveals by this very attempt that he flees *agnoia*, ignorance, and concealedness, and that he pursues *epistasthai*, knowledge, and the having-there-in-disclosedness of being."[32] *Aporia*, according to Heidegger's interpretation of its Greek sense, names, then, a most singular but also most fundamental transitory situation of the human being in his or her relation to the world. It describes a constitutive moment in that relation in which Dasein becomes aware of its ignorance, of the discrepancy between what it familiarly knows and what it does not know, but it is also a moment in which such a sense of not knowing a way out triggers a will to get through even though there is no practical urge to do so. Yet, however elementary this transitory stage may be, it should never be valorized for its own sake. Even though the moment in question is characterized by the impossibility of getting through, it is only a stage in which Dasein is "underway," or "on the way," and that thus needs to be understood from the end of the way. Heidegger writes: "Yet *aporein* has not in itself any independent and positive meaning, it has only the functional meaning of the correct pursuit of the knowledge of being itself." This knowledge is no longer the knowledge that one familiarly has, the knowledge that one has by accident, and that, in a circumspective mode of relating, one brings to things in the world. Rather in the *diaporein*, or the will to get through the impasse, "one seeks to gain an understanding of the thing from the thing itself. The positive steps in *diaporein* are nothing other than the presentification of the determined thing. The way and the direction of the *aporein* lead from the environment (*Umwelt*) to the world.

This occurs in such a manner that the *aporein* does not concern itself with that which one only encounters by chance and that happens to attract attention. Rather, the *aporein* implies that *Dasein* gets itself on the way with the result that that which has always already been there now attracts attention. Where there is such *aporein*, there exists this getting-oneself-on-the-way, the on-the-way to."[33]

Undoubtedly, the prime thrust of Heidegger's discussion of *aporein* is to show that Dasein by itself aims at a disclosure of Being for the sake of Being and that the possibility of *sophia* is rooted in this independent way of being of Dasein. But in the course of his investigation, Heidegger has also provided us with a more fundamental understanding of aporia and its pervasive function for philosophical thought. To conclude this Heideggerian analysis of *thaumazein* and *diaporein*, let me then try to spell out what these insights are. To begin with, I should emphasize that the impasse in which Dasein finds itself caught in a circumspective or natural understanding of the world shows that Dasein qua Dasein knows, in a certain way, of that "which has always already been there"—Being (of the *da*, of the "there"), first and foremost—but does not get through to it. Only because Dasein already has a certain knowledge—a foreknowledge of the world as such, of Being itself, a knowledge of which it is capable precisely because it is Dasein—can it experience an impasse at all and feel compelled to find a way out. The knowledge that Dasein qua Dasein has of Being in advance of all explicit knowing is the horizon from within which *aporein* becomes meaningful. Although Heidegger's analysis of the Greek notion of *aporein* is strongly colored by his concern with a fundamental ontological analytic of Dasein, this analysis shows, beyond a shadow of a doubt, the following things: first, Dasein experiences aporias only because it already has a fore-understanding of Being—that is to say, of what will lay the aporias to rest; second, to find a way out of an aporetic impasse is clearly within the reach of Dasein, and, I add, no special tricks are required to do so; third, that which one has to get through is the unfamiliar "what has always already been there," in traditional terms, the One, the whole, Being, and ultimately, in Heidegger's fundamental ontology, the Being that Dasein *is*, and of which Dasein has a certain preconception from the outset. Finally, Heidegger's elucidation of the status of *aporein* clearly establishes that the aporetic impasse is the transitory passage to *theorein*, in short, to philosophical thinking. Here too, it is important to bear in mind that, if Dasein is capable of finding its way to philosophical thought, it is because—as its experience of getting stuck demonstrates—it has already a tendency to look at things for the sheer sake of looking at them. Aporia, then, is an experience, and it is a concept that reveals something about the nature and the task of thinking itself. Indeed, if thinking encounters impasses to begin with, it is primarily because its "object" is, to use more traditional terms, the One, the whole, totality, and so forth. Yet thinking cannot become aware of its task without running into aporetic situations. This task consists in thinking the whole as such, the whole against whose backdrop thinking experiences aporetic wonder. Aporias of thinking are the breaking points at which thinking becomes philosophical thinking—that is to say, a thinking that is distinct from familiar understanding and that which thinks something—the whole—that is distinct from what it comprises.

Philosophical thinking—that is, the kind of thinking that the aporias call for in order to break the deadlock to which they give rise—cannot, in principle, be made to tremble by way of a mode of aporia-solving that relies on contrivances, stratagems, or schemes. The entire distinction between *episteme* and *tekhne*, or *mechane*, on which Kofman rests her argument is an intra-philosophical distinction, and thus it already presupposes the birth of philosophy in aporetic wonder. As the founding aporias of philosophical thought itself, the aporias from which philosophy arises are, in their essence, anterior to those with which sophistry confronts philosophical thought. Anterior to the sophist *tekhne* of cunning problem solving is the philosophical approach to aporias. Only by exposing itself to aporias in a manner that allows for the overcoming of them does thinking acquire the independence and sovereignty that no sophist trick is able to challenge.[34] Is this, then, to assert that the way that philosophical thought relates to the aporetic successfully reduces it to a, however important, transition point? Does the aporetic let itself be reduced to nothing but a condition of philosophical difference? If, indeed, no thinking comes into its own without enduring an aporetic experience, does this not imply that the condition of possibility of thinking also points to the limits of thinking? In other words, if aporia is so essentially tied to thinking, is this not to suggest that thinking is a considerably more complex "thing" than the philosophical tradition has led us to believe? To answer these questions, I return briefly to Derrida's elaborations on aporia.

Because Derrida broached this issue early on and continued his analysis later in very different contexts, any adequate discussion of aporia

in his writings would at least have to take stock of his analyses of the Aristotelean aporias of time and of Heidegger's remarks about them in "Ousia
and Gramme" and regard as well his later reflections on the constitutive
role of aporia in thinking responsibility, singularity, and performativity.
Here, however, I will only consider the text *Aporias*, which is not only most
likely Derrida's most elaborate text on aporia, but also the text in which
aporia becomes most explicitly linked to the possibility of thinking. The
analysis of the question of aporia in this work centers on the crucial chapters 46–53 in *Being and Time* in which Heidegger delimits and defines
what he calls the full existential concept of death, that is to say, a concept
that is not only "at the very heart of the existential analysis," but on which
the very possibility of a fundamental ontology of Dasein rests.[35] As Jean-
François Courtine has pointed out, these are chapters in which Heidegger's procedure is "remarkably aporetic or better diaporematic."[36]

Throughout the analyses of the chapters in question, Derrida shows
to what extent Heidegger's philosophical enterprise, with all its essential
distinctions, is grounded on the possibility of rigorously demarcating Dasein's relation to death, in other words, the possibility of distinguishing
"properly dying" from other modes of death such as perishing and demising. Indeed, as a thinking enterprise, *Being and Time* is not only engaged
in all kinds of border settings, delimitations, and demarcations; as a
philosophical enterprise of thinking characterized by such operations as
rigorous separation, division, and distinction—what the Greeks called
diairesis—it also requires a founding distinction capable of being thought,
or intuited, *as such*. For *Being and Time*, the distinction between properly
dying and perishing or demising plays this role of a foundational distinction. Now Derrida argues that, if it were possible to demonstrate that that
fundamental distinction cannot be made as rigorously as Heidegger
claims, the whole of *Being and Time* would not, therefore, necessarily collapse, but would trigger shockwaves through its whole edifice. More precisely, what exactly it is that thinking accomplishes in this work may need
to be reconsidered. Before proceeding to demonstrate that the way Heidegger conceives of properly dying, indeed, harbors an unsolvable aporia,
Derrida makes the following statement:

If, in its very principle, the rigor of this distinction were compromised,
weakened, or parasited on both sides of what it is supposed to dissociate (*veren-
den/eigentlich sterben*), then . . . the entire project of the analysis of *Dasein*, in its
essential conceptuality, would not be discredited [trans. mod.], but granted another

status than the one generally attributed to it. I am thus increasingly inclined to read ultimately this great inexhaustible book in the following way: as an event that, at least in the final analysis, would no longer simply stem from ontological necessity or demonstration. It would never submit to logic, phenomenology, or ontology, which it nonetheless invokes. . . . The event of this interrupted book would be irreducible to these categories, indeed to the categories that Heidegger himself never stopped articulating. . . . *Being and Time* would belong neither to science, nor to philosophy, nor to poetics. Such is perhaps the case for every work worthy of its name: there, what puts thinking into operation exceeds its own borders. The work exceeds itself, it surpasses the limits of the concept of itself that it claims to have properly while presenting itself. But if the event of this work thus exceeds its own borders, the borders that its discourse seems to give to itself . . . then it would do so precisely at this locus where it *experiences the aporia*.[37]

What clearly transpires from this passage is Derrida's indebtedness to the classical appreciation of aporia that I have referred to. As an event— a work worthy of the name—*Being and Time* is rooted in an experience of aporia. Rather than simply ruining it, such an experience is, as Derrida later establishes in the text, its very possibility.[38] For Derrida, the aporia is intimately linked to the possibility of thinking and its operations of distinguishing, delimiting, and demarcating. But as it is already possible to gather from the above passage, there are significant differences as well between Derrida's appraisal of aporia and that of the classical tradition. For one, aporia in Derrida is not merely heuristic, a temporary, transitional state to be overcome. Aporia is much more intimately linked to the differentiating, conceptualizing, and hierarchizing tasks essential to philosophical thought in Derrida than in Plato and Aristotle. Rather than being understood from the vantage point of its possible solution, the unpassability that it signifies according to its concept is taken seriously. An aporia is an aporia only if it is truly *amechanon*. As a consequence, the aporia cannot be made to withdraw backstage after it has provided the possibility for rigorous and consistent thinking. Instead of being a transitory phase toward thinking, it becomes, in Derrida, the very "medium" of thinking. While recalling the numerous places in his work where the notion of aporia imposed itself upon him, or where he found himself tied up or paralyzed by aporias, Derrida remarks that he never tried "to move . . . against or out of the impasse but, in another way, *according to* [*selon*] another thinking of the aporia, one perhaps more enduring."[39] Unlike classical philosophical thought, with its eagerness to make a quick deal with aporias because it is intent on overcoming them as soon as possible, this more enduring thinking of aporias is less impatient. It seeks to hold out the experience of aporia without the temptation of giving in to the desire to get or finding a quick fix to what, by definition, ought to be an impasse. A first and highly significant consequence of sustaining or supporting aporia is a change in the concept of aporia itself. Suffice it to say that in the "plural logic of aporia" developed in *Aporias*, the identity of the aporia as a non-passage owing to impermeability is shown to imply references to other ways of non-passage: first, to the impasse due to the absence of any border to cross—that is to say, to total permeability—and second, to non-passage as the result of an elementary milieu that does not allow "for something that could be called passage" in the first place.[40] But philosophical thought, that which is made possible by the aporia, is also affected when the aporia is thought more patiently, more enduringly. This other thinking of the aporia is a thinking that models itself after, in conformity with, or along with the aporia. Derrida broaches this kind of thinking in a reevaluation of Heidegger's claims in *Being and Time* concerning the status of this very same work. Assuming that Heidegger's work is a work of philosophical thought and a work of rigorous distinctions and flawless deductions and constructions based on one fundamental distinction, the discovery that this distinction is profoundly aporetic forces one not to discredit the whole of *Being and Time*, but rather to account for its achievement in a different way than that which Heidegger himself presents. Rather than needing to be conceived as a work whose every step is a function of ontological necessity, or whose unfolding is commanded by what Heidegger terms "thinking," *Being and Time* appears to endure at all moments its own impossibility. And in this it is, as Derrida notes, an event, that is, a singular unique performance of "philosophical" thought.

At this point, it needs recalling that Heidegger defines death in terms of the ultimate possibility of Dasein—that is to say, of a being whose nature it is to always be ahead of itself and that therefore is a being characterized by potentiality-for-being (*Seinkönnen*). Since being-toward-death is Dasein's ultimate possibility, Heidegger calls it the possibility of impossibility. After extensive analyses difficult to summarize, which, consequently, can only be rendered here in the barest outline, Derrida argues that although Heidegger does not explicitly say so, his admission that the "ultimate possibility is nothing other than the possibility of an impossibility," signals what Derrida calls a "unique" and "ultimate aporia."[41] On the one hand, Heidegger holds that to face death as Dasein's ownmost singular possibility is the condition in which it comes most properly into its own; on the other hand, he defines this possibility as the impossibility of any existence, or propriety, whatsoever, that is, as the possibility of being-able-no-longer-to-be-there. The possibility of impossibility thus becomes indistinguishable from the impossibility of possibility. Derrida remarks that Heidegger never lends "the least attention or the least thematic interest to the logical form of the contradiction or to what goes against meaning or common sense. In the persistence of this apparently logical contradiction (the most proper possibility as the possibility of an impossibility), he even seems to see a condition of the truth, the *condition of truth*, its very unveiling, where truth is no longer measured in terms of the logical form of judgment."[42] One may perhaps wish to object to Derrida's construal of this contradiction that, in fact, no such contradiction exists in Heidegger's text. On the level of intention, this is certainly the case insofar as the contradiction has already been domesticated and put to work for philosophical thinking by means of an apophantic *as*. Indeed, as Derrida demonstrates, it is by way of Heidegger's understanding of "the possible *as* the impossible" and the contention that authentic Dasein is capable of relating to the impossible *as such*—to the impossibility of Dasein, that is, death—that Heidegger endures the aporia and turns it into the very condition of truth and into the beginning of his philosophical discourse. But, adds Derrida, when authentic Dasein faces the possibility of impossibility of Dasein "as such," it faces, at the same time, the possibility of an end of being able to face all end as such—that is, the end as such of all "as such." If, for Heidegger, death, as the possibility of the impossibility of Dasein, sets absolute limits when Dasein faces this possibility as such, the equally originary possibility of the impossibility of any "as such"—that is, of all appearing of death *in propria persona* to Dasein—also shows death to erase the limits that it itself makes possible. Derrida writes: "To mark and at the same time to erase these lines, which only happen by erasing themselves, which only succeed in erasing themselves [*n'arrivent qu'à s'effacer*], is to trace them as still possible while also introducing the very principle of their impossibility, the principle of ruin, which is also their chance and which promises the line while compromising it in parasitism, grafting, and divisibility."[43] Aporia is thus not something negative. It is also what allows the limits constitutive of philosophical thinking to be drawn, but, as limits that are neither pure nor undivided, they are crossable and consequently impossible limits. Far from being a flaw, the fundamental aporia of death in *Being and Time* represents the condition from which philosophical thought draws its very possibility; at the same time, however, this enabling condition undermines the claims that philosophical discourse makes for itself. Derrida holds that the constitutive limits of philosophy only come into being by effacing themselves. Differently said, what the aporia makes possible is no longer something called philosophy. Neither is it thinking, if thinking is understood from its ability to draw indivisible lines. If the aporia at the heart of *Being and Time* makes all limits problematic (that is, crossable), it is still not a work of *Dichtung*, or poetics, in the sense Heidegger understands the term *Dichtung*, namely, as what parallels the path of thinking. Nor is it a work of literature. Its founding aporia does not relieve us from the task of thinking what it is most singularly. Unrelentingly, and without ever hoping to put the question to rest, thinking must pursue this task.

Thinking, Without Wonder

Philosophical thinking is not philosophical without the pretense to universality. However, would such a pretense not require philosophy to make its beginning in an experience that is common to all, or that could at least be recognized by anyone as his or her own? Furthermore, would then the claim to universality not also imply that the experience cannot be an extraordinary one? Would it not imply that, on the contrary, the experience can only be an ordinary one—that is, an experience of everyday life? But, from its inception in Greece, philosophy has maintained that it originates in a break with the ordinary. Philosophy claims a rift in everydayness and the opening of a distance within which the ordinary suddenly comes to stand in a relation of opposition to the thinker; this is an extraordinary experience, the experience of wonder. In the sensation of *thaumazein*, philosophical thought erupts as metaphysics, as thought in rupture with and beyond nature. In addition, it opens up an abyss between the philosopher and the life of the community, in short, from all that is human. Can such extraordinary experience rightly claim to be able to be recognized by everyone? The extraordinary experience is a pathos, an affect, a sentiment that occurs and that one suffers; it is an event and thus singular. But is the beginning of philosophy in a pathos not then also a patho-logical, especially if it is entirely incomprehensible to the community? Is it not then a pathogenic beginning? Moreover, how can a pathos so singular as wonder be the ground of philosophy as a universal discourse? Might it not be necessary then to revisit the extraordinary experience of wonder if one seeks to secure philosophy's claim to universality? And if this is necessary, could it also be that such revisiting could lead to a reconception of the universal? Furthermore, might not the way in which the relation between the experience that causes the irruption of philosophical thought and the universal itself need to be renegotiated?

The feeling of wonder that provokes philosophical thinking is a shock unlike any other shock caused by individual things that can strike us as curious, strange, or surprising. It is a shock that is incomparable to any other commotion. Its violence has no equivalent because it challenges all unreflective faith in its entirety. To hold that philosophy originates in wonder is thus also to assert the uniqueness of this pathos. Only the shock caused by wonder possesses the required violence to initiate a passage from *doxa* to philosophy—that is, from the relativity of opinions and beliefs to what is shareable by all, hence, universal. However, if this extraordinary, highly unique, and uncommon experience of wonder that unsettles everydayness provokes philosophical reflection, is it not because this experience reveals something that concerns everything and everybody, despite—or rather because of—its exceptional, even patho-logical, nature. The very extraordinariness of the feeling of wonder must not be understood solely from and in view of the ordinary that this feeling interrupts. When this feeling interrupts ordinary experience, the relativity of everything ordinary comes into view. The feeling of wonder is, therefore, the feeling of awe in the face of and the marvel at something that, in distinction from the world of *doxa*, is universally binding.

That wonder should lie at the origin of philosophy—and should indeed constitute its sole origin—has been so well established that it has become self-evident, ever since, Plato in his *Theaetetus*, and Aristotle in his *Metaphysics* recognized in this pathos the power to break with *doxa*. Not that this is any longer surprising. However, when philosophers have spoken of wonder, they have not always meant the same thing—attributing wonder, for example, to different sources in a range of different subjective experiences. Even though Plato, for example, does not explicitly state what causes wonder, it is generally acknowledged that it is a question for Plato of the perception of, and even an admiration for, the invisible whole—the

non-phenomenal totality, or the world in its entirety—that is manifested
in the retrait of particular phenomena. For Aristotle, however, the notion
of wonder implies that the subject is conscious of an aporetic situation,
that is, the subject is unable to understand something. Wonder is linked to
the perplexity that arises whenever one confronts unusual phenomena—or
phenomena that, though familiar, have suddenly become strange or alien.
So, although *thaumazein* is acknowledged as the sole origin of philosophy,
it has been subject to all manner of interpretation throughout the history
of philosophy. Indeed, because wonder possesses this structure, which
contains rupture, it has become related to certain other experiences that
have the capacity to shake the subject to its very core. For this reason, different affects, such as anguish, horror, stupor, and even nausea, have thus
come to adjoin Platonic marvel and Aristotelian perplexity, but the very
origin of philosophical thinking in *thaumazein* has never, to my knowledge, been called into question. Would it not be appropriate to wonder at
this lack of wonder about the very notion of wonder?

However, it has been remarked that in modernity such wonder in
the face of an order in which each thing has its proper place is no longer
the affect that awakens philosophical thought. According to Hans Blumenberg, "Neither enthusiasm before the infinite in the style of Giordano
Bruno, nor Pascal's fright at this abyss contains anything of the tranquility
required for the pure theoretical contemplation that the cosmos of the
Greeks made possible." Whereas for Bruno and Blaise Pascal the affects
caused by the unfathomableness of the infinite, or the abyss, motivate the
leap into the transcendent, for a Leonardo da Vinci—for whom the experience in question is no less determinant—these affects become the occasion for inventing a way to bridge the abyss, connecting one fixed point to
another, one edge to the other. From this, Blumenberg concludes that "insofar as modernity sees itself at all confronted with philosophical problems
of a specificity of its own, they arise from discomfort, that is, from John
Locke's 'uneasiness,' and no longer from wonder."[1] Uneasiness, whether in
the shapes of enthusiasm, of fright, or of starting back (in self-affirmation),
is no doubt no longer of the order of wonder, but as the double response to
the abyss demonstrates (the relation to God, or the search for a bridge), it
shares structural elements with wonder. If modernity knows any *philosophical* problems of its own at all, it is only because the philosophical is to be

traced from the double possibility of being struck by wonder: wonder at the difference that opens within the world (whether the World, the Opening, or the transcendent) or at the difference that divides it, hopelessly and aporetically, in view of some way out.

Wonder, not before particular things, but before the whole—in the opening of which things come to light—both characterizes philosophy and separates philosophy from myth, which, unmindful of wonder, knows everything ahead of time. This pathos, surprising the subject, is that of the luminous opening (within the world) of all appearances; it is, in its very novelty, the experience of marveling that things should be there, that there should be the world rather than nothing at all. Even though this is at first a silent experience, wonder grants itself to language in the form of a question, in the innumerable questions that philosophy poses and seeks to resolve. Wonder, which both happens to the subject and overcomes the subject, is a *Stimmung*, or, more precisely, the *Grundstimmung*, of philosophical thinking. As such, once experienced, it continues to attune that kind of thinking that translates wonder into questions and in whose responses thought seeks to explain and to justify that there is something rather than nothingness.

In the same fashion as the philosophies that preceded it, phenomenological thought emphasizes wonder as the beginning of philosophy or theory, with perhaps even more force than before, since it conceives of itself as a renewal of philosophy. In his reflections upon the beginning of the theoretical attitude in ancient Greece, Edmund Husserl understands *thaumazein* as what provided the occasion for the break with the practical and mythical attitude characteristic of the world of *doxa*. Before all else, it is a question of marveling, in a purely contemplative mode, at the strange fact that beyond particular phenomena there is a world of objectivities (geometric idealities) that represent the universal horizon of individual, particular worlds. But, the disconcerting experience in *thaumazein* of an irruption of foreign elements (such as universal idealities) into the everyday world continues to resonate throughout the whole of phenomenological research, particularly insofar as this research includes consideration of a transcendental phenomenology of the ego and of the essential structuring forms of the lived experiences of the *Lebenswelt*. According to Husserl, what inspires the wondering of transcendental phenomenology, and also constitutes it in the first place by providing it with an object of its own, are the universal structures of the subjective acts that constitute the world. Martin Heidegger, however, who affirms that the Greeks were principally engaged in wondering at the notion that beings exist only by virtue of the opening of Being in which they present themselves, determined that the principal task of philosophy is the safeguarding of what provokes this wonder: Being. In contrast to Husserl, for whom *thaumazein* is on the order of a curiosity and, as such, is the first form of philosophy as theory, for Heidegger in *Being and Time*, the wondering contemplation of beings, *thaumazein*, produces only incomprehension; however, what may first appear as the irritation of having met some obstacle on the path to understanding gives rise to the will to forge a path through the aporia toward Being, in whose clarity particular beings show themselves and forge relations between themselves. Heideggerian phenomenology, by serving as a safeguard of Being as that which is the most stupefying, does not attempt to overcome wonder, no matter how unsettling it may be, in order to transform itself into a merely theoretical mode of thought; on the contrary, it seeks to hold itself at this very point where wonder holds sway, as the very condition of thinking through the most astonishing of all astounding things: Being itself.

Contemporary French philosophy, whether it belongs to a Bergsonian current or whether it is inspired by phenomenological research, has not ceased to interrogate the conditions under which thinking becomes thinking, especially philosophical thinking. Gilles Deleuze, for example, in the process of examining this act that causes thinking to emerge from thinking itself, has been led to radicalize rather extravagantly the implications of philosophical pathos, to such an extent that he recognizes thinking only as the results of break-ins, of violence, or of the actions of enemy forces. However, for Jean-François Lyotard, for whom philosophy's task is contained in the single question, "What is thinking?," thought can only be said to occur, and could only be said to be worthy of the name thinking, if the pathos by which it justifies itself consists not only in being astonished about the fact that something happens, but also in that it could have *not* occurred. In Lyotard's thought, which is astonished by the fact that there are events, rather than that there is something instead of nothing, *thaumazein* does not exclude the terror latent in the real possibility, as Auschwitz continues to demonstrate, that (the) Nothing can happen. Breaking sharply with that tradition, which has always affirmed Being and which continues to affirm Being, Lyotard claims that we are forced to think by our experience of the abyss of nothingness.

But in what way does wonder figure in the thought of Jacques Derrida? Is *thaumazein*, in whatever form—admiration, perplexity, terror, nausea, and so forth—presented in Derrida's work as a theme worthy of philosophical reflection? Is there, within Derrida's work, an interrogation of the pathos with which Derrida's own thinking begins, which, explicitly taken up, would provide the tone or the key to all of his reflections? Is it possible to define a fundamental tone (*Grundstimmung*) with which all of Derrida's writings would be in tune? No doubt, one would have to reread all of Derrida's works before even attempting to answer these questions. However, just at this point, I would like to interject the impression—a provisional impression, one to be modified hereafter—that, at a first glance at least, Derrida doesn't appear to treat *thaumazein*, neither in the history of thinking nor in his own thinking. Shouldn't one be astonished that Derrida's thought has not dealt directly with this extremely powerful theme in the history of philosophy, which is decisive for any reflection that tries to answer what it means to philosophize? If my impression is correct (even as it is also superficial), this lack of reference to the question of wonder is certainly not due to some negligence on Derrida's part. But should one imagine that Derrida scornfully mistrusts this respectable, venerable *philosopheme*, just as he would have scorned its several reinterpretations within the history of philosophy? Are we to believe that his thought would end up being a thinking bereft of any of the astonishment and wonder that philosophy has declared to be its own origin? Is this even possible? After all, what would a thinking be without wonder, with neither an origin nor a beginning in a pathos, without a point of origin with which to begin in the first place? It would, without a doubt, be the end of philosophy.

For what is, as such and as a whole, to come into relief, it must manifest itself to a beholder, to a subject who then marvels at the wonder that there is something rather than nothing. Obviously, the feeling of wonder necessarily presupposes a subject, the human being. However, this subject

can experience what is as such and as a whole—the World in all its autonomy—only if he or she is severed and excluded from it. The intrinsic, or
"organic," link of the subject to the world must have been ruptured in order for the World as such to manifest itself and for a feeling such as wonder to occur. Undoubtedly, once what is, as such and as a whole, has
manifested itself to the human being in its own right, his or her presence
within the world can become an issue. And yet, only because the human
being is detached from the world—as a subject who stands in a face-to-
face relation with the world in its entirety—can the latter appear to him or
her as such. *Thaumazein* as the origin of philosophical thought contains,
therefore, the outlines of a metaphysics of the subject, the conception of
an anthropology, as well as of the elementary features of humanism.
Might this be the reason why all explicit reference to the problematic of
philosophical wonder is oddly absent from Derrida's work?

It is generally acknowledged that Derrida has been critical from
early on of the concept of experience and that he has even spoken of the
necessity to "exhaust the resources of the concept of experience before
attaining and in order to attain, by deconstruction, its ultimate foundation."[2] Setting aside Derrida's appropriation of the concept for his own
thought—in the shape, for example, of "the 'experience' of *differance*,"[3]
but above all, of the experience of aporia, or the impossible—let us emphasize that, according to *Of Grammatology*, "'experience' has always
designated the relationship with a presence, whether that relationship had
the form of consciousness or not."[4] Experience is a metaphysical concept
that presupposes a "relationship with a plenitude, whether it be sensory
simplicity or the infinite presence of God," and, consequently, the absence
of the trace.[5] Now, if wonder is indeed of the order of a pathos, wonder
occurs in an experience of something—the cosmos, the whole, the
World—that has the status of an "entity" that is self-contained, fully self-
present, intelligible all by itself, and free from all references and traces.
From this perspective, a thinking such as Derrida's that seeks to extricate
itself from metaphysics cannot, it would seem, accommodate *thaumazein*
as a pure experience in which philosophical thought originates.

Deconstruction, for having brought philosophy back to what is heterogeneous to it, is often seen as having tolled the death bell of philosophy

itself; however, if the deconstruction of philosophy justifies itself by virtue of the relations philosophy maintains with its others, it is only because philosophy does not allow itself to be reduced to its others. Philosophy cannot be reduced to any of its others, and it has others only insofar as it cannot be reduced to them. It only relates to them and permits itself to be corrupted by these others on the condition that it be irreducibly different from these others. Moreover, the fact that philosophy cannot be converted to its others explains Derrida's interest, which led him to all of philosophy's strategies of concealing the relations that it actually holds with its others. It has never been sufficiently noticed that Derrida forcefully affirms that there is a certain irreducibility of the philosophical, with all of its demands, and what is concomitantly promised with it. With Edmund Husserl, first, Derrida has said that any project that would have proceeded factically to explain the birth of philosophy is doomed to fail to the extent that any such project, even that which may have been carried out with the greatest competence and with the greatest of methodological rigor, would have explained everything *but* philosophy itself, which is to say, "this rift in the finite" and "the openness of the infinite" in which the factical (e.g., any possible domains of inquiry, whether they be geographic, economic, sociological, cultural, historical, etc.) acquires its meaning.[6] With Heidegger, and against Emmanuel Levinas, Derrida has underscored the absolute and exclusive resistance of Being to any metaphor, as well as the impossibility of reducing Being's origin by reducing it to some eponymous being, such as breathing, for example. This way of accounting for Being by relying upon metaphor explains the entire empirical history of Being, "except precisely for the essential," namely, that a particular *being*, like breath, was at one point thought to be a metaphor, coming thereby to signify Being or that which is irreducible to any being. The moment of thought that consists of tearing open the beingness of a particular being for the sole purpose of establishing it as a metaphor for Being, this moment of thought that is "the emergence (*percée*) of thought itself," cannot be reduced to any ontic point of origin. Philosophical thought is precisely this: "*une percée*," that is, a breakthrough.[7] It implies a radical liberation, a decisive rupture with facticity and the discourse of facticity. By presupposing the tearing open of the world, the origin of philosophy cannot simply be of this world. But how is it, then, that a factual sentiment like wonder can give birth to philosophy? Can a feeling such as wonder awaken philosophical thought without having undergone a transformation of its very nature as a feeling, without ceasing to be what it literally is? Should not wonder have been considered *as* the origin of thought, in the process becoming something other than a simple state of the soul, in order to have become worthy of its name as the beginning of philosophy? Would this not also be the recognition of the intrinsic irreducibility of philosophical thinking to the factical world, which would finally explain why *thaumazein* is not evidently thematized in Derrida's thought? As long as wonder is understood as a sentiment, however extraordinary, wonder fails to explain anything essential, especially not the origins of thinking, unless its extraordinariness consists precisely in this—namely, that its sensible nature is torn open so to be able to refer to the rift in what is, in short, by no longer being a sentiment to begin with.

According to metaphysical thought, as forms of sensibility and pure subjective states, feelings, emotions, and sentiments are secondary compared to the intellect and reason. But metaphysical thought has also conferred a title of nobility to certain feelings that set them apart from the lower forms of human consciousness. Undoubtedly, *thaumazein* is one, if not the most important, among those nobler affects because it is seen as the very origin of philosophical thought. Although no longer fully of the order of the sensible, *thaumazein* is still not an operation or representation of the intellect. It is a feeling that is barely a feeling anymore, a form of awareness of what is universal that is not yet intellectual. Does such a proto-synthetic affect not obfuscate the rift in sensibility that must be thought for philosophical thinking to reveal what in it is irreducible? Something that also links it structurally—that is, most intimately—to a non-thinkable tear within what is?

One must also make a distinction between thinking and philosophy: what Derrida calls "thinking" can be reduced neither to technology, nor to science, nor to philosophy. Thinking calls into question all of philosophy's values, including what is supposed to be fundamental, or originary, or radical, as well as the unquestioned authority of the principle of reason to which philosophy has submitted itself and that thinking interrogates—not in the name of the irrational, but in the name of reason itself insofar as reason is an unconditional call to form a critique of all imaginable conditionalities. Strictly speaking, even the word "thinking" itself, which carries a certain weight ever since Heidegger appropriated it in order to designate the self-collection and the gathering of Being, is in danger of appearing too excessive when one compares it to Derrida's modest aims in employing the term. In short, what Derrida terms "thinking" exists apart from whatever "philosophical thinking" might have been understood to hitherto mean. Would it not follow from this that such a thinking would be obliged, indeed, owe it to itself, to interrogate the wonder to which philosophical thought owes its birth, insofar as this birth in wonder is an unquestioned presupposition? Is not thinking in need of inquiring into wonder as its merely conditional origin? Thinking as such cannot originate in something like wonder or astonishment: not simply and not uniquely. But if thinking is not born in a pathos that occasions a rupture with the world of *doxa*, how does it come about? What is it that causes its advent?

According to Husserl, wonder, in a properly philosophical sense, is summoned by the universal structures of subjectivity that constitute the world, whereas for Heidegger, wonder arises whenever one realizes that beings *are*, that beings show or present themselves in the perpetually self-hiding clearing of Being as such. One might provisionally characterize Derrida's thinking, on the one hand, as an exploration of the relations that obtain between the same (homogeneity, identity, selfhood, presence, life, as well as philosophy as an entity to itself) and the other (not only with the others proper to thinking or to philosophy, but also with some unforeseeable other, the other to come) and, on the other hand, as an attempt to articulate the laws of these relations, for example, by the use of the notions archi-trace, différance, supplementarity, the re-mark, and iterability. Wouldn't these laws, which in *The Tain of the Mirror* I took the liberty, yet not without some evidence in Derrida's writings, to call infrastructures, be themselves the occasion for some sort of philosophical pathos? Is there anything astonishing about these laws, above or beyond any consideration of particular laws? Is there, moreover, any philosophy that may be inferred from these laws? These structures have nothing to do with the notion of the whole, or with the harmonious order of the universe, which Platonic philosophy marveled at. However, they are idealities, and thus could merit the wonder that Husserl reserves for the essential forms that constitute the founding acts of consciousness. But the structures in question are not only enabling structures; their very iterability implies an element of othering with the result that rather than simply repeatable identities, they also assign limits to what they bring about. As structures of possibility and impossibility, they may curtail any contemplative admiration. If, furthermore, these structures are the occasion for a kind of puzzlement about the aporias that lie at the heart of the relations between the same and the other, it does not follow therefore that they constitute a transitional passage toward *theorein*. But, even if one is not struck by wonder in front of these infrastructural laws and does not *admire* them, do these laws leave thinkers and thinking necessarily cold or indifferent? Is the *Grundstimmung* of Derrida's thinking, indeed, a kind of impassivity [*impassibilité*]—a thinking *outside* the domain of wonder's influence?

All the same, the text, "The Laws of Reflection: Nelson Mandela, in Admiration," tells us that Nelson Mandela *forces* us to admire him, chiefly because of his own admiration for "the law itself, the law above other laws" and for his having made of this admiration a combative power. There is no doubt but that the term "admiration" refers in this context primarily to the first of René Descartes's six primitive passions, and one should not be surprised that admiration was the first among Descartes's passions, since, translating emotion, wonder, surprise, and questioning, all directed to what Descartes named the "extraordinary," "admiration" suggests, as Derrida notes, cognition. Admiration, indeed, "enables understanding [*elle donne à connaître*]."[8] Just as Hannah Arendt has shown, *thaumazein* is above all an admiration of something that forces one to admire; as a result, this sentiment that Derrida admits to feeling before Nelson Mandela not only forces Derrida to admire, but also to reason (on the topic of the laws of reflection)—"admiration reasons"—referring as well to philosophical wonder, which is, as Husserl affirmed, the first form of philosophy as *theoria*.[9]

When rereading Derrida's texts from the perspective of the questions raised above, one notices not only copious references to feelings, sentiments, affects, and emotions, but also the presence of an inextricable link between feelings and rationality within the operation of the thinking of deconstruction—if indeed there is any such operation, that is, a "deconstructive" labor in view of the production of an effect, or work. The transcendental or quasi-transcendental investigation of the conditions of possibility and impossibility is regularly accompanied in Derrida's texts by what one may only characterize as an interrogation in the style of a transcendental aesthetics. For example, in *The Other Heading*, the axiom, regarding "a very dry necessity," according to which there can be no identity (of present-day Europe) that does not carry within it a self-differing, is preceded by an axiom that belongs to the order of a *feeling*, namely, that feeling expressed by Derrida, which is that a certain Europe, however dated it may already be, does not yet exist and still remains to come.[10]

Certainly, in Derrida's texts, wonder does not play the classical function of occasioning philosophical thought; however, philosophical thought, as such, that is, as a thought that is destined or addressed to someone, does presuppose the experience of a wound—a wound that is not necessarily caused by some event that should have happened only once, and to which the figure of the philosopher should have responded consciously, but a wound that would be a priori precisely in the measure that thinking is a response to a call, a demand, or an injunction that causes philosophical discourse to submit to shock after shock and to traumatism after traumatism. We read: "A philosophical discourse that would not be provoked or interrupted by the violence of an appeal from the other, from an experience that cannot be dominated, would not be a very questioning, very interesting philosophical discourse."[11]

How is it that wonder would be the very origin of philosophy without already containing, on a purely contemplative and not yet discursive level, the whole of philosophy? When, in *Theaetetus*, Socrates remarks that Hesiod was correct to have held such consideration for Iris, the daughter of Thaumas, it is because Iris, in her capacity as a messenger, instructs us on no lesser subject than that which Thaumas contemplated with admiration and with stupefaction: through the character of Iris, wonder is translated into speech and into discourse. Husserl's interest in understanding what motivated the passage from what he calls "uniquely, simply [*blossen*] *thaumazein*" to *theoria* and, strictly speaking, to science, presupposes this particular genealogy, and, as a result, the passage to speech, if not to writing, in all of its idealizing and universalizing turns. But, as such, this passage is merely the means through which wonder understands itself and gains hold of itself, developing in the process what it was already when it was mere bare-naked wonder. Wonder is a *philosopheme* that contains already, by itself, the whole of philosophy. Have we not already seen that philosophical discourse, which establishes wonder as the beginning of philosophy, shows wonder to be structured by all of the major metaphysical oppositions: active/passive; sensible/intelligible; myth/logos; particular/universal? As an integral part of the whole of philosophy, wonder cannot, therefore, escape deconstructive vigilance. Furthermore, is not wonder also, in itself, a still larger part than this whole, in the sense that wonder forms not only the matrix or grid of philosophy, but, at least to the extent that philosophical thinking would be neither mechanical nor sclerotic, that very thing to which all of thought's motions refer, as a sort of *Grundstimmung* of philosophy? But by what right can a pathos such as wonder assume the role of affecting thinking in all of its forms and with all of its ramifications?

According to Heidegger, what is most questionable (*bedenklich*) is the fact that we still do not think. Thinking, understood as the apprehension of Being—that is, of that which alone provokes wonder—does not yet take place, first and foremost because that which needs to be thought has turned away from human beings. Human beings will learn to think only if they learn to unlearn what thinking has meant hitherto. In short, thinking must still be learned in the opening of oneself to what is the most astonishing (Being) for thought to be possible in the first place. If thinking does not yet occur, it is precisely because we have not yet begun to wonder. Thinking's task, in advance of apprehending Being in wonder, is for the time being limited to prepare the advent of what, according to Heidegger, is only a possibility of philosophy that still has not been actualized. For Derrida, thinking too is still to come. As "the experience of the condition, of conditionality, of the ex-position of a limit, the exposition *to* a limit," thought does not yet engage the unconditional to which it must respond in order to be thought in the first place.[12] Yet, such exposition, or exposure to the unconditional, to what arrives, and to what overcomes us, imposing itself unconditionally without giving any notice, is such that thinking seems to be the *impossible* itself. If there has ever been thinking, if it ever took place, it would have had to occur as a response to an unpredictable event so singular as to give rise to an equally singular act of thought, for thinking is truly thinking only on condition that it meets an impossible demand. But what is the status of wonder in this impossible thinking? Is wonder, then, also something that cannot simply be presupposed, something whose conditions of occurring link it—indistiguishably perhaps—to terror as much as to a promise?

I recall first of all that, in the process of becoming *theoria*, wonder becomes the thinking of that which, at the very moment of its inception, had provoked the *Stimmung* in question in order to transform it into an object of knowledge. Philosophy begins with astonishment, with the recognition of lacking all clues, only to be immediately transformed, at least since Aristotle, into the project of seeking principles, *arche*, causes. What up to that moment gave rise to wonder quickly becomes ordinary again. I provisionally suggest the following: in thinking through that which calls forth thought, thought has thought all there is to think, especially if thought includes itself in the process. It would have thought everything, except for what is most essential, namely, the event of *thaumazein* itself, independently of its determinations as admiration, puzzlement, terror, or nausea. When Derrida evokes "*la pensée de ce qui reste à penser,*" does not what remains after philosophy would have, at least in principle, thought everything—the whole—consist precisely in the very event of astonishment within the singularity of its irruption into the everyday? And yet, if, in order to be conceived as a responsible response to the affect of wonder, inasmuch as it is an event, the thinking of wonder is to do justice to wonder itself in its singularity, the affect of wonder can be only one of several possible shocks that force thought to happen. For, indeed, if one considers wonder in its character as an event, wonder is not only necessarily plural, but it also may just as well only be one event among many others.

Understood as an event, as something that happens to thought and that forces it to think, wonder is no longer the wonder described by philosophy, containing within it the whole of philosophy. Wonder, insofar as it is an event, whether it be determined as admiration, as perplexity, as horror, as anguish, as stupor, as nausea, and so forth, is something that comes upon us, that happens to us, and that imposes itself upon us in an unconditional manner. It is on the basis of the notion of such an unconditionality—which, for example, exists in that wonder that effects a breach within the regions of the visible and the transparent—that Derrida thinks thinking, that is to say, philosophy as originating in *thaumazein*, as the discourse of reason that, through the mode of calculation, makes judgments about conditionality, about limits, and about the possible. This thinking of thinking—not to be mistaken for a philosophy of philosophy—can no longer be said to have a single origin; it no longer begins with bare wonder alone. And, indeed, insofar as it responds to the event, its origins are plural, which amounts to claiming that it no longer has an origin to begin with, beginning, rather, "*Wherever we are:* in a text where we already believe ourselves to be."[13] Thinking, no longer possessed of a single origin, no longer contents itself with simply unfolding that which announced itself in the very bareness or nudity of such an origin.

Thinking in a text—which is here to be understood as a "text, in the infrastructural sense that we now give to that word," that is, as a system of references which could be either a text in the usual sense of, for example, a philosophical text, or a public discourse, or even the text of the situation of our time—owes its birth to the recognition that thinking, philosophical thinking, for example, is always necessarily "held within" [*prise*] and "overtaken" [*surprise*] by a language and a logic constituting a system that cannot be dominated by thinking: this system has always "sufficiently *surprising* ressources" to which discourse, whatever is said, is always otherwise than what is intended.[14] The wonder that causes thinking would thus be nothing less than an awareness of being overtaken by the resources of that in which one is caught. Consequently, thinking amounts to the production of a structure that consists in the relation of a particular thought to the resources of a system that overtakes any particular thought and, indeed, in which it is captured. Conversely, however, thinking has a duty to catch unawares and overtake those discourses that are today dominant—among which one may count not only philosophical discourses, but also more particularly juridico-political discourses—by confronting them with the available resources of our philosophical heritage. According to this latter task, thinking does not consist solely of the critical demand for responsibility, which asks of those in power to account for their discourse in the name of the heritage that encloses them; thinking also serves, here, to recall to those in charge that this heritage carries with it a certain responsibility, and promise.

   Would surprise, stupefaction, astonishment, or *ébranlement*, belong completely among the objects that thinking analyzes and deconstructs, namely, philosophical or juridico-political discourses? It would then be the case that thinking should no longer have anything to do with wonder, which would be nothing more than another of deconstruction's objects. However, if wonder is to be deprived of its traditional privilege, it is perhaps also because wonder is not astonished nearly enough. If thinking no longer knows any wonder, is it not, precisely, because wonder hardly shocks at all, only just enough to give rise to some desire or will to know or to master whatever it is that lies at its source? Even as thought begins with the event, whether an event of surprise or some other sort of event, it leaves wonder behind. Yet, if thinking is summoned by the event—by the unforeseeable, unconditional coming of the other, whether this other be a person or a thing—is it not subject then to a violent shock, a shock still more violent than that of wonder? Provoking thought, as though it were responding to this very call, this overturning, unsettling shock even risks destroying the very possibility of a response at all. What makes thinking thinking, before all else, is the inevitable risk that shock might, rather than provide the occasion for philosophical thinking, just as well be its extinction. Only on condition that the shock that triggers thinking is not immediately supplanted by an effort to achieve knowledge about its cause, but threatens thinking in its very possibility, does thinking have a chance to occur. Dispossessing wonder, opening itself to the event, to unconditionality, to that which or to whom might arrive, thought no longer understands anything of wonder anymore; rather than allowing itself to know wonder, to summon it for interrogation, it grants it its status as an event. In this case, however, there is no longer any wonder anymore, or rather there is still more wonder than one thinks.

Notes

INTRODUCTION

1. Jean-François Lyotard, *The Differend: Phrases in Dispute*, trans. G. Van Den Abbeele (Minneapolis: University of Minnesota Press, 1988), xii.

2. Immanuel Kant, *The Metaphysics of Morals*, trans. M. Gregor (Cambridge: Cambridge University Press, 1996), 186, 209.

3. Immanuel Kant, *Critique of Pure Reason*, trans. N. K. Smith (New York: St. Martin's Press, 1965), 422–423. See also Jacques Derrida, *Rogues: Two Essays on Reason*, trans. P. A. Brault and M. Naas (Stanford, CA: Stanford University Press, 2005), 171.

4. Derrida, *Rogues*, 118.

5. Ibid., 125–127. See also my review article of this work by Derrida (in particular, on the notion of "auto-immunity"), "In the Name of Reason: The Deconstruction of Sovereignty," *Research and Phenomenology* 34 (2004): 289–303.

6. That this is also true of Foucault is one of points made by Leonard Lawlor in an essay "Un écart infime (Part II): The Blind Spot in Foucault," forthcoming in *Philosophy and Social Criticism*.

7. Martin Heidegger, "Letter on Humanism," in *Basic Writings*, ed. D. F. Krell (New York: Harper & Row, 1977), 193.

8. Hannah Arendt, *Ich will verstehen. Selbstauskünfte zu Leben und Werk* (Munich: Piper, 1996), 74.

9. Martin Heidegger, "Was heisst Denken?" in *Vorträge und Aufsätze* (Pfullingen: Günther Neske, 1959), 140.

10. Martin Heidegger, *What Is Called Thinking?* trans. J. Glenn Gray (New York: Harper & Row, 1968), 244.

11. Martin Heidegger, "The End of Philosophy and the Task of Thinking," in *Basic Writings*, 376.

12. Heidegger, *What Is Called Thinking?* 5.

13. Heidegger, "The End of Philosophy," 377–378 (trans. mod.).

14. Ibid., 378–379.

15. Arendt, *Ich will Verstehen*, 110.

16. Jacques Derrida, *Fichus. Discours de Francfort* (Paris: Galilée, 2002), 21.

17. Heidegger, *What Is Called Thinking?* 4; Theodor W. Adorno, *Metaphysik. Begriff und Probleme* (Frankfurt/Main: Suhrkamp, 1998), 198.

18. Martin Heidegger, "Science and Reflection," in *The Question Concerning Technology and Other Essays*, trans. W. Lovitt (New York: Harper & Row, 1977), 164.

19. Heidegger, "The End of Philosophy," 377.

20. Heidegger, "Letter on Humanism," 240.

21. For an interesting and thorough historical (and sometimes witty) account of the category of continental philosophy as a species of philosophy distinct from analytical philosophy, see Simon Glendinning's "What Is Continental Philosophy?" in *The Edinburgh Encyclopedia of Continental Philosophy* (Edinburgh: Edinburgh University Press, 1999), 3–19.

22. But if it is true that there is no primacy of theory in Derridean thought, it is also true that today at least the sciences are no longer simply driven by theory. As Hans-Jörg Rheinberger has forcefully shown, it is "experimental thinking" that drives scientific research. See Hans-Jörg Rheinberger, *Experiment, Differenz, Schrift* (Marburg: Basilisken Presse, 1992), 22.

23. Jacques Derrida, "Some Statements and Truisms about Neologisms, Newisms, Postisms, Parasitisms, and Other Small Seismisms," in *The State of Theory*, ed. D. Caroll (New York: Columbia University Press, 1990), 63–94.

24. Richard Rorty, *Contingency, Irony, and Solidarity* (Cambridge: Cambridge University Press, 1989), 125.

25. Derrida, "Some Statements and Truisms," 87.

26. Given the thoroughly different ways in which "critique" has been understood, even a history of the concept (*Begriffsgeschichte*) of critique encounters special difficulties. See the introductory remarks to Kurt Röttgers, *Kritik und Praxis. Zur Geschichte des Kritikbegriffs von Kant bis Marx* (Berlin: Walter de Gruyter, 1975), 1–17.

27. Werner Schneiders, "Vernünftiger Zweifel und wahre Eklektik. Zur Entstehung des modernen Kritikbegriffes," *Studia Leibnitiana* 17, no. 2 (1985): 146–150.

28. Kant, *Critique of Pure Reason*, 9.

29. For the prehistory of the modern concept of critique, see, in particular, Schneiders, "Vernünftiger Zweifel und wahre Eklektik," 143–161. For a discussion of Kant's precritical concept of critique and its indebtedness to the emergence of aesthetics as a philosophical discipline in the eighteenth century, see Röttgers, *Kritik und Praxis*, 25–31.

30. For this history of dissolution of the concept of critique, see Röttgers, *Kritik und Praxis*, 63ff.

31. Martin Heidegger, *What Is a Thing?* trans. W. B. Barton and V. Deutsch (South Bend, IN: Regnery/Gateway, 1967), 119–120.

32. Ibid., 120. But the origin of Kant's concept of critique in the emerging discipline of aesthetics is not limited to the establishment of something general over

against the particular. Whereas in the first half of the century, critique concerned the rules of the judgment of taste and was still indebted to the established logic of the school, the concept of critique, as a result of the increasing awareness during the late Enlightenment period of the specificity of the realm of aesthetics, acquired the meaning of rational cognition by way of empirical concepts. Although the discipline of aesthetics did not abandon its concern with general rules according to which aesthetical objects, or objects of art (*techne*)—objects that have the character of man-made products—are to be judged, the latter were no longer considered to be of a logical, but of an empirical nature. This understanding of critique, which was transposed from the domain of aesthetics to other domains, is equally important for Kant's understanding of the term.

33. Gilles Deleuze, *Nietzsche and Philosophy*, trans. H. Tomlinson (New York: Columbia University Press, 1983), 89.

34. Ibid., 88.

35. Ibid., 86–87.

36. Ibid., 197.

37. Philippe Lacoue-Labarthe, *Heidegger: La politique du poème* (Paris: Galilée, 2002), 60.

38. Derrida, *Rogues*, 174–175. In *The Other Heading*, Derrida speaks of the duty not only to cultivate "*critique, . . . the critical idea, the critical tradition,* but also submitting it, beyond critique and questioning, to a deconstructive genealogy that thinks and exceeds it without yet compromising it." *The Other Heading: Reflections on Today's Europe*, trans. P. A. Brault and M. Naas (Bloomington: Indiana University Press, 1992), 77. See also Derrida's *Specters of Marx: The State of the Debt, the Work of Mourning, and the New International*, trans. P. Kamuf (New York: Routledge, 1994), in particular, pages 87–91 and 162–163, as an example of the continuity between Marxism's critical legacy and deconstruction.

39. Jacques Derrida, *Points . . . Interviews, 1974–1994*, trans. P. Kamuf et al. (Stanford, CA: Stanford University Press, 1995), 54; Jacques Derrida, *Sauf le nom* (Paris: Galilée, 1993), 77.

40. "Hypercritique," however, is not always understood by Derrida in this sense of uncompromising vigilance. As illustrated in Chapter 1, in "Force of Law," in the context of a discussion of Benjamin's "Critique of Violence," Derrida uses the term "hypercritique" to refer to Benjamin's attempt to achieve pure and uncontaminated distinctions—that is, something that from a deconstructive point of view is bound to fail.

CHAPTER I

1. Jacques Derrida, *Points . . . Interviews, 1974–1994*, trans. P. Kamuf et al. (Stanford, CA: Stanford University Press, 1995), 54.

2. Jacques Derrida, *Psyche. Inventions de l'autre* (Paris: Galilée, 1987), 390.

3. Jacques Derrida, *Le problème de la genèse dans la philosophie de Husserl* (Paris: PUF, 1990), 12, 30.

4. Walter Benjamin, "Critique of Violence," in *Selected Writings: Volume 1, 1913–1926*, ed. M. Bullock and M. W. Jennings (Cambridge, MA: Harvard University Press, 1966), 236–252 (hereafter cited in text as *CV*); Jacques Derrida, "Force of Law: The 'Mystical Foundation of Authority,'" *Cardozo Law Review* 11, nos. 5–6 (1990): 919–1045 (hereafter cited in text as *FL*).

5. Benjamin's hermetism has found its hitherto most judicious treatment in Bernd Witte, *Walter Benjamin—Der Intellektuelle as Kritiker. Untersuchungen zu seinem Frühwerk* (Stuttgart: Metzler, 1976).

6. The German original is quoted from Walter Benjamin, *Gesammelte Schriften*, vol. 2, 1 (Frankfurt: Suhrkamp, 1977), 179–203.

7. Derrida, "Force of Law," 979. In this context, see also Walter Benjamin, "Program of the Coming Philosophy," in *Benjamin: Philosophy, Aesthetics, History*, ed. G. Smith (Chicago: University of Chicago Press, 1989), 1–12. In this essay, Benjamin argues that the fundamental Kantian distinctions between epistemology and metaphysics and criticism and metaphysics are "not of principle importance."

CHAPTER 2

1. Philippe Lacoue-Labarthe and Jean-Luc Nancy, *L'Absolu littéraire. Théorie de la littérature du romantisme allemand* (Paris: Seuil, 1978), 30. In a passage not taken up into the English translation (*The Literary Absolute,* trans. P. Barnard and C. Lester [Albany: State University of New York Press, 1988], the authors describe Benjamin's thesis and note that "it did not fail to create a 'revolutionary' effect in traditional romantic studies." Winfried Menninghaus, *Unendliche Verdopplung. Die Frühromantische Grundlegung der Kunsttheorie im Begriff absoluter Selbstreflexion* (Frankfurt/Main: Suhrkamp, 1987).

2. Menninghaus, *Unendliche Verdopplung*, 71, 41.

3. Ibid., 42.

4. Walter Benjamin, "The Concept of Criticism in German Romanticism," in *Selected Writings: Volume 1, 1913–1926*, ed. M. Bullock and M. W. Jennings (Cambridge, MA: Harvard University Press, 1996). All page references in this chapter refer to this edition.

5. In a letter dated November 8, 1918, to Ernst Schoen, Benjamin says that writing his dissertation is not wasted time: "What I have been learning from it, i.e. insight into the relationship of a truth to history, will of course hardly be at all explicit in the dissertation, but I hope it will be discerned by astute readers." In another letter to Schoen dated April 7, 1919, he remarks: "A few days ago I completed a rough draft of my dissertation. It has become what it was meant to be: a pointer to the true nature of romanticism, of which the secondary literature is completely ignorant—and even that only indirectly, because I was no more

allowed to get to the heart of romanticism, i.e., messianism (I only dealt with its perception of art) than to anything else that I find very relevant. Had I attempted to get to the heart of romanticism, I would have cut myself off from any chance of achieving the expected complicated and conventional scholarly attitude that I personally distinguish from the genuine one. But I hope to have achieved the following in this work: to deduce this state of affairs from the inside out." Walter Benjamin, *The Correspondence of Walter Benjamin 1910–1940,* ed. G. Scholem and T. W. Adorno, trans. M. R. Jacobson and E. M. Jacobson (Chicago: University of Chicago Press, 1994), 136, 139–140.

6. Since Benjamin does not let up on his criticism of the Romantic concept of art criticism in the second part of the dissertation—in fact, quite the opposite is true—it would seem that the peculiar fruitfulness that some Romantic propositions have gained in the theory of art to which Benjamin alludes presupposes a critical dismantling of their specifically Romantic underpinnings.

7. Friedrich Schlegel, *Kritische Schriften* (Munich: Hanser Verlag, 1970), 424.

8. Indeed, it is highly doubtful whether the Romantic "idea" or Absolute is an idea in the Platonic sense. See my "Ideality in Fragmentation," in Friedrich Schlegel, *Philosophical Fragments,* trans. P. Firchow (Minneapolis: University of Minnesota Press, 1991), xxviii–xxx.

CHAPTER 3

1. Walter Benjamin, *Selected Writings: Volume 1, 1913–1926,* ed. M. Bullock and M. W. Jennings (Cambridge, MA: Harvard University Press, 1996). All page references in this chapter refer to this edition.

2. See Bernd Witte, *Walter Benjamin—Der Intellektuelle als Kritiker. Untersuchungen zu seinem Frühwerk* (Stuttgart: Metzler, 1976), 55–57.

3. Gershom Scholem, *Walter Benjamin und sein Engel. Vierzehn Aufsätze und kleine Beiträge* (Frankfurt/Main: Suhrkamp, 1983), 53–54. See also: Gershom Scholem, *Walter Benjamin: The Story of a Friendship,* trans. H. Zohn (Philadelphia: The Jewish Publication Society of America, 1981), 94.

4. Witte argues that Benjamin's practice of tying autobiographic experiences of a private nature into his critique of Goethe's novel, in which the debate with Goethe's life serves also to clarify his own personal situation, can plausibly be retraced to his readings of Kierkegaard (and Hermann Cohen). According to Witte, this existential relation is the source of his critique's ethical categories according to which life and work are to be judged. Witte acknowledges that, as regards in particular Benjamin's relation to Jula Cohn, "the connection between the private biography of the critique and literary critique goes well beyond merely anecdotal interest," and he concludes that, "therefore, the layer of meaning of his text concerns properly only the author himself and the privileged reader named by the dedication" (Witte, *Walter Benjamin,* 63). For Witte, the reduction of the communicative function of critique to that of a dialogue between the author and

a loved one, and to a medium for the author's self-understanding, accounts for the extreme and esoteric subjectivism of Benjamin's critique. Witte's book is still by far one of the best—that is, most perspicuous—books on Benjamin, precisely because of its hostility to the early works of Benjamin. Witte only highlights the private nature of the critique, the extreme individualism that it advocates, as well as the esoteric theology at work in the text, in order to dismiss them as contrary to what critique should be. However, it needs to be argued that even though this essay is highly autobiographic and interwoven with private issues, the presence of these strains in the text are a form of what today is called the singularity of signature of all texts. Something similar is true of Benjamin's highly esoteric theology. With it, Benjamin touches on essential aspects and implications of critique that before never became thematic in that way.

5. This is, of course, a question concerning the relation between the work and the life of its author, a question that continued to occupy Benjamin from, at least, his early study of two poems by Friedrich Hölderlin, in which he distinguishes between two extreme functional unities, that of the poem and that of life, up to his essay on Goethe's *Elective Affinities*, and beyond.

6. In part 3 of the essay in which Benjamin sets up Ottilie as an allegory of the work of art (see Witte, *Walter Benjamin*, 69–79), and in which he also gives the most extensive account of his theory of art, the "idea of art criticism" is characterized as the impossibility of unveiling (*Unenthüllbarkeit*). "Never yet has a true work of art been grasped other than were it ineluctably represented itself as a secret." And Benjamin adds: "Such veiling is divinely necessary at times, just as it is also divinely determined that, unveiled at the wrong time, what is inconspicuous evaporates into nothing, whereupon revelation (*Offenbarung*) takes over from secrets." Revealed, "the object in its veil," that is, the beautiful object, would become "infinitely inconspicuous," infinitely plain. Although both revelation and beauty hold in themselves historical-philosophical orders, beauty, in contrast to revelation, "makes visible not the idea but rather the latter's secret" (351).

7. In "Theorie der Kunstkritik," which is a first draft of the section of part 3 of the essay devoted to the question of "the ideal of the problem," Benjamin defines "ideal" as follows: "The ideal of the problem is an idea, which is to be called an ideal because it does not refer to the immanent form of the problem, but to the content of its answer which transcends it, even though this occurs only through the concept of the problem as the concept of the unity of its answer." Walter Benjamin, *Gesammelte Schriften*, vol. 1, 3 (Frankfurt/Main: Suhrkamp, 1974), 833–834.

8. According to Bernd Witte, Benjamin's notion of the "ideal of the problem" is a synthesis of Goethe's and the early Romantics' positions on the theory of art. He writes: " 'Ideal' designates the formed content, in a Goethean sense, of the artwork, which includes at the same time its secret, that is, its fundamental impenetrability to critique, whereas the concept of 'problem' refers to the infinity of the

idea in the sense of romantic philosophy." Witte, *Walter Benjamin*, 45. For a discussion of the "ideal of the problem," see page 88.

9. Benjamin's theory of philosophy as a sibling of beautiful art is not without resemblance to Heidegger's distinction between poetry (*Dichten*) and thinking (*Denken*). The differences and similarities of the two thinkers in this respect will be taken up on another occasion.

10. Apart from the fact that marriage is "one of the most rigorous and objective articulations (*sachlichsten Ausprägungen*) of human life," and that it is the occasion for the rediscovery of material content in the later writings of Goethe, marriage, is, perhaps, also well suited to shed light on how matter and content interlink in the material content, precisely because of its relational character. Furthermore, marriage is not simply a formation of human life; it is one through which a content imprints itself on human life, and this content is, for Benjamin, of transcendent, that is, divine, origin. For a reading of "Goethe's Elective Affinities" that emphasizes the systematic significance of the imagery of the seal, and the imprint, for understanding the essay in question, see Fritz Gutbrodt, "Wahl: Verwandtschaft. Benjamins Siegel," *MLN*, 106, no. 3 (1991): 555–588.

11. For Benjamin, Kant's cluelessness regarding the material content of the facts of the matter, whether of marriage or just anything else, is clearly linked to his indebtedness to the Enlightenment. Poverty of material content, that is, of the moral or ethical significance, and ultimately, of the theological meaning, of a subject matter, is a "crucial feature of the German if not of the entire European Enlightenment, [and] an indispensable precondition of Kant's life work, on the one hand, and of Goethe's production, on the other" (298). Benjamin's anti-Enlightenment stance would need a separate study.

12. Of relevance here are, in particular, pages 61–64, from Immanuel Kant, *The Metaphysics of Morals*, trans. M. Gregor (Cambridge: Cambridge University Press, 1996). Let us also point out that although Benjamin uses both terms of *moralisch* (moral) and *sittlich* (ethical), it is not entirely clear from the text whether Benjamin's essay intends a sharp conceptual distinction between the moral (*das Moralische*) and the ethical (*Sittlichkeit*). However, if ethical judgments concern only human beings, and if moral philosophy is to rigorously establish that fictional characters cannot be the objects of an ethical judgment, there may be a hierarchical relation between these concepts. Indeed, the debate with Kant's *Metaphysics of Morals* at the beginning of the essay is the opening prelude for a discussion throughout the essay of *Sitten* and *Sittlichkeit* in which, as we will see, the ethical is shown to be rooted in a face-to-face relation of the individual in his or her creatural singularity with God. Since, ultimately, the critique of works, although distinct from biographism, will seek to discover in them the caesural trace of a decision and of an awakening of the author to responsibility, an authentic biographism, one that is predicated on a conception of the ethical intimately interwoven with theological considerations, guides Benjamin's reading of Goethe's novel in the essay.

13. Sigrid Weigel has shown the pervasive importance for Benjamin's essay of this motive of the beyond, or divine, that juts into all orders of human life. See Sigrid Weigel, "On the Dialectic of Divine and Human Order in Walter Benjamin's 'Goethe's Elective Affinities,'" in *Walter Benjamin and Romanticism*, ed. B. Hanssen and A. Benjamin (New York: Continuum, 2002), 197–206.

14. Benjamin's claim that the "origin [of love] is the presentiment of a life of bliss [*des seligen Lebens*]" (352), shows, that morally speaking, and with respect to its truth content, marriage, as the expression of continuance in love, is produced "by the highest powers" (301).

15. In his account of *Elective Affinities* in the encyclopedia essay on "Goethe," Benjamin provides a more historical and sociological explication for the predominance of the theme of decay of marriage in Goethe's novel. See, "Goethe," in *Walter Benjamin, Selected Writings*, Vol. II, 1927–1934, Cambridge, MA: Harvard University Press, 1999, p. 182.

16. In a manuscript page, Benjamin notes that when love becomes vacillating, and marriage flounders, "the sacramental also becomes transformed into the mythic." Speaking of the couples in the novel, he notes that for them "it is not love that is primal, but the situation in which the old sacramental powers of the dissolving marriage seek to settle in between them as mythic, or natural powers." Benjamin, *Gesammelte Schriften,* vol. 1, 3, 837–838.

17. Ibid., 835–837.

18. Chapter two of Benjamin's essay concludes with the statement: "Thus, if in the novel the mythic is considered the thesis, then the antithesis can be seen in the novella. Its title points to this" (333).

19. This does not mean that, as Goethe seems to have suggested, "inner ethical struggle as an object of poetic construction" would be excluded from poetry. Benjamin writes: "Indeed, what would remain of the drama, of the novel itself?" (312). Notwithstanding the possibility of poetic depiction of ethical strife, it remains that fictional characters are not to be judged like human beings, that is, ethically.

20. A further conclusion is "that, according to ethical laws, passion loses all its rights and happiness when it seeks a pact with the bourgeois, affluent, secure life. . . . In the mute constraint that encloses these human beings in the circle of human custom, indeed of bourgeois custom, hoping there to salvage for them the life of passion, lies the dark transgression which demands its dark expiation. Basically they flee from the verdict of the law that still has power over them" (343).

21. The manuscript titled, "Kategorien der Ästhetik," which is a first draft of sections of part 2 and 3 of the essay, explores the concept of form in some greater detail. See Benjamin, *Gesammelte Schriften,* vol. 1, 3, 829–830.

22. As Marc Sagnol has argued, "this strange concept becomes intelligible once one understands that it is a first version of the concept of allegory as it ap-

pears in the book on German Tragic Drama." Marc Sagnol, "Les 'Affinités électives,' roman non tragique," in *Global Benjamin. Internationaler Benjamin-Kongress 1992*, vol. 1, ed. K. Garber and L. Rehm (Munich: Wilhelm Fink Verlag, 1999), 677f.

23. In an essay that explores the various facets of the concept of the expressionless, and in particular its relation to the sublime, Winfried Menninghaus emphasizes, from the start, the close filiation of the Benjaminian concept to the Jewish prohibition of image worship. Winfried Menninghaus, "Walter Benjamins Metamorphosen der Bilderlosigkeit," in *Für Walter Benjamin*, ed. I. Scheurmann and K. Scheurmann (Frankfurt/Main: Suhrkamp, 1992), 170.

24. Benjamin's essay "Goethe's Elective Affinities" intersects here, as in several other instances, with propositions made in the early essay "Language as Such and on the Language of Man."

25. Presumably a husband (in any case a man) is the author of such a commanding word, but it's not he, but the commanding word itself that thus brings out the truth from the woman. It cannot be the husband or any man, because otherwise the latter would be in the position of representative. Representation, however, as is clear from the essay, belongs to the order of myth. Let us also point out that in a manuscript titled "On 'Semblance,'" related to the passage under discussion, Benjamin refers to "the discourse of a liar (*Rede eines Lügners*)," which the commanding word interrupts in order to bring out the truth. (Benjamin, *Gesammelte Schriften*, vol. 1, 3, 832). In none of the passages reference is made to a husband, or a man.

26. This errant totality is that of nature "as it appears in the symbolic artwork rounded off by aesthetic semblance so as to form a totality in which all details find their justification." Witte, *Walter Benjamin*, 78.

27. Yet that of which Mozart had a premonition is not yet the full material or truth content of the marital relation, according to Benjamin.

28. Although Benjamin is critical of the "totalitarian" character of the mythic, and of the construction of heroic life as a totality, this is always only in the sense of what he terms an "erring totality." Thomas Dörr, who also mistakes this critique for a deconstruction, understanding the latter in a Schlegelian sense as a destruction, does not seem to be aware of the fact that, for Benjamin, totality, in a way similar to Kant, for whom it is a concept of reason, thus not directly intuitable, or presentable, is an unfathomable characteristic of ethical life. Thomas Dörr, *Kritik und Übersetzung. Die Praxis der Reproduktion im Frühwerk Walter Benjamins* (Giessen: Focus Verlag, 1988), 69–70.

29. For a critical account of Benjamin's interpretation of this sentence, see Witte, *Walter Benjamin*, 80–82.

30. Benjamin defines the symbolic as "that in which the indissoluble and necessary bonding of truth content to material content appears" (318). See also page 322.

CHAPTER 4

1. Martin Heidegger, *Nietzsche*, vol. 1, *The Will to Power as Art*, vol. 2, *The Eternal Recurrence of the Same,* trans. D. F. Krell (San Francisco: Harper & Row, 1991).

2. Heidegger, *Nietzsche*, vol. 1, xxxix.

3. Ibid., 4.

4. Jacob Grimm and Wilhelm Grimm, *Deutsches Wörterbuch* (Leipzig: Hirzel, 1854).

5. *Trübner's Deutsches Wörterbuch,* ed. Alfred Goetze (Berlin: de Gruyter, 1939).

6. J. C. A. Heyse, *Handwörterbuch der deutschen Sprache* (1833; repr., Hildesheim: Olms, 1968).

7. Martin Heidegger, 1. *Nietzsches Metaphysik. 2. Einleitung in die Philosophie. Denken und Dichten, Gesamtausgabe,* vol. 50 (Frankfurt/Main: Klostermann 1990), 84.

8. Heidegger, *Nietzsche*, vol. 1, 4–5.

9. Martin Heidegger, *What Is a Thing?* trans W. B. Barton and V. Deutsch (South Bend, IN: Regnery/Gateway, 1967), 119.

10. Martin Heidegger, *Nietzsche: Der Wille zur Macht als Kunst, Gesamtausgabe,* vol. 43 (Frankfurt/Main: Klostermann, 1985), 277, 279.

11. Heidegger, *What Is a Thing?* 119–120.

12. Martin Heidegger, *Introduction to Metaphysics,* trans. G. Fried and R. Polt (New Haven, CT: Yale University Press, 2000), 67.

13. Ibid., 65.

14. Ibid.

15. Ibid., 120.

16. Ibid., 65.

17. Martin Heidegger, *Erläuterungen zu Hölderlins Dichtung, Gesamtausgabe,* vol. 4 (Frankfurt/Main: Klostermann, 1981), 60.

18. Ibid., 196. In Heidegger's analysis in "Language" of Trakl's "A Winter Evening," intimacy becomes determined as the very middle from which the intimate "divides itself cleanly and remains separated." Intimacy here names the middle from which the extremes are held apart (*auseinander*) so that they are at one with each other (*zueinander einig*). Martin Heidegger, *Poetry, Language, Thought,* trans. A. Hofstadter (New York: Harper & Row, 1971), 202–204.

19. Heidegger, *Nietzsche*, vol. 1, xxxix–xl.

20. Heidegger, *Nietzsche, Gesamtausgabe,* vol. 43, 275–276.

21. Martin Heidegger, *Contributions to Philosophy (From Enowning),* trans. P. Emad and K. Maly (Bloomington: Indiana University Press, 1999), 131 (trans. mod.).

22. Heidegger, *Nietzsche,* vol. 1, 4–5. In the addendi to the lecture on "Nietzsche's Metaphysics," from 1941–1942, as well as in the lecture "Introduction into Philosophy. Thinking and Poetry," from 1944–1945, Heidegger conceives of

Auseinandersetzung not only primarily as a confrontation with Nietzsche, but as well as a debate that secures "our thinking: that which is thought-worthy for us" (84). He writes: "'*Auseinandersetzen*': Thinking confronts thinking (*Denken setzt sich mit dem Denken auseinander*). Only thus can one thinking encounter another. Only in this manner is there response (*Entgegnung*). In this manner alone, thinking frees itself from standing against one another in opposition (*aus dem Gegen der Gegnerschaft*)—into the belonging into the same" (87). "In an *Auseinandersetzung* the thought that addresses us and our own thinking bring themselves into a relation of opposition. With this separation (*Auseinandertreten*) the distance perhaps occurs from which an appreciation matures of what constitutes one's own essentiality and the unattainable strength of the encountered thought. Genuine *Auseinandersetzung* does not track down weaknesses and mistakes, it does not criticize, rather it brings historically encountered thinking before our thinking, and into the open of the decision that, as a result of the encounter, becomes inevitable. Therefore, we can think about the historically encountered thought of Nietzsche, as well as of all other thinking, only through *Auseinandersetzung*, through which alone we are included into the fundamental feature (*Grundzug*) of historically encountered thought, in order to respond to it in a historical manner." Heidegger, *1. Nietzsches Metaphysik. 2. Einleitung in die Philosophie. Denken und Dichten, 98.*

23. Heidegger, *Nietzsche, Gesamtausgabe*, vol. 43, 276.

24. Ibid.

25. Heidegger, *Nietzsche*, vol. 1, 5.

26. Heidegger, *Nietzsche, Gesamtausgabe*, vol. 43, 277.

27. Heidegger, *Contributions to Philosophy*, 127.

28. Heidegger, *1. Nietzsches Metaphysik. 2. Einleitung in die Philosophie. Denken und Dichten*, 100.

29. Martin Heidegger, *Vier Seminare* (Frankfurt/Main: Klostermann, 1977), 24.

30. Heidegger, *Contributions to Philosophy*, 124.

31. Heidegger, *Nietzsche, Gesamtausgabe*, vol. 43, 276.

32. Heidegger, *Nietzsche*, vol. 1, 4.

33. Ibid.

34. Heidegger, *Nietzsche, Gesamtausgabe*, vol. 43, 278.

35. Heidegger, *Contributions to Philosophy*, 126 (trans. mod.).

36. Ibid., 130.

37. Ibid., 119.

38. Ibid., 125.

39. Ibid.

40. Ibid., 130.

41. Ibid., 131.

42. Ibid., 123.

43. This is perhaps the point to anticipate a possible objection to the preceding developments. It might be argued that the confrontation between Heidegger and Nietzsche as we have outlined it, would correspond, at best, to Heidegger's treatment of Nietzsche in the lectures on "The Will to Power as Art," whereas in the later lectures, Nietzsche will become restricted to such a degree that it would be truly misleading to still characterize it in terms of an *Auseinandersetzung.* Yet, let us recall that the "Author's Foreword" from 1961 prefaces "all Volumes." Indeed, is not the radically constricted Nietzsche of the later lectures—in which the completion of metaphysics becomes "reduced" to, or "substituted" by technology as the fulfillment of metaphysics, precisely the opponent at its strongest—"unfolded from the innermost depth of his work to what is most extreme about him"—as required by all genuine *Auseinandersetzung?*

44. Heidegger, *Nietzsche, Gesamtausgabe,* vol. 43, 278.

45. Ibid., 277.

46. Ibid.

CHAPTER 5

1. If meaning has a pragmatic aspect, in other words, if it is constructed by way of acts, discursive or not, such construction yields to prescriptive norms and takes place in view of a desired effect. With the acknowledgment of the pragmatic comes, therefore, the practical obligation to critically address the values that regulate performance. Judith Butler's analysis of gender difference is a case in point. Rather than necessary and natural in origin, gender reality is, as Butler has argued, a product of sustained social performance, a cultural artifact, in short. To speak here of "performative" is to suggest that the gendered body is "a dramatic and contingent construction" (139), a "fabrication" (136), rather than the expression of a "preexisting identity by which an act or attribute might be measured" (141). But to call it a performative construction is also to say that the acts, gestures, and enactments through which the illusion of an self-identical gender-core is created are "effected with the strategic aim of maintaining gender within its binary frame" (140). As the result of a "the tacit collective agreement to perform, produce, and sustain discrete and polar genders as cultural fictions" (140), the performative dimension of gender reality exhibits a prescriptive axiomatics whose function, according to Butler, is to regulate sexuality "within the obligatory frame of reproductive heterosexuality" (136). Awareness of the performative nature of the gender distinction brings with it the practical obligation to question and to displace the axiomatics and subvert the finality pursued by it. This finality consists in imposing a binary frame on sexuality. Butler conceives of the performative, in this context of gender construction, as what permits to bring about the dualism required by the hegemonic system of reproductive heterosexuality. It is with this duality that Butler takes issue (and, perhaps, with the performative itself insofar as the latter serves primarily to engender the illusion of a natural binarism). What

she opposes to it is a proliferation of parodic performances through which sex and gender become denaturalized and by which the social constructions of the masculine and the feminine are destabilized again. But by repeating differently the cultural performances in order to subvert the binarism of the gender norms enforced through cultural performance, does one in fact escape what one seeks to revoke? Does one not remain tributary to the performative (at least insofar as it is conceived as fabricating binarism)? Finally, does one thus not even run the risk of neutralizing the performative altogether? Judith Butler, *Gender Trouble: Feminism and the Subversion of Identity* (New York: Routledge, 1990).

2. Jacques Derrida, *Limited Inc* (Evanston, IL: Northwestern University Press, 1988), 69–70 (trans. mod.). All page references in this chapter refer to this edition.

3. Samuel Weber, "Program," in *Glyph. Johns Hopkins Textual Studies*, vol. 1 (Baltimore, MD: Johns Hopkins University Press, 1977), x–xi.

4. These then current misreadings consisted, in particular, in imputing that permanence is the defining characteristic of the written over the oral word; in the massive use of the grid of the absence-presence opposition to construe the meaning of Derridean concepts; in the assumption that with writing or text, deconstruction would argue for the simple absence of intentionality; and so forth. "Limited Inc a b c . . ." counters these assumptions by Searle on pages 50–59.

5. I am referring to the essay "De la subjectivité dans le langage," republished in Émile Benveniste, *Problèmes de linguistique générale* (Paris: Gallimard, 1966), 258–266. Austin's speech act theory is explicitly discussed in the essay from 1963 titled "La philosophie analytique et le langage" (idem, 267–276). The receptivity of French thought for speech act theory may even be retraced back to Jean-Paul Sartre's analyses, in *What Is Literature?* of the speaker's situatedness, being always "en situation."

6. To the extent that "Sarl opposes to ['Signature Event Context'] an argumentation that in fact has been borrowed from it . . . Sarl can be said to have understood *Sec* quite well" (54), Derrida remarks. "'Discourse from/to-*Sec*' or 'it reapplies' [*ça rapplique*]" (47) signals, in "Limited Inc a b c . . . ," this gesture in the "Reply" of borrowing arguments from Derrida's essay in order to criticize it. In the "Afterword: Toward an Ethic of Discussion" that concludes "Limited Inc a b c . . . ," Derrida also notes "that, *sometimes*, *certain* bitter and compulsive enemies of deconstruction stand in a more certain and more vital relationship, even if not theorized, to what is in effect at stake in it than do *certain* avowed 'deconstructionists'" (140).

7. See Chapter 4, "Toward an Ethics of *Auseinandersetzung*."

8. Needless to say, with what I have just shown, the meaning of the reference to the alphabet, and its first three letters, in "Limited Inc a b c . . ." is not exhausted. When Derrida remarks that Searle accuses "Signature Event Context" of certain statements that are not to be found in the essay, the reference to "the *a b c* of reading" (trans. mod.) signifies the elements, or rudiments, of a reading, the

minimal rules of reading, which Searle does not observe but to which the essay itself adheres (87). Indeed, this reference to the alphabet echoes Edmund Husserl's
repeated use of this image and may well serve as a reminder of the elementary
rules and functions of phenomenologically rigorous analysis and thought. See
Ernst Wolfgang Orth, *Edmund Husserls 'Krisis der Europäischen Wissenschaften
und die Transzendentale Phänomenologie* (Darmstadt: Wissenschaftliche Buchgesellschaft, 1999), 144. Noting that in the essay in question, he presupposed "the
knowledge of a certain *a b c* of classical philosophy," Derrida suggests that Searle
does not fully master the rudiments of the profession given that, for example, he
misses the meaning of the term "modification" as signifying "modal determination: the contraction of a substance or an attribute into a mode or a modality"
(100). The *a b c* that Searle has at his disposal (106), would thus be a limited *a b c*,
limited to its first three letters. Speaking of Searle's "narrow definition of writing
as the *transcription* or *representation* of speech" that he brings to his reading of
"Signature Event Context," he is said to "thereby adhere to a certain interpretation of phonetic writing, indeed to the alphabetic model, to the *a b c*'s of logo-
phonocentrism" (79). The "other *a b c*" that is referred to, and that would be
required to get a real debate underway (106), is one that takes responsibility for
the entirety of the presuppositions and implications of metaphysics, or logo-
phonocentricism, and that hence does not limit its responsibility to the first three
letters of the alphabet. Jürgen Habermas' account of the Derrida-Searle debate
flouts the *a b c* of reading even more bluntly than Searle. Holding that Derrida's
essays on Austin and Searle lack transparency, Habermas bases his discussion,
rather than on a reading of Derrida's texts themselves, on Jonathan Culler's summary account, and oriented interpretation (at times in a deManean vein, such as
when he concludes that according to Derrida any interpretation of a text would be
a misinterpretation), of the two essays in his *On Deconstruction.* From Culler's in-
terpretative reading of Derrida's debate of Austin and Searle, Habermas then accuses Derrida of making not very clear (einleuchtende) links, of intending a
relativism of meaning, of claiming that idealization amounts to arbitrary logocentric acts, or of making deliberately paradoxical statements, and so forth. Jürgen
Habermas, *The Philosophical Discourse of Modernity: Twelve Lectures,* trans.
F. Lawrence (Cambridge, MA: MIT Press, 1987), 195–199.

9. Revisiting the Derrida-Searle debate, Stanley Cavell objects to Derrida's discussion of Austin on the grounds that Derrida, who, he claims, has not been sufficiently aware of the philosophical climate of the Anglo-American academic world
from the mid-1940s through the 1950s, does not recognize that with his speech act
theory Austin takes issue with then dominating positivism whose major representative was A. J. Ayer. He writes: "Derrida does nor recognize—or attach particular
significance to—Austin's argumentative move, taking performatives as counter-
examples to a philosophical thesis, as, whatever else, a specific and (then) current

counter to logical positivism, specifically to positivism's notorious claim that utterances other than statements are lacking in a measure of rationality, or say adequation to reality" (50). More generally, Cavell deplores that by centering exclusively on Austin's theory of performatives, Derrida (and Searle) has contributed to impoverishing Austin's philosophy and bringing about "the current near-oblivion into which his name has fallen, except for the work on performatives" (60). Not only that, according to Cavell, the exclusive attention to the theory of performatives causes Derrida to miss "the extent of Austin's differences from the classical and/or academic philosophers with whom Austin, as much as Derrida, is at odds" (48). Derrida's neglect of other Austinian works, such as the latter's theory of excuses to which after all the reference in *How to Do Things with Words* to Euripides' tragedy *Hyppolytus* would gesture, would have caused him to overlook the overall concern of Austin as a thinker with the finitude of human action, the tragic condition of man, and the resulting weariness of all "obtuse and devious profundity" (70). Reassessing Austin's theory of performatives against the backdrop of these philosophical concerns, Cavell interprets the reasons for the infelicity to which, according to Austin, all utterances are prone by way of the limits of what the human as a finite being can possibly bear. Responding to the question of "what it betokens about utterances or action that they suffer, say, imitations," he writes: "It betokens, roughly, that human utterances are essentially vulnerable to insincerity (you may say false consciousness) and that the realization that we may never know whether others are sincere or genuine (I do not exclude the first person) is apt to become unbearable. (We might say that it returns philosophy's attention to the fact that human life is constrained to the life of the mind, such as it is)" (58). The ills that inevitably accompany all human utterances rather than having the "profundity" of structural, and quasi-transcendental laws, as Derrida holds, would thus be anthropological and have their origin in the limits of the human mind alone. Yet, as the "Afterword: Toward an Ethic of Discussion" recalls, when Derrida speaks of law, convention, or the iterability of the mark, it is "beyond all human speech act. Barring any inconsistency, ineptness, or insufficiently rigorous formalization on my part, my statements on this subject should be valid beyond the marks and society called 'human' " (134). Cavell's lack of attention to the structural implications of the infelicities that can always, hence necessarily, befall speech acts—a disregard in the name of the "devastatingly banal" (60) that Austin associates with the ordinary—is evident as well in his discussion of Derrida's description of Austin's postponement of a "general theory." Holding that in "Signature Event Context" Derrida was not aware of the work of Austin beyond *How to Do Things with Words,* Cavell avers that on the two occasions at which Austin refuses to go into the general theory of speech acts, he actually is speaking of not only of two different theories, but two theories he developed elsewhere—a theory of pretending and another of excuses (both of which are featured in Austin's *Philosophical Papers*), and Cavell thus concludes that "when Austin says he is 'excluding' the theories from his discussion, the obvious sense is that they are simply not being rehearsed in this place" (52). However, from what we have seen so far, the "general theory" Derrida contends is being deferred by Austin is a theory that would account for the necessary possibilities that can befall any act of speech as structural possibilities and that therefore have to be taken into account in the very definition of what constitutes an act of speech. Neither of Austin's two theories, however, meets this expectation. Stanley Cavell, *Philosophical Passages: Wittgenstein, Emerson, Austin, Derrida* (Oxford: Blackwell, 1995).

10. Jacques Derrida, *Margins of Philosophy,* trans. A. Bass (Chicago: University of Chicago Press, 1982), 297.

11. Jacques Derrida, "Two Words for Joyce," trans. G. Bennington, in *Post-Structuralist Joyce: Essays from the French*, ed. D. Attridge and D. Ferrer (Cambridge: Cambridge University Press, 1984), 155.

12. What is true of Derrida is true of Jean-François Lyotard as well. Their reference to categories of speech act theory implies a radical recasting of this theory. In "Discussions, or Phrasing 'After Auschwitz,'" (in *The Lyotard Reader*, ed. A. Benjamin [London: Basil Blackwell, 1989]), Lyotard remarks that in his pragmatic observations about "the phrase 'Auschwitz,'" no "'wild,' unquestioning use of certain notions borrowed from pragmatics" is made. "In reality, no *use* at all is being made of them" (371). Pointing out that his phrastic approach implies a displacement of man given that "man" (in the shape of addressor or addressee) is a function of phrase universes, more precisely, an instance in such a universe, he adds that, therefore, his "phrases do not arise from the human sciences, nor from pragmatics in particular" (372).

13. Jacques Derrida, "Avances," in Serge Margel, *Le Tombeau du dieu artisan* (Paris: Minuit, 1995), 19.

14. Jacques Derrida, "Ulysses Gramophone," in *Acts of Reading,* ed. D. Attridge (London: Routledge, 1992), 298.

15. Ibid.

16. Ibid., 302.

17. Jacques Derrida, "Declarations of Independence," *New Political Science* 15 (1986): 9.

18. Derrida, "Ulysses Gramophone," 300–301. See also my "On Responding Responsibly," in *Inventions of Difference: On Jacques Derrida* (Cambridge, MA: Harvard University Press, 1994), 227–250.

19. Derrida, "Declaration of Independence," 10.

20. Derrida, "Avances," 40.

21. Ibid., 29.

22. Jacques Derrida, *Monolingualism of the Other; or, The Prosthesis of Origin*, trans. P. Mensah (Stanford, CA: Stanford University Press, 1998), 67.

23. Derrida, *Monolingualism*, 68.

CHAPTER 6

1. Jacques Derrida, "Some Statements and Truisms about Neologisms, Newisms, Postisms, Parasitisms, and Other Small Seismisms," trans. A. Tomiche, in *States of Theory*, ed. D. Caroll (New York: Columbia University Press, 1990), 71. See also p. 81.

2. Derrida, "Some Statements and Truisms," 81–82.

3. Jonathan Culler, "Resisting Theory," *Cardozo Law Review* 11 (July/August 1990): n. 5–6, 1565.

4. Derrida, "Some Statements and Truisms," 83.

5. Derrida writes: "By the word 'jetty' I will refer . . . to the *force* of that *movement* which is not the *subject, project,* or *object,* not even rejection, but in which takes place any production and any determination, which finds its possibility in the jetty—whether that production or determination be related to the subject, the object, or the rejection." Derrida, "Some Statements and Truisms," 65.

6. Ibid., 79.

7. Ibid., 82.

8. For what follows, it may also be of interest to invoke Callias of Athens' *Grammarian's Tragedy*, also referred to as *grammatike theoria*, that is, as the procession of the letters of the Greek alphabet. See, Athenaeus, *The Deipnosophists*, trans. C. B. Gulick, vol. 4 (New York: G. P. Putnam's Sons, 1930), 531–563, as well as Egert Pöhlmann, "Die ABC-Komödie des Kallias," *Rheinisches Museum für Philologie* 114, (1971): 230–240.

9. Joachim Ritter, "Die Lehre vom Ursprung und Sinn der Theorie bei Aristoteles," in *Metaphysik und Politik. Studien zu Aristoteles and Hegel* (Frankfurt/Main: Suhrkamp, 1977), 18.

10. On Plotinus, see, for instance, Heinz Heimsoeth, *Die sechs grossen Themen der abendländischen Metaphysik und der Ausgang des Mittelalters* (Darmstadt: Wissenschaftliche Buchgesellschaft, 1981), 207; for Hegel, I refer to Werner Beierwaltes, *Identität und Differenz* (Frankfurt: Klostermann, 1980), 171–172.

11. Ritter, "Die Lehre vom Ursprung und Sinn der Theorie bei Aristoteles," 21.

12. Philippe Lacoue-Labarthe and Jean-Luc Nancy, *The Literary Absolute: The Theory of Literature in German Romanticism*, trans. P. Barnard and C. Lester (Albany: State University of New York Press, 1988), 102.

13. Lacoue-Labarthe and Nancy, *The Literary Absolute*, 16.

14. Friedrich Schlegel, *Lucinde and the Fragments*, trans. P. Firchow (Minneapolis: University of Minnesota Press, 1971), 254.

15. In "Vom Wesen der Kritik," Schlegel holds that the first condition of all possible understanding is the contemplation of the whole (*Anschauung des Ganzen*). Friedrich Schlegel, *Kritische Schriften* (Munich: Carl Hanser, 1971), 395.

16. Schlegel, *Lucinde and the Fragments*, 248.

17. In correction from the translation by Peter Firchow in *Lucinde and the Fragments*, who was unaware, it seems, of the fact that "intellektuale Anschauung," is a philosophical *terminus technicus*.

18. Friedrich Schlegel, *Dialogue on Poetry and Literary Aphorisms*, trans. E. Behler and R. Struc (University Park: The Pennsylvania State University Press, 1968), 85.

19. Schlegel, *Lucinde and the Fragments*, 248.

20. Ibid.

21. Friedrich Schlegel, *On the Study of Greek Poetry*, trans. S. Barnett (Albany: State University of New York Press, 2001). All page references in this chapter refer to this edition. Schlegel, *Dialogue on Poetry*, 78.

22. Schlegel, *Dialogue on Poetry*, 102.

23. Ibid., 54. Rather than signaling the critic's arrogance and self-validation, the contention that a theory of poetry must be poetic, and that criticism must espouse literature—an idea the Romantics called "productive criticism"—is a strict consequence of their understanding of theory as a contemplation of the universal in fragmentary shape of an individuality.

24. Even though it is only after 1797, and as Arthur O. Lovejoy has argued, upon reading Schiller's text on "Naive and Sentimental Poetry," that the "interesting" characteristic of modern poetry is made the positive hallmark of Romantic poetry, this essay involved in what would seem to be a rather negative appreciation of modern poetry, already contains the major philosophical presuppositions that will inform Schlegel's thought in the period of the *Athenaeum*, and well beyond, at least up to the *Windischmannschen Vorlesungen* from 1804 and 1806, that is, the core of his writings during what is called early German Romanticism.

25. Schlegel, *Lucinde and the Fragments*, 175.

26. Friedrich Schleiermacher characterizes the contemporary cultured contemners of religion's "rage for calculating and explaining [*Verstehen*]," as an operation of dissecting into pieces and anatomizing (*zerstückeln und anatomieren*)," which suppresses sense. He writes: "They seek to grasp nothing in and for itself, but only in special aspects, and therefore, not as a whole, but only piecemeal. To inquire or thoroughly examine whether the object they would understand is a whole, would lead them too far. . . . But all must be used for some excellent purpose, wherefore they dissever and anatomize. This is how they deal with what exists chiefly for the highest satisfaction of the sense, with what, in their despite, is a whole in itself, I mean with all that is art in nature and in the works of man. Before it can operate they annihilate it by explaining it in detail. Having first by decomposition robbed it of its character as art, they would teach and impress this or that lesson from the fragments." Friedrich Schleiermacher, *On Religion: Speeches to its Cultured Despisers*, trans. J. Oman (Louisville, KY: Westminster/John Knox Press, 1994), 124, 128.

27. August Wilhelm Schlegel, *Vorlesungen über dramatische Kunst*, vol. 1 (Stuttgart: Kohlhammer, 1966), 93.

28. Friedrich Schiller, *On the Aesthetic Education of Man in a Series of Letters*, trans. R. Snell (New York: Frederick Ungar, 1965), 107.

29. Ibid., 135.

30. Friedrich Wilhelm Joseph Schelling, *The Philosophy of Art*, trans. D. W. Stott (Minneapolis: University of Minnesota Press, 1989), 291, note 8.

31. I borrow the expression "aporetic intensity" from Edward Booth, *Aristotelian Aporetic Ontology in Islamic and Christian Thinkers* (Cambridge: Cambridge University Press, 1983), 26.

32. For a detailed discussion of Paul de Man's theory of reading and how it is to be demarcated from what Derrida calls reading, see Rodolphe Gasché, *The Wild Card of Reading: On Paul de Man* (Cambridge, MA: Harvard University Press, 1998).

33. Paul de Man, *The Resistance to Theory* (Minneapolis: University of Minnesota Press, 1986), 10. When de Man claims that it is "not *a priori* certain that literature is a reliable source of information about anything but its own language" (11), it is clear that knowledge about language itself is possible, and that even if it is negative knowledge, it is a priori certain knowledge.

34. Georg Wilhelm Friedrich Hegel, *Phenomenology of Spirit*, trans. A.V. Miller (Oxford: Oxford University Press, 1979), 467–468.

35. Schelling, *The Philosophy of Art*, 40.

36. De Man refers to what I call "individuality" here—namely the sensible representation of an idea (or ideal), which, as far as the realm of art (and history) is concerned, presupposes a possible interaction between the so different worlds of the intelligible and the sensible—under the titles of the "phenomenal" or "aesthetic." I address de Man's critique of the supposedly Cratylist underpinnings of aesthetics, in short, the understanding of aesthetics as ideology, in *The Wild Card of Reading*, 124–146.

37. Aristotle, *The Complete Works*, vol. 2, ed. Jonathan Barnes (Princeton, NJ: Princeton University Press, 1985), 1555.

38. Some readers of de Man have already suggested a possible relationship between his work and negative theology. Richard Rorty, for instance, on the sole basis of de Man's claim that language, in literary or poetic language, functions according to different principles than those of the phenomenal world, concludes that reading such a language, one that provides information only about itself, is worshipping a "Dark God," "a way of mourning a *Deus absconditus,* of participating in a divine absence." Richard Rorty, *Essays on Heidegger and Others: Philosophical Papers*, vol. 2 (Cambridge: Cambridge University Press, 1991), 114–115. See also 116, 117.

39. Georg Lukacs, *Soul and Form*, trans. A. Bostock (Cambridge, MA: MIT Press, 1978), 15 (trans. mod.).

CHAPTER 7

1. René Wellek, *Concepts of Criticism* (New Haven, CT: Yale University Press, 1963), 282.

2. René Wellek, *Discriminations: Further Concepts of Criticism* (New Haven, CT: Yale University Press, 1971), 17.

3. René Wellek and Austin Warren, *Theory of Literature* (New York: Harcourt, Brace, 1956), 50.

4. J. Hillis Miller, "Presidential Address 1986: The Triumph of Theory, the Resistance to Reading, and the Question of the Material Base," *PMLA* 102, no. 3 (1987): 281–291.

5. Georg Wilhelm Friedrich Hegel, *Aesthetics: Lectures on Fine Art*, vol. 1, trans. T. M. Knox (Oxford: Clarendon Press, 1975), 378. All page references in this chapter refer to this edition.

6. Walter Benjamin, "The Concept of Criticism in German Romanticism," in *Selected Writings: Volume 1, 1913–1926*, ed. M. Bullock and M. W. Jennings (Cambridge, MA: Harvard University Press), 1996.

7. Ulrich Weisstein, *Einführung in die Vergleichende Literaturwissenschaft* (Stuttgart: Kohlhammer, 1968), 36.

8. Friedrich Schlegel, *Lessings Geist aus seinen Schriften,* quoted in Wellek, *Discriminations*, 29.

9. Wellek, *Discriminations*, 29.

10. Wilhelm Dilthey, *Der Aufbau der geschichtlichen Welt in den Geisteswissenschaften, Gesammelte Schriften* (Leipzig and Berlin: Teubner, 1927), vol. VII, 130; Karl Reinhardt, *Vermächtnis der Antike,* 2nd ed. (Göttingen: Vandenhoeck & Ruprecht, 1966), 439–441.

11. Nelly Tsouyopoulos, "Die Entdeckung der Struktur komparativer Begriffe in der Antike," *Archiv für Begriffsgeschichte* 14, no. 2 (1975): 153.

12. Ernst Robert Curtius, *European Literature and the Latin Middle Ages*, trans. W. R. Trask (Princeton, NJ: Princeton University Press, 1978), 15–16.

13. Georg Wilhelm Friedrich Hegel, *Philosophy of Right*, trans. T. M. Knox (Oxford: Clarendon Press, 1985), 29.

14. August Wilhelm Schlegel, *Vorlesungen über dramatische Kunst und Literatur*, vol. 1 (Stuttgart: Kohlhammer, 1966), 17.

15. Ibid., 21.

16. Ibid., 19.

17. Ibid., 18.

18. Friedrich Schlegel, *Literary Notebooks 1797–1801*, ed. Hans Eichner (Berlin: Ullstein, 1980), 111.

19. Ibid., 124.

20. Ibid., 111.

21. Ibid., 177.

22. Alfred Baeumler, *Das Irrationalitätsproblem in der Aesthetik und Logik des 18. Jahrhunderts* (Darmstadt: Wissenschaftliche Buchgesellschaft, 1981), 139–140.

23. Ibid., 296.

24. Georg Wilhelm Friedrich Hegel, *Science of Logic*, 2 vols., trans. A. V. Miller (New York: Humanities Press, 1969), 420.

25. Edmund Husserl, *Logical Investigations*, 2 vols., trans. J. N. Findlay (New York: Humanities Press, 1982), 343.

26. Only because the Romantic idea of a comparative study of poetry and the arts has been universalist in thrust was it conceivable at all that Friedrich Schlegel could devote himself to a study of the non-European spiritual culture of India. *In principle*, the universal allows for a relation with the Other, even with what is inassimilable.

27. Martin Heidegger, *Einleitung in die Philosophie. Denken und Dichten, Gesamtausgabe*, vol. 50 (Frankfurt/Main: Klostermann, 1990), 137.

28. Ibid., 138.

CHAPTER 8

1. Hans Blumenberg, "Light as Metaphor for Truth: At a Preliminary Stage of Philosophical Concept Formation," in *Modernity and the Hegemony of Vision*, ed. D. M. Levin (Berkeley: University of California Press, 1933), 53–54.

2. Michel Foucault, "Theatrum Philosophicum" *Critique* 282 (November 1970): 908.

3. In this context, see Derrida's critique of the idea that metaphysics can be unseated through a reversal of Platonism, in *Spurs: Nietzsche's Styles,* trans. B. Harlow (Chicago: University of Chicago Press, 1979). For his own account of how theater combines with philosophical thought, I refer to "Plato's Pharmacy," in *Dissemination*, trans. B. Johnson (Chicago: University of Chicago Press, 1981). See also my analysis of that relation in the chapter devoted to Derrida's concept of reading in *The Wild Card of Reading: On Paul de Man* (Cambridge, MA: Harvard University Press, 1998), 149–180.

4. Hans Blumenberg, *Das Lachen der Thrakerin. Eine Urgeschichte der Theorie* (Frankfurt/Main: Suhrkamp, 1987). All page references in this chapter refer to this edition. A first version of this text appeared under the title "Der Sturz des Protophilosophen—Zur Komik der reinen Theorie, anhand einer Rezeptionsgeschichte der Thales-Anekdote," in *Das Komische. Poetik und Hermeneutik VII* (Munich: Fink, 1976), 11–64. The present context does not permit a comparison of the two versions.

5. Hans Blumenberg, *Begriffe in Geschichten* (Frankfurt/Main: Suhrkamp, 1998), 193.

6. As indicated in the latest version of the Thales anecdote in Jacques Taminiaux, *The Thracian Maid and the Professional Thinker: Arendt and Heidegger*, trans.

M. Gendre (Albany: State University of New York Press, 1998), even with Heidegger, the potential of the anecdote has not been exhausted. In Taminiaux's study of Heidegger's discussion of the Aristotelian notions of *phronesis* and *praxis*—in which he argues, pitting Aristotle against Plato, that Heidegger, in total disregard of these notions' embeddedness in a practical philosophy, reinterprets them to fit Plato's conception of the *bios theoretikos*—Hannah Arendt is shown to oppose these Heideggerian moves in the name of a thinking that originates in Aristotle's notion of the *bios politikos*, and whose understanding of theory is not alienated from the human beings' practical concerns. Arendt, Taminiaux asserts, laughs with the laughter of the Thracian maid at the philosopher's theoretical and political fallacies. He writes: "The professional philosopher, toward whom Arendt's dismissive attitude is directed following the Thracian maid's mocking of Thales, is the individual who by devoting himself totally to the thinking activity has elevated this human aptitude—which is only one among others—to the rank of absolute" (132–133).

7. Plato, *The Collected Dialogues,* ed. E. Hamilton and H. Cairns (Princeton, NJ: Princeton University Press, 1980), 879 (174 a–b).

8. Ibid., 1174–1175 (47 a–d).

9. Ibid., 879 (174 b–c).

10. As thus becomes clear, with the anecdote about Thales and the Thracian maid, Plato not only inscribes the position of anti-theory into theory itself, but anti-theory is a strictly philosophical position, intelligible only in view of what theory aims at, and hence it is a moment within theory itself. It is appropriate, therefore, that several of the variations of the anecdote, in particular the latest one by Taminiaux, can make of the Thracian maid the true philosopher.

11. Barbara Herrnstein Smith, *Belief and Resistance: Dynamics of Contemporary Intellectual Controversy* (Cambridge, MA: Harvard University Press, 1997), 80.

12. Plato, *The Collected Dialogues*, 850 (145 b–c).

13. Henry George Liddell and Robert Scott, *A Greek-English Dictionary* (Oxford: Oxford University Press, 1978), 1613.

14. Hans-Georg Gadamer, "In Praise of Theory," trans. D. J. Schmidt and J. Steinwand, in *Ellipsis* 1, no. 1 (Spring 1990): 96 (trans. mod.).

15. That *theoria* is contemplation of the divine is even more obvious with Aristotle. See Hannelore Rausch, *Theoria: Von ihrer sakralen zur philosophischen Bedeutung* (Munich: Fink Verlag, 1982), 11–12, 143ff.

16. Ibid., 12–14.

17. Ibid., 37.

18. Wlad Godzich evokes the Greek institution of the *theoroi* to argue that from the start, theory, for the Greeks, is a public and not a private act carried out by a lone cogitating philosopher. *The Culture of Literacy* (Cambridge, MA: Harvard University Press, 1994), 165.

19. Rausch, *Theoria*, 34.

20. Ibid., 17.

21. Ibid., 34.

22. Karl Kerényi, *The Religion of the Greeks and Romans*, trans. C. Holme (New York: Dutton, 1962), 153.

23. Ibid., 144. For what follows, it is not insignificant to note that Kerényi understands the being-seen that is intimately tied up to seeing as a being-known. He writes: "In the Greek sense Existence is seeing and being-seen, or more exactly, knowing and being-known, or most exactly at all, being and being-known" (150).

24. Rausch, *Theoria*, 180.

25. Taminiaux, *The Thracian Maid*, 105.

26. Ibid., 95. However suggestive, the gesture by which Aristotle becomes squarely opposed to Plato is highly problematic. Plato's philosophy is not exclusively a celebration of the *bios theoretikos*. After having exited from the cave, and contemplated the light, the philosopher returns intent on freeing the inhabitants of the cave from the fetters of darkness. It is certainly the case that Aristotle was the first to have recognized the domain of the practical in its own right, but this does not mean at all that *theoria* has become secondary. *Sophia* is inextricably connected to *phronesis*. "One is certainly wrong," as Gadamer has remarked, "when one denigrates the priority that . . . [Aristotle] did grant the theoretical life by describing it as his platonic inheritance. Quite the contrary, Aristotle was the first to establish the independence of the practical-political question of the good from its older form which was theoretically oriented to cosmology. He opened his investigation into human praxis, the *Ethics*, with the compact sentence: 'All striving in knowledge and deeds and choices aims at the good.' But it is just as obvious to him that theoretical interest does not need a legitimation either, and that it animates every human being." Gadamer, "In Praise of Theory," 88; see also 98. If *phronesis* depends on *sophia* and *theoria* in Aristotle, knowledge of the good remains the final standard of practical life. From what we have seen about the Greek notion of *theoria* and the inseparable connection of knowing and seeing that this notion implies, it follows that what is seen, and thus known, is always seen as form, figure, or shape. For this reason, the known is, to quote Kerényi, "as actual and consequently as certain, indeed, as efficacious, as anything which is immediately and clearly seen." Kerényi, *The Religion of the Greeks and Romans*, 145. Yet, for the Greeks, as Kerényi has recalled, moral or practical ideas, such as justice and honor, are no exception in this regard. Rather than being experienced affectively, they are understood as steady forms, or figures of being, hence as objective realities, as it were, that, as such, inevitably invite the look of *theoria*, of a seeing that beholds them, precisely, in this actuality that is theirs. In other words, conceived as forms—forms to which they owe their actuality—moral ideas require theoretical knowledge (147). (The German original is considerably more precise

than the English translation. See Karl Kerényi, *Die Antike Religion: Ein Entwurf von Grundlinien* [Düsseldorf: Eugen Diederichs Verlag. 1952], 108–109.)

27. Taminiaux, *The Thracian Maid*, 98, 91.

28. Blumenberg, "Light as a Metaphor for Truth," 34.

29. Richard Alewyn and Karl Sälzle, *Das grosse Welttheater. Die Epoche der höfischen Feste* (Hamburg: Rowohlt, 1959), 21–22. Except for the backstage, the theater stage in the Middle Ages was surrounded on all sides by the public. Alewyn writes: "Only the theater stage of the Renaissance withdraws from the public and now faces the auditorium breadthwise and with little depth, like a line. The more the baroque period unfolds, the more the depth of the stage increases, with the effect that the relations become reversed. The convex stage of the Middle Ages is replaced by the concave stage of the baroque, a funnel widely open that sucks the spectators into its depth" (59).

30. Plato, *The Collected Dialogues*, 878 (172 c–d).

31. Ibid., 879 (173 c).

32. Ibid., 878 (172 c–d).

33. Ibid., 879 (173 d).

34. Ibid., 879 (174 c).

35. Ibid., 879 (173 e).

36. Ibid., 880 (174 e).

37. Ibid., 881 (176 b).

38. Blumenberg, "Light as Metaphor for Truth," 54.

CHAPTER 9

1. Eugen Fink, *Studien zur Phänomenologie 1930–1939* (Den Haag: Martinus Nijhoff, 1966), 194. As Pierre Thévenaz remarks, rather than "*archaeology* which is the science of antiquity," Husserl "could well have availed himself of the neologism *archology.*" Pierre Thévenaz, *What is Phenomenology? and Other Essays*, trans. J. M. Edie et al. (Chicago: Quadrangle Books, 1962), 180.

2. Fink, *Studien zur Phänomenologie 1930–1939*, 195; Tadashi Ogawa, *Grund und Grenze des Bewusstseins. Interkulturelle Phänomenologie aus japanischer Sicht* (Würzburg: Königshausen & Neumann, 2001), 125.

3. "Dass unter diesem Titel eine Wissenschaft notwendig sei, die als eine wahrhaft so zu nennende 'Archäologie' jenes Letztursprüngliche und alle Ursprünge des Seins und der Wahrheit in sich Beschliessende systematisch erforschen und in weiterer Folge uns lehren soll, wie aus dieser Urquelle aller Meinungen und Geltungen jedwede Erkenntnis in die höchste und letzte Vernunftform gebracht werden kann." Edmund Husserl, *Erste Philosophie (1923–24)*, part 2, HUA, vol. 8 (Den Haag: Martinus Nijhoff, 1959), 29–30. An as yet unpublished manuscript (C 16 VI) is titled "Phänomenologische Archäologie. Rückfrage auf das Ich. . . ." I thank Rudolf Bernet for this reference.

4. Husserl, *Erste Philosophie (1923–24)*, 28.

5. Michel Foucault, "Monstrosities in Criticism," *Diacritics* 1, no. 1 (Fall 1971): 60. I would like to thank Bernhard Dotzler for the reference to this debate.

6. *Kant's gesammelte Schriften,* ed. Preussische Akademien der Wissenschaften, vol. 20 (Berlin: Walter de Gruyter, 1942), 341.

7. Ibid., 343.

8. Ibid., 344. Françoise Proust prefaces her discussion of Kant's reference to a philosophical archaeology in her work, *Kant. Le ton de l'histoire* (Paris: Payot, 1991), with the observation that with Kant "a period poses for the first time the question of what it is, of its actuality, and no longer of its position with respect to a past (a tradition), or its place with regard to a hoped for future (of the stages that are still to be met after it). The question that it poses concerns its present, and the meaning of its present experiences" (308). The transcendental thrust of Kant's philosophical archaeology, characterized by a "diagnosing and prognosing" inquiry, is consequently limited to the exhibition of possibilities that concern the present alone. Proust's deep indebtedness to the work of Foucault is evident in the following lines: "Archaeology does not seek to exhume under the continent of the present (or the present continent) a hidden continent that has disappeared, or forgotten *archaisms* that would need to be brought back to the surface in order to account for them, to explicate or, at least, to understand them. The transcendental, the *archae*, is not a ground or foundation. It is the condition of possibility, that is, that which makes something possible; what provides something with its condition and its nature as a possible nature; what makes it rise and raised as something possible. The archaeologist ferrets and noses out. He is in quest . . . of possibles, traces of the possible, of possible traces, yet not of those possibles that have sunk themselves into the real, that have 'realized' themselves, but possibles that were only possible (that 'could be,' 'could have been,' 'are on the verge of,' 'are in the process of germinating,' 'are still born'), or are only traces. For the trace signifies that a possible not only cannot become lost, but can only come and return, eternally under the form of an other possible. Every past possible is a *possible* present, a possible *present*" (312).

9. *Kant's Gesammelte Schriften*, 342.

10. Ibid., 343.

11. Ibid., 341.

12. Maurice Blanchot, *Michel Foucault tel que je l'imagine* (Paris: Fata morgana, 1986), 26.

13. Michel Foucault, *The Archaeology of Knowledge & The Discourse on Language*, trans. A. M. Sheridan Smith (New York: Pantheon Books, 1972) (hereafter cited in text as *AK*).

14. As Bernhard Waldenfels has noted in the chapter of his *Phänomenologie in Frankreich* devoted to Foucault's debate with phenomenology, Maurice Merleau-Ponty's version of phenomenology has been instrumental to Foucault's reception

of phenomenology. Bernhard Waldenfels, *Phänomenologie in Frankreich* (Frank-furt/Main: Suhrkamp, 1983), 523ff. For a more extensive analysis of Foucault's in-debtedness to Merleau-Ponty, see Leonard Lawlor, *Thinking Through French Philosophy. The Being of the Question* (Bloomington: Indiana University Press, 2003), 24–46.

15. Michel Foucault, "On the Archaeology of the Sciences: Response to the Epistemology Circle," in *Aesthetics, Method, and Epistemology: Essential Works of Michel Foucault, 1954–1984*, vol. 2, ed. James D. Faubion, trans. R. Hurley (New York: The New Press, 1998), 309–310.

16. Jacques Derrida, *Archive Fever: A Freudian Impression*, trans. E. Prenowitz (Chicago: University of Chicago Press, 1996), 1.

17. Michel Foucault, "Michel Foucault explique son dernier livre," in *Dits et écrits 1954–1988*, vol. 1 (Paris: Gallimard, 1994), 772.

18. Ibid.

19. In Charles Péguy's *Clio*, also subtitled, "Dialogue between History and the Pagan Soul," History remarks about one of the jokes that she cracked that "all her jokes are always very witty. This is at least what everybody always tells me. Because the joke is archaeological, naturally, like everything I am doing. In general when I crack a joke everybody admits that it is very funny, because I hold many chairs in the University of the Government." Charles Péguy, *Clio* (Paris: Gallimard, 1932), 10.

20. Claude Lévi-Strauss, *The Savage Mind*, trans. G. Weidenfeld and Nichol-son Ltd. (Chicago: University of Chicago Press, 1966), 242 (trans. mod.).

21. Gilles Deleuze, *Foucault*, trans. Sean Hand (Minneapolis: University of Minnesota Press, 1988), 18. See also Blanchot, *Michel Foucault tel que je l'imagine*, 46–47, on the fictional nature of his writings.

22. The whole passage from Claude Lévi-Strauss that I referred to in endnote 20, runs as follows: "On the one hand [archives] constitute events in their radical contingence (since only interpretation, which forms no part of them, can ground them in reason), and, on the other, they give a physical existence to history, for in them alone is contradiction of a completed past and a present in which it survives, surmounted. Archives are the embodiment of eventhood."

23. Richard Rorty, "Foucault and Epistemology," in *Foucault: A Critical Reader*, ed. D. C. Hoy (Oxford: Basil Blackwell, 1986), 43.

24. What Foucault calls *episteme*, rather than a form of cognition or a kind of rationality, represents the whole of the relations that at one given historical junc-ture unite the discursive practices against whose backdrop epistemological figures, the sciences, and formalized systems emerge. The *episteme* "is what, in the positiv-ity of discursive practices, makes possible the existence of epistemological figures and sciences" (*AK*, 192).

25. Ludwig Landgrebe, *The Phenomenology of Edmund Husserl*, trans. D. Wel-ton (Ithaca, NY: Cornell University Press, 1981), 52, 56.

26. Ibid., 60.

27. Jacques Derrida, "Eugen Fink, *Studien zur Phänomenologie, 1930–1939*, La Haye, 'Phenomenologica,' (21), M. Nijhof, 223 p.," in *Les études philosophiques*, 4 (1966), 549–550.

28. Jacques Derrida, *The Archeology of the Frivolous: Reading Condillac*, trans. John P. Leavey, Jr. (Pittsburgh, PA: Duquesne University, 1980) (hereafter cited in text as *AF*). In several instances, the translation has been modified.

29. Etienne Bonnot De Condillac, *Essay on the Origin of Human Knowledge*, trans. and ed. Hans Aarsleff (Cambridge: Cambridge University Press, 2001).

30. Ibid., 5 (trans. mod.).

31. Ibid., 15–16.

32. Ibid., 216.

33. Ibid., 209–210.

34. Ibid., 202 (trans. mod.).

35. Jacques Derrida, *Edmund Husserl's Origin of Geometry: An Introduction*, trans. John P. Leavey, Jr. (Boulder, CO: Nicolas Hays, 1978), 50 (trans. mod.).

36. Condillac, *Essay on the Origin of Human Knowledge*, 5 (trans. mod.).

37. Michel Foucault, *The Birth of the Clinic: An Archeology of Medical Perception*, trans. A. M. Sheridan Smith (New York: Random House, 1973), 92 (trans. mod.).

38. Ibid., 116 (trans. mod.).

39. Ibid., 117.

40. Derrida's elaborations in *Of Grammatology* on "the catastrophic form of archaeology," already anticipate his archaeological interpretation of the frivolous. Jacques Derrida, *Of Grammatology*, trans. G. C. Spivak (Baltimore, MD: Johns Hopkins University Press, 1974), 257.

41. Jacques Derrida, *Speech and Phenomena and Other Essays on Husserl's Theory of Signs*, trans. David B. Allison (Evanston, IL: Northwestern University Press, 1973), 6.

42. Condillac, *Essay on the Origin of Human Knowledge*, 6.

43. Citing Condillac, Derrida writes that "the confused ideas that regulate our actions, the prelinguistic and presemiotic judgments, and mute analysis 'make us act'" (97). The activating quality of the language of action that precedes the language of signs can be compared to the meaning of any of the expressions analyzed in *Speech and Phenomena*, which meaning attests to the presence of the non-expressive in expression itself.

44. The conditions of meaning are essentially the same as those of the loss of meaning. In the chapter of the *Essay* dealing with the genius of languages, Condillac writes, "Now that I have shown the causes of the ultimate progress of language, it is relevant to look into the causes of its decline; they are the same" (193). Indeed, the man of genius advances language by inventing "new expressions within the rules of analogy or with as little deviation from those rules as possible" (190). But this deviation is also that which sets into motion the ruin of a language. And Derrida adds, "The archeology of the frivolous is this deviation of genius" (68).

45. Edmund Husserl, *Die Krisis der Europäischen Wissenschaften und die Transzendentale Phänomenologie*, Husserliana, vol. 6 (Den Haag: Martinus Nijhoff, 1962), 360, 393.

46. Friedrich A. Kittler, "Thermodynamic und Guerilla. Zur Methode von Michel Foucaults Archäologie des Wissens," *Trajekte* 2, no. 4 (April 2002): 16–21.

47. Foucault entirely dismisses the difference between the empirical and the transcendental, and with it ultimately the difference that thinking makes when he suggests that any "search for the origin, for formal *a prioris*, for founding acts . . . never discovers more than a series of empirical facts" (*AK*, 203–204).

CHAPTER 10

1. Gilles Deleuze, *Nietzsche and Philosophy*, trans. H. Tomlinson (New York: Columbia University Press, 1983) (hereafter cited in text as *NP*).

2. Gilles Deleuze, *Proust and Signs*, trans. R. Howard (London: Athlone Press, 2000) (hereafter cited in text as *PS*).

3. Gilles Deleuze, *Difference and Repetition*, trans. P. Patton (New York: Columbia University Press, 1994) (hereafter cited in text as *DR*).

4. See Paola Marrati, *Gilles Deleuze. Cinema et philosophie* (Paris: Presses Universitaires de France, 2003), 11, 121–122.

5. Gilles Deleuze and Félix Guattari, *What Is Philosophy?* trans. H. Tomlinson and G. Burchell (New York: Columbia University Press, 1994), 37.

6. But what about the fact that, in *What Is Philosophy?* Deleuze and Guattari juxtapose a philosophy no longer viewed capable of freeing itself from the image of thought (lest it ceases to be philosophy?) to the sciences, and the arts, all of which are definitely equivalent and definitely (violently) creative undertakings? Apart from thus depriving philosophy of the privilege and priority that it enjoyed in the earlier works, does this not also suggest that the standpoint from which these three types of discourses and practices are analyzed is no longer that of philosophy, but rather of a kind of thinking that itself, consequently, is no longer subject to any image whatsoever?

7. See also in this context the reference, in *Difference and Repetition*, to Michel Foucault's conception of "the classical world of representation," which Deleuze aligns with "the four iron collars of representation" discussed in the chapter "The Image of Thought" (*DR*, 262).

8. Plato himself is partially excepted from Platonismus. Even though "Platonism already represents the subordination of difference to the powers of the One, the Analogous, the Similar and even the Negative," and difference is here "like an animal in the process of being tamed, whose final resistant movements bear witness better than they would in a state of freedom to the nature soon to be lost: The Heraclitean world still growls in Platonism." Deleuze consistently rejects

reading Plato on the basis of Aristotle's critique of Plato and in line with Aristotelean requirements (*DR*, 59).

9. Deleuze and Guattari, *What Is Philosophy?* 82.

10. Ibid., 54–55.

11. Immanuel Kant, *Critique of Judgement*, trans. J. H. Bernard (New York: Hafner Press, 1951), 115.

12. In the final chapter of *Difference and Repetition*, Deleuze discusses in great detail the four transcendental illusions in question, all of which are said to "distort" the nature of difference and repetition (*DR*, 265–270).

13. As we will see later in this chapter, such denaturalization is intimately linked to raising empirical givens to the level of the transcendental, or infecting the empirical with the transcendental, in short, by confusing levels of thought.

14. As Marrati has argued, in his reevaluation of the image in the works on cinema, Deleuze approaches the image in a way that is different from Heidegger's conception according to which the image rests on the representation by a subject. Marrati, *Gilles Deleuze*, 38–40.

15. Martin Heidegger, "The Age of the World Picture," in *The Question Concerning Technology and Other Essays*, trans. W. Lovitt (New York: Harper & Row, 1977), 129–130.

16. Ibid.

17. One could easily argue that in the chapter "The Image of Thought," from *Difference and Repetition*, Deleuze seeks to make good on what, Descartes and Kant, in particular, sought to accomplish, namely, to begin from the ground up. But that also means to transcend the business of cognition, which, as Deleuze argues, prevents (to the extent that cognition is re-cognition, and hence tributary to the more general problematic of representation) such a beginning in the first place.

18. Since Deleuze's credits Plato for having kept alive, by remaining mindful of the pre-Socratics' insights, what he calls in reference to Antonin Artaud "a generalized thought process which can no longer be covered by the reassuring dogmatic image" (*DR*, 147), while being also "the first to erect the dogmatic and moralizing image of thought which neutralizes the text and allows it to function only as a 'repentance'" (*DR*, 142), a comparison of his reading of Plato with that of Derrida in "Plato's Pharmacy," would be warranted. Although Deleuze also admits that the structures of the image of thought are only "effects" produced by the presentation of difference, "rather than being conditions that subordinate difference and make it something represented" (*DR*, 145), he has also a tendency, when it comes to determining something (thought, for instance), to do exactly what he reproaches Plato for, namely to determine it "in terms of separate contraries (*contraire separé*)" (*DR*, 142). He thus opposes the "new vision of the *Republic*" to the other dialogues, in particular to the *Theaetetus*, even though the

vision in question is also compromised in the *Republic* by the "*Theaetetus* model [that] continues to act in a subterranean manner." As I have argued in an analysis of "Plato's Pharmacy," for Derrida, the disseminating structures of thought are inseparably tied to those structures of thought that seek to master dissemination. One cannot have one without the other. See my analysis in "Giving to Read," in *The Wild Card of Reading. On Paul de Man* (Cambridge, MA: Harvard University Press, 1998), 149–180.

19. Deleuze and Guattari's treatment of Husserl in *What Is Philosophy?* still echoes this denunciation of all mixing. Indeed, Husserl's notion of an *Urdoxa* is for both authors an instance, precisely, of a confusion of levels. Let me also note that the fact that *Difference and Repetition* makes frequent recourse to literary examples does in no way suggest a mixing of two genres, philosophy and literature. Literature is enlisted only where it brings the philosophical points home more poignantly than philosophy itself.

20. Let me also point out a third sense of representation, according to which a representation is the mathematical expression of something. Leibniz's conception of the monad's *repraesentatio mundi* is to be understood in this sense.

21. Gilles Deleuze, *Empiricism and Subjectivity: An Essay on Hume's Theory of Human Nature*, trans. C. V. Boundas (New York: Columbia University Press, 1991), 30. As this concern with mixing levels of thought demonstrates, Deleuze's critique of representation remains consistent from this early work on to at least *Difference and Repetition*.

22. Ibid., 121.

23. For an excellent treatment of singularity in Deleuze, see François Zourabichvili, *Deleuze: Une philosophie de l'événement* (Paris: Presses Universitaires de France, 1994).

24. This statement occurs in the context of a discussion of the distorting interpretation of power as the object of a representation. Deleuze writes: "The mania for representing, for being represented, for getting oneself represented; for having representatives and representeds; this is the mania that is common to all slaves, the only relation between themselves they can conceive of, the relation that they impose with their triumph. The notion of representation poisons philosophy: it is the direct product of the slave and of the relations between slaves, it constitutes the worst, most mediocre and most base interpretation of power" (*NP*, 81).

25. Deleuze, *Empiricism and Subjectivity*, 90. In *Bergsonism*, the "superior empiricism" is construed as an empiricism "capable of stating problems and of going beyond experience toward concrete conditions." These are none other than "the difference in kind," or what Bergson termed, "différences de nature." Gilles Deleuze, *Bergsonism*, trans. H. Tomlinson and B. Habberjam (New York: Zone Books, 1991), 30.

26. *Difference and Repetition* echoes this concern with pluralism when Deleuze opposes multiplicity to the metaphysical dyad of the One and the multiple.

27. If Deleuze takes issue with the whole of the history of philosophy, it is, first and foremost, because philosophy never made good on the necessity to radically break with *doxa* (except for very few attempts, such as, for example, those of Spinoza and Nietzsche).

28. For Deleuze's critique of the Husserlian notion of *Urdoxa*, see, for instance, the following passage where, after having accused Kant of multiplying rather than overcoming common sense, he writes: "Must not the same be said of phenomenology? Does it not discover a fourth common sense, this time grounded upon sensibility as a passive synthesis—one which, even though it constitutes an *Urdoxa*, remains no less prisoner of the form of *doxa?*" (*DR*, 137).

29. Ute Guzzoni, "Das Erstaunliche und die Philosophie," in *Information Philosophie* 2 (2001): 10.

30. Gilles Deleuze, *Différence et Répétition* (Paris: Presses Universitaires de France, 1968), 188.

31. Plato, *The Collected Dialogues*, ed. E. Hamilton and H. Cairns (Princeton, NJ: Princeton University Press, 1980), 766 (523b–c).

32. Julia Annas, *An Introduction to Plato's Republic* (Oxford: Clarendon Press, 1981), 218.

33. In this context, let us also mention that, by linking the philosophical to the extraordinary, Deleuze subscribes to the paradigm *episteme/doxa* without questioning it. For the linkage of the extraordinary to this paradigm, see Bernhard Waldenfels, *In den Netzen der Lebenswelt* (Frankfurt/Main: Suhrkamp, 1994), 35–38. It may be appropriate to note here that, in *Introduction of Metaphysics*, Martin Heidegger, after having quoted Nietzsche's statement that "A philosopher . . . is a human being who constantly experiences, sees, hears, suspects, hopes, dreams extraordinary things," holds that "philosophizing . . . is extraordinary questioning about the extraordinary." Martin Heidegger, *Introduction to Metaphysics*, trans. G. Fried and R. Polt (New Haven, CT: Yale University Press, 2000), 13–14.

34. Eugen Fink, *Studien zur Phänomenologie 1930–1939* (Den Haag: Martinus Nijhoff, 1966), 183.

35. Edmund Husserl, *The Crisis of European Sciences and Transcendental Phenomenology*, trans. D. Carr (Evanston, IL: Northwestern University Press, 1970), 285.

36. Furthermore, in distinction from most of the tradition that has viewed *doxa* as a preform of philosophy, or conversely, as an apostasy of sorts of the essence of thinking—in short, as vitally connected to, or deriving from, philosophical thought, and hence intimately linked to the latter's intelligibility—the possibility and significance of philosophy is, according to Deleuze, entirely het-

erogeneous to *doxa*. Philosophy does not presuppose *doxa* as a ground; by contrast, only under the condition of relinquishing all possible relations to *doxa* can it accomplish what it promises and be the Difference that it announced. It is, therefore, as we have seen, necessarily violent.

37. What Deleuze's discussion of the *concordia facultatum* shows is to what extent his way of philosophizing in *Difference and Repetition*, in spite of all outrageousness and the pathos of radicalization, is conservative. Not only does he seek to undo the discredit in which the doctrine of the faculties has fallen, calling it "an entirely necessary component of the system of philosophy" (*DR*, 143); in the discussion of the fractured I, he holds also on to the idea of the transcendental subject, the difference being only that this subject is no longer formally one, but fractured. But above all, there is, in *Difference and Repetition*, a definite concern with the *system* of philosophy, though such a system is one of discordant faculties raised to the nth power, a system that, rather than unified, is broken up.

CHAPTER II

1. With respect to this last phase of Lyotard's writing, Gérald Sfez remarks: "We can almost speak of a second philosophy of the differend, whose role is not to resolve the conflicts, aporias or existing discord involved in the use of the term—which it was never intended to do—but to discover them differently. We witness a shift in accent that neither resolves nor discredits previous thought. The differend undergoes a change of aspect." Gérald Sfez, "The Writings of the Differend," in *Minima Memoria: Essays in the Wake of Jean-François Lyotard*, ed. C. Nouvet et al. (Stanford, CA: Stanford University Press, 2007).

2. Jean-François Lyotard, *The Inhuman: Reflections on Time*, trans. G. Bennington and R. Bowlby (Stanford, CA: Stanford University Press, 1991), 128.

3. Jean-François Lyotard, *The Differend: Phrases in Dispute*, trans. G. Van Den Abbeele (Minneapolis: University of Minnesota Press, 1988), xii. All page references in this chapter refer to this edition. For Lyotard's reservations regarding the linguistic discipline of pragmatics, and his attempt to distinguish his own phrastic approach from it, see "Discussions, or Phrasing 'After Auschwitz,' " in *The Lyotard Reader*, ed. A. Benjamin (London: Basil Blackwell, 1989), 371–372. Indeed, the very notion of the "pragmatic" evokes anthropocentricism. See Lyotard, *The Differend*, 76–77.

4. For a discussion of Lyotard's shift from the use of the Wittgensteinian notion of "language games" in *The Postmodern Condition* to the notion of "phrase" in *The Differend*, see for instance Niels Brügger, "Où sont passés les jeux de langages?" in *Lyotard, les déplacements philosophiques*, ed. N. Brügger (Brussels: De Boeck-Wesmael, 1993), 33–53.

5. Lyotard discusses the distinction between articulated and nonarticulated phrases in "Examen Oral: Entretien avec Jean-François Lyotard," in *Lyotard, les déplacements philosophique*, 144–146.

6. Jean-François Lyotard, *The Postmodern Condition: A Report on Knowledge*, trans. G. Bennington and B. Massumi (Minneapolis: University of Minnesota Press, 1984), 23. For a description that betokens the essentially pragmatic nature of the instances of a phrase universe, see pp. 23–24, where Lyotard discusses a phrase whose regimen submits to the rules of scientific knowledge.

7. Lyotard, *The Differend*, xii.

8. These are Lyotard's words (transcribed by himself) in the debate that followed the presentation of his "Discussions, or Phrasing 'After Auschwitz'" at Cerisy-la-Salle, on the occasion of a colloquium on the work of Jacques Derrida in 1980. See *Les fins de l'homme: A partir du travail de Jacques Derrida*, ed. P. Lacoue-Labarthe and J.-L. Nancy (Paris: Galilée, 1981), 314.

9. For a discussion of the resurgence of the norm of honor in contemporary social, cultural, and political life, see *Ehre: Archaische Momente in der Moderne*, ed. L. Vogt and A. Zingerle (Frankfurt/Main: Suhrkamp 1994).

10. Jean-Jacques Rousseau, *Emile or on Education*, trans. A. Bloom (New York: Basic Books, 1979), 272.

11. Lyotard, *The Postmodern Condition*, 82.

12. Jean-François Lyotard, *The Postmodern Explained: Correspondance 1982–1985*, trans. D. Barry et al. (Minneapolis: University of Minnesota Press, 1993), 72.

13. Kathleen Freeman, *Ancilla to the Pre-Socratic Philosophers* (Cambridge, MA: Harvard University Press, 1983), 19.

14. For an analysis of the shift from the code of honor to the concept of dignity in contemporary democratic societies, see Peter Berger, "On the Obsolescence of the Concept of Honour," in *Revisions: Changing Perspectives in Moral Philosophy*, ed. S. Hauerwas and A. MacIntyre (Notre Dame: University of Notre Dame Press, 1983), 172–181.

15. Aristotle, *The Complete Works*, ed. J. Barnes (Princeton, NJ: Princeton University Press, 1985), 2164 (1361a 25–30).

16. Ibid., 1731 (1095b 20–25) and 1773 (1123b 20).

17. If honor is only the highest of all exterior goods and not the highest in general (the highest good is truth and is of the order of the *bios theoretikos*), it is because it is, after all, "superficial": "it is thought to depend on those who bestow honour rather than on him who receives it, but the good we divine to be something of one's own and not easily taken from one." Ibid. (1095b 20–30).

18. Jean-François Lyotard, *Just Gaming*, trans. W. Godzich (Minneapolis: University of Minnesota Press, 1985), 54–55.

19. Theodor W. Adorno, *Negative Dialectics*, trans. E. B. Ashton (New York: Continuum 1997), 381.

20. Theodor W. Adorno, *Metaphysics: Concept and Problems*, trans. E. Jephcott (Stanford, CA: Stanford University Press, 2001), 38.

21. Adorno, *Negative Dialectics*, 391–395.

22. Adorno, *Metaphysics*, 125.

23. Ibid., 20.

24. Ibid., 25.

25. Ibid., 69.

26. Ibid., 19–20.

27. Ibid., 51.

28. Adorno, *Negative Dialectics*, 391–392.

29. The restrictive locution "at least" (*du moins*) in "at least . . . to save the honor of thinking," suggests a defeat of all attempts (by thinking and other efforts) to give the differend its due. In this, the maxim "to save the honor of thinking" conforms to the current use in French of "*sauver l'honneur*," which is used on the occasion of defeat (of a soccer team, for instance), and marks an effort not to lose face.

30. Jacob Rogozinski, "Lyotard: Differend, Presence," in *L'esprit créateur* 31, no. 1 (Spring 1991): 110.

31. Ibid., 112–113.

32. For Geoffrey Bennington's and Jean-François Lyotard's responses to Rogozinski's paper at the Centre Sèvres, see *Témoigner du différend: Quand phraser ne se peut. Autour de Jean-François Lyotard*, ed. P.-J. Labarrière (Paris: Editions Osiris, 1989), 85, 123, 126.

33. Geoffrey Bennington, *Lyotard: Writing the Event* (New York: Columbia University Press, 1988), 144–145, 153.

34. *Questioning Judaism: Interviews by Elisabeth Weber*, trans. R. Bowlby (Stanford, CA: Stanford University Press, 2004), 118.

35. This priority is explicable insofar as the cognitive discourse is the locus of truth. Tilman Borsche, in a superb essay, has shown that Lyotard's achievement in *The Differend* consists in having displaced the problematic of truth from its locus in the proposition or statement, a locus that it has enjoyed since Plato (who unseated the Presocratics' assumption that the locus of truth is the name), or rather since Platonism until today. Lyotard situates its locus in actual discourse, that is, in the temporal interlinkage of phrases, by departing from the Platonist model of truth according to which truth is an invariable and is independent of the addressor and addressee of phrases. In thus focusing on the event of phrases, Borsche argues, Lyotard is much closer to Plato himself, that is, to the dialectic in the dramatic shape in which it can be found in Plato's dialogues. See Tilman Borsche, "Orte der Wahrheit, Orte des Widerstreits. Zur diskursiven Bestimmung von Bedeutung nach Lyotard," in *Fremde Vernunft. Zeichen und Interpretation*, vol. 4, ed. J. Simon and W. Stegmaier (Frankfurt/Main: Suhrkamp, 1998), 113–138.

36. Alain Badiou, "Custos, quid noctis?" *Critique* 450 (November 1984): 860; see also 854. Bennington makes a similar remark in *Lyotard: Writing the Event* when he writes: "In general, this insistence on the application of the rules of the cognitive genre to cases which might not come under its jurisdiction is the most

common form of *différend* discussed by Lyotard (despite his insistence on their multiplicity)" (145).

37. When Lyotard remarks that to "distinguish between phrase regimens . . . comes down to limiting the competence of a given tribunal to a given kind of phrase" (5), it is clear that this distinction serves to keep illicit demands in check and to recall a tribunal (or a genre of discourse) to the area in which it can make reasonable demands. A main rationale for distinguishing between phrase regimens is to prevent unnecessary and irrational differends. Such fundamentally illicit differends arise from the extension of demands to account that are legitimate in certain discourses, to objects that, that for essential reasons, defy such demands. Thus there clearly are avoidable differends.

38. See also Lyotard, *The Postmodern Explained*, 61–62.

39. If the cognitive phrase comes after a silence, it is (perhaps) because all phrases hold at bay the threat that nothingness could be a real possibility.

40. Lyotard, *The Postmodern Explained*, 107.

41. This is the moment where a brief reflection on the role of the Notices in *The Differend* may be appropriate. Under the entry "Reader," in the "Preface: Reading Dossier," Lyotard offers up *The Differend* to any philosophically interested reader, "philosophical" here involving only the minimal agreement of not seeking to be "done with 'language' and not to 'gain time.' " Yet, he adds, "for the Notices, a little more professional a reader," is required (xiv). The main body of the work, with its continual fragments of dialogue, in a style not unlike Wittgenstein's *Philosophical Investigations*, is addressed to the general public. The Notices, set in lowercase letters and addressed to the professional philosophers, would at first seem to concern only those who are at some remove from the public or the judge's eye, and who, rather like the intimate circle of the Platonic truth seekers, discuss and instigate the rules for public discourse. Yet, as we have seen from the three Notices discussed so far, they are the spaces in which Lyotard brings to light the hidden presuppositions of the *dialegesthai* and draws the reclusive institution of truth seeking into the open and agonistic space of the *agora*.

42. Adorno, *Negative Dialectics*, 402, 404.

43. Ibid., 364.

44. Ibid., 392 (trans. mod.).

45. Ibid., 362 (trans. mod.).

46. Adorno, *Metaphysics*, 115.

47. Adorno, *Negative Dialectics*, 365.

48. Ibid., 391–392.

49. Tilman Borsche concludes his essay on Lyotard by explaining: "The 'Problem' of thinking does thus no longer consist in discovering 'the' truth of 'the' things, because these are, in the same way, as truth, conditioned, that is, epiphe-

nomena of different discourses. In contrast, what is at stake in the discourse that 'we' are, and through its suitable (conscientious, responsible) linkages, is 'to save the honor of thinking' " (138).

50. This demarcation of Lyotard's reflections on thinking after Auschwitz from the similar concerns of Adorno imposes itself, because Lyotard's reflections admittedly take off from Adorno's elaborations on this issue in *Negative Dialectics*. Nevertheless, an inquiry into what sets Lyotard's reflections apart from Heidegger's attempts to reconceive of the task of thinking may also be warranted, in spite of the disturbing absence of "Auschwitz" from Heidegger's meditations on why we are "not yet capable of thinking." Undoubtedly, the attempt to overcome metaphysical thinking by way of a meditation on the unthought of metaphysics, and the subsequent determination of the nature and task of thinking from the question of Being, has all the looks of a "merely" philosophical exercise, which would be oblivious to certain historical events and thus to their possible unsettling impact on the certitudes of thinking. However, Heidegger's discussion of the nature of metaphysical thought as representational thought in the first part of his 1951 and 1952 lectures, *What Is Called Thinking*, trans. J. G. Gray (New York: Harper & Row, 1968), conjures up a state of affairs as regards the human being's relation to what is. Given the distress and the violence that characterize this state of affairs, it is not without resemblance to what both Adorno and Lyotard seek to address, and that seems to confer an urgency that is not simply "theoretical" upon the effort to go beyond metaphysical thinking. In the context of a debate with Nietzsche, from whom he takes his major clues concerning the reasons why we still do not think, Heidegger determines the kind of relation of the human being that has come to dominate modernity (and hence, the metaphysics of the subject) as representational relating. Such relating not only passes over the human being, but also causes thinking to face what it sets in front of itself as something to be resisted and opposed. Having suggested "that such representing (*Vorstellen*) at bottom sets upon everything it sets before itself, in order to depose and decompose it (*herabzusetzen und zu zersetzen*) . . . [and that] it sets all things up in such a way that fundamentally it pursues and sets upon them (*nachstellt*)," he asks: "What is the spirit of this manner of representation? What type of thinking is it that in thought pursues everything in this manner? Of what kind is the pursuit of thought by man so far?" (84, trans. mod.). To this question concerning the spirit of the kind of thinking whose aim it is to hunt down whatever it sets before itself, Heidegger answers with Nietzsche that it is " '*the spirit of revenge (der Geist der Rache)*.' " He writes: "The pursuit of thought, re-presentation, by the human being so far is determined by revenge, the onset, the attack" (85, trans. mod.). Heidegger wonders toward the end of these lectures whether Nietzsche has truly achieved the deliverance he sought from the spirit of revenge—a revenge that is neither psychological nor moralistic, but, as Heidegger explains, is

metaphysical—with his doctrine of the superman and the eternal recurrence of the same. It is thus safe to say that the Heideggerian attempt to reconfigure the task of thinking in the second part of the lectures must be understood against the background of the Nietzschean determination of the vengeful nature of all thinking up to the present. The notion of thinking that emerges from the last part—a thinking that answers the call of Being—is a thinking that has twisted itself free from the spirit of revenge that has dominated representational thinking. For Heidegger, the representational turn of thinking, which climaxes in the world picture of technology, is not a regrettable accident; in a manner similar to Adorno's and Lyotard's perception of the effects of thinking, he sees it as intimately tied to the very nature of Western thinking. However, the effort to reach back to a more fundamental conception of thinking leads neither to an all-out discrediting of metaphysics, and a subsequent saving of thinking as micrological thinking, nor to seeking the salvation of the honor of thinking by giving the differends caused by thinking their due.

51. *Témoigner du différend*, 119.

CHAPTER 12

1. Jean-François Lyotard, *The Differend. Phrases in Dispute*, trans. G. Van Den Abbeele (Minneapolis: University of Minnesota Press, 1988) (hereafter cited in text as *TD*).

2. With this opening of reality to possible senses, time as a condition of modalization, or more precisely, the future, becomes a constitutive function of the real. No longer "a matter of the absolute eye witness," reality is thus "a matter of the future" (53).

3. Jean-François Lyotard, *Lessons on the Analytic of the Sublime*, trans. E. Rottenberg (Stanford, CA: Stanford University Press, 1994), 53.

4. Ibid., 159.

5. Ibid., 190.

6. Jean-François Lyotard, *The Inhuman. Reflections on Time*, trans. G. Bennington and R. Bowlby (Stanford, CA: Stanford University Press, 1991), 33 (hereafter cited in text as *TI*).

7. If Lyotard's rendering of Kant's notion of the sublime in the *Lessons* is biased in that the sublime is interpreted here as interruptive of the aesthetic of the beautiful, rather than as a necessary complement to it, this is not because, as Gernot Böhme has argued in a sympathetic but also critical essay on the *Lessons*, Lyotard would have read the sublime as a project of art rather than an experience of nature. Gernot Böhme, "Lyotards Lektüre des Erhabenen," *Kant-Studien* 89, no. 2 (1998): 205–218. If at all inspired by the arts, Lyotard's analysis of the sublime in the third *Critique*, yields to the modern arts' systematic and progressive exploration of the elementary or originary constituents of painting, an exploration that

shows the arts to operate *ex minimis,* just as does philosophical thinking (see *TI,* 102–103).

8. Renate Homann, "Zu neueren Versuchen einer Reaktualisierung des Erhabenen. Lyotards Utilisierung einer ästhetischen Kategorie für eine neue Ethik," *Zeitschrift für philosophische Forschung* 48, no. 1 (1994): 43–68.

9. I am bypassing any discussion of the disruption that the temporality of the event thus understood exerts on the aesthetic formal framework—space and time—that according to Kant is required in object formation and object determination. See *TI,* 123–124, and Jean-François Lyotard, *Heidegger et 'les juifs'* (Paris: Galilée, 1988), 60–61.

10. Undoubtedly, not only has Kant considerably simplified Burke's developments concerning the beautiful and the sublime, he has also not fully acknowledged his debt to the latter's inquiry. For an interesting reassessment of Burke's thought, see Baldine Saint Girons, "Kant et la mise en cause de l'esthétique," in *Kants Ästhetik, Kant's Aesthetics, L'esthétique de Kant,* ed. H. Parret (Berlin: de Gruyter, 1998), 706–720.

11. Jean-François Lyotard, *Témoigner du différend. Quand phraser ne se peut,* ed. P. J. Labarrière (Paris: Osiris; 1989), 101.

12. Lyotard, *Heidegger et 'les juifs,'* 65.

13. Lyotard, *Témoigner du différend,* 102.

14. For a discussion of the cabbalistic doctrine of the *Tzim-Tzum* that refers to the godhead's contraction and withdrawal to make space for a world, see Gershom G. Scholem, *Major Trends in Jewish Mysticism* (New York: Schocken, 1971), 260–264.

15. Lyotard, *Témoigner du différend,* 101.

16. Barnett Newman, *Selected Writings and Interviews* (Berkeley: University of California Press, 1990), 174–175.

17. This is not the place to discuss in detail Lyotard's relentless reflection on the relation of Jewish thought to Western thinking. However, for what concerns us here, the distinction in *Heidegger et les "juifs"* between the real Jews and "the jews" is not insignificant in that the latter designate an unpresentable of which the sublime is the negative presentation, and that, he argues, is something that European thinking forgets in a forgetting constitutive of Western thought itself. As to Lyotard's recourse to the pagan, which would also need extensive elaboration, let me only mention that when questioned about its importance for his thinking, he responded, with his usual irony, that it was only a low moment (*un 'sale moment'*). Lyotard, *Témoigner du différend,* 90.

18. Lyotard writes: "Neither the sense of a phrase nor its reality are indubitable. Its sense, because it is suspended to a link with another phrase which will explain it. Its reality, because its assertion is subject to the rules for establishing reality which entail the test of doubt" (*TD,* 66).

19. Jean Améry, *At the Mind's Limits: Contemplations by a Survivor on Auschwitz and Its Realities*, trans. S. Rosenfeld and S. P. Rosenfeld (Bloomington: Indiana University Press, 1980), 39.

CHAPTER 13

1. In all fairness, it must be noted that Habermas criticizes not only Derrida in this respect, but all objectivist and relativist philosophies as well. According to Habermas, it is not possible to hold such views without a performative self-contradiction. See, for instance Jürgen Habermas, *Postmetaphysical Thinking: Philosophical Essays*, trans. W. M. Hohengarten (Cambridge, MA: MIT Press, 1992), 135.

2. Barbara Herrnstein Smith, *Belief and Resistance: Dynamics of Contemporary Intellectual Controversy* (Cambridge, MA: Harvard University Press, 1997), xxii.

3. Herrnstein Smith, *Belief and Resistance*, 76.

4. On this score see Hent de Vries, *Minimal Theologies: Critiques of Secular Reason in Adorno and Levinas*, trans. G. Hale (Baltimore, MD: Johns Hopkins University Press, 2005), 504.

5. Jürgen Habermas, *The Philosophical Discourse of Modernity*, trans. F. Lawrence (Cambridge, MA: MIT Press, 1987), 166–167.

6. Jacques Derrida, *Writing and Difference*, trans. A. Bass (Chicago: University of Chicago Press, 1978), 288.

7. Jacques Derrida, *Mémoires pour Paul de Man* (Paris: Galilée, 1988), 226; Jacques Derrida, *Limited Inc* (Evanston, IL: Northwestern University Press, 1989), 156–158; Jacques Derrida, *Le monolinguisme de l'autre* (Paris: Galilée, 1996), 15–18.

8. Philippe Forget, "Das 'Gerede' vom performativen Widerspruch. Zu Habermas' Derrida-Kritik," in *Allgemeine Zeitschrift für Philosophie* (Stuttgart: Frommann-Holzboog, 1991), 47–57.

9. Jacques Derrida, *The Other Heading: Reflections on Today's Europe*, trans. P. A. Brault and M. B. Naas (Bloomington: Indiana University Press, 1992), 80. In Chapter 5, "More than a Difference in Style," I argued that, for Derrida, a performance in the strict sense, that is, in the sense of a singular event, requires the meeting of, at once, two mutually exclusive imperatives. It follows from this that if ever there has been a performance, it would necessarily have been contradictory.

10. Jacques Derrida, "Force of Law: The 'Mystical Foundation of Authority,'" trans. M. Quaintance, *Cardozo Law Review* 11, nos. 5–6 (1990): 957, 959.

11. Jacques Derrida, *Aporias: Dying—Awaiting (One Another at) the "Limits of Truth,"* trans. T. Dutoit (Stanford, CA: Stanford University Press, 1993), 13.

12. Leonard Lawlor argues that Derrida's interest in the question of aporia is testimony to the indebtedness of his understanding of Husserlian phenomenology to the tradition of interpretation of the latter's thought that begins with

Eugen Fink, and that is carried forward in France by Jean Cavaillès and Tran-Duc-Thao. See Leonard Lawlor, *Derrida and Husserl: The Basic Problems of Phenomenology* (Bloomington: Indiana University Press, 2002).

13. Jacques Derrida, *Le problème de la genèse dans la philosophie de Husserl* (Paris: Presses Universitaires de France, 1990), 32.

14. Derrida, *Aporias*, 13.

15. Sarah Kofman, *Comment s'en sortir?* (Paris: Galilée, 1983), 18.

16. Finally, let me also mention that translated into Latin, aporia becomes, in Quintillian in particular, a rhetorical figure: the figure of *dubitatio*. According to Heinrich Lausberg, an orator who uses this figure either leaves it up to his public to choose between two or more diversivocal or multivocal designations of one thing, raising the question of the seeming impossibility to correctly designate the thing in the first place, or uses it to raise the problem of the meaningful beginning or continuation of the discourse as such. Heinrich Lausberg, *Elemente der Literarischen Rhetorik* (Munich: Max Hueber, 1967), 123. Henri Morier defines it as follows: "Figure by means of which the author or the speaker seems to hesitate between several words, several positions to take, several meanings to give to an action. For the figure to be efficacious, it must reproduce the conditions of truth. We hesitate for multiple reasons, not all of which are not good enough to be revealed: slowness or inadequateness of the mind; lack of memory; poverty of vocabulary; inhibition owing to a feeling of guilt, that is to say, to a veto of moral consciousness." *Dictionnaire de Poétique et de Rhétorique* (Paris: Presses Universitaires, 1981), 377.

17. Plato, *The Collected Dialogues*, ed. E. Hamilton and H. Cairns (Princeton, NJ: Princeton University Press, 1980), 1091–1092 (15d ff).

18. Kofman, *Comment s'en sortir?* 31–32.

19. Ibid., 51.

20. Ibid., 49.

21. Ibid., 59.

22. Ibid., 53.

23. Marcel Detienne and Jean-Pierre Vernant, *Cunning Intelligence in Greek Culture and Society*, trans. J. Lloyd (Atlantic Highlands, NJ: Humanities Press, 1978), 3.

24. Kofman, *Comment s'en sortir?* 15.

25. Ibid., 16.

26. François Châtelet, *Platon* (Paris: Gallimard, 1965), 114–116.

27. Plato, *The Collected Dialogues*, 556.

28. Hans-Georg Gadamer, *Plato im Dialog, Gesammelte Werke*, vol. 7 (Tübingen: Mohr, 1991), 338–369.

29. Aristotle, *Metaphysics*, in *The Complete Works of Aristotle*, vol. 2, ed. J. Barnes (Princeton, NJ: Princeton University Press, 1985), 1554 (982b 15–20).

30. Martin Heidegger, *Platon: Sophistes, Gesamtausgabe*, vol. 19 (Frankfurt: Klostermann, 1992), 126.

31. Ibid., 126–127.

32. Ibid., 127–128.

33. Ibid., 128.

34. The rivalry between philosophy and sophistry could well be construed as one between two ways of approaching and overcoming aporias: in the philosophical mode, aporias are approached in "anamnestic" fashion—that is, on the basis of knowledge gained from a reflection on the knowledge we always already possess of them and that makes it possible to experience them as aporias in the first place; the other way consists in inventing devices that avoid them, but that, at the same time, reproduce them.

35. Derrida, *Aporias*, 77.

36. Jean-François Courtine, *Heidegger et la phénoménologie* (Paris: Vrin, 1990), 313.

37. Derrida, *Aporias*, 32.

38. Ibid., 73.

39. Ibid., 13.

40. Ibid., 21.

41. Ibid., 77, 73.

42. Ibid., 70.

43. Ibid., 73.

CHAPTER 14

1. Hans Blumenberg, *Wirklichkeiten in denen wir leben* (Stuttgart: Reclam, 1981), 8.

2. Jacques Derrida, *Of Grammatology*, trans. G. C. Spivak (Baltimore, MD: Johns Hopkins University Press, 1976), 60.

3. Jacques Derrida, *Limited Inc* (Evanston, IL: Northwestern University Press, 1999), 117.

4. Derrida, *Of Grammatology*, 60.

5. Ibid., 283.

6. Jacques Derrida, *Edmund Husserl's Origin of Geometry: An Introduction*, trans. J. P. Leavy (Stony Brook, NY: Nicolas Hays, 1979), 131–132.

7. Jacques Derrida, *Writing and Difference*, trans. A. Bass (Chicago: Chicago University Press, 1979), 139.

8. Jacques Derrida, "The Laws of Reflection: Nelson Mandela, in Admiration," in *For Nelson Mandela*, ed. J. Derrida and M. Tlili (New York: Seaver Books, 1987), 14–15.

9. Ibid., 13.

10. Jacques Derrida, *The Other Heading: Reflections on Today's Europe*, trans. P. A. Brault and M. B. Naas (Bloomington: Indiana University Press, 1992), 9.

11. Jacques Derrida, *Points . . . Interviews, 1974–1994*, ed. E. Weber (Stanford, CA: Stanford University Press, 1995), 381.

12. Jacques Derrida, *De quoi demain . . . Dialogue* (Paris: Fayard/Galilée, 2001), 200.

13. Derrida, *Of Grammatology*, 162.

14. Ibid., 157–158, 164.

Index of Names

Cultural Memory | in the Present

Jean-Luc Nancy, *The Speculative Remark: (One of Hegel's bon mots)*

Jean-François Lyotard, *Soundproof Room: Malraux's Anti-Aesthetics*

Jan Patočka, *Plato and Europe*

Hubert Damisch, *Skyline: The Narcissistic City*

Isabel Hoving, *In Praise of New Travelers: Reading Caribbean Migrant Women Writers*

Richard Rand, ed., *Futures: Of Jacques Derrida*

William Rasch, *Niklas Luhmann's Modernity: The Paradoxes of Differentiation*

Jacques Derrida and Anne Dufourmantelle, *Of Hospitality*

Jean-François Lyotard, *The Confession of Augustine*

Kaja Silverman, *World Spectators*

Samuel Weber, *Institution and Interpretation: Expanded Edition*

Jeffrey S. Librett, *The Rhetoric of Cultural Dialogue: Jews and Germans in the Epoch of Emancipation*

Ulrich Baer, *Remnants of Song: Trauma and the Experience of Modernity in Charles Baudelaire and Paul Celan*

Samuel C. Wheeler III, *Deconstruction as Analytic Philosophy*

David S. Ferris, *Silent Urns: Romanticism, Hellenism, Modernity*

Rodolphe Gasché, *Of Minimal Things: Studies on the Notion of Relation*

Sarah Winter, *Freud and the Institution of Psychoanalytic Knowledge*

Samuel Weber, *The Legend of Freud: Expanded Edition*

Aris Fioretos, ed., *The Solid Letter: Readings of Friedrich Hölderlin*

J. Hillis Miller / Manuel Asensi, *Black Holes / J. Hillis Miller; or, Boustrophedonic Reading*

Miryam Sas, *Fault Lines: Cultural Memory and Japanese Surrealism*

Peter Schwenger, *Fantasm and Fiction: On Textual Envisioning*

Didier Maleuvre, *Museum Memories: History, Technology, Art*

Jacques Derrida, *Monolingualism of the Other; or, The Prosthesis of Origin*

Andrew Baruch Wachtel, *Making a Nation, Breaking a Nation: Literature and Cultural Politics in Yugoslavia*

Niklas Luhmann, *Love as Passion: The Codification of Intimacy*

Mieke Bal, ed., *The Practice of Cultural Analysis: Exposing Interdisciplinary Interpretation*

Jacques Derrida and Gianni Vattimo, eds., *Religion*